POLITICS IN COLOR AND CONCRETE

NEW ANTHROPOLOGIES OF EUROPE

Matti Bunzl and Michael Herzfeld, *editors*

Founding Editors
Daphne Berdahl
Matti Bunzl
Michael Herzfeld

POLITICS in COLOR and CONCRETE

SOCIALIST MATERIALITIES AND THE
MIDDLE CLASS IN HUNGARY

KRISZTINA FEHÉRVÁRY

INDIANA UNIVERSITY PRESS
Bloomington and Indianapolis

This book is a publication of

Indiana University Press
Office of Scholarly Publishing
Herman B Wells Library 350
1320 East 10th Street
Bloomington, Indiana 47405 USA

iupress.indiana.edu

Telephone orders 800-842-6796
Fax orders 812-855-7931

© 2013 by Krisztina Fehérváry

All rights reserved

No part of this book may be reproduced or utilized in any form or by any means, electronic or mechanical, including photocopying and recording, or by any information storage and retrieval system, without permission in writing from the publisher. The Association of American University Presses' Resolution on Permissions constitutes the only exception to this prohibition.

∞ The paper used in this publication meets the minimum requirements of the American National Standard for Information Sciences—Permanence of Paper for Printed Library Materials, ANSI Z39.48-1992.

Manufactured in the United States of America

Library of Congress Cataloging-in-Publication Data

Fehérváry, Krisztina.
 Politics in color and concrete : socialist materialities and the middle class in Hungary / Krisztina Feh Fehérváry.
   pages cm. — (New anthropologies of Europe)
 Includes bibliographical references and index.
  ISBN 978-0-253-00991-3 (cl : alk. paper) — ISBN 978-0-253-00994-4 (pb : alk. paper) — ISBN 978-0-253-00996-8 (ebook)
 1. Hungary—Social conditions. 2. Hungary—Economic conditions. 3. Hungary—Civilization. 4. Material culture—Political aspects—Hungary. 5. Consumption (Economics)—Political aspects—Hungary. 6. Middle class—Hungary. 7. Post-communism—Hungary. I. Title.
  HN420.5.A8F44 2013
  306.09439—dc23

2013005870

1 2 3 4 5   18 17 16 15 14 13

For my parents
   Deborah S. Cornelius and
   István L. Fehérváry

Contents

	Preface	*ix*
	Acknowledgments	*xiii*
	Introduction: The Qualities of Color and Concrete	*1*
1	Normal Life in the Former Socialist City	*27*
2	Socialist Realism in the Socialist City	*52*
3	Socialist Modern and the Production of Demanding Citizens	*78*
4	Socialist Generic and the Branding of State Socialism	*111*
5	Organicist Modern and Super-Natural Organicism	*139*
6	Unstable Landscapes of Property, Morality, and Status	*164*
7	The New Family House and the New Middle Class	*189*
8	Heterotopias of the Normal in Private Worlds	*220*
	Epilogue	*239*
	Notes	*245*
	Bibliography	*261*
	Index	*281*

Preface

THIS BOOK MOVES between the seemingly disparate worlds of state socialist material culture and postsocialist middle-class life. This structure is an outcome of my own experience of Hungary as two distinct places, separated by time, in which my own status was as implicated in the shifting landscape of identity and belonging as those of the people populating the narrative—and as grounded in the constantly transforming material environment. My fieldwork in the 1990s was focused on the building and renovation practices of an aspiring middle class in a former "socialist new town." The picture of everyday life I came away with was one overwhelmed by economic insecurity and status anxiety, but also one at odds with the world I had known from my travels to socialist Hungary in the 1970s and 1980s. It was a picture easily explained, or so it seemed, by the fall of state socialism and the effects of the neoliberal form of capitalism that then enmeshed the region. And yet there were glaring problems with such a view. It posited Eastern Europe during the state socialist period as an economic and material wasteland, in which the absence of a "capitalist" economy somehow implied the absence of consumer culture—with its accompanying panoply of dreams and frustrations, forms of sociality, and social distinctions. Focused on transformations of material worlds—especially of that particular place called "home"—this book lays bare the ways in which the embodied experience of state socialism, in all its robust materiality, structured the decade after its fall and continues to shape attitudes and practices in the region.

My first trip to Hungary was in 1972, when my American mother bravely ventured across the "Iron Curtain" so that my brother and I could visit my father's family. We traveled to Budapest, the southern town of Mohács, and also to the socialist, planned "new town" of Dunaújváros, where I first became friends with Laura, then aged twelve, and her family. My father stayed behind, sure that if he returned to Hungary, Communist authorities would return him to the political prison system in which he had already spent eight years of his life between 1948 and 1956.[1] After this trip, I returned every couple of years. So began an ongoing debate with him about what was happening in his homeland—one I experienced during the more lenient and prosperous 1970s and 1980s of the Kádár era, and one he remembered from his youth and had seen darkened by the oppression of Soviet Russian occupation and 1950s Stalinist Communism.

In my trips to Hungary, I was embraced as Hungarian despite my kitchen knowledge of the language and mixed parentage. Once past the compulsory ordeal of reporting in to the local police, my presence was valued in ways not in keeping with my age and gender because I was from "the West." When the women retreated to the kitchen after a meal, the men would keep me with them to discuss politics, hungry for what I could tell them of what was going on "out there" (*oda kint*). In return, they regaled me (and each other) with their analyses of otherwise inexplicable state machinations—scrutinizing why authorities had allowed the American film *The Deer Hunter* to be shown, or what it meant that it was suddenly possible to open a savings account of foreign currency when possession of such currency over a small amount was still illegal. The socialist state's combination of secrecy and unpredictability made it appear omniscient and omnipotent, as Daphne Berdahl so cogently observed (1999a). This state also enchanted the material world, making any event that was out of the ordinary seem a potential sign of the behind-the-scenes working of an inscrutable state.

Later, traveling by myself, these trips were framed by tense border crossings with armed guards who inspected train compartments for banned items—not just drugs, but those things feared by a paranoid state: samizdat publications and pornography, computer equipment, cigarettes, and other contraband consumer goods. Once beyond the border, my journals of these trips describe reunions with relatives and friends; wonderful meals and evenings spent discussing politics and life; trips on crowded Ikarusz buses flying by fields of sunflowers; sitting in Old World cafés and swimming in Olympic-size pools; and enjoying the summer ritual of watching Wimbledon on TV with Laura's father, gorging on bowls of dark cherries in their Dunaújváros apartment.

Of particular relevance here was that my material status in socialist Hungary—even as a poor student—was extraordinary. This was true of the purchasing power of the meager amount of foreign currency I brought with me, but also of the cachet I possessed merely through my embodied knowledge of Western goods, fashions, and practices. I also came as bearer of (often requested) artifacts of this material culture: pink Flicker women's shavers, a Fleetwood Mac album, jeans and Cover Girl makeup, Band-Aids and tinted acne medication. In retrospect, the inordinate pleasure I felt I was able to bring with my otherwise modest gifts was central to the dynamic that I now find myself describing in this book: a profound asymmetry in the lifestyle opportunities and the meanings they signify between people who otherwise understand themselves to be of the same status and coeval in the world. John Borneman describes the profoundly complicated mixture of joy/desire and humiliation/resentment that East Germans felt for the "care packages" they received from relatives in the West, often poisonous gifts that implied derogatory assessments of East German consumer goods and living standards while inadequately materializing East Germans' fantasies of "the West" as a consumer utopia (1991:147–49). In my case, my youth, affective ties, and genuine appreciation of the gifts I received in return—from hand-painted tablecloths to albums by the Hungarian disco band Neoton Família—mitigated the potentially ugly interpersonal dynamics associated with such exchanges.

When, in the postsocialist 1990s, my trips became anthropological fieldwork, I witnessed firsthand the long-term effects of this asymmetry in the determination of friends old and new to create Western-standard material worlds. My research questions arose out of seeing the dramatic changes being wrought to the material environment, not just to public, commercial spaces, but in the homes of friends and family. That they had long been dissatisfied with the kinds of material environments possible for them under the socialist state was nothing new. But how was it that in times of such economic uncertainty and social tumult, they felt so compelled to embark on expensive and energy-consuming endeavors to transform their living spaces?

The renewed salience of class and its representation in prestige-oriented consumption were inescapable features of the postsocialist 1990s, and I saw this clearly in how people I knew re-evaluated themselves, their relationships, and the future prospects for themselves and for their children. Still, I was unprepared for the overwhelming sense of status-related anxiety, strained and defensive social relations, and "materialistic" preoccupations I encountered. These impressions were most likely exaggerated by my focus on that part of society in Hungary most concerned with maintaining respectable social status: people aged from their twenties to early sixties, working full-time jobs or running new businesses, often with children to provide for. Moreover, my own standing in the country as an American Hungarian had been transformed from nominal insider to marked outsider. The post-1989 influx of condescending Westerners arriving to "teach" Hungarians about capitalism and democracy (for a price), who were vocal about the inadequacy of Hungarian living conditions, generated enormous resentment. The greatest ire was reserved for the Hungarian émigrés who returned after 1989 to influence politics, to take advantage of cheap prices, to seek business opportunities, or to live well on their Western pensions. This negative image was combined with the older stereotype of the "American uncle" arriving home in a Mercedes with gifts, flaunting wealth achieved through low-status professions.[2]

A defining moment came in the early stages of fieldwork, when a Romanian ethnographic filmmaker, Gabriel, and his wife, Adina, a film scholar, came to visit me in Dunaújváros, where I was doing my research. This town of 57,000 people had been built as a planned, model socialist city in the 1950s and was made up almost entirely of the monolithic, concrete block apartment buildings that—in the West—had become the paradigmatic symbol of oppressive, Eastern European Communist regimes. When Gabriel and Adina compared the town to their own experience in socialist housing blocks outside Bucharest, however, they were impressed by its cleanliness and the good state of repair of buildings and streets. They were also charmed by the many weekend bodegas and summer cottages owned by city dwellers on the outskirts of nearby villages. But Gabriel, himself committed to ethnographic documentation of village religious practices, could not understand my project. Especially after being shown several newly built homes in emerging suburban neighborhoods in these same villages, he wondered: What was the point of studying such material practices with no ostensible objective of spiritual transcendence? Over the next year, I came to see that "transcendence" was exactly what was at stake in postsocialist transformations to domestic space (Miller 1994, 2005). This transcendence was not the kind Gabriel had in mind, a transcendence *beyond* the realm of the material. Instead, it was transcendence *via* the material—more concretely, the material of the highly ideologized, value-laden sphere of the family home.

Acknowledgments

I HAVE ACCRUED many debts in the undertaking of this long project. It would be impossible to acknowledge everyone who has helped me to produce this book through conversations and suggestions, advice in research and writing, personal encouragement, and practical support, as well as inspiration through example. And yet a number of people over the years have remained singularly influential. The late Edward T. Hall, my early mentor, sometime boss, and valued friend, first introduced me to nonverbal communication and the unnoticed effects of the built environment and spatial practice. At the University of Chicago, I had the privilege of working with exceptional teachers. I offer my heartfelt thanks for years of intellectual inspiration and professional guidance and support to Leora Auslander, John L. Comaroff, Nancy Munn, and especially to Susan Gal. I was also fortunate to receive generous help from Seteney Shami, William H. Sewell, Jr., and Paul Friedrich in the early stages of this research. Anne Ch'ien played a pivotal role for all graduate students in anthropology.

The book has benefited enormously from the generous readings made by friends and colleagues at different phases in the writing. David Altshuler, Laura Ring, and Miklos Vörös gave me invaluable feedback in earlier stages. The book manuscript itself has been immeasurably enriched by the thoughtful insights, criticisms, and suggestions made by Éva Huseby-Darvas, Miranda Johnson, Paul Johnson, Lara Kusnetzky, Paul Manning, Ildikó Porter-Szűcs, Jason Pine, Michele Rivkin-Fish, Liz Roberts, and Geneviève Zubrzycki. In the context of workshops and publications, Melissa Caldwell, Jennifer Patico, Olga Shevchenko, Rachel Heiman, Carla Freeman, Mark Liechty, and Robert Foster have been insightful interlocutors. The influence of Dominic Boyer, Drew Gilbert, Jessica Greenberg, Andy Graan, and Marko Zivkovic dates back to our time together in the Anthropology of Europe workshop. I have cherished the suggestions, support, and friendship of Martha Lampland and Maya Nadkarni, fellow anthropologists of Hungary; the influence of their scholarship is evident in these pages.

A few individuals sacrificed time and effort to read the manuscript in its entirety. Dale Pesmen drew on her many talents to help me turn the first complete draft into a book manuscript; I can't thank her enough for her intervention at a critical moment. Zeynep Gürsel lent her formidable ethnographic eye, incisive questions, and writing skills to later stages and made the process so much more enjoyable. The detailed comments made by Brad Weiss, Zsuzsa Gille, and Brian

Porter-Szűcs shaped the last rewriting of the book. Erika Büky contributed skillful editing as well as observations from her own half-Hungarian background.

At the University of Michigan, the vibrant atmosphere and warm collegiality I have experienced in the Department of Anthropology has surpassed all my expectations for academic life. I am profoundly grateful to my colleagues and students for their inspiration, guidance, and support. In particular, Alaina Lemon, Gillian Feeley-Harnik, and Webb Keane were a constant source of energizing intellectual exchange, friendship, and good advice. I also want to thank Tom Fricke, Judy Irvine, Stuart Kirsch, Bruce Mannheim, Joyce Marcus, John Mitani, Erik Mueggler, Andrew Shryock, and Carla Sinopoli for their wit and sustained support. I would be remiss if I did not express my vast appreciation for the staff in the Anthropology Department, as well as for the staff of the Center for Russian, East European and Eurasian Studies.

In Hungary, I benefited greatly from the intellectual engagement, guidance, and friendship of a number of individuals. In Budapest, my thanks go to Judit Bodnár, Tamás Hofer, the Urban Institute (especially Katherine Mark), Attila and Andrea Pók, Pál Péter Tóth, Klára Gyires, Emőke Tomsics, László Kontler, and Viola Zentai. I was also generously advised by Katalin S. Nagy, Viktória Szirmai, Miklós Miskolczi, Mária Pataki, Ilona Fehér, and Aliz Torday. In Dunaújváros, I received invaluable assistance from sociologists Éva Kántor and Attila Kiss at the Dunaújváros Technical College; staff at the Intercisa Museum; staff at the Land Registry Bureau, especially Zsuzsa Létai; Klára Stossek at the Dunaújváros City Library; journalist Mária Kazai; and the members of the Pentele Friendship Circle. I cannot express enough my appreciation to all the people in Dunaújváros who graciously welcomed me into their homes.

The following friends and family enriched my time in Hungary in numerous ways, both personally and professionally. My thanks go to Zsuzsana Fehérváry and László Czakó; Endre and Ida Fehérváry, both now deceased; Diana Dobiz-Plézer and her family, especially Mária Dobiz and (the late) István Dobiz; Timea Zupkó Móró and János Móró; János Balatoni and (the late) Érzsébet "Cinci" Balatoni; Erzsébet Svarda; Virág Stossek and her family; the Szűcs family, and Levente Bagossy and his family.

I would like to acknowledge the staff at the University of Indiana Press for their careful production of this book, especially Rebecca Tolen, Nancy Lightfoot, Sarah Jacobi, Michelle Sybert, Drew Bryan, and the editors of the Anthropology of Europe series, Matti Bunzl and Michael Herzfeld. I continue to be grateful for the early support and inspiration of the late Daphne Berdahl, who remains keenly missed. Thanks to Scott Webel for compiling a fine index. Kinga Benkes and Ágnes Hasznos helped with Hungarian translations and diacritics, and Jen Morris helped with the bibliography.

Funding for primary fieldwork was provided by grants from the Fulbright Commission and the Social Science Research Council (IREX). Follow-up trips in 2008 and 2010 were supported by the University of Michigan Department of Anthropology. A fellowship from the American Council for Learned Societies (ACLS) funded one year of writing. Additional funding for book production and color plates was provided by University of Michigan's Office of the Vice President for Research. I am grateful to these institutions for making this research possible.

Most importantly, I thank my family for their patience, bottomless reserves of support, and love throughout this process. My father, István Fehérváry, overcame his early skepticism of this endeavor to become a staunch and loving supporter. My mother, Deborah Cornelius, encouraged my interest in Hungary and in the Hungarian language at a time when it was not popular to do so. She has been an inspiration in her own work in Eastern European history. The intellectual, personal, and practical contributions she and Matthew Hull have made to this book from the very beginning are incalculable. My mother-in-law, Ann Hull, used up her vacation time to live with us for six weeks to watch the kids so I could write, and she has been steadfast in her support of my professional life. My cousin, Moira Killoran, gave me wise counsel during a critical stage in the writing process. My brother, András Fehérváry, made his apartment my home base in Budapest and has offered good advice and given me confidence ever since. Finally, my love and appreciation go to Matthew Hull, my partner in just about everything—who happily threw in his lot with me and this project. His visits to Hungary during fieldwork, and mine to Pakistan, provided us with fascinating contrasts and insights. I am more grateful than I can say for our life together and for the gift of our children, Alex and Zsofia.

POLITICS IN COLOR AND CONCRETE

Introduction

The Qualities of Color and Concrete

In november 2010, two decades after the fall of the state socialist system in Hungary, the glossy headline of an interior decorating magazine on a Budapest newsstand caught my eye: "Gray, grayer and grayest!" The words were a startling provocation in a place where gray had come to stand in for the Eastern European material and political landscape during state socialism and remained an image the country sought to escape. "We tend to associate gray with what is boring, but there are a thousand kinds of gray, and when combined with colors its varieties are endless," wrote the author as she described a lush interior of multiple textures and hues of gray created by a decorating firm called Zinc. The accompanying photo featured silver frames and silvery satins, a velvet armchair in gun-metal gray, coal-colored pillows strewn on a soft, light gray carpet, and a lamp shade the color of anthracite. "Just look around," she enthused, "how these furnishings evoke the dawn fog, the rain-soaked highway, the pebbles on the lakeshore! . . . But here in our home [Hungary], everything gray is bad. The weather is gray, the people are gray, gray is all that is dull, depressing, uninteresting. It's time to rehabilitate the gray!" (Kelemen 2010).

In Hungary, gray is far more than a color. It is an aesthetic quality that powerfully links material environments with political affects. Gray evokes not just a landscape dominated by concrete block housing, but a whole array of impressions and sentiments. During socialist times, Western observers often invoked the grayness of Eastern Europe as a shorthand for their perceptions of life behind a dark Iron Curtain, of enforced poverty and the fatigue of daily provisioning, of unsmiling salesclerks, scarce goods, and the lack of colorful advertising and commerce. In these accounts, color often signified the pleasures and possibilities of capitalist consumption, of the freedom to express one's identity through style. In the political rhetoric of the 1990s, the claim that state socialism failed because the state could not satisfy the consumer desires of its population became uncontroversial. "Capitalism" rapidly displaced "democracy" as the ultimate victor of the Cold War, and color became a powerful tool for asserting its legitimacy (Manning 2007a).

For Eastern European dissident intellectuals and émigrés, however, the grayness of the material world during the socialist period was iconic not so much of deprivation as of political repression.[1] Run-down built environments, industrial pollution, second-rate consumer goods, and uniformity were indexes less of scarcity than of an oppressive and negligent state. Desire was less for consumer goods in and of themselves than for a kind of political-economic system that allowed for creative productivity, intimate social relationships, aesthetic pleasures, and free expression without fear of state retribution. But gray continues to color both perceptions of the region from elsewhere as well as the desires and ambitions of an aspiring middle class in Hungary to achieve membership in a wider community of value. Such expectations were inculcated during the socialist period, for state socialism had promised to provide citizens with the material goods and environments necessary to realize the well-being and dignity of modern citizenship.

The planned city of Dunaújváros, where I conducted my fieldwork, had come to epitomize the gray of state socialism. Founded as Hungary's model socialist town in 1951, it was first named Sztálinváros, or City of Stalin. Throughout my years of visiting the mill town, from the 1970s through the 1990s, Hungarians I encountered from Budapest or other historic towns couldn't contain their disapproval: "Why would anyone want to go there?" they cried, distancing themselves and indeed the country from everything the city stood for.[2] Dunaújváros was regarded as the ugliest city in Hungary, the much-publicized exemplar of Soviet city planning and emblematic of Hungary's subordination to the Soviet Union. Indeed, its distinction as the first planned socialist city in Hungary had long served to link it with other such cities in the Soviet bloc—and consequently denied it an identity as organically Hungarian. For many, it was a reminder of a tragic history in which Communist rule had suppressed or distorted Hungary's bourgeois-democratic development, forcing this small, central European country to undergo a Soviet rather than a "normal" Western-style modernization.[3] In Dunaújváros itself, residents were acutely aware of this stigma, yet many fiercely defended the town's credentials as a modern, Hungarian city—the successful realization of a centuries-long dream that Hungary would one day produce its own steel. After 1989, its residents took on the double burden of trying to incorporate the city into a Hungarian landscape that was itself being incorporated into a European one. The city was thus an ideal site in which to investigate how the socialist state had forged new relationships among the state, material goods, and people, and how these were being transformed in a postsocialist environment.[4]

This book explores the interpenetration of politics and materialities, particularly of the multitude of meanings and affective powers embedded in the qualities of lived space.[5] The moral, spiritual, and economic struggles of the postsocialist period crystallized a material aesthetic for a livable, normal, and respectable life for middle-class Hungarians. But clearly such an aesthetic did not arise overnight, emerging fully formed out of some supposed state socialist material wasteland. Rather, it was the product of everyday experience of the robust and politically charged material culture that developed over the four decades of the socialist period, much of it centered on the home. Qualities of things—colors like orange and gray, substances like wood and concrete, shapes like right angles and organic curves—came to provoke affective responses to the sociopolitical and economic ideologies with which they were aligned. The affective powers of such qualities outlived the regime that generated them, shaping the way a socialist-era middle class negotiated the postsocialist 1990s and constituted a new middle class.

Aesthetic Regimes and Transforming Cosmologies

The material transformations to Hungarian domestic space from the 1950s to 2000 both reflected and produced understandings about the value of citizens in society and the nature of the political and economic regime governing them. In the chapters that follow, I have divided this period of fifty years not into decades or political eras, but into five distinct "aesthetic regimes," or politically charged assemblages of material qualities that have provoked widely shared affective responses.[6] These aesthetic regimes I refer to as Socialist Realism, Socialist Modern, Socialist Generic, Organicist Modern, and Super-Natural Organicism.[7] Although these successive regimes built upon and against their predecessors, one did not replace another so much as coexist and overlap with it and turn into something else. The temporalities of the material world are often out of sync with other temporalities (Pinney 2005).[8] Thus, while these aesthetic regimes often contained political ideologies, they could also take on new meanings and values completely at odds with the politics that had given them life.

As in planned cities across the region, the built form of Dunaújváros was intended to bring into being an ideal social order and socialist modernity—providing its citizenry with housing, health care, employment, and equitable distribution of wealth.[9] This socialist modernity was to be free of the existential insecurities created by a market economy and at the same time realize a universal modern "good life," one centered on the nuclear family. Consumption of mass produced goods was never inimical to communist ideology, as a socialist modernity depended on the promise of modern mass production and the industrial division of labor. Contrary to the intentions of an original communist avant-garde, however, the *Socialist Realist* aesthetic promoted by Stalin produced monumental residential buildings that were supposed to signal to the common man a grandeur commensurate to the value of the working classes who occupied them. In Hungary in the 1950s, this Socialist Realist aesthetic regime inhered in buildings of solid, neoclassical design that contained apartments made of "quality" materials such as ceramic tile and wood parquet. Stalinist furnishings were recognizably upwardly mobile, echoing bourgeois elements like lace curtains and heavy furniture (chapter 2).

After the Stalin era came to an end in the mid-1950s, politicians throughout the Soviet bloc were faced with populations tired of sacrifice and increasingly aware of the growing prosperity in the postwar West. This was particularly true of the

Hungarian regime after it crushed the popular uprising of 1956. As the Cold War escalated, overall quality of life for citizens became part of the ongoing rivalry between the two superpowers and their ideologies. As elsewhere in the Soviet bloc, in the 1960s the Hungarian state ramped up its production of the components of a modern and civilized lifestyle: an urban apartment, outfitted with a refrigerator and television, and, for those in the more highly valued professions, a car and a weekend cottage in the countryside. Under the "benevolent" leadership of party secretary János Kádár in the 1960s and 1970s, the Hungarian state's commitment to this goal earned it the nickname "refrigerator socialism." Hungary's material prosperity relative to other Soviet bloc countries was made possible by what became known as "goulash communism," or a combination of central planning with economic reforms and a high tolerance for a second or informal economy.

The policies of the Kádár era contrasted starkly with that of the Stalinist era, but both shared the goal of modernizing through materialities. Socialist Realist design was associated with the oppression of the Stalinist regime, and so a socialist version of International Modernism rose to take its place. A *Socialist Modern* aesthetic regime (chapter 3) was made up of residential apartment blocks of prefabricated panel concrete and furnished with modern, mass-produced décor. From 1960 until well into the 1970s, media discourses promoting Socialist Modern successfully devalued once-treasured furnishings like ornate armchairs and created value and expectations for lightweight and multifunctional alternatives. Dark and heavy materialities, saturated with history and class hierarchies, were replaced with the clean, light, and mobile materialities of a future-oriented modernism. These modern furnishings were linked with Western designs, but were also iconic of socialist visions for an egalitarian, civilized society.

Although capitalist consumer culture is usually blamed for aligning the quality of people with the qualities of goods, it was under state socialism that Hungarian citizens learned to judge themselves by their appropriation of modern commodities—from new apartments to colorful plastic kitchen trays. The phrase "Show me your home, and I'll tell you who you are!" was a widely used expression in publications throughout the era. The promotion of socialist consumerism is often presented as a paradoxical or self-defeating endeavor, and not just because of the shortages of state-produced goods. Socialist ideologues in the 1960s, who identified the values of communism with asceticism and anticonsumerism, saw the rise of a socialist consumer culture in the 1960s as the resurgence of petty bourgeois mentalities, corrupting the socialist project, and they blamed women especially for fostering "refrigerator socialism."

And yet to see socialist regimes' promotion of modern apartments and furnishings as forms of communist propaganda or as mere equivalents to capitalist projects of creating consumer-citizens misses the larger story. In fact, the state actively cultivated citizens with demanding material standards, or *igények*. As

I show in chapter 3, producing citizens with high expectations for modern material worlds was integral to the project of creating a utopian society. The goal was not to promote invidious distinctions but to lift people out of poverty and backwardness to full membership in a modern, socialist society—a goal shared with other "developmentalist" states during this period (see Mazzarella 2003 for socialist India). The working classes and agricultural poor were to be empowered to take their rightful place in society, and thus, in Bourdieu's formulation, to transform their embodied sense of their social place (1984). The socialist state prioritized the material project of becoming modern, often positing the modernity of the West as the norm, above other modes of attaining social respectability.[10]

But the state production and distribution system was never able to make this level of a modern "good life" available to all citizens. Instead, by the 1970s, such a modern consumer lifestyle had become the hallmark of a socialist "middle stratum" (*közép réteg*). This middle stratum had much in common with the modern middle classes that emerged after the Second World War in Europe and the United States, defined by their relation to new materialities and professional work rather than by inherited class status (Patterson 2011). While acknowledging that people in the West lived in larger spaces and had nicer cars, many Hungarians in this broad stratum were willing to accept that the social welfare guarantees they enjoyed as members of a socialist society made up for these shortcomings.

Over time, the Socialist Modern aesthetic became discredited. As people moved into panel-construction buildings and lived with furnishing that broke easily or did not age well, the value of these materialities (along with their embedded ideologies) was subverted. It became transformed into what I call *Socialist Generic*, or the materialities of Socialist Modern negatively valued (chapter 4). Citizens struggled to achieve a modern life in conditions where the necessary commodities were scarce, compelling them to forage and barter in the second economy, use networks to obtain goods from the West, and engage in do-it-yourself provisioning for everything from vegetables to fashionable dresses. Instead of realizing a modern, utopian society, the materialities of state-produced goods and housing became affectively aligned with the impersonal and bureaucratic state. This aesthetic regime was epitomized by the stripped-down modernism and uniformity of the concrete panel apartment blocks that were built all over the region in the 1970s. The difference between Socialist Modern and Socialist Generic lay not in their materials and design, but in which qualities were attended to, how they were evaluated, and what they communicated about the state's regard for its citizens.

Because much of the population had no choice but to move into such generic environments, a vernacular aesthetic was deployed to appropriate and "humanize" them, for example by putting thick sheepskin coverings over lightweight, mass-produced sofas. I refer to this aesthetic regime as *Organicist Modern*, or an embrace of natural materials and organic forms in a structural opposition to Socialist Generic (chapter 5). Increasing awareness of the detrimental effects of industrial pollution reinforced the sense that the hubris of state socialism had violated the laws of nature. In the context of Soviet occupation and an abstracting, civilizing state, these ideals for an environment in harmony with nature also drew on a primordial Hungarian culture embodied in traces of ancient folk music, dance, and material culture. Instead of marking a return to bourgeois or peasant materialities, however, Organicist Modern transformations attempted to realize some of the promises of Socialist Modern such as qualities of "openness." This Organicist aesthetic also aligned with values of autonomy and the natural order of things, and so were affectively and materially linked to the second economy and market reforms of the 1970s and 1980s.

After 1989, Organicist Modern aesthetics moved from a marginalized position to become the official design ideology of the new, fully independent Hungary. At the same time, it was transformed by this new context as well as by shifts in the materials used to realize it. A *Super-Natural Organicism* emerged as "nature" was enhanced by new technologies into high-quality commodities circulating in a globalizing marketplace (chapters 5, 6, and 7). These commodities, from weather-resistant woods to pressure-treated roofing tiles, continued to evoke an anti-Communist morality, but now also signaled the superiority of the classes that could afford them. Meanwhile, those most affected by the retreat of the welfare state, the proletariat, became aligned with a shabby and crumbling Socialist Generic. Although the socialist state had been concerned with social equality, it firmly established the correspondence between the qualities of people and the qualities of the materials surrounding them. This correspondence was seamlessly taken up by commercial rhetoric in the 1990s, legitimating the free market and, with it, social inequalities.

The material preferences and practices of the 1990s and 2000s have arisen out of and realigned expectations once developed for a socialist modernity, expectations generated by Socialist Modern forms and their ideological framing. Frequent invocations of "normal" and "livable" material worlds thus reflect aspirations for the enduring but elusive prospects of the modernity and dignity once promised by the socialist state (chapter 1). The efforts of people in Dunaújváros to transform their homes to meet new standards were about more than status distinctions. They were continuing efforts to create spheres of normalcy for themselves and their families.

Materialities and Their Qualities

Studies of material culture as consumption have tended to focus either on the use of consumer goods for status, distinction, and exclusion, or on consumption itself as a pleasurable activity, one that allows people to express their identities and realize themselves. But the consumption and use of material goods is usually about far more than this. It can be a labor of sacrifice for others rather than a form of self-indulgence, particularly within the family where provisioning for others can express affection, impose ideas about nutrition or respectable dress, or demonstrate values of thriftiness or of generosity (Miller 1987, 1998). Consumer practices and the material goods that people bring home to give to others or to consume with them (from food and entertainment to medicine and utilities) thus play a central role in the ongoing constitution of those social relationships (Carrier 1995).

Anthropologists have tended to focus less on modern consumption than on the problem of the commodity form as a theoretical category. This approach, though central to critiques of capitalism, has obscured the role of material things in the world. Material goods reflect, mediate, and constitute social relations, but they also do much more. They can extend or limit human powers, experience, memory, health, and well-being.[11] Cars and refrigerators, for example, make possible suburban communities—not merely as status symbols but as machines that enable people to live at a distance from workplaces and food sources. Moreover, because cars and refrigerators depend upon infrastructures of roads and electric power, they can be litmus tests for the extent to which a nation-state can make possible such lifestyles.

The qualities of those cars and refrigerators also matter. They can stand in for differences between people, as in the oft-cited comparison between the East German two-cylinder Trabant and the West German Mercedes, each automobile indexing radically different production regimes and with them radically different political understandings of how resources should be concentrated or distributed (chapter 8). To posit consumer goods as simply status symbols or the products of advertisers' manipulations is to dismiss the important ways in which such goods can ease or increase labor burdens, prolong the life of foods and people, transport people or maim them, provide people with pleasures or poison them. Class position is generally indexed by the extent to which people have control over their material worlds; indeed, this control over the powers of the material is part of what constitutes that class position.

Finally, material objects can provoke powerful affective responses with their qualities, designs, or aesthetic assemblages.[12] While discursive framing, socialization, and previous encounters with particular materialities play a role in these responses, they cannot determine the phenomenological and affective experience of them. Such experiences can help to constitute, reinforce, or challenge shared understanding of the workings of the social, political, and economic order. Examining these relationships demands a theoretical approach that explores how our embodied experience of materialities contributes to the process of signification. Scholarship using the materially grounded semiotics of Charles S. Peirce (1955) does just this.[13]

Central to my approach to the material is a focus on material properties or qualities not limited to the level of culturally recognized objects. This allows us to think beyond the subject/object dichotomy and consider how qualities and their combinations can produce affective responses that may or may not come to constitute a recognizable aesthetic regime.[14] In Peircean terms, sensuous qualities of objects and substances have the potential to become "qualisigns." The color gray, for example, counts as a qualisign, as does a texture like softness or a property like luminosity. To be comprehended as a qualisign, a qualia such as a color must also appear in multiple realms (objects, substances, bodies). The qualia of gray in a rug, for example, is shared by a slab of concrete, a dawn fog, and pebbles on the lakeshore. By definition, this gray inheres in or is "bundled" with other material properties (Keane 2005:188–89), such as the rug's texture, absorbency, fragility, and perhaps its tendency to show stains.

Focusing on the qualities inhering in things gives us a way to think about how a variety of seemingly unrelated objects can be united into a coherent style—an aesthetic. This capacity of a quality to appear across a variety of objects, materials, or substances allows for the homologous alignment of these domains and in turn contributes to the significance we attach to such qualia. This significance is not arbitrary but is informed by a kind of resemblance—or iconicity—between the qualia and the meanings or sentiments it comes to evoke.[15] Anne Meneley (2008) has shown, for example, how olive oil's "luminosity" (as fuel for light or as imbuing luminous properties to other materials) lends itself by iconic extension to concepts like spirituality, power, and life force. Iconicity thus characterizes the relationship between sensuous qualities of things, affective resonances, and how we might take these up in language to describe concepts, values, or emotional states. The alignment of domains as homologous through particular qualia is not fixed, but obtains power in and through the work of continuous social practice.

Perceptual qualities can form the basis for a unifying "aesthetic" by linking materialities to one another through common associations. For example, particular colors (reds, oranges, and browns), textures (wool, wood), aromas (cinnamon, musk) and so on can all become associated with physical warmth. Although the iconic relationship between red and heat is not arbitrary, it is also not deterministic. Red can just as well be associated with the coldness of watermelon or the rawness of red meat. These complex associations via sensuous perception are linked but not determined by more stable cultural associations. For some, these colors, textures, and aromas might exude the welcoming warmth of a "homey" interior, but for others they trigger repulsion, associations with the decay of a different generation or the earthy impurity of a different class. In this way, aesthetic regimes that are grounded in particular material properties become aligned with wider sociocultural values in ways that seem to inhere in the material, naturalizing, for example, the relationship between state socialism and qualities of grayness, or capitalism with color.

Only some of the material properties of things available for perception can be taken up for signification at any one time. Our attentiveness to *particular* qualia of a thing is affected by convention, training, and context—but it can always change depending upon circumstances. For example, the fossilized tree resin we call amber has a wide variety of potential qualia: it is transparent, has a golden color, can burn, and also has electrostatic properties. Only a few of these potential qualia are salient for someone who is appreciating amber as a material for jewelry. This "excess" in the material qualities of objects, as Webb Keane observes, can act as "vehicles of transformative pressure on . . . systems of meaning and of pragmatic action" or provide openings to new possibilities for meaning and action (2006:200). In other words, unexpected transformations arising from the material (like a wooden cabinet door warping or a color fading) draw our attention to different qualia and force a revaluation of the object. Similarly, changing circumstances can suddenly draw attention to qualia of things not salient before.

In Nancy Munn's account of Gawa, value-producing transformations of the material world are stable historically: things and people are reciprocal agents of each other's value, but the material itself does not catalyze disruptive transformations. Heavy, rooted trees are regularly transformed into light canoes that transport Gawans swiftly over the fast-moving water. The social ideal is for people to feel satisfied with only a little food and be able to leave plenty to give away and thus expand Gawan fame across time and space; moreover, "light" bodies are full of life, quick, and unencumbered by excess weight—an ideal shared with canoes and contrasting with passive and heavy states of sleep, illness, and death (Munn 1986). Any deviations from these trajectories are assumed to be the work of sorcerers who try to arrest and invert such positive transformations.

For more turbulent histories, we need to look at how radical changes to people's material environments become implicated in transformations of value that can reconfigure sociopolitical cosmologies. Such affective powers of the material, as I see it, arise from habituated engagement with densely valued materialities, materialities that are aligned homologously across different domains. They can become a form of embodied politics that pre-empt deliberation and can conflict with discursive understandings.

A Peircean approach calls into question the need for a theory of objectification, in which subjects and social relations "objectify" themselves in the material (Miller 1987). This objectification approach relies on the assumption (building on Hegel) that human beings come into consciousness by recognizing their difference from objects and other persons in a first stage of alienation, an alienation of the subject that is overcome via a Hegelian dialectic (Miller 1987). But what if we reject this a priori alienation and instead begin with the body (and embodied subject) as a material entity immersed in and engaged with a material context (including that of other animate materialities) that pushes back, merges with, extends, transforms but is never absent (cf. Merleau-Ponty)? This material is also a priori structured by the social, as Mauss observed for the body long ago (Mauss

1973), but not necessarily in ways that divide subjects and objects. Socialization draws our attention to particular aspects of the material and makes sense of these interactions in time and space, as we learn to recognize discrete objects and attach significance to them. But this significance is inseparable from embodied experience of these materialities or those intuited to be their equivalents (i.e., having one's engagements structured by past experience with like materialities). Such an approach does not preclude the possibilities of a subject or of subjectivities, nor does it discount the power of materialization.[16] It does, however, remove the need to posit objectification as the overarching principle for understanding the multiplicity of the material and its ever-changing possibilities. Moreover, unlike a theory of objectification, a theory of qualisigns allows us to investigate materialities that may never achieve the status of objects, with consequences for subject formation.

Anthropology and the Materialism of the Communist Project

The socialist state's reorganization of the material—from the "means of production" to housing to consumer goods—confounds conventional definitions of the material in capitalist contexts. What does a consumer culture look like under conditions that are fully monetized and commodified but not "capitalist"? In what sense was socialist citizenship also a form of consumer citizenship?

In its aims of total transformation of society, the state socialist project was a thoroughly "materialist" project, as well as a thoroughly modernist one. The state's investment in the powers of the material world to transform society and human consciousness provides rich terrain for exploring parallel concerns in anthropology about the relationship between the material environment, social life, and political subjectivities.

Communist Materialism

The "thesis" of historical materialism provided the justification for Communist Party rule as well as of a state-run, centralized economy. For Marx and Engels, the foundation of society is determined by its relations of production, or the how the social order is structured by ownership of the means of production, the organization of labor power, and the development of productive technologies. This material "base," however, is often obscured by a "superstructure," or the legal structures, ideologies, and prevailing moral codes that reinforce social hierarchies that are fundamentally based on economic power. The historical progression of this materialist thesis is that societies move through historical stages of such material configurations dialectically, always driven by expansions in productive capacity. When the communist revolution erupted in Russia, however, the Soviet Communist Party consolidated its powers by claiming the ability to lead society to the final stage of communism with its knowledge of the scientific laws of Marxism-Leninism.

Labor power was central to the theory of historical materialism. Manual labor in particular had the ability to transform the material world, and in the process produce people as human beings. Labor as a productive, social activity had the capacity to transform consciousness, and so would forge workers into socialist citizens. Indeed, labor was the activity that constituted one as a full member of society, as part of a nation of "working people" (*dolgozó nép*) (Stewart 1993:192). This Communist doctrine, while theoretically elaborated in Marx's writings, also echoed the work ethic of central European agricultural classes, except that it was now directed toward producing the prosperity of the collective rather than self-sufficient autonomy.

Communist Modernism

Communism was also modernism's greatest champion, sharing its faith in the ability of human rationality and technical power to transform the world (Bauman 1991). Like other social reformers of the time, communists did not blame the miseries generated by the industrial revolution—of overcrowded, filthy cities and the exploited working classes—on new technologies and rationalized systems of labor, but on the chaos and injustice created by a capitalist system. On the contrary, these new powers of production were to be harnessed by careful planning and used to end hunger, stave off disease, and provide a decent quality of life for all citizens. "Godless communism" did indeed condemn institutionalized religion for conditioning the working masses to await reward for their suffering in an afterlife, but communism also invested the mundane, material world with godliness in the form of gargantuan factories, planned cities, and collective residential forms. These were all to be harmoniously integrated into a larger, egalitarian, and humane social order.

Early Communist Party leaders in the Soviet Union had ideas for how to restructure material relations at their base, but the material order that would emerge from this restructuring was another matter. What would a communist society look like once the means of production had been redistributed? Radical architects and designers, many of whom were members of the early-twentieth-century avant-garde, stepped in to provide the "design of socialism" (Stade 1993). In sympathy with communist ideas, they believed radical social transformation was only possible with a complete rupture from the past, by taking people out of their familiar surroundings and immersing them in a material world stripped of all conventional signs and decorative artifice. This theory applied to buildings but also to everyday objects, furnishing, clothing, and even typefaces, all designed so that form followed function. Such honest materialities, they believed, would have the power to modernize and civilize as well as to foster collective sentiments and egalitarian social formations. Designed as a total environment, the early avant-garde claimed that the planned city could cause "the most backwards of nations to jump directly into the most modern of worlds" and thus skip undesired stages of historical development (Holston 1989:78).

Architects and designers regarded their work as part of the transformation of base and not of superstructure, but such claims brought them into conflict with the Communist Party power structure, where only the party could be the arbiters of economic base (Groys 1992). During Josef Stalin's decades in power, the doctrine of Socialist Realism demoted all cultural production to superstructure. Cultural producers were to perform the less important work of representing transformations in the material base. Moreover, Marxist materialism conceptualized modernizing development as one of stages and so spoke in terms of the "road" Soviet states had to travel rather than the leap advocated by the modernist avant-garde. For Stalin, this painful process could be "sped up" via mechanization and the powers of central planning, but not avoided. And yet, despite the persecution of avant-garde artists and designers, socialist new towns carried forward many modernist city planning principles, particularly the notion of building on a tabula rasa and designing cities as organized totalities.

After Stalin's death, modernist theory and design had a determining impact on the eventual look and feel of state socialist worlds in the Soviet Union and also in Eastern Europe. By midcentury, modern architecture had become International Modernism, a predominant symbol of modern state and corporate commercial power worldwide, rather than a tool for avant-garde revolutionary social transformation. This prestige, conjoined with its former revolutionary pedigree, contributed to its appeal. But socialist use of modernist forms continued to diverge from modernist orthodoxy in its understanding of the role of representation. The Communist Party never accepted the notion that consciousness could be transformed simply through the shock of exposure to radically unfamiliar materialities. Instead, the public had to be educated in how they were to experience and be transformed by them. Campaigns, seminars, slogans, news media, statuary, staged demonstrations, and even socialist advertising and packaging were all recruited for this task.

Soviet orientation to the material was from the beginning one of "ideology in infrastructure," in Caroline Humphrey's felicitous phrasing, as the state attempted to use the materiality of dwellings to produce new social forms and moral values (Humphrey 2005:39–40; see also Buchli 1999). And yet, while "the built environment made material certain precepts" and actively contributed to "the conceptual worlds of Soviet people," this did not happen in any straightforward way (Humphrey 2005:40). The buildings, furnishings, and other infrastructure constructed under state auspices did not have the determining effects theorized and desired by designers, planners, and party ideologues—even with explicit discursive framing. At the same time, the daily pleasures and (more often) struggles with these material forms, along with the often contradictory values and ideologies that saturated them, became part of how they were understood and experienced. In the study of these materialities, then, the challenge is to take the role of discourse and representation into consideration without allowing them to swallow up and entirely contain the possibilities of the material.

Anthropologists tend to agree with communist modernists that everyday engagements with the materialities of the house/home can produce, reinforce, and transform persons as social beings.[17] Even though the modern household is not arranged to homologously reflect and reinforce coherent social cosmologies to the degree of the Kabyle house (Bourdieu 1977), it remains a site that is shaped by and powerfully refracts shifting social norms and ideals through materialized aesthetics.[18] But anthropological research continuously demonstrates that human beings are rarely transformed by material forms according to the intentions of architects or designers. People confound attempts to change their behavior and forms of sociality unless they are willing participants. Nonetheless, the house as home remains an attractive site for social reformers, as they continue to see in its material forms the power to "engineer" social change.

I understand the house/home to be prototypically (but not always) a "subject-centered space" (see Munn 2004, after Merleau-Ponty) and thus embodied space. The dwelling as a built structure materializes ideal boundaries between inside and outside, the regulation of food and bodily waste (Douglas 1970). It is therefore ideally associated with physical and psychological shelter and sustenance; a place protective of vulnerable states (sleep, undress, intimacy, sickness, emotional distress); a place to store possessions; for hospitality; and for defining members of a household. The degree to which a house/home fulfills these capacities varies tremendously. Many adult men in Dunaújváros, for example, felt more at home in the local bar than in their apartments, where the only space they could claim as theirs was the armchair in front of the TV. Nonetheless, such a domestic space is usually constructed as the space *from* which one goes out into the world, for better or worse (Rulwert 1991).

Binaries Materialized

Scholars of socialist Eastern Europe and the Soviet Union find they have to contend with the numerous binary oppositions that are unavoidable in the region. The socialist state's project of creating an alternative modernity was built upon a diametric opposition to bourgeois capitalism as it was understood to exist in the West. The Cold War, as Katherine Verdery has noted, was "more than simply a superpower face-off" with "broad political repercussions. [It] was also a form of knowledge and a cognitive organization of the world" (Verdery 1996:4). The broader repercussions of the Cold War magnified and reinforced the opposition between communism and capitalism (or "democracy" as it was more often called in the West) and aligned it with other oppositions that continue to shape our political discourse as much as they do politics in the region: the private versus the public, the market versus the state, the individual versus the collective.

Scholars and journalists have tended to reproduce these binaries in describing everyday life during the socialist decades. They generally presume that, as anthropologist Alexei Yurchak puts it, "Socialism was 'bad'" (2006:5), and thus valorize everything and everyone that seemed to oppose it. Yurchak's achievement is to demonstrate how many people in the Soviet Union, particularly urban, educated youth coming of age in the last decades of the Soviet era, neither resisted nor embraced socialist ideology and state activities. The everyday life of "late socialism," he argues, was characterized by attempts to "live normally" without paying attention to politics one way or another. People went through the motions of political obligations, expending a minimum of effort and personal investment. Outright dissidence and resistance was, for this generation, just as problematic as enthusiastic participation because it lent far too much credence to a communist ideological project that had long been lifeless (2006).[19]

In Hungary too, the extent to which everyday life was politicized varied enormously depending upon the time, place, and the part of society in question. For example, consumption was far less politicized than it was Romania (see Verdery 1996:27–29)—in part because goods and venues for goods were more abundant.[20] Youth wearing blue jeans in the 1970s tapped into a complex set of significances, as jeans were not just from the capitalist West but were also the uniform of Western youth rebelling against forms of authority, including capitalism. By the 1980s, jeans had become fairly mainstream (Hammer 2010). Moreover, much consumption was promoted by state organs, and people sought out and purchased goods for a variety of reasons. Families and individuals were more than willing to purchase state-produced furnishings and move into state-built apartments while they implied upward mobility and modern lifestyles (chapter 3).

At the same time, we must acknowledge that at other times, goods and spaces were wrapped up in these very binaries, as apartments built by the state became refuges from it, or the failings of particular consumer goods became direct signs of the state's intent. The binary that organized the others was the opposition between an amoral public sphere and an idealized private sphere. While these oppositions were constantly shifting in discourse, depending upon the context (Gal 2002), they were nonetheless often fixed in the material.

Public and Private, Us and Them: Socialities of Production and Exchange

In its attempts to tear apart and then reassemble the social, political, and material, the state intervened in people's ability to produce and to exchange—both practices that anthropologists have considered critical for the making of society and personhood. Following Marx, many anthropologists have taken to heart that human beings realize their "species being" through "production" or their active transformation of the material world—turning nature into culture.[21] Following Marcel Mauss, they have demonstrated that social relationships are created and maintained through the exchange of material things (including people).[22] In its ambition to transform society and human nature, Soviet communism targeted these areas for intervention, but in centralizing control over production and exchange, the socialist state produced new forms of subjectification. In order to regulate production, the state abolished private ownership of material resources and productive technologies. While this prohibited one part of society from exercising monopolistic control over the means of production, it also curtailed people's ability to make things for private use or for sale to others. The state also attempted to abolish all forms of private, unmediated exchange. While this helped to eliminate usury, ruinous pricing, and exploitative employment, it also disrupted the social relationships that emerge through material exchange.

Of course, the state was unable to carry through these principles, and throughout the Soviet bloc, a second or informal economy of private production and exchange operated alongside and intertwined with the "official" economy (Sampson 1987). Because of the quasi-legal status of this second economy, it was often experienced as opposed to and autonomous from the official economy and by implication from the state. The second economy, however, was parasitic on the first for materials, technologies, and even the time workers "stole" from the state when they made goods for private use during regular working hours. Despite this drain on state resources, the second economy bolstered the socialist economy as a whole by plugging some of the gaping holes created by top-down, centralized planning. Because it was made up of people working through social networks, providing (usually) small amounts of food, goods, and services where they were needed, as well as providing alternate distribution systems, it contributed to the overall viability of the socialist economy. The second economy was one of the ways people "domesticated" state socialism and made it functional (Creed 1998). In Hungary, the state's implementation of economic reforms beginning in the 1960s allowed this second, informal economy to thrive, contributing to the country's relative material prosperity and its reputation as the "happiest barracks in the bloc."

Despite the entangling of public and private economic spheres in practice, the highly politicized and visible form of state intervention in economic activity contributed to the conceptual polarization of public and private. The unofficial, informal second economy and its materialities were idealized as a private sphere of relations between citizens without the interference of the state, and indeed often at state expense. Meanwhile, the formal, official, centralized economy was aligned with the public of the bureaucratic state as a monopoly producer, distributor, retailer, and employer.²³ Likewise, the sphere of family life and individual interests was idealized as a semiautonomous, apolitical, and sacred private opposed to the profane, politicized public sphere of the state.²⁴ Because these ideological contrasts between public and private often corresponded with formal and informal social relations, they reinforced a pervasive and simplistic moral dichotomization pitting "them" (the communist state) against "us" (the oppressed population).²⁵

The notion of such a "unitary state," as Paul Manning (2007b) calls it, situated over and against "the people," was widespread in the region (and in the work of Cold War scholars).²⁶ The socialist state was of course not a monolithic, omniscient entity, with all parts moving in concert toward a unified objective. It was made up of persons and organizations with diverging interests and structural conflicts. In the realm of housing and official consumer culture, for example, there was little agreement on how to produce material goods that would be both attractive to consumers and inexpensive to produce. Nonetheless, from the vantage point of citizens, the state was often conceptualized as the unitary entity controlling what happened in society, *even if* at times those citizens themselves constituted the state as architects, bureaucrats, producers, managers, salesclerks, and so forth. The state's role as the abstract source for most goods, branded as Socialist Generic, contributed to this impression (chapter 4). This appearance of hegemonic unity may have constituted the state's greatest vulnerability, as it unified an otherwise fragmented opposition. As Bauman puts it, "The doorstep on which to lay the blame [was] publicly known and clearly marked, and for each and any grievance it [was] *the same doorstep*. Conflicts that otherwise would remain diffuse . . . tend[ed] to be subsumed under one overriding opposition between the state and society" (1991:40).

Materialities of Public Space and Private Property

The ideological division between state and people, public and private, found a physical basis in the "simple geography of socialism" (Lampland 1995:273). The public spaces of the state, from bureaucratic office buildings and empty town squares to the stairwells and hallways of high-rise apartment buildings, were supposed to be collective spaces but in practice were spaces no one claimed. The unifying aesthetic of Socialist Modernism across residential and institutional buildings contributed to the perception that these public spaces, even in apartment buildings, belonged to an impersonal, unitary state. It did not help that this kind of architecture infamously rejected sheltering spaces for social congregation. In contrast, as much of this book demonstrates, people strove to transform the interiors of apartments into heterotopic private spaces utterly distinct from the building that surrounded them. There were of course many places on the state socialist landscape that escaped this reduction into private or public, such as forests and parks, swimming pool complexes, amusement parks, and churches, but the ubiquity of Socialist Generic architecture, particularly in places like Dunaújváros, became the paradigmatic materializations of this conceptual divide.

This simple geography of socialism was reinforced by the state's policies on property. By eliminating most intangible forms of property (such as stock), the state reinforced a notion of property as tangible and physical material—whether of the movable variety (*ingóság*) such as jewelry, cash, or a car, or fixed (*ingatlan*) like real estate. Furthermore, by eliminating any private property that could be used for profit, the state effectively reduced the "private sphere" to the household, meaning possession of one family-occupied permanent dwelling of limited size and a garden plot or vacation cottage. The curtailment of nonresidential property and investment options meant that for the population of homeowner/occupiers, investing finances, time, and energy into the apartment or family house and garden plot was the only way to achieve family prosperity or accumulation (*gyarapodás*) (Kunszabó 1983). The residential property not only became the main repository of family wealth but also the production site for many second-economy activities.

This bifurcation of society into public (or state) and private family-based property grounded evaluations of moral conduct. Taking resources, goods, and equipment from the state was widely accepted and sometimes considered a moral imperative, but strict rules of respect for private property were supposed to govern relations between private individuals.[27] By the 1980s, opposition intellectuals began to see the liberal political possibilities of the private sphere and to view the robust second economy as a potential space for civil society. György Konrád, the writer most associated with this view, believed that "official premises belong to the state, homes to 'society.' Home and free time: these are the spatial and temporal dimensions of civic independence" (Konrád 1984:202).

Some scholars have argued that property rights were insecure during the socialist era in a theoretical sense (Bunce and Csanádi 1993; Verdery 1996:298), but family-occupied housing was made a basic human right. State-owned apartments, once allocated, were practically inalienable; they stayed in a family through inheritance and could not be sold (though they could be traded for another state apartment). In the case of family houses, the sense of inalienability was reinforced by the tradition that property, often built through a family's own labor, should remain in a family's possession over generations. Kinship and property relations thus mutually constituted each other. Idealizations of "home" were linked to the materiality of "house," as evidence of family permanence (Miller 1994; Pine 1996). Locating such permanence in the family home became paramount in the 1990s, a time of social upheaval and economic crisis (Shevchenko 2009). Public resistance to the introduction of property taxes is evidence of enduring assumptions that the material home was an inalienable private sphere. The rise of a real estate market, while encouraging people to think of property as a commodity, has also intensified people's anxieties about losing their homes.

As in many places in the world, the home was an intensely moralized, value-laden space during state socialism. The ongoing and severe shortage of housing only heightened the values Hungarians placed on their homes. The economist János Kornai tried to normalize this attention to domestic space by reference to the West, arguing that Hungarians "take the English view that 'their home is their castle.' Most family life takes place within the walls of the home. . . . [It] is an embodiment of autonomy and one of the physical guarantees of the chance to retreat into private life" (Kornai 1992:456). But Kornai shared the sentiments of writers throughout the Eastern bloc who delineated the doorway to their yard or apartment as the sacrosanct boundary between what was "ours" and what was "theirs." "Apartments were for us mythical cult objects . . . they were life prizes," recalled the Croatian writer Slavenka Drakulic. "An apartment, however small, however crowded with people and things, kids and animals, is 'ours.' To survive, we had to divide the territory, to set a border between private and public. The state wants it all public—it can't see into our apartment, but it can tap our telephone, read our mail. We didn't give up: everything beyond the door was considered 'theirs.' . . . What is public is of the enemy" (Drakulic 1992:91–92).

This definition of the home (particularly the apartment) as a private space in stark opposition to a hostile world outside it shares much with Michel Foucault's notion of the heterotopia, particularly in how such spaces relate to other sites "in such a way as to suspect, neutralize, or invert the set of relations that they happen to designate, mirror or reflect" (1986:24). He distinguishes these spaces from utopias, which "have a relation to society and existing spaces through analogy": heterotopias "are absolutely different from all sites that they reflect or speak about" (Foucault 1986:24). For Foucault, ordinary spaces like the workplace or the home in France did not qualify as heterotopias. But in Hungary, as I show in chapters 5 and 8, private domestic spaces had the potential to be the ultimate heterotopic spaces, defining the world outside of them through difference and having the power to envelop and transform their inhabitants.

Of course, the apartment or house could never live up to such ideals for family autonomy and privacy. Even inside one's apartment, one could not escape the presence of neighbors and dependence on the state for services (however unreliable) such as water, electricity, and heating. Even rural homes without utility services were dependent on other forms of public infrastructure, such as buses and roads (Lefebvre 1991). Homes are also embedded in the larger society through interactions with neighbors, the neighborhood, town, and the state. And despite its idealization as a world beyond matters of self-interest, the home remained a locus for consumption and provisioning, for maintaining social relations through hosting, and for the display of social status.

After the fall of state socialism, tropes of the home as offering sanctuary from a hostile, intrusive, and "not-normal" public sphere remained entirely in keeping with socialist-era formulations (chapter 8). But in the 1990s, new private spaces such as the interiors of luxury cars were emerging, with heterotopic possibilities of the sort that Foucault originally conceptualized. Renovated apartments and the new ideal of a free-standing family house with an enclosed garden exemplified an anti-socialist heterotopia. Correspondingly, formulations of private and public were undergoing subtle transformations calibrated with new expectations for normal life. New residential spaces came to be places where a normal life could transpire, contained within but isolated from the continuing not-normal world surrounding them.

Mass-Produced Gifts, Do-It-Yourself Commodities

In some respects, the contrast between public and private, them and us, neatly replicates the analytic distinction in anthropology between economies of alienated commodity exchange and those of socially embedded gift exchange (cf. Gregory 1982). Anthropological accounts of postsocialist Eastern Europe and Russia are often tempted to reproduce this framework, aligning the socialist era with the personal relations of the second economy and opposing them to the harsh new world of capitalist commodity exchange. In these accounts, home production of fresh vegetables, sausages, and *pálinka* (fruit brandy) are celebrated not just as adaptations to regimes of scarcity and impoverishment but as forms of re-embedding production and exchange in local networks and modes of realizing personhood in the face of capitalist alienation (Ries 2009; Smith 2003).

There is no denying the gustatory pleasures and personal satisfaction that some of these forms of material transformation and exchange achieved for their producers. Analysis of state socialist economies, however, do much to scramble anthropological assumptions about the nature of the commodity and of the gift that were taken from contrasting capitalist and precapitalist economies (though most scholars now acknowledge that this stark division between the two has been overdrawn). Shortages intensified the commodity status of goods produced by the socialist state. When people throughout the region joined lines forming in front of shops without knowing what was being sold, they did so in the knowledge that whatever was being offered could be used to procure something else: thus they thought of the good entirely in terms of its abstracted exchange value. In contrast, mass-produced commodities from the West often appeared in the country as already singular and embedded in social relations—the very qualities of an appropriated gift. At the same time, many home-produced goods were made not to be singular, handcrafted creations, but in order to replicate commodities—such as fashionable clothing and home décor—whose images circulated in the popular media but which were not available in material form.

These peculiarities of state socialist material culture challenge anthropological axioms about the alienated nature of commodities in modern, industrialized societies. In centralized, authoritarian economic systems, the experiences of alienation and appropriation are decoupled from the commodity status of material goods and inhere instead in the context of exchange and in the specificity of the goods, including their distinct materiality. The Hungarian experience underscores the fact that in a time when the material worlds that surround us are almost entirely made up of commodities, the commodity status of objects tells us little about them and what they do in the world.

By focusing on materialities, I track the contradictory sentiments that people had for do-it-yourself production as well as for the second economy and its personalized networks of exchange (chapters 3 and 4). From the perspective of the neoliberal market reforms that transformed and often disrupted people's lives after socialism, scholars have sometimes romanticized socialist relations between people and the objects of their labor, as well as the social relations upheld by personal exchange networks. But urban Hungarians' dreams and expectations of a more normal life were often centered on disentangling material needs from social relationships. These expectations were fostered by socialist representations of a modernity to come, one that emphasized the freedoms offered by modern divisions of labor, impersonal forms of exchange, and the tangible separation of productive and reproductive spheres, allowing for idealized relationships seemingly free of obligations. The disillusion with the decentralized market system that has emerged over the last two decades has, in part, arisen from the persistence of the "not-normal" conditions assumed to be a legacy of socialism, in which whom one knows matters more than what one does in attaining personal and familial prosperity. As Georg Simmel noted long ago, the rationalization of exchange through money brings with it social alienation but also freedom from the burdens of obligation (Simmel 1978). By the 2000s, many of the new middle class in Dunaújváros had given up on the idea that such idealized relations existed anywhere in the world and had come to think that doing things through connections was fairly "normal" everywhere.

History, Economy, and the Demise of the Second World

The metaphor of the Iron Curtain dividing East from West, or dark, colorless and oppressive communism from bright, colorful, and democratic capitalism, has obscured the actual porousness of this boundary to the flow of commodities, images, and aspirations—not to mention economic exchanges in the forms of loans (from West to East) and labor (from East to West, especially in the 1980s). Moreover, it obscures the fact that economic, political, and technocultural phenomena, from the OPEC oil crisis to the spread of television, affected all of Europe, producing a coeval and entangled history.

Since the fall of state socialism, the spatial Cold War divide has been reconstructed as a temporal one, with the region's (communist) socialist past being opposed to a (capitalist) postsocialist future. This view has obscured continuities within the region as well as connections across this geopolitical divide. Rather than understand "postsocialism" as a phenomenon unique to the former socialist states, it should be seen as part of a wider shift to neoliberal policies and rising corporate power that were fortified ideologically by the fall of socialism and economically by the opening of formerly socialist consumer and labor markets.[28] The Hungarian economy over the past two decades has thus been part of a postsocialist global economic system, rather than the remains of a state socialist one.

Hungary had been moving in the direction of "postsocialism" for decades before 1989, with its market reforms and its promotion of consumer society.[29] The state's tolerance for a second, or unofficial, economy allowed for the limited growth of private entrepreneurship and contributed to rising standards of living, although the socialist "good life" was also subsidized by massive foreign debt. By the late 1970s, the Hungarian economy slowed and began to shrink, in part because the oil crisis had led to deteriorating terms of trade with the West. In the 1980s, the burgeoning foreign debt forced the party to retract its commitment to the basic principles of a social welfare state, increasing prices of basic consumer goods and introducing unemployment. Economic reforms gradually legalized private enterprises and firms. Although the Communist Party retained political control, by the end of the 1980s, it allowed for substantially different agendas between Communist electoral candidates, setting the stage for the relatively peaceful negotiations leading to the political transfer of power in October 1989. The end of Communist Party rule and Soviet occupation is thus referred to in Hungary as the "system change" (*rendszerváltás*) rather than a "revolution" or a "transition" from one system to another (a convention I follow here).

The system change nonetheless was a moment of fundamental transformation in Hungary. The supposed "transition" from state socialist to democratic capitalist systems brought into relief processes that had been taking place more gradually elsewhere: the protracted decline of the modernist welfare state and the rise of a neoliberal version of capitalism, with all of its contradictions (Comaroff and Comaroff 2000:298). The expanding media of the 1990s, now uncensored but pressured by market forces, published extensive statistical measures of the economy and social life. Between 1989 and 1997, per capita income declined in real terms by more than 30 percent, falling to pre-1980 levels.[30] With inflation, purchasing power dropped by 22 percent (the difference made up for by depleting savings), and per capita consumption was down to 1978 levels by 1996. By the end of 1997, the state-owned sector had shrunk from more than 75 to 21 percent. These shifts made things like telephones far more widely available but contributed to the astronomical increase in prices for utilities once owned and subsidized by the state.

The new regime, pressured by the IMF and other foreign financial and political institutions, embarked on radical decentralization and privatization, selling off state-owned corporations and interests, largely to foreign buyers. Foreign corporations were also attracted by Hungary's highly educated population of workers, from skilled factory hands to computer programmers, willing to work for a fraction of the wages of their Western European or American counterparts. The "entry" of the east European states into a global, capitalist economy was thus a misnomer for opening these countries to Western corporate capital which saw the region as a source of cheap labor as well as a new market for its goods—lowering prices to drive out local competitors or simply buying them up.

From a system of "mandatory labor," as some dissidents had called it, the massive layoffs from state companies or those privatized led to rising unemployment rates—particularly among youth, the elderly, and unskilled or agricultural labor. At the same time, the period saw a continued rise in white-collar workers and entrepreneurs and a rapid increase in service sector employment. The dramatic visibility of income disparities contributed to growing pressures to mark oneself and one's family as part of an emerging middle class.

While the unstable middle classes in Hungary share the anxieties of middle classes elsewhere, their experience reveals with particular poignancy how the fall of state socialism has reconfigured what it means to be middle class globally.[31] With the loss of a "second world," there is no longer a middle ground between First World and Third World citizenship—nor an alternative to so-called First World standards. The dream of a universal middle class, one that came with the national objective to extend modern prosperity to all citizens, died with state socialism. The penalty for slipping out of this middle class now is to suffer the consequences of falling into the denigrated state of a Third World underclass of people that do not count as full-fledged citizens.

Research Data and Methods

My insights into the interplay of political, economic, and aesthetic shifts in Hungary over five decades come from a variety of sources. In addition to research conducted in Budapest in archives and in general on national trends, media, and housing, I did archival work at Intercisa, the local museum in Dunaújváros, at the Land Registry Office, and at the steel mill library. I conducted formal interviews with professionals in Dunaújváros and Budapest (real estate agents, city planners, engineers, architects and interior designers, directors of the large housing cooperatives, city government officials, journalists and magazine editors, steel mill officials, home savings loan agents, and so on). I also talked with furniture and building supply store workers, as well as with people in the construction industry: builders, plumbers, painters, contractors, and producers of building materials. Through the sociology department at the local Junior Technical College, I took part in a door-to-door survey, investigating how people in different city sectors evaluated the quality of life in their neighborhood (based on criteria such as access to services, shops, parks and play areas, pollution, and transportation) as well as their attitudes toward such new phenomena as foreign companies and entrepreneurs. The bulk of my time, however, was spent with people in the course of their daily lives. During my fieldwork, I met with residents in more than eighty different houses, apartments, lofts, and summer or weekend cottages in Dunaújváros and its suburbanizing villages.

Fieldwork in the City

Fieldwork in a modern, urban environment where most people hold full-time jobs and are occupied at night with family and television has its unique challenges. Friends and new acquaintances were always pressed for time, but I also learned to avoid calling people in the evenings during prime-time television hours. Many professionals, understandably, granted me just one audience. Consuming the services of hairdressers and aestheticians was a way of guaranteeing regular, structured conversation sessions, as well as experiencing an important aspect of everyday life for many adult women in the city. Several women I met who owned *kozmetika* (aesthetician) businesses were married to influential men in the city, and their salons were places through which information circulated about real estate, business transactions, and city and factory politics, as well as more personal gossip. Horseback-riding lessons with a friend gave me an entree into pursuits favored by the local, aspiring middle classes and elites, while visits to the local fitness salon provided a window onto a segment of society attuned to new signs of embodied status (i.e., bodybuilding, tanning). I taught English conversation at a private language school, and often visited the village "elders" making up the Pentele Friendship Society. Finally, I had the questionable honor of joining for a short time Dunaújváros's semiprofessional women's soccer team, an activity not considered suitable for respectable young women. Nonetheless, I was exposed to working-class and youth culture through this ragtag team of players, aged thirteen to twenty-seven, who by and large regarded soccer as a potential avenue of escape from the city.

Except for some of the families I met through the housing survey and the soccer team, most of my contacts considered themselves part of a respectable middle-class society, albeit in very different ways. My roommate Judit, even though she worked at a low-paying job as a graphic designer, considered herself above factory work since she had gone to the *gimnázium,* or the academically oriented high school, rather than the technical school attended by most working-class kids. Her parents were white-collar professionals from "good families" in nearby villages. Her younger sister's upcoming marriage to a boy from a respectable working-class family was a source of considerable family tension.

To my initial surprise, I discovered that in this town of nearly sixty thousand, those individuals or families who assumed they belonged to this group usually knew each other or knew of each other. A young woman working as a radio journalist was following in her father's footsteps and had gone to the *gimnázium* with another young couple I met while looking into an Amway-like corporation selling Chinese herbal medications. The city planner, it turned out, regularly played bridge with the president of one of the housing associations I had interviewed. My main contact at the Land Registry Office was on familiar terms with a local politician and pharmacy owner whom I had met in his capacity as one of the town's first real estate agents. A factory manager, himself active in selling herbal medications, introduced me to the village elders in the Pentele Friendship Circle. These coincidences, of course, were anything but. In Dunaújváros during the state socialist period, the worlds of the steel factory management, hospital professionals, and the local government—which encompassed the housing bureaucracies and all educational, cultural, and media institutions—had been interlinked. "Respectable society" in town had become defined less by family background than by professional position and education, income and consumption patterns, attendance at cultural events, and style of dress. Coming from a good family was important but it was neither a guarantee of membership nor an absolute precondition. The stability of this social strata was under assault in the late 1990s.

Materialities as Evidence

Much of the evidence for my arguments about the relationship between material aesthetics and political affect comes not from informants' explicit statements but from the material culture and materials themselves. The material world vastly overwhelms our capacity to describe it in discourse, and so much of our phenomenological, sensual experience remains largely unarticulated. On the one hand, the material objects and substances we live in and with form a taken-for-granted backdrop that constitutes a deceptive "humility of objects" (Miller 1988). Indeed, aesthetic choices are often made unconsciously even though they are structured by the social, just as these choices (and everything that constrains them) communicate worlds of information about a person to others (cf. Bourdieu 1984). Just as such information cannot be easily captured with words, so our experience of the material cannot be reduced to language. Because it is "beyond words," as Leora Auslander argues, material culture can provide rich sources for "grasping the affective, communicative, symbolic and expressive aspects of human life" (Auslander 2005). Material arrangements constitute an expressive semiotic realm, so photographs of interiors (along with knowledge of their material qualia) constitute powerful evidence for the ways people attempted to "make" their domestic spaces. Similarly, the material design of products—whether handcrafted or mass-produced—constitutes a form of affective communication from producer (or source) to the consumer or user.

I draw liberally on cultural artifacts such as films, television shows, advertisements, newspapers, home furnishing and women's magazines, "do-it-yourself" instruction manuals, and museum exhibits, as much for the evidence they provide of the material and its contexts as how they talk about it.[32] During the socialist era, these media were by definition sponsored by the socialist state or one of its ministries, but what this meant for press "freedoms" varied enormously depending on venue, topic, and era. Some topics, such as architecture or the housing situation, were heavily politicized. In contrast, media coverage of home furnishing customs fell into the less heavily policed (and less prestigious) categories of women's and domestic issues.[33] The local Dunaújváros newspaper, particularly the back pages and women's section, provided a wealth of information about everyday life.

Print media often carried pieces in which journalists adopted the inclusive "we" to articulate the attitudes and assumptions of the average reader. This was not simply journalistic convention: when people learned I was interested in a certain topic, they often regaled me with opinions that had a similar "set piece" character, reflecting their individual perspectives and idiosyncrasies but also echoing the sentiments of others as well as those appearing in the paper. These conversations were ethnographically rich as both reflections of cultural perspectives and evidence of how readers were discursively interpellated.

Among national media sources, particularly important was the national magazine *Lakáskultúra* (Home Furnishings). From its inception in the mid-1960s, this popular and influential publication was estimated to have been read by well over a tenth of the population regularly. Until the 1990s, *Lakáskultúra* presented the lived-in and often cluttered homes of ordinary, "modern" Hungarians rather than interiors designed by professionals. It focused especially on those moving into or living in urban apartments, through photographs, floor plans, and interviews. It also offered "professional" advice to readers, occasionally pictured the home of a celebrity, and contained advertising for products manufactured by state firms or sold at state consignment warehouses. I interviewed *Lakáskultúra*'s founding editor, one of its main photographers, and several contributing journalists. While sensitive to the editorial aims and political guidelines under which this staff operated, I found *Lakáskultúra* to be a valuable source of visual and discursive information about middle-stratum Hungarians' ideals for their homes as well as the constraints within which they actually lived. After 1989, a host of new interior-furnishing and also house-design publications came on the market and were well received. *Lakáskultúra* retained its popularity alongside these new competitors, even after it was bought by the German media conglomerate Axel Springer in the early 1990s. While it continued to feature the homes of "real" Hungarians, these homes increasingly had the mark of professional interior designers.

People's reactions to films and advertisements, their attitudes toward homes presented in home-design magazines, and their discussions of television shows are usually performances of morality and "taste." But in the rapidly changing media and commodity worlds of 1990s postsocialist Eastern Europe, these reactions—however inarticulate—also illuminated shifting understandings of the social and cultural landscape.

In the chapter that follows, I provide the perspective of my main fieldwork in the mid-to-late 1990s that motivated me to go back and "dig up" the materialities of the socialist era. This period was marked by uncertainty and instability, one in which my interlocutors sought to find or create for themselves a normal life defined in part by material goods and living spaces. At the same time, their experience of rapid change was shaped by more enduring understandings of Hungary's position between East and West, and by an abiding sense of the importance of material order for evaluating one's own and others' moral character and well-being.

1 Normal Life in the Former Socialist City

The New Normal

In the mid-1990s in Dunaújváros, half a decade after the fall of state socialism, long lines once again formed in front of shops, but now for lottery tickets. An editorial on the front page of the local newspaper attempted to articulate the sentiments of the people standing in these lines, people still living in concrete apartment blocks, whose standard of living had declined rather than improved in the tumultuous years since the incursion of market capitalism.

> Most people know... that unfortunately in this world it takes a lot of money for a full life. If you want to update your library, travel, see the world; if you want to have a livable home, drive a normal car, and occasionally have a respectable dinner—for these you need a small fortune. (*Dunaújvárosi Hírlap*, June 3, 1997)

Throughout my fieldwork, people used terms like "livable," "normal," and "respectable" to refer to services, goods, and material worlds that met their expectations of life after the end of state socialism. New telephone systems, automatic teller machines, twenty-four-hour convenience stores, and courteous sales clerks were amenities that many Hungarians associated with the dignity accorded respectable citizens of a "First World." In contrast, they understood obsolete technologies and infrastructures, corruption and rude behavior, and the frantic pace of everyday life to be vestiges of a discredited socialist system. Scholars have reported similar uses of "normal" throughout central Eastern Europe and the Baltics during this period, as people used it to refer to things that were clearly extraordinary in their local context, but were imagined to be part of average lifestyles in Western Europe or the United States.

One could argue that such a normalizing discourse is precisely the mechanism by which older forms of consumption are replaced by newer, more elaborate forms. But that explanation forecloses a different set of questions: Why were such material environments and consumer goods normalized in these countries rather than explicitly marked as of European standard, as they were in Russia in the same period (Shevchenko 2009:128)? What functional and aesthetic qualities endowed certain places and things with such idealized normalcy, given that the ability to distinguish what counted as normal was not self-evident to outsiders like me?

The discourse of the normal indexed a profound adjustment of identity set in motion by the sudden geopolitical shift of these countries from Soviet satellite to aspiring member of a reconfigured "Europe." Once envied within the Soviet bloc as the most western (and thus modern) of the socialist states, these nations suddenly found themselves situated on the undefined eastern border of greater Europe, with all the loss of prestige this entailed. After 1989 they were in the unenviable position of having to prove their westernness in a new context—to themselves as much as to a European Union reluctant to grant them membership. Hungary was disproportionately affected by this shift in status, having once been a popular vacation destination for residents of other Soviet bloc nations, who had regarded it as a paradise of freedoms and consumer affluence.

But closer attention to the Dunaújváros editorial suggests that the "full life" promised by winning the lottery was not a new desire and thus not one that can be fully explained by Hungary's entry into a global capitalist economy. While the imagined lifestyles of respectable citizens in Western Europe were certainly a model for the aspiring middle classes in Hungary, the full life referenced here is not one of mimetic transformation. Desire for high-quality comforts, conveniences, and health care, as James Ferguson (2002) has argued, is not the same as imitation and loss of cultural authenticity. It is a claim to membership in a wider society where citizens enjoy the tangible benefits of advanced technologies and economic prosperity. Qualities in material goods such as durability and functionality, innovative styling, and user-friendly or beautiful design were material evidence of the well-being that many people had long assumed their counterparts in Western Europe enjoyed. This well-being was made possible by a private life that ensured harmonious family relations, hard work rewarded with the means for dignified living, and a state that treated its citizens with care and respect. As we will see, "normal" materialities were regarded as signs of the emergence of a modern, civilized country, one that conferred citizens with the full humanity accorded to those peoples of coeval status with a First World (Fabian 1983).

In Dunaújváros, as elsewhere in the country, people used this discourse of the normal to evaluate changes to the material landscape after 1989, creating spatial and temporal distinctions between objects and spaces that seemed to be contemporaneous with the West and those that seemed caught in the quicksand of the socialist past. I begin by describing changes to Dunaújváros in the 1990s, providing a sense of how people responded to the changing world around them and how it met or failed to meet their expectations. I then turn to an examination of this discourse itself, including how it built upon two other, more enduring ways Hungarians evaluated material worlds and the kinds of people associated with them. One was a discourse of national identity that alternated between situating Hungary in Europe and "the West," or positing it as an autonomous Magyar country whose authenticity stemmed from its eastern origins. Another was an equally long-standing set of discourses and norms for creating order (*rend*) in the material world. These three discursively explicit and morally loaded ways of evaluating the material environment will begin to ground what appear as conventional middle-class fashioning practices in the particularities of Hungarian history—and thus set the stage for the rest of the book.

A New Landscape

The regime change in Hungary catalyzed swift, ideologically motivated transformations to the built environment, most of them carried out by the first democratically elected nationalist government. The new regime focused on eliminating all symbolic references to the socialist state, communist ideology, and Soviet occupation in public space. As elsewhere in the former Soviet satellite states, the red stars that had graced all public buildings for four decades disappeared overnight. Statues of Marx and Lenin were removed, though some of these were later displayed, somewhat controversially, as socialist "relics" in a tourist-oriented park on the outskirts of Budapest (Nadkarni 2009). Ideologically charged street and place names such as Red Army Road or Lenin Street were literally crossed out, superseded by signs displaying names associated with presocialist Hungarian nationalism, apolitical names from the socialist era, or newly created names reflective of a nonsocialist Hungarian identity. In Dunaújváros, the city council named one street after Zoltán Latinovits, a beloved socialist-era actor, and another after Lajos Kassák, the famous modernist poet, writer, and artist. Elsewhere in Hungary, place names linked to heavy industry were generally equated with state socialism and replaced, but in Dunaújváros, names like Ironworks Avenue remained. For a time, I lived on Foundry Worker Street (*Kohász utca*) and noticed that when I gave my address to clerks in Budapest, they would snicker in disbelief.

As the streetscape changed, so did shop fronts and store shelves. Consumer goods once accessible only through trips to the West or through personal connections became abundantly available in shops, though access to them was now determined by raw purchasing power rather than by connections. The currency used to buy these commodities had also been transformed. Socialist-era symbols on bills and coins were replaced with grand figures from Hungarian history, including King István (Stephen), the founder of Christian Hungary at the turn of the first millennium, and Count István Széchényi, considered to be the founder of modern Hungary. The hefty weight and high quality of the new metal alloy coins, in contrast to the aluminum coins and flimsy bills of the socialist era, were designed to convey the substance and cultural value of European currencies—even as these were giving way to the euro elsewhere in Europe. These changes politicized places, buildings, and objects that had been for the most part, as Maya Nadkarni observed, "unnoticed facets of everyday life" (Nadkarni 2010:194–95).

In contrast to these rapid, largely symbolic changes, a more gradual unmaking of the material world of the socialist state was taking place through production of an aesthetically distinct built environment. The ground floors of city buildings, blackened by decades of exposure to pollution, were painted in bright colors to showcase small shops, restaurants, and boutiques with fanciful window displays, creating a bright commercial corridor for pedestrians. The renovation of one building on a soot-darkened city block sometimes threw the dilapidated state of neighboring buildings into stark relief. In the larger cities, new commercial spaces mushroomed, from postmodern bank buildings, luxury hotels, malls, and private medical clinics to big-box discount warehouses, gas stations, and convenience stores. Billboards, neon signs, and other forms of public advertising, which had been increasing in the last decades of state socialism, proliferated. The restoration of historic castles, churches, and cobbled streets was prioritized by both local and national governments. These artifacts of Hungary's presocialist past could be harnessed to transform the country's image abroad, de-emphasizing its role as ex-Soviet state and evoking its earlier status as part of the Austro-Hungarian empire.[1] Meanwhile, the maintenance of socialist-era buildings, both civic and private, deteriorated as state funds evaporated and unemployment rates rose. This neglect heightened the distinctions between spaces marked as "socialist," and therefore of the past, from those marked as part of the postsocialist present.

Many Hungarians also embarked on transformations of their domestic space. New neighborhoods of single-family homes emerged, contrasting with the apartment blocks that epitomized residential norms under socialism. Those unable or unwilling to make the sacrifices required to build such a house had recourse to interior renovations. In Dunaújváros, some people were only able to repaint their living quarters, but others showed me around new, open living spaces created by adding arched doorways and tearing down walls. Ceramic tiles in bright white or natural tones replaced linoleum floors. And the old, uniform front doors were replaced by doors of carved wood or padded leather or personalized with a brass nameplate. Although these changes were often not visible from outside, redecorating practices were publicized by ubiquitous advertising, specialty stores, television shows, and home decorating publications.

These new construction and renovation projects, undertaken at a time of great economic uncertainty, were often achieved at an expense far beyond a family's means. Nationwide, the average size of new houses was significantly larger than those considered comfortable by the socialist standards of the 1980s (122 square meters), and far bigger than the largest standardized apartments (72 square meters or about 700 square feet). Homebuilders and renovators sacrificed elsewhere in order to use the highest quality materials possible (*Magyar Nemzet,* Oct. 15, 1996), from Italian tiles, German appliances, and American floor heating systems to Hungarian porcelain sinks. And yet as I was shown around these newly transformed spaces, proud residents responded to my admiring exclamations by insisting, "Well, it's totally normal, isn't it?" (*Hát, ez teljesen normális, nem?*). I was bewildered by these reactions. In my experience in Hungary during the 1970s and 1980s, I had often been shown objects or spaces people had been proud of, such as an unusual belt buckle or self-built addition to a weekend cottage—and it had always been appropriate to admire such innovations and mark them as special. At first I wondered whether these statements were aimed at me, either to claim equivalent status with me or making assumptions about what I would think was normal for the United States. But I soon realized that this discourse of the normal was not limited to exchanges with or for the benefit of outsiders (cf. Herzfeld 1997). It was widely used in everyday conversation and in the popular media throughout most of the former Soviet bloc countries.[2]

System Change Comes to Dunaújváros

Given the rapid changes that followed the end of state socialism elsewhere in Hungary, I fully expected the system change to visually transform Dunaújváros equally rapidly, revamping the vast expanses of monochromatic apartment buildings with new colors and distinguishing forms. But in the early 1990s, other than the discreet iron bars on ground-floor windows and the rare outburst of graffiti, it was striking how little seemed to have changed. In fact, after 1989 new building of all kinds ground to a halt and the city became the physical embodiment of what Reinhart Koselleck has called the "one-time future" of a past generation (Koselleck 1985:5). Throughout the country in the 1990s, a common lament was the lack of a "vision of the future" (*jövőkép*) thought to arise from the past. In Dunaújváros, this was a problem of particular significance. Dunaújváros's origin myth as a new socialist city built on a modernist tabula rasa haunted its reputation and self-image. Unlike other towns in the country that had the material artifacts of a precommunist history in civic buildings, churches, and so forth, Dunaújváros had little upon which to build, little materiality of a valued past that could carry it into the future.[3]

By the 1990s, this town of 57,000 had spread out on a plateau on the western side of the Danube and could be divided into thirds. Multistory, residential apartment buildings covered one-third of the total area of about twenty square miles, housing 80 to 90 percent of its population (Figure 1.1). This was the main part of town, where the majority of apartments were two room spaces with a bathroom and small kitchen. A small neighborhood called the "Garden City" (Kertváros) was nestled in the midst of these districts of apartment buildings, where some families had been allowed to build houses for themselves. The steel factory and its grounds spread over the southern third of the new town, separated from the residential areas by a green belt. The final third consisted of the presocialist, run-down village of Pentele to the north, long ago incorporated into the city as the Old Town district (Óváros), as well as an area of single-family houses built over the last three decades of state socialism.

Dunaújváros residents were uncertain of how their city could manage the transition from stigmatized socialist showpiece to "normal," capitalist city. The dairy factory closed in 1995 and the clothing factory the following year. The city hos-

Figure 1.1. The two primary forms of buildings in Dunaújváros: in the foreground, a Socialist Realist residential block from the Stalinist 1950s; in the background, a high-rise "panel" building built in the 1970s. Visible in between are two five-story original concrete panel buildings from the early 1960s. Photo by author, 1997.

pital suffered the fate of medical health facilities throughout the country, namely massive funding cuts, which severely reduced the number of hospital beds and caused the flight of many trained staff, including doctors, to more lucrative private enterprises. Central to the uncertainty about the city's future was the fate of the largely state-owned steel mill (*vasmű*) employing more than ten thousand people in the mid-1990s, or almost a fifth of the city's population. By 1993, the unemployment rate in Dunaújváros had shot up from almost zero to 10.7 percent, though it had stabilized and begun to fall by 1995.

While many older working-class residents continued to identify with socialism, the elderly villagers in the old town of Pentele, most of whom were ambivalent about the new town, regarded the fall of state socialism as an opportunity. A "friendship circle" (the Pentele Baráti Kör) had been meeting once a month for years, sometimes for occasions such as a Hungarian song night (*Nótaest*). They wasted no time in constructing a memorial to the Pentele community members fallen in World War II who had never before been memorialized because they had fought against the Soviets. Next came a memorial to the two hundred local heroes who died in the Hungarian Revolution of 1848, signaling the resurrection of a presocialist Hungarian history and the old village's place within it. The group commissioned an eight-meter-high braided arch of white marble from a local sculptor nationally known for his use of ancient Hungarian symbolism. Erected on a hilltop along the main road into the town, the arch provided a new entry, reframing the angular cityscape behind it (Figure 1.2). In the unveiling celebration, a prominent local artist declared that with this monument, "Finally, there is hope that this city can come to terms with its own past. That it can believe, and make others believe, that what was, *is* now past" (*Dunaújvárosi Hírlap*, Sep. 28, 1990).

Among the other visible changes to the city, some were literally made from the inside out, as apartment privatization gave residents the right to make alterations as long as they did not interfere with the structural integrity of the building. In the higher-quality apartments of brick construction in the city center, built during the Stalinist period, people had more leeway to take down walls and enlarge windows. Some were able to buy or appropriate the attic spaces in these buildings to create spacious loft apartments (*tetőtér*). The city had encouraged such loft building in the 1980s to offset the housing shortage, but had restricted its size and scope. The lofts built in the 1990s, in contrast, took up the space of two or three of the standard two-room apartments below them. The terraces, mansard eaves, and double-story windows of these dwellings offered visible evidence that some people were beginning to enjoy entirely different kinds of private living space.

The steel mill's short-term future was secured in 1994.[4] Because it was the largest and most modern of Hungary's steel factories, the new reform socialist government decided to streamline and eventually privatize it. This development was enough to reassure foreign and domestic investors and allow the city government to initiate construction and reconstruction projects, even though a postsocialist version of downsizing had afflicted other city employers. It was then that the dramatic changes to the landscape in Dunaújváros I had expected in 1990 began to materialize. The city's aging symbols of a discredited modernist utopia now provided a muted backdrop for monuments to a new capitalist era: car dealerships, gas stations, banks, shopping centers, and several new churches. The designs, colors, and materials of these new structures highlighted their difference from the modernist architecture surrounding them. The Opel dealership and gas stations were painted bright yellow and blue. A new bank, clad in mirrored glass, went up next to an oval-shaped, multistory shopping complex, providing a sharp contrast to the large but faded modernist cubes that housed the socialist department store and national savings bank. As a socialist new town, the only churches in Dunaújváros had been in the old village, and the churchgoing population had been negligible. But by 1996, the support arches of an enormous cathedral, financed in part by German Catholics, rose to break the angular uniformity of socialist-era residential estates that surrounded it (Figure 1.3). Nearby, a Lutheran-Calvinist church of red brick with curving lines was being built in a Hungarian Organicist

Figure 1.2. Brochure including a map of the city and sporting the new crest. The photograph is of the new memorial, a braided arch forming a gateway into the city.

Normal Life in the Former Socialist City | 35

Figure 1.3. Catholic cathedral under construction in 1996, made of concrete panels and steel and designed by an architect trained in Hungarian Organicist school principles. Photo by Matthew Hull.

architectural style, another Western-financed effort that had targeted the socialist city as an ideal place to begin undoing four decades of "godless communism." And, although fairly small, the city's Mormon temple was said to be the first in Eastern Europe. (This affected my fieldwork, as I was often mistaken at first for a proselytizer. Most people's only direct experience with Americans was with the "polite young men" who were regarded with sympathy and yet irritation for their unwillingness to leave once they got their foot in the door.)

Before the new shopping center was finished, budding entrepreneurs turned ground-floor apartments in the panel-construction buildings into small shops and boutiques, ignoring the laundry hanging from the apartment balconies above (see Figure 1.4). A centrally located set of residential buildings housed an unbroken strip of small shops, offering an assortment of goods, from brand-name clothing and jewelry to pet care and computer products. These tiny shops marked their absolute difference from the unadorned, concrete architecture encompassing them through ornate facades ranging from industrial chic design to carved wooden entrances (see Plates 6a and 6b). Nicknamed "boutique row," the shopping strip quickly acquired cachet and became a popular meeting place. The city council responded by replacing the asphalt sidewalks with rose-colored paving stones

Figure 1.4. Window shoppers enjoying the spectacle of boutiques with colorful and eclectic façades set into the ground floors of five-story concrete panel residential buildings. Photo by Matthew Hull, 1997.

and added landscaping and parking. A young couple who took me there for a stroll commented that it came close to being a "normal" space and that they felt "as if it is already the West." At the same time, they complained about the lack of a "normal" café in town, discounting the stand-up cafes remaining from the socialist era. Teenagers I met were embarrassed that there was still no McDonald's, reading this as a sign of Dunaújváros's "not normal" status and further evidence it was being left behind in the new order.

Boutique row was rapidly displacing the town's main commercial strip, Ironworks Avenue (Vasmű utca), a four-lane boulevard, often empty of traffic, which ran from the city's central square to the steel factory gates. It was lined with massive, soot-stained residential apartment buildings from the Stalin era. In the early 1990s, several new restaurants and shops had replaced the old state-owned stores that occupied the street level, including a Fotex run by an American Hungarian from California, an upscale (for Dunaújváros) Greek restaurant, and a popular pizzeria named Zanzibar. New kiosks of private businesses carrying brand-name goods were gradually colonizing the state-socialist-era stores, as for example, an entrepreneur who set up a kiosk selling floppy disks and other computer accessories inside the state stationery store. The grand avenue was also falling into disrepair, especially because the town's only hotel, the Arany Csillag (Golden Star), was boarded up—closed under suspicious circumstances having to do with a privatization scam. For decades, the hotel had hosted the big New Year's Eve celebration in town. Its café and restaurant, adjacent to a small gift shop and beauty salon, had been one of the few public places besides the city library where women could sit alone and feel comfortable. It had also been the only place in the city where one could make an international phone call. Equally dilapidated was the movie theater adjacent to the hotel. Soot-stained walls framed the theater's plate-glass window displays, featuring mannequins in Diesel jeans and posters of Hollywood blockbusters. A socialist worker statue had been outfitted in graffiti with the hip-hop uniform of the local male youth—low-slung jeans, pocket chain, and the words "home-boy" inscribed on his rear end.

Throughout the city, spots of incongruous brightness appeared in the form of new technologies. Electric blue phone booths were installed on street corners, but they remained empty for more than a year. This was a bitter blow for many teenagers who were unable to afford the coveted *mobil,* or cell phone, and had eagerly anticipated the possibility of a little privacy for their conversations. ATM machines were installed in public spaces throughout the city. One had even appeared in the entrance to the steel mill, a monumental piece of Socialist Realist architecture with an internationally famous mosaic depicting the alliance of Hungarian peasants and heroic workers. When I commented on the poetic irony of this juxtaposition to the city planner, who had approved the installation, she refused to see the humor in it. "Why not? ATMs are a normal part of modern cities!" Within a year, the steel mill was dispensing wages automatically into bank accounts, resulting in long lines of workers each payday in front of the city's ATMs.

Elsewhere in the city, small twenty-four-hour grocery stores and other shops—many offering an eclectic selection of low-quality goods from shampoo to curtains—opened in the ground floor of apartment buildings. Most people welcomed these for their color and their convenience, but others grumbled that they were signs Hungary was going the way of the Balkans, as they more resembled their stereotypes of ad hoc bazaars in contrast to orderly, "European" shopping venues. Restaurants opened and closed with regularity. People I talked to assumed they were money-laundering operations for organized crime, given the inability of most families to eat out. As in the past, tiny roadside or doorway bars were regularly filled with men who had just finished a factory shift or were about to begin one. Several pizzerias thrived, offering their mostly youthful clientele inexpensive pizza with exotic sounding names and served with ketchup. A large disco and techno music venue called Remix opened on the outskirts of town and was packed on the weekends. I went there with girls from the soccer team, some as young as fourteen.

In many other respects, life in Dunaújváros continued as before. The three shifts of the steel mill (ending at 6 AM, 2 PM, and 10 PM) set the rhythms of the workday. Most men rode their bikes to work, while women took the bus or walked and came home weighed down by the daily groceries. Each Saturday morning, as they had for years, shoppers (mostly women) with baskets converged on the marketplace to do their weekly produce shopping, although the variety of goods as well as their prices had increased exponentially. The city tried to create more parking spaces to accommodate new cars on the road, although by my count two-thirds of the cars in town were older socialist makes and were often kept parked as owners could no longer afford gas. (Even so, by the mid-1990s there were seven car dealerships within the city limits.) The density of the buildings and districts made most areas of the city accessible by bus or even by foot, and young people could easily walk to meet one another. It took about forty minutes to walk from the city center to the far side of the newest and most distant district, built in the 1980s.

On the weekends, couples were often out in matching track suits with their children, riding bicycles. People walked their dogs or went jogging in the embankment park high above the Danube, or climbed the hundreds of concrete steps leading down to the water. This area doubled as a modern sculpture garden, the terraced grass full of steel structures with fading paint that most residents considered an eyesore, another legacy of the bad taste of socialism. On summer weekends, people who still had weekend cottages or garden plots in nearby villages spent their time there. Others escaped the heat at the large swimming-pool complex dating from the early 1970s, which included an Olympic-sized outdoor pool and an expansive park with volleyball courts, snack bars, and playgrounds. On winter evenings, most people stayed indoors and watched television.

Throughout Hungary, the repudiation of socialist materialities and practices was central to the establishment of a collective and individual identity in a transformed present. It was no wonder, then, that the city council rejected out of hand a suggestion to capitalize on the city's socialist origins and turn it a living museum of state socialist architecture.[5] The suggestion was made by the first postsocialist director of the city's tourism office (a professor of sociology at the technical college and not a city native). He later told me he believed it rankled both those who wanted to distance the city from its state socialist past and also those for whom state socialism was not yet something to be declared dead.[6] Instead, the council and the steel factory management embarked on aggressive modernization campaigns to shed the city's associations with communism and transform its image into one welcoming of capitalist reform and cutting-edge business processes. They made plans for an Innovation Center with a polytechnic institute and an incubator for small businesses. The town also sponsored an annual American car festival that attracted thousands, and invested heavily to renovate the old and dilapidated village area of town to imbue it with "historic charm" (*történelmi hangulat*).[7] The steel factory courted international investment with glossy ads in airline magazines. It had also commissioned a coffee-table book celebrating the factory's fiftieth anniversary, a narrative that distanced it from the megalomaniacal visions of a Stalinist regime and instead presented it as the ultimate realization of the modernizing dreams of the nineteenth-century Hungarian national hero Count István Széchényi (Horváth 2000).

Discourses, Cultural Categories, and the Material

The Abnormality of Socialist Everyday Life

The "discourse of the normal" in the 1990s marked the system change as a transformative moment—particularly in the way it created distinctions between the denigrated material remains of state socialism and those materialities considered acceptable for a postsocialist world. And yet this discourse was far from new. In the interwar period it had been used to refer to what was modern and up-to-date, and as we will see, it was one that was taken up as a modernizing discourse by the socialist regime. This discourse has some similarities with the normalizing pressures of modern, standardized behaviors and ideals that Warner describes for the United States (drawing on Foucault and Canguilhem), in which the norm as a statistical average and as a normative, middle-class ideal combine and are internalized (Warner 1999:52–60, 69). In Hungary, as in many east European countries, such normalcy is idealized and has its own local history in disciplinary institutions. But there is a critical difference. The responsibility for the inability to conform to such norms is not so much internalized as externalized, projected onto political, economic, and social systems that fail to provide the necessary conditions for achieving normal life, with crucial effects on for the constitution of subjectivity.

The Hungarian *normális* is taken from the Latin and has much the same meaning as "normal" in English: according to norms, standards; what is customary, normative, ordinary and average; in addition, what is nice, natural, healthy, dependable, rational, sane (Bakos 1994). In the classic Hungarian-English dictionary, *normális* is translated simply as "normal" but with two telling examples linking conditions and people. The first is the notion of "under normal conditions" (*normális körülmények között*), and the second of a "not normal person," defined as someone who is crazy (Országh 1987:768). As we have seen, synonyms for "normal" include "livable," "respectable," and "fit for human beings," while equivalent expressions for "not normal" (often said with exasperation), include "unbelievable," "catastrophic," and "inhumane." *Normális* could also be used (at times sarcastically) to refer to the familiar and authentically Hungarian in contrast to the newfangled and strange—as in not being able to find a "normal sausage" anymore among the burgeoning Chinese, American, and other foreign fast-food establishments in Budapest. As we've seen, the meanings of "normal" and "not normal" vary by speaker and with context—whether it is used seriously or with sarcasm, or whether it is applied to people, to organizations, or to the material environment. What counts as "normal" is always open to contestation.

Not mentioned in either dictionary, though, is the countercontextual use of "normal" that arose during the socialist period to describe the extraordinary, and the corresponding use of "not normal" (*nem normális*) as a way to criticize the familiar and the expected. This use originated in the perception—common in the Soviet bloc—of the profound "abnormality" of an everyday life under conditions of constant material shortages, all-encompassing bureaucratic entanglements, and the anxiety of living with an unpredictable, paternal state (Fitzpatrick 2000). In the 1990s, the phrase "This is not normal!" retained this connotation but also signified disappointment in the system change for not ushering in the "normal" accompaniments of a market economy and modern society more quickly. Not only had the anticipated high-quality commodities, service-oriented businesses, and trustworthy establishments failed to appear, but people also felt that their hectic lives of anxious rushing about (*rohangálás*) had not changed. As Ildikó, a successful manager at the steel factory, once explained to me: "Here, it's still not enough to work hard at several jobs. You have to go through friends to get things done. You can't simply make a phone call, but must do errands in person. It's not possible to trust a professional to take care of house-building or repairs, so you have to do it yourself. And if you come home at night tired, you can't go out to eat somewhere but have to cook. All these things burden a person, make them feel that they are scattered in all directions at once."

At the same time, people were acutely aware of the counterfactual nature of the "normal"; they knew that things they now referred to as "normal" were anything but. For example, a scholar in Budapest mused about her new, spacious apartment by saying, "I know it's normal, but it's going to take some time to get used to." Similarly, a young man on a bus nodded out the window at a silver car flying by, commenting to his seatmate ruefully: "If everyone had a car like that, that would be normal!"

Occasionally, new and unexpected changes brought on by market capitalism and democracy were deemed "not normal," but again, state socialism was often implicated in the lawless and disorderly form these new institutions had taken because of the legacy of socialist, dysfunctional systems and the attitudes they produced. Like some eerie inversion of Socialist Realist discourse, which posited the future-in-the-present with hope (Fitzpatrick 1992), the discourse of *normális* posited the past-in-the-present with bitterness, that is, the abnormal way the state socialist past interferes with a "normal" present.

This way of talking was particularly used by Hungarians who felt entitled by their profession or their family's status to a dignified, "European" standard of living. In constructing certain material worlds and consumer practices as "normal," they disassociated themselves from the stigmatized material culture of a "not normal" state socialist modernity.[8] Many of Hungary's former socialist middle class complained, as did the editor remarking on the lines in front of the lottery kiosk, that to live a "normal" life in this world was impossible without a fortune. But those people who had been able to acquire high-standard material environments also peppered their talk with such bitterness.[9] On the one hand, they complained about the extraordinary difficulties of achieving such worlds given the realities of the Hungarian economy of the 1990s and the "not normal" context of daily life. On the other, they felt unable to enjoy the fruits of their labors, given the mixed implications of such lifestyles in a society transforming its moral standards and systems of value. As we will see in chapter 6, visible signs of prosperity were burdened by associations with corruption, illegal entrepreneurial activities, and abuse of privilege, as well as by associations with a *nouveau riche*. Normalizing relatively extraordinary living conditions by reference to a Western European context was an important way of deflecting charges of illegitimate gain and maintaining respectable middle-class status. One woman, for example, described herself as belonging to a "middle stratum, not rich but not poor." Her new, spacious loft apartment had become "entirely normal" for her, but when guests came to visit they "took a deep breath with the feeling of space." She admitted that "the average Hungarian doesn't live like this, but in horrible oppression." And indeed, for many of the people hardest hit by economic reforms, loss of benefits, and chronic unemployment, socialist times came to be remembered as a time of relative prosperity and thus the "normal" compared to present-day difficulties (Búriková 2004:2; Creed 2010; Greenberg 2011).

Hungarians generally used "normal" to refer to economic, political, and social systems rather than to inner states of being or spirituality—much as Norbert Elias (1978) described the use of the term "civilization" in nineteenth-century England and France. When applied to people, *normális* indicated someone who was well-behaved, polite, and dependable rather than imputing anything more profound about their character, not even a good-hearted humanity. At the same time, "normal" systems were seen to be necessary conditions for the possibility of "normal" social behavior and private life, with consequences for the construction of personhood. A dissident political opposition in the last decades of the socialist era had often equated the "normal," as it was associated with what is natural and healthy, with forms of market capitalism and the bourgeois middle classes of European states, including those of the presocialist era in Hungary. Such institutions were thought to produce forms of order—legal, political, and economic systems—that not only worked "normally" in the West but created the conditions necessary for a "normal" life.

As in other places in the former Soviet bloc, many Hungarians had a sense that "not normal" conditions forced otherwise decent people to behave unethically (see also Pesmen 1999:1–2; Wedel 1986:151–52). This is what Ildikó meant when she complained about having to use friends to get things done. But Hungarians approached this dilemma differently than the Russians Dale Pesmen knew in Omsk, where people "who called themselves 'normal' either appealed to the value of their poverty, or, at least, mentioned that a 'normal' level of material comfort ought never to be achieved at another's expense" (1999:1). To become wealthy or politically powerful—that is, to achieve a "normal" material life—one had to be "abnormal" inside. Hungarians employed the reverse logic: one had to try to achieve "normal" standards of living in order to live an ethical, spiritually meaningful life, one that provided the conditions for harmonious relationships with one's family.

In the 1990s, Hungarians continued to imagine that somewhere out there was a place where people did not have to behave in these abnormal ways and could be treated and treat others with respect. When I pressed people to specify which country best exemplified their understanding of "normal," however, answers were vague and indecisive. Maybe it was England for its civility, or Germany for its roads. Maybe it was the Netherlands, where one man told me he was still amazed by the memory of seeing a bus there pull up to the curb and "kneel" to let a disabled passenger board. "Now *that's* a normal country!" he exclaimed, a place where the material world was in the service of citizens and not the other way around.

Discourses of National Identity: Hungary between East and West

Evaluating aspects of one's existence in this way arises from enduring discourses of identity in which peoples on the periphery of a conceptual West position themselves in relation to it. For centuries, political elites had to contend with charges of economic and political "backwardness" from their Western European counterparts. Susan Gal (1991) has written that they have engaged in "attempts to adopt western (European) models of material and technological advancement, 'civilization,' bourgeois life, and liberal democracy" on the one hand, and on the other engaged in the "contrary attempt to reject domination, first by demanding political independence and then by valorizing national identity; the creation or recreation of folk traditions and the assertion of indigenous spiritual values felt to be superior to those of the west" (1991:443). This dualism echoes Norbert Elias's (1978) analysis of the ways a rising German middle class in the eighteenth century countered France's hegemonic claim on "civilization" by positing their own superiority in the realm of a folk spirituality or *kultur*. Thus, ironically, "even the indigenist position, while ostensibly rejecting Europe, adopts western European ideals and the western image of a world of bounded, culturally differentiated social units" (Gal 1991:443; see also Graan 2010:841; Živković 2011).

Gal argues that the historic tension between the desire for Hungary to become more like a modern Europe and the contrary impulse to remain unique and independent has generated a "dual classification system" penetrating Hungarian culture (Gal 1991:443), where "West" and "East" constitute a kind of symbolic opposition with which virtually every social and cultural difference can be expressed and symbolized (Hofer 1991:161). Thus, the ways Hungarians classify everything from social groups to commodities are inextricably bound up with reference to the world beyond the country's borders and systems of distinction elsewhere (contra Bourdieu 1984). Depending on the situation, Hungarians use this East/West opposition to evaluate aspects of Hungarian life as varied as institutions, public behavior, hospitality, driving etiquette, consumer goods, toilets, punctuality, and women's fashion.

Western or European qualities, however, are not always positively valued and can suffer in comparison to indigenous analogues. The oppositions between terms West/East, Europe/Hungary, Hungary/Orient, modern/traditional, and so forth, shift in value depending on context (Gal 1991). As with Elias's civilization/*kultur* distinction, European civility can be associated with a cold, formal alienation and contrasted with Hungarian warmth and generous hospitality. Likewise, the ease but "superficiality" of Western friendships (generally specified as American) can be opposed to the allegedly less casual but more enduring and deep bonds between Hungarians. As we will see, this particular affective difference was deployed in the socialist period to distinguish the humanity of the "Hungarian people" from an alien, socialist, bureaucratic state, and then again, in the 2000s, from an equally alien, bureaucratic European Union. In the 1990s, though, the postsocialist discourse of the normal momentarily fixed Europe and the West, capitalism and parliamentary democracy, as the hegemonically positive norm for Hungary, aligning the East with a Soviet-imposed state socialism.

Hungarians I met over the years were acutely aware of how Hungary was represented in the Western European and American press.[10] One positive stereotype emerged after the Hungarian revolution of 1956, presenting Hungary as a nation of freedom fighters who were oppressed and tragically cut off from Europe by the Soviet Union. Socialist Hungary was regularly admired by Western politicians and journalists for its mixture of central planning and market innovations, dubbed "goulash communism." But even before 1989, Hungarians were also being tarred with the stereotypes that were to dominate a Euro-American imagination after socialism's collapse: impoverished, frumpy masses threatening to flood Western Europe, overwhelmed with crass desire for material goods but lacking the taste to make appropriate distinctions among them (Berdahl 1999b). People in Dunaújváros still smarted from the memory of humiliating treatment in Austria in the mid-1980s, when travel restrictions were lifted and Hungarians traveled in numbers to Vienna's main shopping street, Mariahilfer Strasse. A common sign had admonished them in broken Hungarian: "Magyar, No Steal" (*Magyar Nem Lopni*). The lived effects of this stigma showed in people's interpretations of interactions with "Westerners." An eighteen-year-old friend from Dunaújváros's women's soccer team was still outraged at the insult that a teammate had suffered at the hands of her host family while working as an au pair in France: they had apparently tried to instruct her in how to use their VCR, "as if she'd never seen one before."

The many critiques of the construct of "Europe" and its provincializing powers are relevant for Eastern Europe and the ways it has been constituted as "backwards" (e.g., Chakrabarty 2000), and yet this relevance is complicated in places like Hungary, with its own history of identification with a colonizing European empire. Accordingly, the West has played a more ambiguous role in national and other identities (Gal 1991). Historically, the bourgeois and gentry classes tended to regard themselves as European, and thus Europe was considered as much a part of one's own identity as something to be rejected as foreign. After the fall of socialism, a European standard became the measure of an idealized identity not only in the project of reuniting with Europe in the present, but for many, to reconnect Hungary with its own presocialist, bourgeois-democratic historical trajectory—one that communist rule had suppressed or distorted. Once released from the Soviet sphere, Hungarians demanded recognition of their European identity based on the nation's history, culture, education level, and professionalism, pointing to Hungarian contributions to Western civilization in fields as disparate as theoretical physics, classical music, and Hollywood cinema. With the removal of all apparent obstacles to rejoining Europe, the consensus in the 1990s was that the country must strive to become what it would or should have been if its history had followed a "normal" course.[11] As the realm of the possible was perceived to have expanded dramatically for citizens within this changed national context, so too did internalized expectations for realizing a "normal" life.

Ordering the World: Normative Materialities

The discourse of the "normal" became an evaluative measure, comparing Hungary to an external, partially imagined referent. "Normal," however, also built upon local systems of evaluation, and in particular on the role of the material in constituting personhood. *Normális* thus builds upon and in some cases is used as a synonym for the Hungarian word *"rendes,"* meaning "orderly" or "proper." The cultural concept of order has tremendous significance for the relationship between property and propriety, between physical and moral cleanliness, and for hierarchies and gendered divisions of labor. Sense of self and self-respect comes in large part from how one is evaluated by one's community, and central to this evaluation is the relationship between a person and his or her materialities. A person's value stems from how demanding that person is (*igényes*) for the material quality and state of his or her home, garden, car, animals, children, clothes, and body. The term *igényes* has no adequate translation in English but has positive connotations roughly equivalent to having exacting standards or discerning requirements for one's material world, of not settling for less. In some parts of the world, status is marked by the other people or servants who do this kind of labor, but in much of provincial Hungary, care for one's materialities remains a crucial index of a person's work ethic, ordering abilities, and character.

For this normative culture, to create "order" of various sorts is to return things to a positive state, to repair something, to make things right (*rendbe jön, rendbe rak, rendbe hoz*). In villages and provincial towns in the region, norms for order have traditionally extended from tidiness within the home to the yard outside, extending to the perimeter of one's property—always delineated by a gated fence or wall. It is the visible result of what Martha Lampland describes as a "rivalry of diligence," in which "constant, productive activity" is central to the construction of morality, respectability, and of self within a widely shared peasant ethical system (1995:316–23). This constant activity is not arbitrary, but must be purposeful and directed toward the maintenance and improvement of the family property.[12] With a few exceptions, work done for a wage for someone else was a sign of relinquished autonomy, building up their material prosperity at the expense of one's own (Lampland 1995:ch. 2). From this perspective, the importance of a material world over which a family has direct physical control becomes clear (see also Verdery 2003:178–81 for Romania). The socialist state encouraged such practices. In villages around Dunaújváros, many houses still displayed faded signs proclaiming that they had been awarded the distinction of "Clean Yard, Tidy House" (*Tiszta udvar, rendes ház*).

Such norms for order were not limited to the peasantry. Laura's mother, for example, remembered that when she was growing up as the daughter of a fairly prosperous shoemaker in her provincial town, a tuft of grass growing between the stones of the yard elicited moral censure. Similarly, the yards of weekend cottages throughout the socialist period and into the 2000s were meticulously tended, including the area just in front of the mandatory fence. These owners would not cut the grass or trim the hedge one centimeter over the line dividing their property from their neighbors'—not out of ill-will, but out of respect for culturally shared notions linking social worth to the orderly maintenance of property. To have done so would have been to insult the neighbors' work ethic.

Gender was reinforced by the division of labor in these ordering practices. For women, being *rendes* implies caring not only for their own bodies but those of their children, husband, and elderly parents as well. On a bus in Budapest, I watched as a little girl was coached by her grandmother to fold her cloth handkerchief, matching up the corners and putting it in her bag without wrinkling it. When she failed, her grandmother admonished, "No boy will want to marry such a disorderly girl!" As this anecdote reveals, while women are conventionally held responsible for creating order in the home, men internalize a demand for this order—as well as the right to rebel against it. Men were generally assumed to be responsible for order in the social world: of their families, of politics.[13] Many men also held themselves to high standards of orderliness at home, but we will see how at times their masculinity demanded that they rail against the constraints imposed by women's ordering powers. Women I asked about this agreed that it was almost expected of men that they display a certain level of unruliness and to feel entitled to abandon self-control now and then, especially when drinking.

For respectable Hungarians in Dunaújváros, order and cleanliness were inseparable concepts. While I rented a room from Judit, a divorced graphic designer in her early thirties, I learned to wash, dry, and put away my dishes and utensils immediately after using them; to wash the stove, replace the stove cover and top it with a decorative cloth after each use; and not to splash water on the tiles in the renovated bathroom when I took a shower. I once came home to an angry note, for I had left in a rush and had forgotten my dirty coffee cup in the sink. Judit's sister had come to visit and had interpreted my slovenliness as entitlement, assuming that I expected Judit to clean up after me. Other women boasted to me that they got down on their hands and knees and washed the kitchen floor every night before going to bed. Some were explicit in comparing their standards for cleanliness favorably to those of Germans, widely considered to be the cleanest and most orderly peoples in the region.

Such norms for order were collectively reinforced. If I tried to leave someone's home with an item that had been given to me, I was not allowed to take it without a bag. If I stepped off of the brick pavers by the bus stop and onto the gravel, I was reprimanded with sharp stares until I returned to them. Such orderliness was inseparable from evaluations of character, such as being nice, decent, good, upright, respectable, punctual, and dependable. For example, an elderly gentleman scholar in the village greeted me at our first meeting with the following: "I could tell right away you were a *rendes* person, because you came on time!" Conversely, someone who was not *rendes* was someone who was not to be trusted. Orderly behavior (*rendes viselkedés*) is to behave properly. To be disorderly (*rendetlen*) is not only to be untidy or messy, but to be tardy, careless, and negligent, even to be a troublemaker. In Dunaújváros, a woman's exacting "orderly" appearance—meaning cleanliness, grooming (especially of nails), pressed clothing—indexed her propriety. A woman was beyond reproach even if she wore revealing modern clothing such as a transparent blouse, as long it was clean and pressed and as long as she was moving through public space, tending to her tasks. Conversely, disheveled clothing and aimless standing around drew looks of fierce disapproval; indeed, the local prostitutes could be identified less by what they wore than by where and how they stood. It was precisely this connection between order and respectability that made unwashed blue jeans such a potent countercultural form of dress in the 1960s and 1970s, especially among Hungarian university students, beyond their symbolic and material connection to a decadent West. The material properties of jeans, tight at the crotch and durable enough for the wearer to sit on the ground, violated viscerally held norms for propriety and cleanliness. In the face of an "otherwise, vulgar, dishonest, and defaced world of middle-class culture," the dirty jeans stood for "a sense of purity and authenticity" (Hammer 2010:141).[14]

For the mainstream population, however, disorderliness was used to justify the fate of the poor and marginalized. The president of the largest council housing estate in Dunaújváros made regular visits to evaluate families who had requested an apartment. He told me that he often encountered "a mess, two big dogs, and beer bottles in the corner. I don't give these people a chance." He boasted that he told them outright what he thought: "If I were them, I wouldn't have the gall to ask for an apartment. First, I have to make order for myself!" Such people were undemanding of their material worlds or *igénytelen,* and such complacence was equivalent to laziness and moral degradation. Non-Magyar ethnic groups as well as lower classes were evaluated according to perceptions of their orderliness or, conversely, laziness. The Germanic Schwab (or *Sváb*) populations fairly numerous in western Hungary were known for their orderliness, just as in the 1990s Chinese immigrants were often favored over local Roma because they were thought to be cleaner and harder-working.

Despite the overwhelming terms in favor of order and the normal, exceptions continued to be made for some people who were "not normal" in their habits or who were allowed to transcend the realm of "order" (*rendkívül*), someone or something extraordinary. A theater director I knew was a paradigmatic example, someone very well-liked and admired but who rarely behaved like a "normal" person. Like Russians in the socialist city of Omsk, Hungarians seemed have a sense that a certain abnormality or eccentricity was considered acceptable—even necessary—for creative people (Pesmen 1999:3). Intellectuals and teachers were often accorded the distinction of being highly civilized, and perhaps for this reason were considered above the normative demands of orderly cleanliness. As a female sociologist in Dunaújváros explained, "I have so much to read—I don't have time to be an order fanatic (*rendmániás*)."

At times in Hungarian history, as Hofer has shown (1984), a valued characteristic of national identity has been precisely its (masculine) disorder, manifested in qualities once associated with the Hungarian Protestant gentry in the eastern part of the country—generosity, passion, rebelliousness. At other times, such values would be subordinated to those associated with an Austrian law-abiding order and calculating restraint, more prominent in the western half of the country, where there were more Schwab ethnic Germans (Gal 1993). With market reforms came renewed appreciation for values ostensibly embodied by this largely Catholic, rural ethnic group, values aligned with the capitalism of Weber's "protestant ethic": diligence, frugality, rational investment, austerity but respect for material accumulation (Kovács 1990, cited in Gal 1993). Any previous romanticization of Hungarians as embodying "transient" sociality (to use Miller's term [1994]) had, for the moment, given way to ideals of control and restraint.

Demanding Materialities after the System Change

With *rendes*, respectability inheres in the visible labor a person or family expends to order their material self and possessions rather than in the amount or value of those possessions. *Normális*, on the other hand, takes the nuances of *rendes* and locates them in a modern, commodified world. A young woman of twenty related to me how in high school she was often chided by her peers for using an old backpack and wearing a dress her mother had made for her years before. They used to say to her, "What's wrong with you? You aren't normal!" She explained, "It is no longer enough to be clean and neat, to have one's clothes in order (*rendben*). Now one has to have brand names and other status symbols."

Indeed, the most effective sign of participating in a transformed social order was with prestigious consumption—such as fashionable clothes, brand-name accessories, and a new cell phone. A reporter for the local paper, Márta, remarked with bitterness that her salary didn't allow her to dress properly for her profession. She was sure that when she went on assignment wearing the same old, worn boots, people whispered, "That woman has low standards, lacks self-respect" (*Igénytelen a nő!*). "This isn't normal!" she cried. "I know what would be appropriate to wear, how to look, but I simply can't afford it."

Hungary's changing geopolitical status had suddenly recontextualized Western goods that had long been regarded as special. Now their abundance and availability for cash created confusion in how people were to respond to them. To mark oneself as part of a new, European middle class, it became necessary to regard such goods as part of a normal, everyday life, even if they were prohibitively expensive relative to average incomes. Other things that people had long prized were being re-evaluated in the 1990s. In rural areas, for example, the "modern" indoor bathrooms installed by peasant families wealthy from the second economy during the 1970s and 1980s had often only been used for display, and family members continued to frequent the outhouse. But after 1989, these bathrooms were put to use.[15]

Integrating Hungary into a Western-standards material world meant that such standards had to be normalized. Sigrid Rausing (1998) has written of the incentives in postsocialist Estonia to normalize the meanings and values of objects once considered unfamiliar or exotic. Newly available but expensive Western consumer goods such as jeans and detergent could no longer be "occasions for surprise, enthusiasm or confusion," but had to be "redefined as already taken-for-granted" (Rausing 1998:190). Normalizing or even denigrating such goods not only endowed individuals with a timeless "European" and "anticommunist" identity, but it identified them as successful participants in the capitalist economy (Rausing 1998:208).

At the same time, responses to the influx of goods and what they represented were often more ambivalent. Younger generations in particular had an expression they used when they encountered a product with some kind of unexpected but inessential innovation. One evening in 1996, I joined a small but lively gathering at a friend's apartment in Dunaújváros. At some point, a young woman named Klára picked up a juice carton with a new (at the time) handy screw-top opening and muttered, "Pure American!" (*Tiszta amerikai!*) as she poured herself a glass. The expression usually expressed appreciation for Western designs maximizing user comfort, particularly in contrast to state socialist products, but it also carried with it a note of amused disbelief and disdain for such frivolous inventions, so sincerely dedicated to the pursuit of comfort and ease.

Heterotopias of Normalcy

The increasing visibility of new, postsocialist spaces sharply contrasted with and transformed the significance of the older spaces around them, creating disjunctures in temporal and spatial experience. These "normal" spaces were much like those Foucault describes as heterotopias, spaces that manage to invert the set of relations governing spaces outside of them, and thus are "absolutely different from all sites that they reflect or speak about" (Foucault 1986:24). And indeed, some of these new spaces—brightly lit gas stations in the middle of agricultural fields, malls with fantasy themes, luxury cars speeding through the landscape—were seen to be "absolutely different" from and opposed to those spaces associated with the socialist era, most notably aging commercial spaces, bad roads, and the crumbling concrete of residential areas.

But the Hungarian landscape in the 1990s could not be so easily divided into static socialist and postsocialist material worlds (Vörös n.d.). Even in Dunaújváros, many spaces marked as "normal" resulted from transformations to the built environment made in the 1980s. Even so, these buildings were understood to conform to a postsocialist aesthetic and were thus incorporated into the logic of "before" and "after" stories. The outdoor farmer's market that had been built in the late 1980s was considered a "normal" material space, in part because it was made of exposed brick and surrounded by an arcade-like building housing small shops. To my untrained eye, a house built in the 1980s might look new, just as my apartment-mate's reupholstered socialist-era couch could have come right out of a recent IKEA catalog. Friends and acquaintances were surprised at my inability to perceive aesthetic differences that to them clearly distinguished the products of the postsocialist era from those produced during state socialism. More than just postmodern trends, these differences were linked to impressions of quality and to perceived intent in design and production, all of which carried affective powers.

Middle-class aspirants' insistence on the normalcy of such environments was not merely a way to justify luxury and comfort. It elucidated the depth, tenacity, and character of expectations that had been fostered over the socialist period. "Not normal" conditions remained after the fall of state socialism, but their persistence did not dampen expectations for the private, material spaces of new houses, "American" open-plan kitchens, and luxurious bathrooms. Desire for such "normal" spaces stemmed from a cultural logic that cast them as conducive to imagined, idealized lives—places that produced "normal" people and where a "normal" life could transpire, insulated from the "not normal" world surrounding them. This project of transformation through the material was made salient by the ideological and aesthetic project of "building socialism" of the preceding forty years.

In order to show the power of this notion of "normal" to shape practices and subjectivities, particularly in exerting intense social pressures on individuals to transform themselves through their material worlds, I turn in the next chapters to the state socialist period. The mass consumer society and modern consumer subjectivities fostered by state socialist materialities led people to equate modern standards of living with the self-value and dignity merited by a "modern" citizen. Elite taste makers propagated the importance of domestic material culture for the development of a modern citizenry, but at the same time, the private, domestic sphere became idealized as a site of autonomy and refuge from an intrusive state and the "abnormal" social, economic, and political conditions it fostered.

2   Socialist Realism in the Socialist City

In April 1950, workers began clearing land on an orchard-covered plateau overlooking the Danube River some sixty kilometers south of Budapest. Curious villagers from the nearby settlement of Dunapentele learned that the workers were building barracks for a new steel mill. They were soon to discover that the site had also been selected for the massive project of building Hungary's first socialist "new town." The factory was to provide steel for an anticipated war with the West, but the new town, named Sztálinváros, or City of Stalin, was to model the socialist utopian society to come. Like other new towns being built throughout the Soviet bloc, it was intended to demonstrate the ability of a Communist Party–led, centrally planned, socioeconomic system to effect a wholesale transformation of society and to usher in an alternative modernity, one that avoided the misery of capitalist urbanization and industrialization.[1]

In contrast to the disorder of the existing industrial cities and backward villages, this new town was to feature a modern division of labor in which each member of a literate citizenry contributed to the working of the whole. Publicity campaigns promised a "good life" for the entire population, a life epitomized in modern urban living with central heat and indoor plumbing—comforts that were still rare in the countryside. The rational organization of labor would ensure that residents and workers in the new town could purchase rather than produce the goods they needed and enjoy the novelty of leisure time to be spent in cultivating the self.

The city was to be the Stalin era's most impressive embodiment of Socialist Realism, the doctrine by which all forms of representation were to model the country's socialist future. It also reflected residual modernist avant-garde understandings of the transformative powers of a built environment planned as an organic totality. Such convictions in the agentive powers of the built environment to transform consciousness were subordinated to the Marxist-Leninist principle that the powers of physical labor, and thus the literal "building" of socialism, was to transform habits and mentalities. Yet the new town was to retain basic modernist city elements: garden belts, totality, axes, planning.

As a testament to the socialist system, the new town was both a success and a failure. While it provided attractive images and material evidence of the promised socialist way of life, it fell short of offering adequate food, shelter, and employment (much less education and health care) for most of those who had actually built it. Most significantly, the regime's failure to make good on promises of providing new, modern housing in an egalitarian fashion established enduring social inequalities.

Postwar Rebuilding and the Communist Takeover, 1945–1948

Hungary entered the Second World War late, reluctantly siding with the Germans against the Soviet Union in the hopes of regaining territories lost after the First World War (Cornelius 2011). This decision had disastrous consequences. The war destroyed a quarter of the country's industrial capacity, paralyzed its transportation system, and damaged or leveled three-quarters of the buildings in Budapest. Military maneuvers had stymied agricultural activity, and at least half of the country's livestock had perished. Stiff reparations to the Soviet Union, Yugoslavia, and Czechoslovakia created intense inflation (Berend and Ránki 1985:179–80). The population of about ten million had been devastated by the loss of an estimated 500,000 in war-related battles, 400,000 Hungarian Jews locally or in German camps (Szelényi et al. 1988:7) and, in the final stages of the war, 600,000–700,000 POWs sent to labor camps in the Soviet Union (Stark 2006:251–52). The difficulties of the reconstruction period were compounded by the loss of an additional 5 percent of the population to emigration, a high proportion of which were from the most educated classes (Molnár 1990:103; Róna-Tas 1997:35).

In 1945, Hungary's newly elected coalition government, headed by the Smallholder's Party, embarked on the radical reconstruction of its war-torn space. It began by breaking up large estates and redistributing land to the peasantry in an attempt to fulfill an idyllic vision of Hungary's future as a small, modern, agrarian democracy, a "Denmark on the Danube" (Szabó 1988:690). The years 1945–1947 were a time that many Hungarian historians in the 1970s and 1980s nostalgically remembered as a genuinely democratic and progressive moment, made possible by the departure of the aristocratic class that had staunchly opposed reform of the semifeudal order. In the waning days of the war, large land- and factory owners had fled before the advancing Soviet army, and local village committees often took the initiative in dividing land and distributing it to the landless. In towns, workers took over abandoned factories and restored production in a wave of de facto nationalization (Hare 1988:116). Reconstruction and progressive reforms proceeded rapidly under a provisional government. It began to restructure the bureaucracy and to improve the communication network, social security system, and health services in the countryside. "People's colleges" were set up to expand education opportunities for peasant youth (Gáti 1986:68).

As in much of postwar Europe, the challenge of reconstructing the country had a unifying effect. The era was dominated by themes of building for the future. A younger generation of intellectuals was drawn to the modernist movement, identified as simultaneously international and Hungarian because of the active participation of Hungarians in early avant-garde art and architectural movements.

Many building professionals saw modernist architecture as the most important tool for the development of a new society, based not only on the legacy of Hungarian urban sociology and city planning, but because both CIAM (the International Congress of Modern Architecture) and Soviet constructivism offered architects and city planners a primary role in that process (Szirmai 1988:94). Hungarian architects and engineers who had left a country inhospitable to their avant-garde ideas during the conservative interwar period returned, seeing opportunity in the rubble—a modernist tabula rasa on which to implement long-desired modernization and social reform (Szirmai 1988). It was a time of building the country anew rather than restoring an old order (Szabó 1988).

Despite its minority stake in the new coalition, the Communist Party wielded enormous influence through its alliance with the Soviet forces that continued to occupy the country and its control over the Ministry of the Interior and economic council. It began by pushing through the nationalization of heavy industry, mining, electrical generating facilities, and the financial sectors. By 1947, the ten largest banks had been nationalized (Hare 1988:117). Communist Party leaders also led negotiations with the Soviet Union over the terms of Hungary's burden of war reparations and granted the Soviets control over the five largest heavy industrial firms (Róna-Tas 1997:35–36). Along with other countries in the Soviet sphere of influence, Hungary was pressured to decline massive reconstruction aid from the U.S.-sponsored Marshall Plan. Instead, the country was forced into exploitative trade agreements and "joint ventures" with the Soviet Union (Borhi 2004:140). The overwhelming damage the Soviet Union inflicted on these central European economies through a systematic program of economic extraction is often neglected in descriptions of the economic backwardness of the region.[2]

The Great Transformation: Stalinist Modernization

In 1948–1949, the Communist Party eliminated its opposition and took control of the country. Plans for social reform and modernization were intensified. The agricultural population, which made up more than 50 percent of the nation's inhabitants, was to be transformed into a modern working class; correspondingly, agriculture was to be sacrificed to industry to transform the country into a "land of iron and steel." As Zygmunt Bauman observes, the Communist regime's objectives were grounded in the modernist dream of a total transformation of society, from its economic, political, and social structures to human consciousness itself: "It was under communist, not capitalist, auspices that the audacious dream of modernity, freed from obstacles by the merciless and seemingly omnipotent state, was pushed to its radical limits: grand designs, unlimited social engineering, huge and bulky technology, total transformation of nature" (Bauman 1991:38–39).

The first five years of Communist Party rule saw the radical overhaul of Hungarian economic and social structures and the consolidation of one-party rule. The party nationalized all privately owned media, eliminated religious organizations and private schools, centralized and co-opted all formal and informal civic activities and associations (from the boy scouts to chess clubs), and eliminated the right to private property. As part of this process, all independent architectural, engineering, and construction businesses were combined and controlled by one central planning office, which was then responsible for the design and administration of all construction projects in the country. This strict control over all sectors of society was justified by the need to ensure, as István Rév writes, that "the billions of individual acts contributed to the gigantic task of social construction . . . the grand social vision of the planner" (1987:337).

Ironically, this "great transformation," as Ákos Róna-Tas (1997) calls it, managed to produce the very historical process that the Hungarian economic-historian Karl Polanyi had attributed to capitalism in the industrialized West—namely, the disembedding of economic transactions from local social worlds (Polanyi 1944). Put another way, the state's centralized economic structure severed previous forms of local economic exchanges and the social relationships they maintained. Economic transactions had been deeply embedded in local social relationships and forms of production. But instead of being absorbed into the abstracted world of capitalist markets, where producers and consumers are often separated by vast distances and remain unknown to one another, these local economies were taken up into the abstracted and impersonal bureaucracy of the centralized state. In the process, much private production and exchange became criminalized.

The Stalinist state had begun the nationalization and industrialization of agriculture in the late 1940s, first by confiscating land that had recently been given to the landless peasantry, and then through a largely unsuccessful attempt to collectivize agriculture. It used punitive taxation and compulsory deliveries of produce and livestock to push people into collectives, policies that greatly exacerbated the hardships already faced by villagers. General hostility toward the regime was intensified by policies that criminalized practices that had long been central to rural life, such as slaughtering one's own pig.

To deal with private property in housing, larger owner-occupied houses and apartments were appropriated by the state and carved into smaller units, or homeowners were forced to share their space with other families. For the next four decades, Hungarian law limited families to one permanent winterized dwelling that they either owned or had been allocated by the state. This law eliminated and vilified in one stroke the category of the landlord, effectively prohibiting anyone from using their control over property to exploit others. Shortages of housing pressured the state into allowing people to sublet apartment space from time to time, but in principle only the state could control rental housing in the name of the peoples' welfare and not for profit.

Along with landlords, all other professions that were seen to control means of production or to be exploitative were eliminated. Bankers, industrialists, and other "profiteers" were obvious targets, but the prohibition extended to small business owners such as grocers, traders, and small merchants. Any capital, machinery, inventory, or other material resources owned by such businesses were commandeered by the state. Building on existing prejudices, the party vilified retailers as members of a capitalist class who made their living by exploiting others rather than by the "sweat of their brow." After 1949, even artisans producing essential goods, industrial workers in small workshops, and small shopkeepers were excluded from the ranks of the "working people," a category limited to manual laborers (Róna-Tas 1997:41). By 1953 there were few private chimney sweeps, canners, distillers, printers, bakers, or butchers still in business, at least with a license. Small construction enterprises also disintegrated (Róna-Tas 1997:44).

As a consequence of these policies, a bureaucratic and punitive state apparatus now mediated and controlled the very human activity that Karl Marx had insisted was essential for people to realize their species being: productive and creative labor above and beyond need (Marx 1963). It was also to mediate the socioeconomic activity that Marcel Mauss had shown was essential for creating and maintaining social relationships: durable exchange relations (Mauss 2000). Such localized forms of productive labor and exchange would be replaced, in theory, by an economic system envisioned as an abstracted totality, with all parts working for the whole. The model for this system was the modern factory, with the entire nation and its working-age population conceptualized as one centrally organized, efficient, and rational space (Róna-Tas 1997; Scott 1998). People laboring in factories and collective farms would produce what economic planners at the center decided the society needed based on ideological principles. This "collective wealth" would then, again theoretically, be equitably redistributed. But the centralized economy was never able to produce what the population needed, nor was the state able to insert itself into all forms of exchange relationships. Instead, the system itself produced new forms of localized production and exchange, transforming the conditions through which people engaged with the material.

Unmaking and Reconstituting Social Hierarchies

Although the party's longer-term goal was to "proletarianize" the peasantry, equally critical at this early juncture was the elimination of "enemies of the people." In discourse and iconography, entire categories of people were classified as "parasites," "conspirators," "saboteurs," and self-interested enemies of social reform. Show trials were one of the more macabre forms of public pedagogy. The populace was required to listen to trial proceedings on the radio and was thus taught to recognize the more subtle signs of a "class enemy" habitus. The 1949 General Electric show trial was an exercise in the vilification of the bourgeoisie. Lifestyle, dress, furnishings, manner of speaking, vocation, and family background were used to identify individuals predisposed to be hostile to a redistributive type of economy (Rév 1991). Denotation in this era became literal, linking specific objects and aesthetic forms indexically to desired or prohibited social behaviors or backgrounds (Buchli 1999:56–62). The dangers of being taken for a "bourgeois" generated a reverse self-fashioning, as people attempted to shed any signs of bourgeois culture. Wearing creased pants to work in 1950, an elderly engineer told me in the 1990s, was enough to brand one a class enemy. At the same time, the peasantry and working classes were enticed to work in the new socialist town through the promise of benefits such as modern apartments, radios, and bicycles, while workers who vastly exceeded their quotas were given such "bourgeois" luxuries as fur coats (György 1992). While many Hungarians were confused by the proliferation of political arrests and secret police activity, intense class antagonisms stemming from Hungary's modernization process allowed for this systematic characterization of "enemies of the state."

The drive to eliminate the bourgeoisie in Hungary was complicated by the fact that, historically, it had never cohered as a social class. In the half-century before the communist takeover, anyone below the rank of the aristocracy might qualify as middle class, including the independent business and trade community, the civil service dominated by a déclassé gentry, and the intellectual and professional classes (teachers, doctors, lawyers, engineers, and so on). This heterogeneous population had been fractured by ethnic and religious divisions, particularly between the more conservative Christian gentry, who were increasingly impoverished but clung to their titles and ranks, and an assimilating, urban Jewish bourgeoisie prominent in industry and business and also heavily represented among the professions. Further confusing the issue, these so-called middle classes had tended to reproduce the highly codified culture of the traditional nobility rather than develop the independent civil society assumed to be characteristic of a Western European bourgeoisie (Gyáni et al. 2004:343–57).

In the early 1950s of the Stalin era, anyone falling into this diffuse middle-class category was evaluated on the basis of their background and their family's political past. The best they could hope for was to be categorized as an "intellectual"—based on their parents' occupations as cultural or technical intelligentsia—and allowed to work. If their documents classified them with an "X," designating a class enemy, they could be barred from university admission, excluded from higher positions in the workplace, and, for a time, deported to rural villages.

Cinci, a woman in her seventies when I met her in 1996, told me what had happened to her in the 1950s. Her story was paradigmatic of those people targeted by the early Communist regime as class enemies. Like many of the gentry, her father's family had steadily lost its wealth and position in the interwar period, even after he married a Jewish woman from a prosperous family. Cinci was nonetheless educated in good schools and spoke fluent Italian, French, and German. One day in the early 1950s in Budapest, her husband—like so many others—was taken by the secret police as an enemy of the people and disappeared into the prison system. She gave birth to a son close to nine months after his arrest. As the wife of a class enemy, she was barred from all employment, even though her extended family depended on her for their livelihood. In desperate straits, she did what many other women did in her situation: she capitulated to official pressure to divorce her husband in absentia. She eventually met and married an architectural draftsman of peasant-worker background. Sheltering her with his class status, he moved them to Sztálinváros when he was offered an apartment for his skills. But even then, Cinci could only find menial work; she was a floor guard at the town museum when I met her. She claimed she had been shunned by the city elite because they envied her education and skill with languages, though I wondered if she was also penalized for flaunting signs of her former class status.

The state's need for trained professionals to implement its massive industrial expansion program ran counter to its rhetoric of class warfare. It was forced to create unofficial opportunities for members of the old middle classes (Mark 2005: 505–506). In fact, as the need for competent professionals became more apparent, it became easier for persons of the former "exploiting classes" to "ritually cleanse themselves of their class stigma" by "'erasing' their bourgeois backgrounds and inventing new 'class conscious' versions of their pasts," or taking a working-class job or marrying into a lower class, as Cinci had done (Mark 2005:506). Many people stigmatized by their class backgrounds found anonymity and sanctuary in the emerging city of Sztálinváros (Miskolczi 1980:11–21); even the children of wealthier peasants labeled as "kulaks" sought refuge in the town (Szelényi et al. 1988:176). At the same time, some professionals of obviously upper-class backgrounds were labeled as "intellectuals" and—particularly if they agreed to join the party—offered privileges like nice apartments to lend their expertise to state projects.

These implicit and explicit social pressures were reinforced by brutal repression. Between 1951 and 1953 alone, the police prosecuted 850,000 people (nearly 10 percent of the population) for minor offenses (Róna-Tas 1997:60). More than 100,000 people were imprisoned for "political" crimes. Political arrests by the secret police, always carried out in the dead of night, were followed by beatings, interrogations, and torture before any judicial proceedings had taken place. Political prisoners were routinely executed (Fehérváry 1989). As elsewhere in the Soviet bloc, state secrecy and control over information flows, combined with an adherence to "rational" procedures such as legal trials and material evidence of legality such as official documents, stamps, and uniforms, seemed to replicate familiar modes of legitimate (albeit authoritarian) state procedures and obscured the extent of the state's human rights violations.

Rebuilding and Re-education

The new socialist states did not implement social transformations through coercion alone. They began building a new social and material order to replace the one they were destroying, offering tangible benefits and using symbolic-ideological means of persuasion (Verdery 1991:427–28). Education campaigns promised to raise national literacy rates. Thousands of young people from rural areas headed to cities for work in factories and in pursuit of a better life, and women were integrated into the workforce whether they wanted to be or not. Class-based quotas for higher education and for professional positions, as well as sanctions on class privileges, offered unprecedented social mobility—for a time. During this time in Eastern Europe, "there was always something to celebrate," the Czech writer Milan Kundera wryly noted:

> Old wrongs were righted, new wrongs perpetrated, factories were nationalized, thousands of people went to jail, medical care became free of charge, small shopkeepers lost their jobs, aged workers took their first vacations ever in confiscated country houses, and we smiled the smile of happiness. (Kundera 1981:91–92)

Socialist Realism

In Hungary as throughout the Soviet bloc, publicity and re-education campaigns followed the Soviet example, implementing the representational doctrine of Socialist Realism first introduced in the Soviet Union in 1930. Stalin had understood that a largely uneducated, rural populace would resist communist ideology and social reforms and that they would have to be educated in the ideological and practical aims of a socialist system. Drawing on his background in linguistics, he developed Socialist Realism as a doctrine to assist people in correctly understanding the "reality" (or conditions of existence) they saw before them. In a direct attack on the revolutionary avant-garde, he argued that the proper work of cultural producers (including visual artists, playwrights, journalists, and architects) was to produce representations that "reflected and modeled the developing socialist reality dialectically" (Fitzpatrick 1992). Rather than creating socialist forms, these cultural producers should be helping people to visualize the monumental buildings being raised at a muddy site. Instead of participating in the reordering of base, they were to produce superstructure to reveal, to unenlightened eyes, the utopian socialist future being constructed in the present.[3]

Just as in the Soviet Union, Hungarian public space became intensely politicized. Even before the war had ended, memorials to the Austro-Hungarian Empire and the interwar regime were demolished and replaced with monuments to the Red Army "liberators" (Fowkes 2002). Portraits of Stalin and the Stalinist Hungarian leader Mátyás Rákosi were ubiquitous. Drapery, posters, and flags covered up traces of a presocialist past in the statuary and ornamentation on buildings (György 1992). Banners and signs admonished people to build socialism and pull out reactionary elements by their roots. Loudspeakers were set up in villages to reinforce the one-way, monologic communication from party to people found in newspapers and radio.

New or remodeled cultural centers became an arena for socialist pedagogy, describing and modeling the new society through film, theater, and literature. People from all walks of life were compelled to attend night or weekend classes in Marxism-Leninism. While copies of Marx in Hungarian translation were unavailable, political dictionaries and phrase books provided an "accessible" form of the scientific principles of Marxism-Leninism for "any worker or peasant who wished to acquaint himself/herself with the 'task and goal of Communism'" (Lampland 1987:83).[4] The creation of a socialist society during this era was also one of Sovietization (Swain 1992:53–84). The publishing sector was dominated by translations from the Russian into Hungarian of instruction manuals, novels, and textbooks. As in most countries, the state also transmitted social values through the educational process, such as in the following example from a fourth grade math textbook used in Sztálinváros in 1952: "A Stakhanov's weekly pay is 237 forints. How much does s/he earn in 4 weeks?"[5] At the same time, learning Russian became compulsory (and resented) in all the Soviet bloc countries, not just as a form of solidarity with the Soviet Union but because it was considered the language of the vanguard and thus the best language to "carry the message of Communism" (Lemon 1991:5).

New, elaborate sports facilities reflected the regime's concern with healthy and productive bodies, and clubs were to be "workshops for the transformation of men" (Kostof 1985:703). Campaigns valorizing physical labor in urban settings lent a romantic heroism to the mundane reality of factory life and worked to smooth out the contradictions between the values of manual and mental labor (Siegelbaum 1988). Stakhanovites, or workers said to have vastly exceeded their production quotas, were made into local celebrities and rewarded with prestige, gifts, and, most importantly, apartments (Miskolczi 1975).

Idealized representations of the proletariat, figured as the youthful and vigorous New Socialist Man, were contrasted with derogatory images of the bourgeois classes. Aging, decrepit figures in top hats and tiaras aligned metonyms of wealth and power with the grotesque. Public space was filled with images celebrating the working-class heroes, trowels in hand, who were building socialism through hard work and self-sacrifice. Statues, murals, posters, and plays glorified the muscled but disciplined body of the proletarian worker holding a hammer aloft and paired with the robust body of a female peasant wielding a scythe. The objective of transforming the agricultural population into an urban proletariat was reflected in this gendered difference, naturalizing the superiority of industry over a subordinated agriculture.[6]

By the time it was implemented in Hungary, Socialist Realism had become a codified form of representation and discourse in the USSR. Nonetheless, its implementation in the building of a planned, socialist new town brought to the surface tensions between party officials and cultural producers. They shared a conviction in the powers of the material world to effect the transformation of society, but their theoretical perspectives diverged on the place of architecture and home furnishings in this scheme.

Sztálinváros: Campaigns for the Socialist City, 1950–1956

The decision to build a steel mill in a country with no iron ore was often characterized by critics of the regime as typical of the megalomania of Stalinist industrialization policies. But Hungarian political elites in the nineteenth century had aspired to national self-sufficiency in steel production, even then seen as an index of modernization. While Budapest and some other urban centers had experienced a degree of industrialization before the turn of the century, modernization in the provinces had been obstructed by lack of capital and the continuing political power of the landed gentry (Gáti 1986; János 1982; Miskolczi 1980). Steel production remained an important goal for the interwar regime of Miklós Horthy, which had developed plans in the 1930s to build a steel factory outside of the town of Mohács, on the Danube River near the Yugoslav border.

Though the steel factory reflected long-standing aspirations to industrial power, the centerpiece of the Stalinist project was building the socialist city. It would not only provide an industrial heart for the new socialist nation-state but also, and more importantly, it would transform society in its image and through its very materiality. The first public announcement for Sztálinváros came five months after building began, not from the minister of industry but from the minister of culture. "The pride of the 5-year Plan," József Révai announced, was the building of a new steel mill and adjoining city in order to "double our iron and steel production, speed up our industrial development, agricultural modernization and cultural elevation" (*Szabad Nép*, Oct. 13, 1950, in Miskolczi 1980:62). According to publicity at the time, workers at the site insisted that the new town be named after the Soviet leader, "The City of Stalin," or Sztálinváros.

For the next three years, from 1951 to 1953, the project was the focus of massive publicity campaigns and enormous expenditure.[7] Daily radio reports and photos to put up on workplace and apartment bulletin boards encouraged the population to follow the progress of raising Hungary's first socialist city and witness the heroism of the workers building it.[8] It was referred to in party speeches, featured in films, taught about in schools, and depicted in Socialist Realist style on an arsenal of medals, certificates, and other mass-produced awards. Many of these featured a young working-class couple in profile, facing a glorious future represented by modern apartments and factory smokestacks.[9] During 1951–1953, more than twenty-three newsreels and short films, in Socialist Realist style with triumphant music and optimistic themes, were made to publicize the city-factory. Most celebrated the workers building the workers' city, focusing on the city's modern apartments. Others documented foreign dignitaries visiting the fledgling socialist country's crowning achievement or publicized events such as the Sztálinváros soccer team's decimation of their Budapest rivals. A local journalist, Miklós Miskolczi, later wrote about the city's exemplary status at the time. The very name "Sztálinváros emanated power: a mention in a store that the desired goods were for Sztálinváros, and clerks rushed to fill orders; if a child mentioned that his father worked in Sztálinváros, he gained immediate acceptance into training schools. Perhaps the most convincing evidence that the city had attained sacred status was that only someone from Sztálinváros could joke with its name: 'Stalin'" (Miskolczi 1980:14).

Conflicting Ideologies of Material Transformation

The story of how the city was designed and built in the early 1950s is in part a story of the struggle between two groups and the asymmetrical power relations between them. On one side were political officials representing the pragmatic and ideological interests of the party. On the other were cultural producers, particularly architects and designers, struggling to retain their professional autonomy in a highly politicized environment. Stalinist party politicians saw architecture as merely part of a representational superstructure. From this perspective, the material world as such has no agency: the city's transformative power lay in the collective *labor* of building it.

For modernist-influenced architects like Sztálinváros's master planner Tibor Weiner, however, the "honest" forms of modernist architecture no longer falsely represented an underlying base, but actually constituted that base. The material form of the city as an organic totality, carefully designed to promote egalitarian sentiment, was itself the technology for transforming consciousness. As such, it played a direct rather than mediating role in social transformation. Removing people from their familiar environments and inserting them into a radically new material context, they surmised, would shock residents into abandoning their traditional ways. Instead of being transformed into a modern, working class through the process of building the socialist city, residents would be transformed by living in it.

These diverging perspectives resulted in forms of publicity that were often contradictory but nonetheless cohered insofar as they instilled expectations for higher standards of living in much of the population.

Building Socialism, Transforming Consciousness

The Communist Party made explicit its expectations for the transformative effects of the project in the party directive of November 25, 1950 (reproduced in Balogh, Föglein, and Szakács 1986:289–95). Work on the project was to forge the working population—particularly malleable youth—into an exemplary socialist working class. The city site itself was to model party organization and socialist life and consequently establish loyalty to the party and the new political order. But it was participation in the physical labor of the building process itself—the embodied activity of constructing a new society under transformed conditions of production—that would do the work of transforming consciousness.

In these campaigns, communist authorities built upon the compatibility between Marx's insistence that man realized his species being through creative transformation of nature and the peasantry's valuation of physical labor and its fruits. They invoked the Hungarian term *rendes*, connoting a proper and ordering engagement with the material world. Social identity and the construction of self were profoundly tied to the active transformation of the material world and the display of the products of this labor. Communist regimes attempted to redirect the virtues of transformative physical labor away from private property and toward "collective" property, seeing in private property the grounds for invidious distinction, pride, and the social censure of those unable to meet normative material standards.

Numerous construction, industrial work, and beautification campaigns throughout the socialist period were based on the contention that physical labor (especially collective labor) had transformative powers and could rehabilitate even the most morally corrupt persons, from class enemies to Roma (gypsies).[10] This notion certainly held for the convicts and prostitutes sent to Sztálinváros to be "rehabilitated" through construction and factory work. But the benefits of shared physical labor were to be extended to people from all over the country and from all walks of life who were transported to the site for a few weeks or for a "voluntary" Sunday of consciousness-transforming construction work. In 1951 alone, more than thirty thousand Hungarian citizens came by train, boat, and truck to "build socialism," at an expense in transportation and board that far outweighed the value of their labor (Miskolczi 1980:71). Young people in particular were recruited. Over three summers, the Communist Student Youth Association (DISZ) brought thousands of high school and university students to the muddy site for two-week camps. High school students were encouraged to "Meet in Dunapentele after Graduation!" (Miskolczi 1980:67). Images of young women in shorts, awkwardly carrying shovels, planks, and corrugated steel bars, giggling in embarrassment or laughing at the festivity of the experience, were splashed over newspaper pages and run in newsreels. The physical experience of laboring on a common project was intended to engender a sense of collective ownership and therefore personal investment in the materiality being built—made explicit in the slogan "It's your country, you are building it for yourself!"

For members of the Communist Party, publicity for the city also had pragmatic objectives: to demonstrate Hungary's loyalty to the Soviet Union and at the same time convince a skeptical and largely anti-Soviet population that this road to modernization was in the nation's best interests. In its campaigns, the party appealed to a sense of national independence (Szabó 1988:690), asserting that industrial production would make the country more *autonomous* while increasing its military powers. Unlike agriculture, which was vulnerable to the vicissitudes of nature, the steel industry was to offer economic security.

A Quasi-Modernist City: Transformation Through Material Form

Soviet town planning shared many aspects of modernist city planning, including the importance of designing cities as organic totalities, dividing industrial areas from residential areas with a greenbelt, and imagining systems of transportation as arteries ferrying people between them. But with the intensification of Stalinism after 1950, modernism in all its forms had to be rejected, at least rhetorically, as elitist and too closely aligned with the West. In manifestos and articles, socialist master planners described new socialist cities in terms of their diametric opposition to the chaos and disease of Western cities—exactly as modernist cities had once been described—and yet they were also differentiated from the designs of modernist cities now seen as alienating, overly ambitious, and capitalistic. The planners of socialist cities also had to embrace a shift from the avant-garde's mantra "form follows function" to the Socialist Realist credo "socialist in content, national in form." In practice, "national in form" meant adorning buildings with references to folk or historic motifs, undermining the modernist principle that a building's function be transparently legible from its form, free of ornamentation or references to other places or times. A Socialist Realist building was to clearly represent its function and status through architectural flourishes. The importance of critical institutions such as cultural centers and party headquarters, for example, were to be proclaimed to all with the appropriate monumentality.[11]

And indeed, most of the architecture built in the new town in its first decade was of moderate Socialist Realist design, of solid structures with neoclassical elements that lined the streets and formed interior courtyards. (Hungary avoided the elaborate "wedding cake" variety of Socialist Realist architecture found in the Soviet Union and in some east European capitals.) On the main avenue, these buildings featured substantial covered portals and heavy balconies that evoked turn-of-the-century buildings from Budapest to Bologna (see Figure 2.1). The rest of the residential quarters were built as four- to five-story, massive courtyard buildings covering the perimeter of a city block, with secluded interior yards and green parks. Entrances to individual apartment buildings opened off of these interior spaces.

In keeping with Socialist Realism's use of conventional symbols, apartment furnishings were designed to appeal to the working classes by deploying qualities associated with European bourgeois materialities (see Dunham 1990). The room of a 1950s worker apartment, reconstructed for a local museum exhibit, was a scene of bourgeois domesticity: a living room sofa and upholstered armchair, lace doi-

Socialist Realism in the Socialist City | 65

Figure 2.1. Arany Csillag (Golden Star) Hotel on Vasmű utca, Sztálinváros, mid-1950s. Photo used by permission of the Intercisa Museum, Dunaújváros.

lies, framed wedding photographs, a radio, and women's fashion and home economics magazines.[12] This Stalinist domestic ideal was reproduced throughout the early 1950s in film clips of new apartments or on the covers of almanacs, and often featured the family gathered for a midday meal around a central table, served by a devoted wife and mother (see Buchli 1999:87 for the Soviet case) (Figure 2.2). This combination of heavy, simplified neoclassical architecture and modest but distinctly bourgeois furnishings came to define a Socialist Realist aesthetic regime in the new town.

While the imposition of Socialist Realism reversed many avant-garde aspirations, Boris Groys has argued that the relevant distinctions between the two aesthetics "arose not because the avant-garde project was abandoned, but because it underwent a radicalization that the avant-garde itself was unable to accomplish" (1992:37). Groys is not referring to the party's return to traditional hierarchies or its attempts to control people through a system of internal passports, restricted movement, and impenetrable borders. Instead, he understands the avant-garde project as predicated on a totalizing aesthetics: a total transformation of society, guided by visionary planning, and imagining a future social order as one of cleanliness, cohesion and modern efficiency, where each part (or individual) unproblematically fulfills its role for the workings of the whole.

We can see the tension between Socialist Realist and modernist ideologies in the designs and writings of Sztálinváros' chief architect, Tibor Weiner, who had

Figure 2.2. Typical image of the Socialist Realist interior and ideal for domestic harmony. Photo used by permission of the Intercisa Museum, Dunaújváros.

been an alumnus of the Bauhaus before going to the Soviet Union to work on planned cities there.[13] Weiner was among the mid-century architects (including the modernist city planners of Brasília a decade later) who submitted to powerful state or commercial forms of authority in exchange for the possibility of planning an entire city as an artistic whole, a *Gesamtkunstwerk*. They were able to rationalize such compromises by holding fast to the avant-garde theory of the transformative powers of the material world, one in which the design of the city would in itself bring about the desired societal transformations—regardless of the politics of the regime granting them the administrative powers to implement their plans (Holston 1989:ch. 2).

From his manifesto, published in 1951, it is clear Weiner imagined himself to be Sztálinváros's "master planner" (Weiner 1951). His city is designed as a unified organism on "virgin territory" or tabula rasa, uniting city and village, with greenbelts dividing residential areas from industrial areas. Abolishing the distinction between center and periphery, his plan ensures that all parts of the city—complying with the "democracy of the socialist order"—will be of the same quality (1951:589). While the plan is structured by a polar opposition between factory and political-administrative city, for Weiner the factory is also important as a model for the city, with its Taylorist efficiency and subordination of the individual to the totalizing whole. The city itself is a factory for social transformation, its central square forming the hub of the "organism."

As in other such planned cities, the organic unity of the whole is reproduced in microcosm in the residential districts. Each district was to be provided with a measure of organic autonomy in the form of smaller centers or microdistricts containing services, culture houses, sports facilities, schools, day care centers, and other institutions. These districts are nonetheless unified by their consistent aesthetic, by their relation to the administrative city center, and through transportation networks conveying people between living and working areas. Weiner's use of the term *kombinát* for the health care and hospital facility (Weiner 1951:591), gestured to Communist parlance for a factory in which all elements necessary for the production of an item were contained under one roof, in this case a hospital-factory, organized to produce healthy humans.

If the planned modernist cities designed for the West were intended to take harried city dwellers, alienated by urban individualism and disparities of wealth, and integrate them into a community through collective work and leisure activities, in the east European and Soviet case, such cities were designed to turn agricultural workers and a downtrodden urban working class into a modern, civilized workforce (French and Hamilton 1979). Weiner's manifesto echoes these aspirations. Peasants used to a life governed by seasonal cycles and patriarchal social relations were likewise to be transformed into a modern labor force by working in factories regulated by clock time and by moving into apartments designed for nuclear families.

Weiner's attempt to sustain, in his manifesto, the ahistorical, decontextualized genre established by Le Corbusier's *Radiant City* (1967) soon descends into the exasperated despair of a man who clearly never had much control over the proceedings (Weiner 1951). He had succeeded in designing some of Sztálinváros's first residential buildings as simple, unadorned, and free-standing structures (Figure 2.3), but when the Stalinist minister of culture József Révai saw them, he temporarily

68 | Politics in Color and Concrete

Figure 2.3. Modernist, free-standing housing cubes from the early 1950s. Photo used by permission of the Intercisa Museum, Dunaújváros.

halted construction on the city. Weiner's "ugly residential cubes," Révai claimed, were evidence of a pernicious formalism that showed that Hungarian architecture remained "far too closely in touch with architectural developments in western Europe" (Aman 1992:19). Weiner was also taken to task for violating the Socialist Realist principle that important buildings must be monumental in size. He had designed the party headquarters as a free-standing "Athenian temple" (as he called it) in the middle of a grand, empty square, but it was still the smallest building in the city center.[14]

As a planned city, however, the model town embodied a totalizing modernity. It separated production (labor) from consumption (residential life) in both space and time, and thus upended the autonomy and self-sufficient production valued in peasant cultures. Workers, male and female, were to occupy specialized niches and take care of their individual needs through modern consumption in the collective spaces of stores, restaurants, laundromats, and child care centers. Workers' apartments were deliberately designed with no space for productive gardens and zoned to prohibit the keeping of livestock, effectively eliminating the possibility of self-provisioning that had been common in much of urban, industrial Hungary (Pittaway 2005:86). Posters from the era tell women that instead of making their own preserves, they should buy them. Illustrations accompanying Weiner's manifesto, tellingly, do not picture the heroic working youth, but show the modern city rendered in line drawings, populated by women in fashionable dresses and high heels and men in suits, strolling past modern automobiles parked on wide avenues.

A Modern Consumer Paradise

Publicity for the city not only had to justify it in ideological terms but also to appeal to the population with the kind of modern life a state socialist system was producing. As a result, some of the promotional materials for the city focused entirely on the benefits that its residents would enjoy, from new, modern housing to transportation systems, shopping centers, and entertainment—all with little to no reference to politics. A color brochure printed in 1952, for example, presents in careful detail the material promises of a socialist modernity in strikingly apolitical terms.[15] At the same time, it follows Socialist Realist doctrine by writing about the future as if it were already present. The uniformity of the various city sectors is offered as a benefit, ensuring that "the buildings furthest from the city center are just as modern and comfortable as in the city center." Instead of having a special quarter for villas, in the new town "there are flower-beds, parks of grass and trees in front of *every* building" [my emphasis]. Sztálinváros would enable residents to live "in a manner worthy of socialist workers." The brochure describes sun-filled apartments, each with a balcony, French doors, and a "beautifully equipped" bathroom with tiles, bath, and shower installed—a sure sign of modernity at a time when having an indoor, private bathroom signified middle-class status (Valuch 1998/99).

Such complete comforts, the brochure proclaimed, were not only for the "home but for the buildings for community life." These included facilities for children—schools, nurseries, and walking paths sheltered from what were optimistically predicted to be "the hundreds of trucks and automobiles rumbling between the steelworks and the river port." A new, modern hospital was to be complemented by sporting venues such as a "modern, indoor swimming pool with sauna." The city boasted a museum, restaurants, and an eight-hundred-seat modern movie theater to satisfy "Sztálinváros's great cultural thirst." "Splendid buses with glass observation decks" would ferry the new town's ironworkers in comfort from their living quarters to the steel combines. The brochure's final blandishment was the announcement that "one of the country's most modern department stores is in Sztálinváros, where the merchandise is so well-stocked that even the most discerning demands (*igények*) can be fulfilled."

The socialist utopia presented in this brochure has little to do with the transforming powers of physical labor (though it does echo modernist principles of the civilizing effects of the planned, modern city). During this period, hardships and suffering were justified by sacrificing for one's children and for the future, but many Hungarians came to consider these promises of a "good life" as the reward to which they were entitled as working citizens of a socialist society.[16] This good life was equated with the modern, and by the end of the 1950s the local paper began to use "normal" to refer to what were considered modern systems, objects, and even venues that the socialist state was bringing into being. In 1959, for example, an editorial in the local paper hailed the impending completion of "the city's second 'normal' movie theater" (*Sztálinvárosi Hírlap*, Feb. 20, 1959).

From Socialist Realism to Socialist Realities

The lavish promises of the socialist city were not to be realized. By 1953, the heavy industrialization and collectivization campaigns, compounded by severe droughts, had pushed the country to the brink of economic collapse. Hungary's agricultural base was devastated, and it was even forced to import wheat, once a primary export. With Rákosi's fall from grace in 1953, the publicity campaigns ended. As the five-year plan's symbolic center, Sztálinváros had generated intense resentment nationwide. Now it was widely condemned as an example of the excesses of Stalinist industrialization. The city's budget was radically cut, and debates continuously resurfaced over its "right to exist" (Miskolczi 1975:127).

Instead of becoming a new heart for the socialist state, pumping out iron and steel to modernize and reinforce the country, the new industrial complex came to be envisioned as a blight, draining the country's strength and leaving the rest of the land impoverished.[17] As the local journalist Miskolczi described it years later, Hungarians elsewhere had been told that the improvements in living standards they were promised had been deferred for the sake of building Sztálinváros. While the rest of the country experienced famine and shortages in construction materials, fuel, consumer goods, and housing, Sztálinváros was portrayed as a cornucopia. Indeed, Sztálinváros was supplied with enough bread that workers were able to take some home to their families in the villages. As the national housing crisis escalated, Sztálinváros had received a disproportionate allotment of the housing budget—even though this fell far short of what was needed to house workers at the site.[18] And while the secret police's reign of terror peaked throughout the land, workers in Sztálinváros were rarely pulled from their beds for midnight interrogations. A joke circulating at the time expressed widespread sentiments: "Now that we have a Sztálinváros, maybe we can have a winter coat" (Miskolczi 1975:128).

In Sztálinváros itself, as in other "socialist new towns" in the region, people experienced contradictions between publicity about the city and the harsh realities of daily life (Dowling 1999; Kotkin 1995; Lebow 1999, 2001). The population grew exponentially, from a few hundred in May 1950 to twenty-eight thousand by the summer of 1952—but only a fraction of these were living in the promised modern apartments (Miskolczi 1980). Workers lived in barrack rooms designed to sleep six to eight people but often housing as many as twenty-two, with rudimentary bathing and storage facilities (1975:71–72). As in new towns elsewhere, the deplorable conditions in these barrack settlements contributed to alcoholism, unrest, and domestic disturbance (Angyal 1976; Miskolczi 1980:24). After the steel works opened in 1954, thousands of people continued to live for years in these uncomfortable barracks.

New residents' experience of the city differed substantially depending on their background, their attitudes toward socialism, and how well the city met their needs. Most of the first immigrants to the city were poor peasant youth from villages one to two days' travel away. They were largely unskilled, and so they accepted construction work on the site mainly to escape the poverty and unemployment in the villages (Pittaway 2005:83). The harsh conditions of rural life had been much exacerbated by Stalinist policies to "industrialize" agriculture, including punitive taxation and compulsory production quotas for crops and livestock. For many villagers during the early 1950s, going to work in industry was seen as little better than surrendering to a state that sought to destroy their way of life, and Sztálinváros came to symbolize all that was wrong with socialism (Pittaway 2005:85). At the same time, these incoming rural construction workers were met with deep resentment by the villagers of Dunapentele. The socialist state had appropriated the farmland of the local villagers to make way for the new city, and incoming construction workers were often housed in their old farmsteads. The new city became a symbol of their dispossession (Lukács 2000:220, cited in Pittaway 2005:84).

For most of the peasant population, local and immigrant alike, the socialist regime's hostility to religion played a major role in their own attitudes toward the new city and represented an "offence against the natural order and their own notions of morality" (Pittaway 2005:84). As one worker explained, "only the most important building is lacking in Sztálinváros, and that is a church. The opinion of the workers is that 'this town has not accepted the good Lord and it has no blessing from him'" (cited in Pittaway 2005:84).

The large number of young, rural workers caused construction delays. In the first year, more than 70 percent of the population was under the age of thirty. Workweeks were a grueling six to seven days, 7 AM to 6 PM. Time off was supposed to be spent collectively, in education courses or at state-sponsored forms of entertainment (Miskolczi 1975:79). But supervisors had difficulty keeping men at the site, and during the week of a harvest, of the *szüret* or wine pressing, or a day a pig was slaughtered, entire cadres would disappear to their villages to participate (Miskolczi 1980).

The combination of inexperienced workers, undersupply, and overly ambitious plans also led to costly errors in city construction. Geologists had discovered that the soil at the site was a porous clay or *lösz* which dissolved when wet, but their recommendations to move the project inland went unheeded. As a result, all pipes had to be encased in concrete. But out of haste or carelessness, workers did not lay the pipes deep enough, and many broke with the shifting pressure of the buildings. In the summer of 1951, an entire portion of the newly built city slid fifty meters down the river bank, costing more than one billion forints to repair (Miskolczi 1980:57).

Over time, recruitment campaigns were fairly successful in appealing to an urban, working-class youth with some skills. They were drawn to the new town by promises of modern luxuries like indoor plumbing (Miskolczi 1980:11–21), but also because of the deplorable housing and work conditions in other industrial areas. When mobilization campaigns failed to attract enough skilled labor, the party issued quotas to district councils and factories to send workers to the new town—though managers of course sent their least-valued workers (Miskolczi 1980). Even political prisoners were brought to work at the site, many of them young men who had been studying for engineering and other professional degrees when they were incarcerated.[19]

The solidarity between the rural and urban working classes was prominently symbolized in the enormous Socialist Realist mosaic set into the monumental factory gates, depicting peasants handing over the first bread of a new harvest to steel workers. But this solidarity remained largely a fiction. The urban working classes were not much more supportive of socialism than their rural counterparts, though for different reasons. "Socialism," in their experience, was equated with despotic management in factories, intense working conditions, and low wages (Pittaway 2005:88). Shared hostility toward the state did little to ameliorate the tensions between the construction workers from villages and the industrial workers from the urban working classes, which often erupted in street brawls (Angyal 1976; Pittaway 2005:87). City authorities acknowledged that part of the problem was that there was not enough work to attract women to the emerging town; they believed a larger female presence would calm and civilize the unruly young men (Miskolczi 1980; Weiner 1963).

Conflicts between social groups in the city were exacerbated by policies of housing allocation. Between 1951 and 1954, only 13 percent of the successful applicants for apartments in the new city had been employed as construction workers, compared to 58 percent who were primarily steelworkers (Pittaway 2005:85). Put another way, the workers who had literally "built socialism" were not the ones who enjoyed the material results. Instead, city authorities viewed them—as well as the peasant residents of Dunapentele—with suspicion. They were assigned to temporary barracks, or continued to commute from their villages, while waiting years for the promised apartments.

Industrial workers, who better fit the idealized profile of the socialist worker, fared better in housing assignments. But even they were routinely assigned to unfinished buildings and had to deal with unfinished kitchens, lack of heating and basic supplies, and a dearth of cultural life. The areas where they were housed became known as *proli* districts, the derogatory nickname for the proletariat. Over time, as conditions improved in the city and repairs to their buildings were made, these industrial workers became local patriots, fiercely defensive of the city to outsiders. They were regarded by later generations as the first wave of an urban proletariat, the "heroic generation" who had participated in the initial building and rapid populating of the city.

The town had great difficulty attracting professionals or members of an intelligentsia (Szirmai and Zelenay 1988:18). Whatever success the party had in luring young doctors, engineers, and party functionaries to the city was through the promise of an apartment and quick promotion to ranks unattainable in other cities, where older and more experienced men and women blocked their paths. Most of these young professionals regarded their stay in the city as temporary and moved away when apartments and positions opened elsewhere. Young doctors and their families were allocated two-room flats with balconies in a building overlooking the Danube, next door to the hospital. I interviewed a man who had been a chemical engineer in Sztálinváros in the early 1950s, living with his wife in one of the few four-room apartments built on the main avenue. They could not say why they had been allocated so much space when the engineer's superiors at the time lived in far smaller apartments. They suggested that officials had taken a person's former living standards into consideration, particularly when housing valuable employees. Her family had been upper-middle class, used to living in one of their villas.[20]

The egalitarian ideal was further undermined by the practice of assigning apartments (as well as colored bicycles!) by profession, thereby segregating the city population by occupation. Thwarting the explicit intentions of planners, apartments in the city center were assigned to doctors, engineers, and party bureaucrats. Skilled workers were given apartments closer to the factory but farther away from the center, while unskilled laborers had to wait the longest and were often allotted apartments in the most densely populated areas (Miskolczi 1980). Workers nevertheless adopted the ubiquitous construction metaphors that drew on the association between transformative physical labor and ownership. This ownership mentality manifested itself at odd times, such as the response from a drunken worker, covered in plaster, when he was denied admittance to the women's hostel: "What do you mean, I can't come in, when I built this house?!" (Miskolczi 1975:79).

In late October 1956, workers and students in Budapest drove Soviet troops out of the country for ten historic days in an uprising against Soviet occupation and influence. Significantly, their "revolution" was not against socialism but in support of a "socialism" that would live up to its ideals. In Sztálinváros, home to the "New Socialist Man," workers defended the steelworks and city *against* Soviet tanks for almost a week after the invasion. Rejecting the association with Stalin and the Soviet Union, they reclaimed the village name of Dunapentele for the new town. Demonstrating an internalization of communist slogans within a nationalist context, spokesmen legitimated their resistance with the following claim: "Dunapentele is the foremost socialist town in Hungary. Its residents are workers, and power is in their hands.... The houses have been built by workers themselves.... The workers will defend the town from fascist excesses but also from Soviet troops" (cited in Irving 1981:534).

In the early hours of November 4, 1956, Soviet tanks rolled back into the country and brutally suppressed what came to be known in the West as the Hungarian Revolution. The turmoil further devastated the economy, disrupting housing construction and fledgling industries that supplied consumer goods. It also quashed notions throughout the region that the Soviet Union would tolerate attempts by satellite states to escape the Soviet orbit. Quietly, Dunapentele once again became Sztálinváros, a name it kept until 1961, when it was renamed Dunaújváros, or "New City on the Danube." But it would never again regain its prominence on the national stage.

Keys to Paradise: Fostering Expectations

By its constant invocation of a utopian socialist future, the early socialist state in Hungary fostered expectations in its citizens, particularly with respect to housing. This intensified even as housing forms, ideologies, and policies were transformed in the following decades. By the end of the 1950s, contradictions were emerging in Sztálinváros over how property was being defined and who was considered a deserving citizen in the eyes of the socialist state. The disconnects between utopian narratives, other kinds of official discourse, and lived experience sent confused messages about who would be allocated an apartment and what residents' legal status would be when they got one.

For workers commuting to or living in Sztálinváros, apartments built by the socialist state had become central to their experience and identity. As the slow process of apartment construction and habitation unfolded, the meanings they attributed to this ever-changing built environment were formed against an official discourse in which building, both literal and metaphorical, was ubiquitous. Speeches and articles constantly invoked plans for the future and extolled the merits of new apartment developments, shopping centers, and services. The local newspaper provided daily tallies of apartments planned, apartments under construction, apartments finished and ready—not to be "moved into" or "rented out," but to be "handed over" as "gifts" to working families.

Officially, those deemed most deserving of apartments were families with children, of low income, and who had been on the waiting list for years while they had labored to "build socialism." Coming from deplorable living conditions was said to strengthen one's case. The working population, however, soon realized with bitterness that professionals and intelligentsia from other cities were allocated apartments out of turn, while other families, more qualified by the above criteria, waited for years. Articles like the following one regularly appeared in the local paper, creating expectations for urban apartments and providing evidence that they were being given, at least some of the time, to those for whom they were intended.

An article appeared in the Sztálinváros newspaper on April 6, 1960 (next to a photo of the 450th television sold in the city that year) that was typical of this genre. It narrated the ceremonial moment when officials handed over the "key to paradise" and recipients joyfully took possession of their new apartment. The reporter began by describing the beginnings of community formation in a newly finished building, particularly among the women and children, and then moved on to describe the apartment and "the craftsmanship of Sztálinváros builders" in loving detail: the "gorgeous, spacious, light rooms, bright yellow wood floors, fashionable balconies," all of which were the result of "many thousands of forints' worth of materials and careful work." (Such descriptions were contradicted by frequent letters to the editor complaining of shoddy workmanship, missing bathtubs, and lack of central heating.) Profiles of a few new residents and their backgrounds followed, and pains were taken to illustrate their economic need as well as their moral character. "The Károly Stiglicz family," for example, "with four children, are moving into the new apartment from a single barrack room. They have been waiting for this day since 1952." When the city councilor hands over the keys, he reminds new residents of their responsibilities in accepting apartments that have cost the state 150,000 to 200,000 forints apiece and admonishes them to "make them beautiful and homey."

This article, like others in the genre, reveals an ongoing problem for the state: how to get residents to invest time, energy, and resources into maintaining state-owned apartments—in effect to take ownership of them. This difficulty resulted in part from ambiguity about legal ownership. On the one hand, apartments remained part of the collective wealth of the people. They were constructed and administered by the state at state expense and leased to residents for a monthly rent so small it barely covered utilities. On the other, they were presented as the gifts of a benevolent state to deserving citizens and were, for the most part, inalienable possessions. Residents had the right to exchange apartments or to pass them onto their children. Nonetheless, any sense of personal ownership was undermined by constant reminders of the state's presence and control: for example, one resident was usually appointed building supervisor and was also entrusted to carry out surveillance on other residents.

State officials increasingly adopted a language of partnership in the hopes that people would take on more of the burden of building and maintaining their own material worlds, even though some refused, saying "that is why we pay rent!"

(*Sztálinvárosi Hírlap*, June 14, 1960). The local paper chastised apartment recipients who were "destroying" their new apartment by tracking in filth, stripping it of metal and tiles, and failing to turn it into a warm home. It points out that for "many people, the new apartment brings tears to their eyes, as they never dared to dream of such a place. The new environment effects a determining change in lifestyle, a cultural effect that raises their standards (*igények*)." The journalist speaks of how moved he is when he goes to some of these "new homes and shares in the new *owner's* proud happiness," and in the next breath asks citizens for help "protecting *society's property*" from those who refuse to change their behavior (*Sztálinvárosi Hírlap*, July 12, 1960, my emphasis).

By the late 1950s, the state was stepping back from the economically untenable position of legislating and controlling all material production and distribution. Contrary to the dominant rhetoric that privileged apartments as the proper form of socialist living, the state also encouraged people to build their own houses to ameliorate the housing shortage. In Sztálinváros, the council set aside an undeveloped "garden city" district for such projects (*Sztálinvárosi Hírlap*, 1959). Reporters tried unsuccessfully to apply the "key to paradise" rhetoric for the new, owner-built houses that intrepid (or desperate) souls were trying to build for themselves, with little or no state assistance. Yet officials were unwilling to relinquish credit for what was being built and their role as benefactors, resulting in an enduring, paternalistic paradigm for citizen-state relations.

By the end of the 1950s, the more traumatic elements of the "great transformation" were already in place (Róna-Tas 1997:77). In 1961, 95 percent of the working population was in state employment, now recruited less by coercion than by workplace perks. While health care and education accrued to everyone regardless of participation in the economy, state employment became the only way to access the benefits offered through the workplace, such as housing assistance, subsidized meals, maternity leave and child care, retirement, cultural and athletic activities, vacation resorts, loans, and even building materials (Róna-Tas 1997:84). By 1962, the state had achieved another one of its major goals, as only 1.6 million people still worked in agriculture and an equal number were now employed by industry—and employment ratios appeared to be reaching the standards of the developed capitalist nations (Miskolczi 1975:127).

This statistical account of socialist modernization belies its contradictory and hybrid nature. Far from realizing the egalitarian society and organic social division of labor envisioned by party officials and modernist city planners, the emerging material forms of the new town epitomized the societal divisions being produced between rural and urban and within urban society. Continuing housing shortages meant that urban employment was not the same as urban living. Large numbers of workers, known as "peasant-workers," lived in rural areas and commuted. Whereas in 1949, 76 percent of the rural population was in agriculture, by the mid-1970s, one-third of villagers commuted to an industrial workplace (Szelényi et al. 1988:29). These modernization numbers also fail to take into account the vast amounts of time and energy "modern" city dwellers continued to spend on self-provisioning, as the state was unable to supply adequate food, clothing, housing, or furnishings for purchase. Finally, even though the built environment constructed in these years laid the foundation for a new, distinctly socialist urban material order (integrating housing, utilities, transportation, consumption, production, services, and so forth), one that produced a "Soviet social " (Collier 2011), it fell far short of the paradise that had been promised.

In an article published in the local paper a few years before his death in 1965, Tibor Weiner summarized some of the "mistakes" officials and city planners had made in conceptualizing the new town. In designing small, two-room apartments, planners had not taken into consideration either a family's changing requirements as children got older, or the desire to live near extended family. Pointing to the new town's dismal record of overcrowding and high rates of divorce, he lamented that "four people can barely fit when the children are little, but when they grow and then if one is a boy and the other a girl, the transaction of a *normal* family life becomes impossible" (my emphasis). Weiner acknowledged the limitations of a fixed ideal for modern living. "In vain did we build what looked like quite high-quality apartments for those times and economic possibilities," he wrote. "We didn't think about larger families or the incessant rise of demands (*igények*) that are part of the development of a socialist society" (Weiner 1963). His regrets would continue to define problems in the emerging town, but he could not have predicted that the quality of apartments in the new town would progressively decline in the 1960s and 1970s, as the state—increasingly conscious of costs and in thrall to the allure of new technologies—sacrificed quality in the name of quantity.

3 Socialist Modern and the Production of Demanding Citizens

IN 1963, THE Dunaújváros newspaper published a particularly strident article on home décor, part of a nationwide campaign to convince residents moving into new apartments to rid themselves of their old, heavy furniture and adopt more appropriate tastes for their new surroundings. The author begins with "What there should not be!" She denounces the complete bedroom set, the permanent dining room, the display cabinet, and the "monstrous wardrobe" (Bars 1963). In the "apartment of today," she proclaims, "furnishings cannot be monofunctional display items but must be useful objects." They cannot have "useless decorations, carved angels, and twirled columns. . . . The fashion is clean lines, low sizes . . . easy to use and clean." To create the all-important open room plan, "furniture is placed against the wall so that the center is left free . . . allowing space for movement, work, comfort, hominess." One multifunctional room, the writer insists, will "better suit the family's time together and the working person's needs," as long as the residents "avoid all that is superficial." She concludes by assuring readers that "lighter, brighter forms and colors will satisfy the modern person's demands (*igény*) for a home."

This chapter picks up from the last in exploring how a distinctively socialist "modern life" came to be produced during the 1960s and 1970s through new forms of housing and furnishing, and with it, a new citizenry that understood themselves to be defined by their consumption habits and modern lifestyles. The state's promotion of a Socialist Modern style encouraged people to abandon a set of materialities saturated with history and class hierarchies and to embrace a clean, bright, and future-oriented modernism. The material properties of prefabricated concrete panel buildings, open plan layouts, and modern furnishings were aligned with "qualities" of a modern future and contrasted with those from a backward past. Publicity about Socialist Modern materialities generated widespread expectations for an urban "good life"—expectations that were in some respects fulfilled and in others bitterly disappointed. Nonetheless, a broad-based, modern citizenry emerged in this era, one with features similar to the consumer-based middle classes emerging in the West but also shaped by the distinctive and interwoven ideological forces and material realities in socialist Hungary.

The material norms for this new lifestyle included a modern apartment, furnishings, and appliances: a refrigerator, washing machine, television, and, for an increasing number of families, a car. A small weekend cottage or summer house in the countryside completed the ideal. State publications encouraged citizens to be "demanding" (*igényes*) of high standards for their material worlds as a mark of their modern mentalities, proclaiming: "Show me your home, and I'll tell you who you are!"

Socialist Modernism and the Kádár Compromise

The embrace of modernism in architecture and furnishings throughout the Soviet bloc was experienced as part of a thaw in formerly prohibitive attitudes toward all things Western. Under Stalin's successor, Nikita Khrushchev, Communist Parties throughout the bloc instituted greater attention to living standards, reduced interference in the private lives of citizens, and made less exacting demands for loyalty to the regime. Khrushschev acknowledged the technological gains Western nations had achieved that allowed them to produce an ever-growing abundance of consumer goods and creature comforts. This technology was now considered ideologically neutral, something a communist system could adopt for its own ends. With this in mind, Khrushchev encouraged international diplomacy, trade, tourism, and scientific and cultural exchange, even with the United States. The Soviets had launched Sputnik in 1957, the first successful space satellite, so it was perhaps not so far-fetched to think—as Khrushchev had boasted—that a socialist planned economy would "catch up to and surpass the west" by 1980 in the realm of consumer goods, living standards, and leisure time.

The political implications of this shift were particularly pronounced in Hungary after the suppressed revolution of 1956, as a beleaguered state attempted to appease a hostile populace and reclaim some political legitimacy. The Hungarian regime shifted investment from heavy industry to the production of housing and consumer goods and encouraged people to focus on improving their private circumstances; in return, it expected political acquiescence. The tenor of this bargain was known as the Kádár compromise, named for party secretary János Kádár, and it was exemplified by his 1962 inversion of the Stalinist (and biblical) slogan "Whoever is not with us is against us." He decreed instead that "whoever is not against us is with us" and quietly released prisoners held for political activities since 1956. Kádár remained in power for three decades until his ouster in 1988. He became known as a benevolent leader, modest in his habits, who oversaw Hungary's development into one of the most prosperous countries in the Soviet bloc.

Kádár's simple semantic shift had vast implications for everyday life. Where once the party required public displays of allegiance, by the early 1960s a citizen's obligation to help "build socialism" was satisfied by a full day's productive work in a factory, a planning office, a daycare center, or a hospital. The party still set the parameters for what could be discussed publicly and how, and it restricted professional advancement for those who were not members of the Communist Party.

But there was far greater room for public debate than before. Reductions in the workweek (from six to five days) and obligatory political activities, alongside increased wages, allowed people to pursue leisure activities and improve their private circumstances.

Hungary was unusual in the socialist bloc for the Communist Party's willingness to experiment with hybrid economic forms, limited privatization, and a high tolerance for second-economy activities. In the late 1950s, the state's second effort to collectivize farms was relatively successful in part because it was more coercive, but also because of the concession that allowed collective farm members to own and cultivate small family plots, and to sell or exchange the produce (Böröcz 1993:87–88). Rural leaders realized that membership in the collective farm would allow them to commandeer resources such as machinery and fertilizer for their own use (Róna-Tas 1997:65–66). For the most part, these family plots were limited to villages where the land (usually around the family house), became the site of productive gardens and pens for chickens, ducks, and pigs. These highly productive and fairly lucrative private agriculture endeavors led to the expansion of second-economy arrangements in other sectors, beginning with small-scale tourism as people rented out rooms at Lake Balaton (Böröcz 1993:88). In the 1970s, there was a proliferation of private, part-time entrepreneurial endeavors such as tire-repair services, pastry shops, and professionals offering private services ranging from electricians to sexologists (Gerő and Pető 1999:119, 173).

Housing and State Legitimacy

The state's ideological commitment to the equitable redistribution of wealth had made adequate housing with modern utilities a fundamental "right" of every citizen. It was to be made affordable through state administration and inalienable through prohibitions on eviction (Ferge 1979:293). Ironically, it was exactly this ideological commitment that made housing shortages so symbolically salient and made housing one of the primary loci through which citizens understood their relationship to the state (Kotkin 1995:160).

The 1960s opened with the party unveiling its Fifteen-Year Housing Plan, meant to provide one million new housing units nationwide. Weeks after the initial announcement, however, back-page clarifications revealed that the state planned to build only 60 percent of these units. Responsibility for the remaining 40 percent fell to private citizens, primarily rural or working-class families, who were to build their own houses (Major and Osskó 1981; see also Molnár 2010). State infrastructure and housing construction policy effectively reduced new housing construction to two, opposed types: the urban apartment and the owner-built house.

The Fifteen-Year Housing Plan became a lightning rod for debates about the direction of socialist society and the dilemmas of growing prosperity. Among some high-profile architects and members of the cultural intelligentsia, the stakes were nothing less than the success or failure of the socialist project (Molnár 2010). In almost all iconography of the socialist future, urban apartment buildings were featured as the appropriate housing form for the development of a classless society, the eventual elimination of private property, and full urbanization. Party ideologues, architects, and design professionals condemned the private family house as a vestige of the past, conducive to individualism and petty bourgeois tendencies (Major 1981:197). In the 1950s, the state had allowed families to build private homes in order to ease the housing shortage (Pittaway 2000), but party ideologues had hoped to gradually eliminate such building.

Over the next three decades, however, people unable to get housing in the city toiled to build housing for themselves in villages, working in the evenings and on weekends to scrounge materials, organize exchanges of labor, and negotiate with (i.e., bribe) state regulators for required inspections and permits (See also Kenedi 1981; Sík 1988). Even as it encouraged this kind of building, the state provided very little in the way of assistance other than sets of plans. In the absence of an established home-construction industry, the challenges of scouring the countryside for scarce materials was endless and involved complicated exchanges and bribes to gain access. Cash and labor were extracted from extended family, friends, and neighbors through a rural system of reciprocal obligations (*kaláka*). Relationships had to be developed in order to find and negotiate with the black market professionals called in to do more complex electrical, plumbing, and roofing work (not to mention taking care of the paperwork) (Sík 1988). Given that construction could take anywhere from two to ten years, many families had to live in the unfinished structures (Miskolczi 1980). Stories abounded of marriages broken by the drawn-out process.

The vast majority of state housing resources were earmarked for modern apartment buildings and infrastructure in urban areas, and the socialist state deliberately withheld funding for residential infrastructure in villages and rural areas. Nowhere was this urbanization policy so marked as in the Old Town area that had been the village of Pentele. Even though it had been incorporated as a district of the emerging city, the village represented the backward materialities and social order that the socialist regime wanted to leave behind: peasant houses, a manor building in disrepair, and a Catholic church. As the new town rose on the plateau above it, Pentele slowly deteriorated under the effects of a building ban and infrastructural neglect. Other settlements within twenty kilometers of the town also had few paved roads and no running water, sewage, or gas mains. People living there had to make do with wells, septic tanks, and solid fuel or gas cylinders for cooking and heat. There were no telephone lines, and public transportation was poor. Villages also suffered from a lack of basic services, such as laundromats, grocery stores, durable goods or clothing shops, movie theaters, and so forth. These disadvantages were particularly hard on women, especially those with jobs in the city (Tímár 1997:4–5).

City dwellers were thus celebrated and privileged over rural residents. Even so, rates of self-built housing rose steadily and eventually surpassed state-built housing in both quantity and quality (Hegedűs 1992:224). But urban housing held its higher status among urban professionals, not so much because of the quality of urban life or the superiority of its materialities as because of the ideological and material denigration of the rural.

Socialist Modern for a Socialist Modernity

The demise of Socialist Realism did not end the communist state's preoccupation with aesthetics. On the contrary, the end of the Stalinist "war on formalism" allowed for the resurgence of modernist principles and ideology-saturated designs.[1] Design historians Susan Reid and David Crowley have argued that by the late 1950s, with increased production of clothing, furniture, and housing, "Style... became an urgent issue," raising new questions: What forms "could meet the needs of and give shape to modern socialist life? What was the appropriate style for socialist modernity?" (Reid and Crowley 2000:3).

Modernism's resurgence throughout the Soviet sphere began with Khrushchev's 1954 attack on Stalinist architecture for its excesses, with its superflous decorations and costly, one-off designs. Party bureaucrats, politicians, and factory managers supported the modernist style primarily for economic reasons and the convenient fact that it had a progressive pedigree. While startup costs were clearly higher than for conventional production, modernist designs and technologies were (wrongly) assumed to be faster, more efficient, and inexpensive because they used factory mass production.[2] It did not hurt that Socialist Modern so closely resembled International Modernism, with its global prestige. In Hungary, the supposed Scandinavian provenance of panel construction and standardized furniture was more likely to appeal to a populace largely hostile to the Soviet Union and at the same time would continue to adhere to egalitarian socialist ideals. A book on the home published in 1958 regales readers with descriptions of "modern home furnishings" as they were adapted in France, Italy, Sweden, and even archcapitalist England and the United States. The book mentions Poland, Czechoslovakia, and East Germany, but makes no reference to the socialist "brotherhood" uniting them or to the Soviet Union's promotion of the style (Bánkuti 1958: 138–76).

Cultural producers in Hungary had various incentives to promote a modernist style. For many, particularly architects and designers, the revival of modernism fulfilled numerous desires simultaneously. For some, it was a return to truly revolutionary and avant-garde ideals after their suppression by the "petty bourgeois" aesthetics of Socialist Realism.³ Hungarian participation in the avant-garde, moreover, aligned modernism with urban cosmopolitanism and against a rural populism (Molnár 2005:115). As the aesthetic of an international cultural elite, it was emblematic of a "modern" and a superior way of living (an aesthetic that party bureaucrats, often less educated and conservative in taste, were unlikely to appreciate). In Hungary as in the Soviet Union, the new discourse of taste was part of a broad "campaign of the cultural intelligentsia to reassert its distinction and reappropriate from Stalinist bureaucrats the intelligentsia's traditional prerogative to define cultural standards in the name of the people" (Reid 1997:177; for Hungary, see Molnár 2010:75). From the late 1950s through the 1970s, the divergent ambitions and desires of politicians, cultural producers, and the consuming public converged enough to ensure the dominance of a modernist aesthetic in the transformation of Hungarian housing and interiors.

Panel Construction

In 1961, ten years after it was founded, Sztálinváros had grown to a population of close to thirty-one thousand people and had been renamed Dunaújváros ("New Town on the Danube"). At this point, most of the population lived in the massive, brick-and-mortar Socialist Realist style apartment complexes along the two central thoroughfares of the new town. Over the next twenty years, however, the population would double, reaching an all-time high of more than sixty thousand in 1980. This growing population would be housed in a Socialist Modern style of architecture: starkly rectilinear buildings constructed of prefabricated concrete panels. This kind of housing construction was based on a technology pioneered in the United States but then developed in the Soviet Union and further modified in Hungary. Indeed, journalists in Dunaújváros presented their city as being on the cutting edge of city planning and socialist design, proudly noting that the first three prototypes of panel buildings were constructed there in 1959—a year earlier than those built and exhibited in Budapest. The local paper extolled the new, man-made materials of these flats: the ferro-concrete walls, the easy-to-clean linoleum flooring, and the durable synthetic paints for the exterior walls. By the 1970s, this kind of monotonous construction had risen up to dwarf the original, Socialist Realist city center.

A Socialist Modern aesthetic regime became inseparable from the economic and political system that brought it into being. But this style of architecture was not unique to state socialism. In the 1960s, governments from London, Copenhagen, and New York City to Moscow and Bombay looked to new, prefabricated housing technologies to solve urban housing shortages. A postwar generation on both sides of the Cold War divide looked to the promises of modern technology and design to provide all citizens with access to the material settings of the "good life."⁴ In the socialist states, these modern materialities were to usher in a socialist modernity that was distanced from the miseries of the Stalinist era and at the same time would avoid the callous social injustices of capitalism. They were to produce not the "New Socialist Man" of the 1950s, but the "Person of Today" (*a mai ember*)—transforming a largely rural population into a modern and "demanding" (*igényes*) citizenry.

The construction of new apartment blocks made of prefabricated panels was a massive and well-publicized undertaking. The state set up a number of housing factories across the country devoted to mass production of housing. The first factory was built in Dunaújváros in 1962 to produce concrete wall sections reinforced with steel bars. These were transported to building sites and then hoisted by crane onto steel frames, where they were bolted into place. These Socialist Modern buildings were first arranged on the landscape as lone figures against an empty background, thus complying with the modernist inversion of the conventional layout of buildings that formed street façades and sheltered interior courtyards (Holston 1989:119–25). In the 1960s, most buildings were low-rise walk-ups, although five-story buildings often had elevators. By the 1970s, construction had shifted to the massive, ten-story monoliths that were often arranged in staggered rows. The floor plans for the apartments themselves had few variations. Most consisted of two low-ceilinged rooms with a small kitchen and bathroom. According to a law passed in 1958, the average apartment size was to be no more than 53 square meters (about 570 square feet) with a ceiling height of 2.7 m (8.86 feet) (Molnár 2010:68). This formula remained fairly constant over the next three decades, so that by the mid-1990s, the average home in Hungary remained less than two and a half rooms.

A vast industry arose to produce the materials necessary for these buildings and to employ the engineers, electricians, plumbers, and other construction workers, and this formed a significant part of economic plans drawn up by central authorities. Future projects and daily achievements were all faithfully reported. The promise of panel construction and its importance for a socialist modernity is encapsulated in the advertisement for a color television in Figure 3.1. The ad plays on a kind of image that was celebrated for decades, a shot of workers using a crane to hoist concrete panel sections into place on new buildings. But here, the modular concrete panel has been replaced with an equally modular panel-sized television.

Some of these panel construction apartments were state allocated, but housing shortages and budget crises soon forced the state to retreat from providing radically subsidized rentals in the 1960s. Much of the construction of the Fifteen-Year Plan took the form of owner-occupied cooperatives, often organized and distributed through a larger firm like the steel factory or other state institutions rather than through the local municipality. Larger cooperatives were run by housing associations that collected fees and did maintenance and repairs. Citizens were

Figure 3.1. Advertisement for the new Videoton television set, circa 1970, with a television replacing the concrete panel on a construction site. "The family's happiness, the family's comfort: The TV!" http://retronom.hu/node/6967. Accessed April 30, 2012.

given the option of buying in to these new construction projects and could get financing through the national savings and loan (OTP). (Employees working at a firm like the steel mill that built or subsidized housing were considered fortunate.) The entrance fees to these buildings, usually paid before the building was constructed, changed the way housing was allocated. Those who could afford the fees benefited from decreased wait times for an apartment; those who couldn't found themselves competing for fewer places. These "buy in" fees increased multifold over time—meaning that by the 1970s only the second and third generation of professional and skilled worker families could afford them. (By the mid-1980s, cooperative building types had completely displaced state-owned building forms.)

For some of those who moved into the new buildings, the change from their previous housing was not necessarily an improvement. In the 1960s, my uncle's family found Dunaújváros's new housing to be more modern but smaller and cramped compared to the house and garden they had left behind in moving from a provincial town. But for many others, these new apartments were miracles of modern comfort. Compared with crowded living arrangements in village houses, which usually had no indoor plumbing and often still had packed-earth floors, a new apartment with an indoor toilet, running water, and central heating seemed an undreamed-of luxury. From 1949 to 1990, the percentage of dwellings with indoor running water rose from 17 percent to 83 percent, while the percentage of homes with indoor toilets rose from a dismal 12.5 percent to 74 percent.[5] Whatever its deficiencies, socialist housing policy indisputably raised standards of living for much of the population.

The Contemporary Style

In Sweden, furnishings compatible with such mass-produced panel architecture were produced by private companies like IKEA (founded in 1943). In socialist Eastern Europe, such standardized, mass-produced "utility furniture" (*típusbútor*) came from the state furniture industry.[6] In Hungary in the 1960s, state media relentlessly promoted the "contemporary style." Furniture exhibitions in Budapest but also in Dunaújváros allowed the public to see prototypes firsthand (*Sztálinvárosi Hírlap*, Oct. 1, 1960). State publicity set these "clean, light, homes with charming atmosphere" against those of a bourgeoisie obsessed with the past. The simple rectilinear shapes, inexpensive materials, and absence of decorative elements kept production costs down (Vadas 1992:161). In contrast to customary practice, in which a couple acquired a complete set of matching furniture as a wedding present or dowry, the consumer of utility furnishings was to buy elements separately and combine them to create shelving or units tailored to the needs of a household. Much of the modern furniture actually produced in the Soviet bloc by the 1960s adopted the Scandinavian modifications of the austere asceticism of orthodox modern designs, in part because it was cheaper to produce than English and German design, which favored steel tubing and glass (Sparke 1986). It was also because Scandinavian design—with its use of natural wood, splashes of color, and more cushioning—had produced a less forbidding style that had been adopted by the upwardly mobile working classes of Western Europe in the postwar 1950s (Attfield 2007; Löfgren 1994; Sparke 1986).

For the next decade, *Lakáskultúra* featured ads and articles promoting modern furniture for every apartment. People who attempted to move their large, traditional furniture into new buildings were ridiculed as stubbornly clinging to old-fashioned ways. One television spot echoed the Laurel and Hardy piano skit by depicting a large woman dressed in a housecoat frantically directing four sweating men who are attempting to move her enormous wardrobe into her modern flat (Papp 1998). A color television spot from 1964 provides a primer in how to adopt modern décor by taking viewers past the classical statuary on the façade of a turn-of-the-century building and in through the windows. Once inside, each velvet-curtain darkened room—packed with large and heavy antique furniture covered with porcelain and crystal on lace doilies—is transformed into a "tastefully decorated modern apartment" (Papp 1998). "They thought of everything but comfort," the voice-over claims as the rooms are shown being liberated from these monofunctional furnishings. The busy wallpaper is stripped away and the rooms are magically transformed into multifunctional spaces with smaller, lighter, and lower rectilinear furnishings.

The great enemy of this contemporary style was kitsch. Taste professionals expressed their horror of superficial and unnecessary objects. Sofa beds need not be covered with spreads, readers of *Lakáskultúra* were told: an embroidered pillow or two would suffice. If readers couldn't afford an entirely new interior, they were instructed to remake their old wardrobes by knocking off carved decorations and replacing carved legs with triangular steel pegs. Ornate gold frames were to be replaced with spare and square silver ones. Articles touted the aesthetic merits of modern porcelain vases and textiles that favored geometric shapes and simple lines over more traditional patterns.

The cultural elite's condemnation of "bourgeois" material worlds was couched in a somatized language of pollution. Modernism was presented as a purifying force that would vanquish the formal, dark, and heavy qualities of bourgeois furnishings beloved by a proper peasantry as much as by an urban middle class.[7] Qualisigns of "lightness" and "cleanliness" were realized in lightweight furnishings, light colors, and the bright light of the sun flooding in through windows liberated of bulky curtains. Sparkling white kitchen appliances, the smooth surfaces of linoleum countertops and floors, and the clean, uncluttered lines of rectilinear furnishings allowed people to wipe away the dust and grime of objects that trapped them in the past. Lightweight furnishings contrasted with the heavy, decorative furniture sets traditionally inherited or acquired at marriage and kept for a lifetime—"inalienable possessions" that were now configured as burdens weighing people down with dark and oppressive materialities. Such objects, they were repeatedly reminded, cluttered spaces, inhibited movement, and collected dust. Expressed in embodied terms, these were materialities not of patina but of stasis and decay. New furnishings, by contrast, could be easily replaced, and they freed people from the fetters of traditional obligations and hierarchies. These qualisigns of lightness aligned with "mobility" and thus extended physical experience to mobility in a transformed social order. Unadorned windows and open spaces would release people from claustrophobic interiors and allow them to "breathe."

Modernizing Materialities and Demanding Citizens

The debates over the aesthetic styles appropriate for a socialist society were part of larger concerns about how such a society could accommodate and exploit emerging forms of consumption. It was clear that new generations were not going to be swayed by a rhetoric of "sacrificing for the future" and that the moral superiority of asceticism had worn thin. The notion of using consumer goods to "modernize" populations had continuities with the Stalin period, when housing and furnishings were considered as potent as the symphony or other institutions of high culture for creating modern, discriminating, cultured citizens. Julie Hessler (2000) discusses how the Soviet Stalinist state in the 1930s saw this potential not only in housing but in retail spaces, salesclerks, and modern commodities, despite the tremendous shortages of consumer goods. Publicity for Sztálinváros had employed a similar tactic in advertising modern department stores and promising abundant modern consumer goods. European bourgeois manners and cultured lifestyles had become the unspoken model for socialist cultivation, just as they had in the Soviet Union (Dunham 1990; Fitzpatrick 1992, 2000; Kelly and Volkov 1998). Socialist Realism's most incisive critique of modernism, after all, had been of its elitist opacity masquerading as transparency, and thus Socialist Realism had attempted to clearly signal to the common man the new status of the working classes with quality materials and recognizably aspirational furnishings.

But the kind of citizen brought into being by new apartments and furnishings in the 1960s was fundamentally different from that of the 1950s. In a seeming paradox, socialist cultural producers encouraged citizens to abandon backward, status-obsessed bourgeois sensibilities by becoming more materially demanding, or *igényes,* and to strive for high-quality, modern living environments. From the perspective of a capitalist, commercial culture, such exhortations sound much like consumer advertising intended to foster invidious distinctions and play upon people's status anxieties. But in an emerging socialist society, raising material expectations was considered a necessary modernizing process in which the home played a central role. Sociologist Zsuzsa Ferge (after Halbwachs) traces this expression to early socialist concerns with the working class and poor peasantry's lack of aspirations and habituation to living with a bare minimum (Ferge 1979: 309–19), of "knowing their place."[8] Lower classes were to be elevated to the level of an ideal socialist citizenry by expanding their sense of entitlement. Instilling the downtrodden with higher levels of "need" was important both to disrupt class hierarchies and as part of a broader modernization and enculturation project.

Exhibiting high standards in one's surroundings and appearance had long been a way of constructing respectability among the well-to-do "proper peasantry" (Fél and Hofer 1969). Moreover, "giving to oneself" (*ad magára*), in the sense of devoting time and energy to the maintenance and improvement of one's physical materialities, was a sign of self-respect and respect for the good opinion of the community. In the hands of professional elites in the 1960s, however, the older notion of being *igényes* was expanded. Being *igényes* now required educated appraisal and appropriation of the ever-changing modern world of commodities as an essential part of one's material order and well-being. A sociologist from a peasant background described his father as a man who "gave to himself," because he was the first person in the village to build the newfangled *sátortető* or tent-shaped roof on his house. A *Lakáskultúra* advertisement from 1967 for new kitchen textiles epitomizes the transformation of this norm, featuring a fashionably coiffed young woman in a colorful apron drying a modern wine glass (Figure 3.2). It proclaims in block type: "Be demanding! Even in the kitchen, make discerning choices!"

The adjacent article on new pots and pans opines, "Our living conditions and lifestyle often cannot keep pace with our changing demands, but the reverse is also common: Our demands do not change as fast as the lifestyles new technological innovations make possible." The author glorifies the advanced level of state production here, but also assumes something else: that a backward population was not sufficiently modernized to appreciate and in turn be transformed by the state's advanced technological capacity. To be a modern, cultured person, the author implies, a citizen should keep abreast of technologies, design innovations, and even fashions and strive to incorporate them into his or her own life:

> Every day, contemporary objects produced with up-to-date technology and design come into circulation.... Cultured dining, table setting, and serving is not a secondary question for home culture. Let us be more demanding and instruct our family members to be so. Let us follow novel things with attention. (*Lakáskultúra* 1967/1:11)

A modern, discriminating subjectivity included high standards for hygiene and housekeeping. A 1977 description of the up-to-date bathroom exemplifies the tone: "The bathroom is the home's most intimate place. This room offers the most opportunities to pass judgment [on a family]. This is where the family's hygienic demands (*igények*) and their level of culture are displayed" (*Lakáskultúra* 1977/5).

Cultivating *igényes* attitudes was part of a modernizing project grounded in scientific progress. Just as the modern housewife was to abandon religious su-

Figure 3.2. Advertisement for kitchen textiles in *Lakáskultúra*: "Be Demanding! Even in the kitchen, make discerning choices!" (*Lakáskultúra* 1967, issue 1).

perstitions and practices, she was also to transform her orientation to what it meant to care for the home—to think of it as a task informed by science and enhanced by rational thinking. Instead of redistributing household labor between men and women, mechanical labor was to solve the problem of this labor altogether. A translation of a *New Scientist* article published in *Lakáskultúra* in 1967 informed Hungarian readers that domestic robots would soon free women from cooking, cleaning, and laundry so they could engage in more fulfilling work for the collective—or enjoy the entertainments made possible by new technological innovations in the form of radios, stereos, and television (*Lakáskultúra* 1967/3:26).

Mária Pataki, *Lakáskultúra*'s founding editor-in-chief, told me in 1997 that the mission of the magazine had been to educate the masses in modern taste. For her, such taste would in itself preclude rather than foment desires for conspicuous consumption, since the kind of person brought forth by modern materialities would, by definition, be *opposed* to bourgeois posturing. Indeed, the goal for socialist society was for the entire citizenry to achieve this modern level of civilization (Reid 2006:252). In this context, socialist citizens were encouraged to be *igényes* as both consumers and producers—to demand quality in both their workplaces and homes.[9]

By the 1970s, the imagery and rhetoric stigmatizing bourgeois furnishings had successfully transformed aesthetic dispositions by inverting older "qualisigns of value." New modern furniture was discursively imbued with progressive ideals and embodied sensations of lightness, cleanliness, mobility, openness, and informality—in a context that aligned such an aesthetic with contemporary trends in the West (see, for example, Bánkuti 1958; S. Nagy 1987; Vadas 1992). Modern styles were embraced primarily by upwardly mobile, younger generations, who, ironically, often made their own versions if they couldn't afford what they wanted or couldn't find it because of shortages in supply. The adoption of the contemporary style—even the stripped-down versions offered by the Hungarian manufacturing sector—was neither an act of rebellious dissent nor an embrace of socialist politicized ideals (Yurchak 2006). By consciously adopting interior furnishing styles that contradicted those of their parents and grandparents, younger generations were "bringing modernity home" (Attfield 1999, 2007). They were opening themselves to the modern norms inhering in these material objects, in part through the embodied social practices the materiality of these furnishings not only made possible but oftentimes dictated.

The coffee table's potency as a symbol of the modern emerged from its design (Attfield 1997). Unlike a traditional dining table where diners sat up straight, close to the table, with bodies only visible from the elbows up, the coffee table invited people to adopt a relaxed, informal posture on low couch seating and opened up the visible space between their bodies. Such furnishings were considered conducive to more egalitarian forms of conviviality, such as having mixed drinks and sharing snacks out of the same bowl. The open floor plan for apartments (made possible by modern building technologies such as plate glass, steel supporting beams, and central heating) embodied a similar social agenda. By removing doors and walls between rooms to create a multipurpose, "democratic" living area, it rejected bourgeois divisions of domestic space, such as the separate kitchen and parlor, which reinforced gendered, generational and class hierarchies (Attfield

1999:76). As I show later in this chapter, this wholesale rethinking of domestic space was turned to different ends in the Soviet bloc.

It is difficult to reconstruct how young Hungarian adults understood panel concrete housing and modern furnishings in this period. But judging from popular music, newspaper articles, and editorials, as well as the pages of fashion and interior décor magazines, they leaned toward the irreverence of their counterparts in Western Europe rather than the dictates of elitist socialist taste makers (see also Hammer 2010; Valuch 2006). Editorials by cultural elites bemoaned the behavior and fashion of modern youth, who with their disrespectful behavior, men wearing women's blouses and "Elvys Priesly" [sic] frothing at the mouth . . . confuse what is 'modern' with what is 'tasteless'" (Dunaújvárosi Hírlap, Oct. 7, 1960). In this atmosphere, many younger, upwardly mobile Hungarians sought to transform their interiors to distance themselves from class hierarchies now seen as old-fashioned.

By the end of the socialist period, a full quarter of the population in the country was housed in urban apartments. In Dunaújváros, the number exceeded 85 percent. The majority of urban apartments were two-room, furnished with the modern "wall unit" of cabinets and shelving, a coffee table with several armchairs, and some kind of foldout couch or sofa—all in a limited range of styles. In Dunaújváros, I was often told, the socialist ethos of egalitarianism had taken hold more than in other places in Hungary. This was reflected in how widely the socialist practice of using the informal mode of address had taken hold here, but also in the reputation the new town had developed for producing *igényes* citizens. They had internalized their entitlement to institutions of high culture, for example, and were bold enough to stride right into a museum of fine art in Budapest instead of cowering outside, as they might once have done.

Social and Material Plasticity

Class and Status, Socialist-Style

In the 1980s, the dissident writer György Konrád pointed out that it was "under Communist leadership that the process of embourgeoisement was given its greatest impetus" (Konrád 1984:149). As a vocal proponent of a bourgeois private sphere, Konrád was clearly amused by this development. But Communist Party members, ideologues, and sociologists had been grappling with the issue of socialist social stratification for some time. Early on, internal critics had voiced concern about the rise of a new Communist Party elite, the earliest and most dramatic of which was by Yugoslav party insider Milovan Djilas. He wrote in the mid-1950s about the power of this bureaucratic class to dispose of the means of production, and he paid for his temerity with prison time (Djilas 1957). Years later in Hungary, Konrád, with sociologist Iván Szelényi, demonstrated how an intelligentsia legitimated its control over redistribution by propagating ideologies in its basic class interest, the most important of all the ideology of a classless society (Konrád and Szelényi 1979). Throughout the Soviet bloc, the public chafed at the visible benefits enjoyed by members of a political elite, from living in villas and driving around in large—often chauffeured—cars to having access to consumer goods through specialty shops not open to the population at large (Gomori 1963).[10]

By the 1960s, the cultivation of *igényes* citizens, the steady increase in standards of living, and the focus on modern materialities facilitated the emergence of a socialist, modern middle stratum, one that had a great deal in common with the middle classes emerging in the postwar West. In Western Europe and the United States, the boom in prosperity had allowed a skilled working class to participate in a consumer society marked by its modernity rather than by class hierarchy. The working-class citizens with more expendable incomes joined the ranks of the middle classes by turning attention and resources toward the consumer project of creating a comfortable "home." In Hungary, the eradication of the propertied classes and the "middle class" of independent retailers and producers in the 1950s opened the way for upward social mobility. This mobility was enhanced by preferential quotas for the peasant and working classes, the shift of agricultural workers to industry, and the mass mobilization of women into the formal workforce (Szelényi et al. 1998:ch.1).

The more radical effects of Stalinist social policies had leveled off by the 1960s and with them the dramatic rates of social mobility (Szelényi et al. 1998:15). In official rhetoric, the term "class" had been done away with, but the influence of traditional class hierarchies lingered on, reflected in the continuing subordination of manual to "intellectual" labor as a new status quo began to take shape.

A new socialist citizenry was emerging that defined itself in terms of its modernity rather than along more familiar class categories (see also Patterson 2011:296–97 for Yugoslavia). Sociology, a discipline rehabilitated in the early 1960s, had modified the Stalinist tripartite division of society (peasantry and working classes, plus an intelligentsia) to produce a more nuanced picture that differentiated social "stratum" by occupation, as well as by education, urbanity, and generation (see Kolosi 1988). It identified a middle range of strata made up of administrators, office workers, managers, professionals (doctors, lawyers, engineers), and cultural producers. Skilled workers increasingly entered the ranks of this group (Kolosi 1988).

In Dunaújváros by the late 1970s, the middle stratum included large numbers of skilled workers married to women in lower-status, white-collar administrative jobs. This group came to define the working-class town's identity from the late 1950s on. Skilled workers that had arrived in the new town in the 1960s were better educated than the older generation and also enjoyed the best of state-supported living: more than 70 percent lived in state flats, compared to 53 percent of those who arrived in the 1950s and 66 percent of those who arrived in the 1970s (Szirmai and Zelenay 1988:78–80). This group increasingly distanced itself from the second largest group in the new town, a "proletariat" made up of unskilled male workers and their families. Only two-thirds of these workers had finished the eighth grade, and they were usually married to women also employed in low-paying factory jobs or other forms of menial labor. This urban proletariat also included so-called peasant-workers, who commuted from nearby villages, whose wives, though categorized as "unemployed," were usually occupied with working a small garden plot and raising pigs and poultry.

At the opposite end of the social spectrum was the state-sanctioned category of "intelligentsia," made up primarily of men with technical degrees as the city attracted and retained very few members of a *humán értelmiség*, or a cultural intelligentsia. Sociologists tended to make a hard distinction between intelligentsia and skilled workers (Szirmai and Zelenay 1988:80), but such distinctions mask how much these categories overlapped by the mid-1970s, as higher-ranking skilled workers became managers and directors, while some of the intelligentsia came from the working class or a rural background. Intermarriage also blurred lines. Class background had become less important for marriage, in part because such a background no longer had the same power to determine life chances, but also because of the limitations placed on the ways such distinctions could be symbolized publicly. Young doctors and engineers who had come to the city for professional reasons often married locally, finding women who came from "respectable" families even if their fathers had only been provincial artisans.

The category of intelligentsia also obscured the small but visible presence of a population that continued to distinguish itself as middle-class or gentry in manners, dress, and social practice, and that had inherited antiques. This group had a cultural influence beyond its numbers, modeling *polgári* social and cultural behavior (Szirmai and Zelenay 1988:88). At the same time, the modern, egalitarian ethos of the new town worked to the disadvantage of middle-class residents who displayed their status in conventional ways. I remember instances from the 1970s when the wives and children of doctors and engineers were accused of putting on "*úri*," or gentry airs. Moreover, their relationships with colleagues were often strained by politics. Unlike many of Dunaújváros's professional and administrative leaders, those in this segment of society generally rejected cooptation by the socialist state, refusing to join the party even if they were denied promotion or positions in which they could do something for their fellow citizens.

The experience of an intelligentsia in the "worker's city" was uneven. Some who had working-class or peasant backgrounds felt at home and enjoyed large social groups and contacts, but a second generation along with professionals who had moved to the city from elsewhere often felt alienated. Some were embittered by their lack of influence in local decision making. Others suffered from a dearth of cultural life and longed to move away (Szirmai and Zelenay 1988:80).

By the 1970s, sociology's growing independence allowed it to investigate the persistence of inequalities within socialist society (Vörös 1997:24). The state's legitimation of a prosperous way of life had paved the way for skilled workers to identify with the interests uniting "the whole of society" (an abstraction) rather than with the working classes in particular (see Ferge 1979:316). Because "the whole of society" was often presented as a modern and civilized population, it also became the normative ideal, defined on either side by those populations deviating from this norm toward poverty (a peasantry or proletariat below) or problematic affluence (in its bourgeois forms or in the conspicuous consumption of party elites). Even though the state largely controlled the means of production and no segment of the population owned much capital, this respectable middle stratum followed the dynamics of a consumer-normalized middle-class culture elsewhere in the world (Liechty 2003; May 1988; Ortner 2002).

Man-Made Modern and Utopian Materialities

Konrád was only partially correct, then, in thinking that state socialism furthered Hungarian "embourgeoisement" (Konrád 1984:149). This new middle stratum had little in common with the bourgeoisie of the early twentieth century. For the generation that moved into new panel apartments and adopted the contemporary style in the 1960s and early 1970s, a new kind of class consciousness was fostered in part through new domestic materialities. As in the West, this generation was being defined by upheavals in attitudes and expectations generated by an unprecedented prosperity, the promises of space-age technologies, and the growth of commercial visual media—television, magazines, advertising, and urban signage. Pop design embodied the zeitgeist of the times, drawing on International Modern design but rejecting its elite pretensions, its authoritarian overtones, its austerity and solemnity, and its insistence on enduring, timeless, and stripped-down forms. Instead, Pop design embraced rapid change, the iconoclasm of popular culture, and commercial design that celebrated bright colors and fanciful shapes. The atmosphere was one of playful irreverence, with an emphasis on cheap, entertaining, and expendable artifacts (Garner 2008:54–56), as well as a rejection of the formal class distinctions and the heavy furnishings of earlier generations. While paper dresses, purple lampshades, and the butterfly chair are paradigmatic examples of this spirit, the early to mid-1960s were also characterized by the proliferation of man-made materials: concrete, synthetic textiles, and, above all, new plastics.

From the perspective of contemporary society, seemingly drowning in plastic, it is hard to imagine a time when plastics and concrete were celebrated as miraculous. Their qualities of versatility and durability were aligned with the modernist promise of transcending the limitations of nature to usher in a bold, new world. Jane Schneider, in her marvelous analysis of the rise and fall of polyester in the United States and England, reminds us that synthetic fabrics were not always taboo, disdained as impure or unnatural (1994). Polyester was initially embraced for its vibrant colors and liberating wash-and-wear qualities, at prices almost anyone could afford. The positive qualities of this synthetic material eclipsed other sensations (or qualia) that later came to the fore and were imagined to be intolerable: static cling and the suffocation implied by describing it as a fabric that doesn't "breathe." Compared to cotton, the production of which entailed back-breaking labor and environmental destruction, polyester was an equalizing fabric—a quality good for the masses—embraced by a postwar generation that represented a new, classless spirit (Schneider 1994).

In socialist Eastern Europe, the powers of industrialization were used to convince agricultural populations with deeply held notions of a "limited good" (Foster 1965) that it would be possible to provide abundantly for all. Technology and manmade materials were thus intricately linked with utopian promises. Mechanization vastly increased productivity. Goods and materials could be produced en masse without the need to extract, harvest, and process natural materials. A colorful ad for plastic trays published in 1967 (Plate 1b) exemplifies this spirit, publicizing the virtues of plastic, its bold, modern colors and its functional strength compared to wood or porcelain: "PLASTIC! Even if you jump on it, it's UNBREAKABLE!" (*Lakáskultúra* 1967).

The state's ideological emphasis on a universal class consciousness as part of its civilizing project contributed to the emerging self-consciousness of a consumer-based middle stratum, where respectability was increasingly imbedded in modern materialities. Older forms of social distinctions lingered, but in Hungary, as Patrick H. Patterson has argued for Yugoslavia, "the new cultural option of belonging to a much more expansive community of consumers gradually worked to undermine [the] importance and to erode the sharp edges of more traditional class categorizations" (Patterson 2011:297).

The Resilience of Old Materialities

Despite the widespread adoption of socialist modern styles by younger Hungarians in particular, the old had not yielded completely to the new. Critics lamented that the ideal of clean lines and uncluttered spaces was still often marred by elements of "petty bourgeois models of the past" such as the display cabinet, planters, porcelain figures, and decorative doilies (S. Nagy 1997). For many older people, modern furnishings remained alien, and they adhered to the traditional norm of positioning a table in the center of the room. Some families of lower-class background still considered modern styles to be above their station, despite public exhortations to be more demanding. Others just found them to be too expensive. People of higher status were often unmoved by rhetoric of the modern and adhered to more traditional tastes. Those that had inherited *polgári* (bourgeois) furnishings might combine them with objects signifying a more modern identity, while others filled entire panel apartments with it—steadfastly refusing to part with these objects as well as their identification with a bygone class status, no matter how old-fashioned these had become (Plate 5b).

Ironically, these "outmoded" tastes were reinforced by state agencies and magazines. The orthodoxy of "good design" was not universally accepted. Many cultural producers and party bureaucrats had tastes that varied significantly from the monochromatic functionalism that dominated design discourse throughout the Soviet bloc in the 1960s (Crowley and Reid 2000; S. Nagy 1997; Veenis 1999). Others were mindful of the diverse tastes of the general public and wanted to provide them with goods they actually desired. As a result, despite the predominance of a modern, contemporary style and the derision of bourgeois kitsch, the state production and retail sector actively promoted *régi*—old or antique furnishings—often in the very same publications that championed the modern. Factories produced furniture and decorative objects entirely out of keeping with the contemporary style. In Budapest and elsewhere, workshops advertised not only reproductions of antique furniture (particularly styles dating from before 1850) but also services to restore or reupholster antique pieces (*Lakáskultúra* 1967/3, 18–19, 31). Hungary's famous porcelain factories manufactured vases with simple, modern shapes, but they also produced elaborately painted animal figurines and gilt bon-bon boxes.

Orthodox members of the cultural intelligentsia condemned these products. A journalist in Dunaújváros, for example, railed against the decorative porcelain figurines and lead crystal displayed in a local shop window in 1963, asking, "Should we be advertising kitsch?" (*Reklámozzuk-e a giccset?*). The local head of distribution defended these goods as having been vetted by the highest levels of the Hungarian design establishment. The journalist retorted by accusing state manufacturing entities of capitulating to public whims and defaulting on their responsibility to produce material goods that would lead to a socialist future. "The problem of kitsch," he insists, "is not a commercial but a political question. . . . The media is not the tool of commercial advertising . . . it cannot shirk its duty" [to help society move forward] (*Dunaújvárosi Hírlap*, July 16, 1963).

The socialist state was not in the position, politically or economically, to enforce the abandonment of traditional styles. Just as the state housing policy officially endorsed apartment construction but included provisions for private house building, state consignment warehouses, or BÁV (*Bizományi Áruház Vállalat*) regularly advertised used and antique furnishings. The campaigns for contemporary furnishings had been so successful that state consignment warehouses were crammed full of old furniture. By 1970, the local paper reported that Dunaújváros's furniture warehouse could no longer accept people's used furniture for lack of space (*Dunaújvárosí Hírlap*, Jan. 6, 1970). At the same time, production of modern furnishings was failing to meet demand. As a result, the cash-strapped state resorted to advertising the surplus old furniture for sale on the back pages of *Lakáskultúra*. Consequently, *Lakáskultúra* featured articles on the appropriate combination of "old and new" furniture along with other enticements to buy older, second-hand furniture. In a 1969 issue, for example, it sponsored a contest that asked readers to cut out small photographs of decorative antiques and paste them into an entirely austere, modern room "in a tasteful way." A book titled "The Dwelling" had provided an early explanation for why such antiques were not to be feared, focusing on the *relationship between* objects rather than the historical provenance of the objects themselves:[11]

> Today [we are] experienced and wise enough to combine the most up-to-date interior designs and forms with antiques. . . . Contemporary interior design is not dominated by a uniform style at all costs, with furniture of smooth lines and objects that are all alike. On the contrary. One does not have to part with objects made, bought or inherited from an older time, even an antique from a century ago. If we arrange our homes with competence, modern furnishings do not preclude the possibility that a Biedermeier commode or empire secretary might elevate a room's beauty and atmosphere. (Bánkuti 1958:170–71)

Alongside its usual articles on middle-stratum Hungarians in modern apartments, *Lakáskultúra* also began to feature apartments in older buildings and furnished in a different style. These homes belonged to members of a cultural intelligentsia—celebrity artists, writers, and theater directors—who were inevitably shown in their high-ceilinged urban interiors furnished with antiques, books, Persian rugs, and original works of art. The genre downplayed the status of these objects as "valuables" and instead described the apartments as filled with "the old," using the term *régi* (old) instead of *polgári* (bourgeois). They were ostensibly acquired as gifts from fellow artists or admirers rather than as family heirlooms and thus shifted in status from symbols of class reproduction to tokens of appreciation. Such persons were understood to have a deep appreciation for the arts and at the same time to be unencumbered by the materialistic desires of ordinary folk. In the hands of a cultural intelligentsia, antiques became objects imbued with historic and personal rather than material value—a different kind of inalienable possession (Weiner 1985). Similar furnishings were considered acceptable in the apartments categorized as "teacher homes" (S. Nagy 1987). Feature articles displayed the desk of a journalist, writer, or professor, piled high with papers, against a backdrop of floor-to-ceiling bookshelves crammed with hardbound volumes. Antique furnishings were never shown in the "inappropriate" settings of *panel* apartments, but only in older interiors with high ceilings and parquet floors where they were understood to be at home.

Socialist Modern and Social Distinction

In socialist Hungary, the relationship between social stratification and wealth was far from straightforward, leading Katalin S. Nagy to find that "the once close tie between remuneration and social status was eroding" (S. Nagy 1987:182–83). State salaries were kept uniformly low, and wealth was redistributed through universal provision of health care and subsidies for transportation, child care, and housing, as well as for consumer goods and cultural events like opera, theater, and concerts. Limitations on property and social censure for the display of class status meant that inequalities were often kept hidden: wealth was reinvested in the home or stored in the form of jewelry, furs, and other material assets.

The second economy created new, entrepreneurial wealth in both state and private or semiprivate sectors, increasing income discrepancies and their materialization in consumption—but not necessarily in keeping with culturally accepted forms of social stratification (Róna-Tas 1997; S. Nagy 1987). During the 1970s, low-status groups such as village agricultural workers, who were able to earn cash through such endeavors as raising pigs, sometimes had higher incomes than urban professionals (though Róna-Tas demonstrates that the extent of this wealth among small producers has been exaggerated [Róna-Tas 1997:ch. 6]). Many were able to build modernized homes to replace peasant houses—though they often retained the tradition of the decorated but little-used "clean room" (*tisztaszoba*) (Hollos and Maday 1983). Higher-status groups, such as professionals and managers, grumbled about these developments, and yet they enjoyed other forms of compensation, such as access to the best apartments and consumer goods, state-sponsored automobiles, trips abroad, and the like. The economic reforms of the 1980s favored white-collar professional and factory workers by legalizing subcontracting and expanding the range for entrepreneurial endeavors. Through it all, urban living retained its prestige over a denigrated rural existence.

In Dunaújváros, state-built housing succeeded in diminishing visible inequalities between social groups (Szirmai and Zelenay 1988:228). Similarly, interior furnishing became increasingly uniform as more people adopted modern styles and were constrained in their arrangement by their apartment's size, floor plans, heating units, and materials, which largely determined where the wall unit shelving and the fold-out sofa had to go (Valuch 2006:35). But attempts to establish material "sameness" through uniform apartment buildings and furnishing did not produce egalitarianism, nor did it inhibit attempts to display social distinction. "A family's lifestyle, the house in which they live, and their home's surroundings are symbolic expressions of their social status/situation," wrote sociologists Szelényi and Konrád in 1969 (cited in S. Nagy 1987:14). By the 1980s, Katalin S. Nagy found in her research on home interiors that if she combined categories from the presocialist era with socialist-era transformations, she could compile a "typology of contemporary Hungarian dwelling interiors" that conformed to social strata (S. Nagy 1987:14, 104–10).[12] At the same time, she too acknowledged the emergence of a "quasi-modern" style as people had to adjust their furnishings to new apartment sizes and layouts and were influenced by the mass media promoting the modernization of interiors.

Outside observers may have seen Dunaújváros housing as remarkably uniform, but residents were acutely sensitive to differences in building types, materials, and location as well as to inequities in housing distribution. Central-city apartment buildings constructed during the Stalin era were valued the most highly for their quality materials and higher ceilings, but also because they were state-owned and allocated—meaning, as we saw in the last chapter, that they cost almost nothing to "rent" and, at the same time, were practically inalienable once allocated. These buildings were by and large occupied by the city's party elites, professionals and their families, and higher-ranking members of the skilled working classes. The few neighborhoods built during this period that had housed the "proletariat" had never been completed to the standards of these other buildings and continued to house lower-ranking working-class people. These buildings had lost any connection to the Stalin era and were called "brick houses" (*tégla házak*) to distinguish them from concrete panel buildings.

Instead of improving over the years, new housing construction and services actually declined in quality and increased in cost as the state confronted mounting financial troubles. Panel construction housing boomed in the 1970s, at the same time when this type of construction was being deemed a failure in the West and demolished. This wave of construction produced the high-rise and high-density buildings that became iconic of state socialism (Plate 4). New city districts further from the center failed to provide adequate services such as child care, grocery stores, transportation, and places to socialize such as coffee shops or movie theaters, as funding was directed entirely to building new housing units. A generation raised in central apartments from the 1950s began their search for housing only to find that new apartments were more expensive and of inferior quality, even as they remained difficult to come by.

For the many thousands of people in need of a home, the waiting period for a state-administered aparment could be more than fifteen years. In Dunaújváros the expression *lakáshoz jutni,* meaning "to obtain, get or come by an apartment," reflected the almost universal obsession with securing a living space. Professionals, technocrats, and other elites continued to have privileged access to housing, but they were still affected by the housing shortage. In the early 1970s, for example,

Margit became eligible for an apartment in Dunaújváros because she had graduated at the top of her law class. Though she and her husband Géza had to marry earlier than they'd intended to qualify for the apartment, they were considered extremely fortunate because they had only lived with her parents in their one bedroom apartment for a year while construction proceeded on their own apartment in a building nearby. Their standing in the community had allowed them to request an apartment near her parents, but they had no say in which unit they would be assigned in the ten-story building, nor in its configuration or quality. Still, the very fact that they had an apartment to themselves and in a central location indicated their privileged status.

Urban housing shortages throughout the country meant that for many Hungarians, particularly of the rural working classes, the only way to acquire a home was to build a house themselves. Typically, those willing to embark on this ordeal were people who had family support networks in rural areas to help with the construction and were also prepared to do much of the physical labor themselves. This implied peasant-worker status. It also implied that the house builders had an interest in taking advantage of second-economy agricultural activities—something reflected in the new house forms emerging in rural areas (Szelényi et al. 1988). By the 1970s, market reforms had made many such self-built village houses into spaces for profitable endeavors such as raising livestock and growing produce. As a result, village houses became larger and more modernized as the decades wore on, but failed to gain urban respectability. What Katalin S. Nagy calls the village modern house of the 1970s was built and occupied by peasant-workers. Unlike the square houses of the 1960s, they were "associated with those elements of society that were once lowest, the children of manor workers (*cseléd*) and poor farmers, now upwardly mobile through second economy and rural possibilities" (S. Nagy 1987). This type of house, from the point of view of an urban intelligentsia, had only one overriding function, that of status representation, with all new, modern furniture and a "super" bathroom no one used. "The whole house becomes a '*tisztaszoba*,'" the "clean room" or decorative parlor in peasant households (S. Nagy 1987:104–10).

The distaste for self-built houses arose partly from a prevalent vision of modernity as consisting of a cultured life in an urban apartment (with weekend retreats to a rustic cottage in the countryside), and partly from the fact that living in urban apartments built by the state had become central to workers' experience and identity as residents of the socialist city. In Dunaújváros in particular, the working classes had internalized the association of family houses with individualism and a betrayal of the collective. A woman of Schwab German ethnic background recalled how her family had been ostracized as "antisocial" when they began building their house in Dunapentele in the early 1970s, making the bricks by hand. And indeed, building the house had been so time-consuming that her father could no longer participate in the collective socializing of workers that went on in factory-owned clubhouses near the Danube. (She noted wryly that others were happy to use the house for social gatherings and celebrations once it was built.)

Dysfunctional Modern

If the state was succesful in nurturing expectations for a modern lifestyle, it undermined citizens' efforts to partake of such a lifestyle by failing to produce the necessary material goods and environments. Hungarian industry managed to produce some of the iconic items of 1960s modernity, and *Lakáskultúra* and other publications made much of the *Kagyló szék* or clamshell chair (an approximation of the butterfly chair) and purple, orange, or black and white upholstery. But production of the high-quality plastics that had revolutionized the consumer goods sector in the West remained a great challenge throughout Eastern Europe, and people had to make do with goods made of the low-quality PVC plastics they had come to dislike during the war years (Stokes 2000). Moreover, even though Hungarian furnishing exhibitions and publicity often featured a variety of colors and forms, the pieces that were made available tended to be conservative and functional and were made of inferior materials.

As with so many other products of Socialist Modern design, in the hands of the state, principles of rationality and efficiency turned into justifications for making housing and furnishing as cheaply as possible. Minimum requirements for space became averages. Unlike the panel construction apartments built during Sweden's "Million Programme," where the average apartment had three rooms totaling about 75 square meters (about 800 square feet), in Hungary, the majority of new apartments were two rooms and about 50 square meters (about 540 square feet), considerably impacting how family life could be organized. The remainder were made up of one-room studios (about 30 square meters) and, more rarely, of three rooms (about 70 square meters). Monotony and uniformity became hallmarks as early designs were reproduced endlessly with minimal alterations.[13] In this respect at least, modernist architects and designers could be seen as the victims of their own ideological success, as their "timeless" and "contextless" designs rendered their services obsolete (Molnár 2010:69–70).

The False Promise of the Socialist Open Plan

The open plan was an example of a design ideal that was distorted by state socialist realities. As originally conceived, the open plan was intended to tear down "false" social divisions by tearing down walls between rooms. Instead, in housing throughout the Soviet states, it was employed not to tear down interior walls but to divide an apartment's small main room into functional zones necessary for a modern life. New apartments continued to be built with walls dividing the kitchen from the main room or rooms. (Moreover, house builders were often turned down for permits if their designs did *not* close off the kitchen from the other rooms!) This room might be divided into atomized zones for working, for a children's corner, for entertaining, and for listening to music and watching television. As illustrated in ubiquitous reproductions of floor plans (Figure 3.3), these independent zones were to be created by rearranging furniture and separating areas with dividers such as bookshelves, hand-crocheted curtains, and risers. In practice, however, having one small room serve as the space for a number of people pursuing disparate activities generated conflict and strife, especially when that room also had to serve as a bedroom, usually for a married couple. This issue was constantly recognized by the press as a "problem."

Dividing the main room in this way required, first, the removal of the traditional central dining table. A taste expert had declared in 1957, "In the lifestyle of today's urbanite . . . eating at home plays a minor role. After a quick breakfast in the kitchen, one has lunch at the workplace" (Szalai 1997). Dining at home was usually relegated to the tiny kitchen, where family members often had to eat in shifts. The loss of a central table had additional consequences. In both peasant and bourgeois households, this table had been the center of home life: it was where the family ate its meals, where schoolwork was done, and where guests were entertained. Even the Stalinist domestic ideal had featured the family gathered around a central table. The open plan eliminated the material conditions for such a family-focused sociality and reconstituted the household as atomized individuals engaged in different, self-directed pursuits.

The piece of furniture most closely associated with Socialist Modern design was the floor-to-ceiling shelving and closet, or "wall unit," which was indispensable in panel apartments with little or no closet space. Wall units stored everything: coats and underwear, bedding and linens, books and decorative objects, entertainment center items (television, radio, record player and records, tape deck), and a bar or cocktail cabinet with bottles, glasses, napkins, and dry snacks or chocolates. These wall units became the centerpieces of the state's furniture industry, as models such as the "Firenze" (Florence) style of 1967 quickly sold out production runs (*Lakáskultúra* 1976/3:2).[14]

Because the main room was also where at least some of the family slept, the sofa bed became another standard piece of furniture. It was usually made of a flat rectangle covered by a fairly stiff pad and upholstered with a durable fabric in a modern print; one side was hinged to allow access to a storage compartment for bedding underneath. It became the norm to strip the sofa bed each morning to remove all traces of a bedroom. This arrangement was often bitterly resented: it obstructed the marital intimacy that was becoming normalized elsewhere in the world and made it impossible to sleep late. For elderly people or those with bad backs, lifting the top of the bed to tuck away the bedding added to the litany of

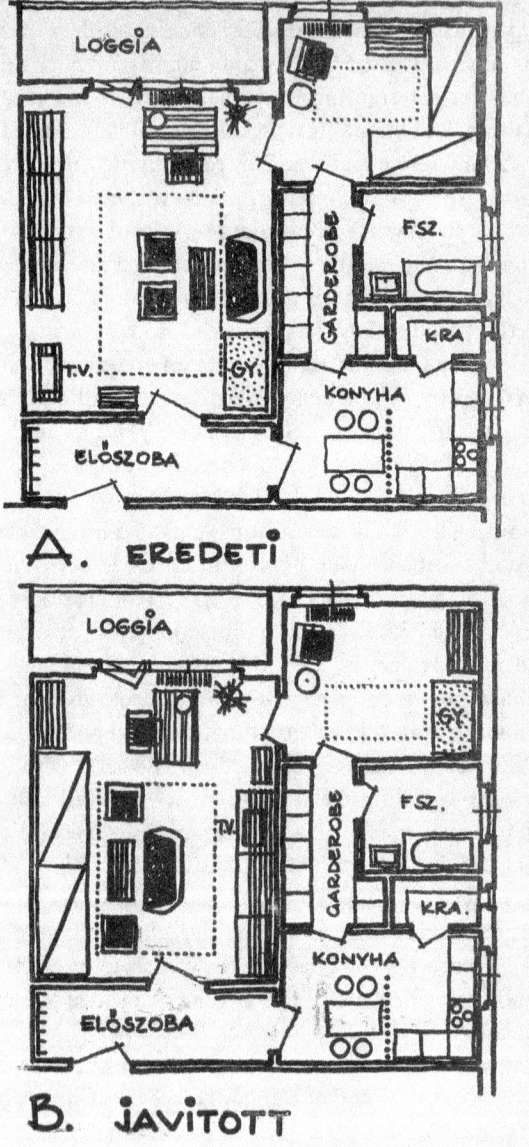

Figure 3.3. "Original" (A) and "Corrected" (B) apartment floor plans of a typical two-room panel apartment. A married couple is expecting a child and have been arguing over how to rearrange their apartment. The editors advise that the most logical solution is to put the child into the small room, and move their beds into the main room. *Lakáskultúra* 1968.

aches and pains attributed to the apartment. In the 1970s, the state reintroduced production of the "French bed" (*franciaágy*), or double-size bed, now in modern styles and featuring a spring mechanism that revealed a space for bedding. This material instantiation of "French" sexuality quickly became a coveted object and status symbol.[15]

Laundry was the bane of women in these apartments. Opening up the entire living space increased the burden of housework, since it made the entire apartment visible; there was no more closing the door on unmade beds or drying laundry (Madigan and Munro 1999). In theory, apartment buildings were fitted with shared laundry rooms. But conflicts arose over sharing the space, especially when clothing disappeared. Women preferred doing the laundry in their bathtubs or, increasingly, with the help of a plug-in washing machine with a spin-dry feature (centrifuge). This feature was prized, because the inconvenience of hanging wet laundry was one of the biggest complaints about small apartments. Men cursed as they knocked their heads on hanging racks above the bathtub. Women hated the hanging laundry scattered around, always ruining the orderliness or *rend* of the apartment.

But even the centrifuge couldn't take care of wrinkled linens. Women groaned when they mentioned the ironing basket, symbol of the ever-present chore, which occupied precious space until they managed to find time for it, usually late at night watching television. The burden of laundering clothes was one of the reasons for the normative nightly bathing ritual. Clean bodies would not dirty sheets and would keep clothes clean longer. Likewise, most people changed out of their street clothes and shoes as soon as they got home and wandered around in their apartments in underwear or a housecoat.

Floor Plan as Spatial Puzzle

The lack of space in modern apartments posed severe challenges for families, and the popularity of *Lakáskultúra* stemmed in part from its acknowledgment of this reality. Especially after the 1960s, it rarely depicted furnishings from trade shows and fairs and never used staged or professionally designed interiors. Instead, it featured the infinitely diverse interior furnishings, room arrangements, decorative inclinations, clutter, and order of real families. A regular feature was its response to readers' requests for expert advice on arranging possessions in a cramped apartment. The magazine's "before" and "after" floor plans included precise measurements of the floor space of each room and the dimensions of each piece of furniture. Interior design professionals suggested how to maximize existing space through replacing furniture, erecting lofts, and creating storage. In the plan in Figure 3.3, for example, a married couple is expecting a child, and they have been arguing over how best to rearrange their two-room apartment. The editors write that the most "logical solution" is to give the child the bedroom, and

Figure 3.4. The space-expanding powers of the Contemporary Style. The illustration (top) makes the room appear enlarged by the open plan, in comparison to the photograph (below). Furniture is drawn at a smaller scale than in the photograph, and the dining table with lace tablecloth is moved out of the center of the room to create a separate zone. A prototypical wall unit replaces the wardrobe for storage. The picture with ornate frame is replaced with two in minimalist frames which are hung lower to make the ceilings appear higher. *Lakáskultúra* 1967(3).

move their beds out into the main room (*Lakáskultúra*, 1968), an arrangement that became the norm. These advisors regularly suggested ways to create the illusion of more space with mirrors, false windows, and paint. Readers followed this design advice, believing out of necessity the professional wisdom that creating a livable home "doesn't depend on the number of meters" but on "some compromise and rational thinking" (*Lakáskultúra*,1976/1:11). Nevertheless, a nagging suspicion remained that living a "normal" life in these spaces might be impossible.

I began to share my friends' fascination with *Lakáskultúra*'s drawings of floor plans and furniture, poring over them like puzzles. Their popularity was enhanced by the extraordinary degree of standardization of living spaces. Housing was described not by number of rooms or bedrooms, but by area in square meters. Everyone in Dunaújváros knew that fifty-three square meters was configured into two rooms with a bathroom and kitchen, and that thirty-two square meters meant one room with kitchen and bath. Seventy-four square meters conjured a luxurious amount of space. Thus readers could easily visualize the kind of space depicted and imagine applying similar schemes in their own apartments or in those of relatives or friends.

Such two-dimensional "representations of space" contributed to modernist design practices of abstraction, practices that allow for extensive manipulation of living space with little accountability for how they are to be lived (Lefebvre 1991: 41). On paper, a floor plan originally designed for a much larger space could simply be reduced to fit a twelve-square-meter room. Similarly, though party officials decreed that the minimum space per person should be nine square meters, in practice this included space taken up by the pantry and the water heater. In drawings of floor plans, designers sometimes manipulated the scale of furniture relative to rooms. Thus, in a 1967 *Lakáskultúra* spread on refurnishing a room (Figure 3.4), the artist's rendering of its transformation (upper drawing) makes the room appear much more spacious by shrinking the furniture and lowering the pictures on the wall.

Do-It-Yourself Modern

As part of the state's modernizing agenda in the 1950s, cultural producers had optimistically appealed to citizens to replace "backward" modes of self-provisioning with purchasing what they needed. A colorful poster of a woman doing her grocery shopping, for example, proclaimed, "Buy preserves! Don't make them yourself." By 1965, however, in the first issue of *Lakáskultúra*, the editor reluctantly acknowledged the existence of do-it-yourself (DIY) practices when she included a section on household tips called "Handyman. *If it's necessary.*" When this became one of the magazine's most popular features, the editors embraced the trend, renaming the section "Home Arts" in 1966. Later, the magazine used the Hungarian expression for DIY, *barkács,* or "cobbled-together" (similar to the French *bricolage*). Over the next twenty years, *Lakáskultúra* was sought after in part for publishing readers' ingenious solutions for organizing cramped spaces and for its attention to DIY ideas.

Citizens who equated modern furnishings with a modern identity but were unable to obtain them or afford them often turned to do-it-yourself production. They were given enthusiastic assistance in the media. A photo of a space-saving folding kitchen table in *Lakáskultúra*, for example, was accompanied by instructions for making one. DIY instructions became wildly popular and were found in local newspapers as well as national magazines, along with books and television clips explaining how to alter a jacket, construct a liquor cabinet, and crochet a dividing curtain (see for example Polster 1961; Várhelyi 1963). Home-made modern décor, however, was something of an oxymoron. Modern furnishings, almost by definition, were supposed to be mass-produced commodities that could circulate in the media as "types" of commercially available tokens. Instead of promoting the exclusivity of singular and unique objects, these images were expressly of commodities that were supposed to be available to all in their replicated form. Consequently, many of the DIY items that people made were attempts to reproduce a commodified good.

DIY practices were framed as modern by aligning them with the DIY craze in the United States and Britain, where such practices were said to provide creative release and autonomy (Atkinson 2006). In the socialist bloc, however, DIY projects were usually a replacement for and imitation of mass production rather than a supplement or alternative to it. Articles on DIY projects still framed them as satisfying hobbies for high-level professional men. A 1975 *Lakáskultúra* features a couple who has just moved into an apartment in Dunaújváros with their three children. The wife is a teacher, but the husband is a physicist who describes how he has spent his time creating the furnishings for the entire apartment out of remnants of old furniture found in a basement, a few purchased items, and cabinets he made from scratch. In another, titled "Handyman Doctor," a pediatrician from Budapest proudly displays his handiwork, all the wood cabinets and furniture in his apartment (Szűcs 1983a). Male readers inspired by these undertakings were likely to be frustrated, however, as many of the magazine's instructions for creating furnishings and renovations called for power tools that were difficult to procure.

Urban DIY practices extended to growing food. Although growing vegetables and tending livestock were disdained as occupations for the peasantry and working classes, the weekend cottage, which became emblematic of the modern good life under socialism, enabled urban "weekenders" to maintain small productive gardens while framing their labors as a suitably modern leisure activity. Skilled workers described tending a "hobby" garden (*hobbi kert*) as a relaxing diversion from jobs requiring intense concentration (Szirmai and Zelenay 1988:212). Members of the white-collar classes and self-professed *polgár* reinforced their modernity by wearing bikinis and listening to transistor radios while they worked (DVH, June 6, 1967). The families of doctors and engineers grew tomatoes, peppers, and varieties of fruit to eat fresh, to preserve, or to make into sweet wine or *pálinka* for the winter. Even though these gardeners were relatively well-compensated for their professional positions, the savings on produce enabled them to budget for durable goods or to travel. Their hobby-garden prizes were a source of satisfaction and pride when shared with friends and neighbors. The fresh home-grown produce, jams, sausages, and liquor (*házi*) was also considered vastly superior to what was available in state stores (see also Smith 2003).

The most extreme form of DIY was the mass movement of "self-build" housing, driven not only by shortages (as we have seen) but also "by western norms of comfort and taste" the state was unable to provide (Szalai 2000:216). Whereas a British volume of model house plans was written to be handed over to a professional building contractor (Finn and Finn 1964), Hungarian versions of the same were meant for the layman building his own house. From the mid-1950s through the 1980s, the state regularly produced do-it-yourself architectural plans for private house builders called "pattern plans" (*mintatervek* or *típustervek*) to encourage higher levels of modernization and more standardized, and aesthetically sanctioned, constructions.[16] A monthly periodical called *Lakásépítők Magazinja* (Homebuilder's Magazine) was finally established in 1982 expressly to help the thousands of men (and women) who were doing their own plumbing, electrical work, tile laying, roof raising, insulating, and so forth. The byzantine process of building a house and its critical role in connecting the second economy to the first was satirized by the writer János Kenedi in a book published in the West in 1981. His ironic use of the state slogan "The country is yours; you are building it for yourself!" reflects the view that life in modern Hungary entailed not only building socialism but also building one's own dwelling, brick by brick.

Although the state had managed to urbanize a large percentage of a once-agrarian population, many city folk became weekend farmers, avid seamstresses, and do-it-yourself carpenters to take care of their everyday needs. Their "leisure time" was thus spent gardening or building houses and became a locus for social life (Burawoy 1992:36, 57). While the products of this kind of labor—from the home-grown tomato to the self-built house—were idealized as self-realizing appropriations of the material world, they could also be the source of intense frustration and resentment, as people grumbled about the difficulties and instrumental social relations of a "not normal" socialist modernity.

Show Me Your Home, and I'll Tell You Who You Are

The expression "Show me your home, and I'll tell you who you are!" was alive and well in socialist Hungary. It referenced not class difference but the "civilizing" notion that a person's material environment reflected his or her moral character, modernity, and respectability.[17] But it was also framed as the expression of a person's individuality and desires in life. In a 1970 article in the Dunaújváros newspaper titled "What is our home culture like?" the journalist writes:

> If we walk into an unknown apartment, we look around a few minutes, and an opinion of the residents usually forms within us under the power of our first impressions. The home is the frame/container for our lives, tailored to our body and to our spirit, [and so] it wears the stamp of our individualism most

completely. It mirrors back and at the same time reveals our relationship to the world, to our wider environment. It even confirms our thoughts, our outlook on the world. (*Dunaújvárosi Hírlap*, Jan. 6, 1970)

In Dunaújváros, as throughout urban Hungary, an economically defined modern lifestyle became the normative "middle" to which most of society could aspire, one centered in a cultivated home. A range of Hungarians from skilled workers to white-collar professionals came to consider themselves as part of a "modern" middle stratum, their status evidenced by urban employment, a modern apartment with amenities, possession of mass consumer goods and media, a summer vacation, and realistic aspirations for a weekend cottage and a car. By the mid-1970s, however, instead of diminished attention to individual interests and greater orientation to the collective, Hungarian society had become characterized by a deepening ideological divide between the public of the state and the "private" of family and individual interests. Instead of participating in a society with a fully modernized division of labor and commodified exchange system, a middle stratum of urban Hungarians divided their existence between what they thought of as "modern" pursuits and forms of self-provisioning that came to be described as "not normal." The socialist project of cultivating demanding citizens had not only produced a new kind of social stratification, but it damaged the credibility of a production system that could not produce materialities that satisfied those discerning demands. A new editor of *Lakáskultúra*, János Balogh, wrote in a resigned tone in a 1985 editorial about "the many obstacles that we [Hungarians] face in shaping our homes according to our standards" (*igényeiket*) (Balogh 1985:7). By then, the dream of a uniquely Hungarian socialist path to the "good life" had ended.

4 Socialist Generic and the Branding of State Socialism

IN THE 1960s, economic reforms injected color, diversity, and forms of abundance into a commercial sphere that had been relatively sparse in the 1950s. The Kádár regime placed new emphasis on quality of life, including the provision of more consumer goods, leisure activities, and forms of entertainment. The department store Luxus opened in Budapest and catered to the segment of the population that wanted and could afford the higher quality and more expensive clothing it offered. At the same time, a chain of new self-service stores appeared, playfully called "ABC" (standing for all the letters in the alphabet) that offered consumers a wide variety of things under one roof and allowed them to access goods without going through a salesclerk. The first state-run warehouse for new furniture opened in Budapest in 1974, called Domus after the Italian design academy (Vadas 1992:183) and in 1976 a new department store chain called Skála opened its glass-clad flagship store in Budapest to great fanfare. The Skála was different from existing department stores in that its wares were supplied by new and more independent cooperative workshops (*szövetkezet*), making for more diverse offerings than previously possible through central planning channels. The Dunaújváros branch of the Skála was housed in a large, windowless set of cubes in a sienna orange. State-sponsored commercial media expanded, including the use of neon signs and television advertising; so did apolitical print media, such as magazines for car aficionados, fisherman, and photographers, as well as for cooking and women's fashion.

The state production sector also increased the manufacture and promotion of socialist brand-name goods, particularly of things that had developed iconic brands in the West: colas, cigarettes, blue jeans, shampoos, and durable technologies such as radios, cameras, and refrigerators. Some firms began to produce under their own logo, and by the late 1970s a few had entered into joint ventures or became subcontractors for Western multinationals, such as Adidas, Levi's, or Coca-Cola.[1] The state stepped up the import of Western consumer goods to supplement domestic production and also imported Western machinery to upgrade domestic capacities for production—going into significant foreign debt to do so. While economic reforms emerged in fits and starts, second-economy activities expanded the range and quality of consumer goods as well as services. The legalization of small-scale family-based businesses in the 1970s increased the availability of "home produced" goods like hamburgers, hand-painted tablecloths, and leather miniskirts.

Yet even as the variety and quality of material goods was increasing, Hungarians blamed the state for foisting upon them goods they considered dull, shoddy, and cheap. This seeming contradiction arose with the development of a Socialist Modern aesthetic regime, as these built environments, furniture designs, and products came to define state socialism. Socialist Modern became Socialist Generic, or an abstracted, mass-produced, and stripped-down version of modernism—epitomized by the massive and monotonous panel construction residential blocks built in the 1970s. State socialist production included a variety of designs and things, but the iconographic dominance of this style cemented a Socialist Generic aesthetic regime as the signature style or "brand" of state socialism.

In previous chapters, I have shown how the utopian promises made by the state became embedded in particular materialities. This chapter explores the political subjectivities that arose out of the everyday necessity of shopping for and living with material goods and environments that were designed, produced, and distributed under state auspices. Dissatisfaction with "socialist" goods and housing generated and reinforced widespread alienation from the party apparatus and bureaucratic state institutions. Citizens judged the value and viability of the socialist economic system as it was embodied in its products, and so shortages of housing and furnishings were evidence of the failure of a state socialist modernity. At the same time, the qualities of these materialities were perceived as indices of the state's regard for its citizenry. Publicity for state products since the 1950s had promised that under socialism, citizens would "live in a manner worthy of socialist workers," where their worth was to be made material in abundant consumer goods and sun-filled apartments with "beautifully equipped" bathrooms. Instead, state production appeared to be stingy with what it produced for them, and the poor quality of available goods communicated the state's low estimation of citizens' demands (*igény*).

Socialist Generic goods circulated with other kinds of objects, and comparisons among these goods was part of what aligned Socialist Generic goods with alienation and abject citizenship. As we will see, objects from presocialist eras conjured images of the past and embodied different systems of value in their quality, materials, and craftsmanship. Objects made in the second economy were by definition and in their materiality aligned with realms that were not of the state. But even some state-produced goods escaped identification with the state, either because they diverged from standardized modernist designs or because they were branded as unique entities.

Finally, people had access to and familiarity with the kinds of Western goods that were available through official outlets or smuggled into the country. The political logic that arose with Socialist Generic goods extended to these Western goods, imbuing them with the power to stand in metonymically for the kinds of consumer lifestyles emerging in the postwar West. The qualities of these goods were seen not just as evidence of a better production system but as iconic of a more humane political and economic system, one that treated citizens with high regard and facilitated the living of a "normal" life. The opposition between state socialist and democratic market systems thus became embodied in their respective products.

Where "Shortage" Falls Short

Anthropological studies of postsocialist consumption tend to rely on János Kornai's characterization of state socialism as an "economy of shortage" (1992). Brief accounts of official consumer culture (rather than of the second economy) focus on the tension, as Katherine Verdery describes it, between the regime's promises "that under socialism the standard of living would constantly improve" and its inability or unwillingness to "make goods available."[2] There is no question that shortages were a dominant feature of state socialist consumer culture and political life. Acute shortages of food and heating fuel in particular, exacerbated by state-dictated price hikes, were the catalysts for many of the political uprisings in the region. Even in Hungary, where food shortages ended by the 1960s, many consumer durable goods such as refrigerators, televisions, and furniture were available only after a waiting period.[3]

Shortage, as Kornai (1992) demonstrated, was central to the workings not only of the centrally planned economy but of the socialist system in general. State firms suffered few consequences for failing to meet production targets and had few incentives to distribute their products effectively. Instead, workers and managers bargained for resources and hoarded scarce supplies in order to maximize their all-important redistributive powers (see Verdery 1991:420–26).

Shortages of certain goods or their availability only in certain places, at certain times of the year, and in certain quantities, gave rise to routinized practices for acquiring them. These depended upon networks that provided information on when something might become available, contacts within the shops, and the willingness to court serendipity—to keep an eye out for a line forming outside of a shop and joining it, even if one did not know what was on sale. An item's value and prestige often had to do with how it was acquired. Furnishing a home required being on "constant alert for tips for when, how and what kinds of home-furnishing objects were currently obtainable; making what couldn't be acquired; and finally, seeking venues for getting goods smuggled in from abroad" (S. Nagy 1997:5). Shortages were the source of intense frustrations, but for many they also contributed to the sense of victory of a successful acquisition (Verdery 1996:27), whether through luck, persistence, special contacts, or networks.

Still, the structural opposition Kornai establishes between a capitalist economy driven by consumer demand and a socialist economy driven by production and supply forecloses the possibility of a consumer society in a supply-side economy (Vörös 1997:17).[4] Moreover, a focus on scarcity fails to engage with the robust materialities of socialist consumption and the conditions of its experience. In Hungary after the 1950s, *hiánycikk* (shortage goods) were often unavailable because state planners had "overlooked" the need for them and not because too few had been produced. They included the kitchen tool used to make Hungarian dumplings (*galuska deszka*); bath plugs that fit the tubs in stock; cosmetics shelves; and the metal boxes necessary for installing electrical wiring in new apartment buildings. As a 1960 editorial in the Dunaújváros local newspaper put it, these things "don't seem important until the moment one needs them, and suddenly they are very important!" (*Dunaújvárosi Hírlap*, Feb. 16, 1960) Some shortages came about when the state discontinued production of a popular item, for example a cabinet for storing bedding (*Lakáskultúra* 1967/3:2)—a problem familiar to Western consumers used to regimes of planned obsolescence. In later years, complaints centered not on shortage but on the limited selection of various types of goods—like cosmetics, jams, or table lamps. In fact, mismanagement often led to the *oversupply* of some things that were not in demand, and not just because they were low-quality products. In 1971, only thirteen Videocolor television sets had been sold in Budapest (population two million) after two months on the market. Color sets were apparently slow to catch on because of the high cost per set combined with limited broadcasting time (cited in Gerő and Pető 1999:225).

The term "scarcity" has been constructed from the perspective of a society characterized by abundance (Sahlins 1972), but as Ina Merkel has argued for East Germany, this obscures local definitions of what counts as scarce and how these perceptions are reflected in daily routines and attitudes (Merkel 1998:283). Indeed, throughout the former Soviet bloc, the new austerities wrought by the end of socialism highlight aspects of *socialist abundance*, not only of unwanted consumer goods, but of sometimes lavish subsidies for food and drink; for cultural events, books, and vacations; for health and child care services; and for basic utilities such as heat—making for warm and cozy apartments in mid-winter Hungary.

Again, a focus on shortages can obscure the significance of practices that arise not from shortage but from constraints on household income (Vörös 1997). In place of the throwaway society that emerged in the West in the postwar era (Packard 1960), state socialist societies maintained a culture of frugality. Zsuzsa Gille has shown that instead of generating enormous waste, as economists would have it, socialist economies established extensive systems for the constant recycling and reuse of consumer goods and resources, systems that rapidly disintegrated after 1989 (2007). Within households, goods were kept for long periods and were well cared for (contributing to norms for neatness), and disposable items were carefully rationed out in full consciousness of their value. An example is the common practice of peeling two-ply paper napkins apart and refolding them for use, something not explained by a shortage of paper napkins (they were readily available) but by the relative imbalance between rising norms for modern lifestyles and limits on disposable income.

Sociality and the Materialities of the Second Economy

The second economy was interconnected with and benefited from the first in two ways: it thrived in the very areas that the first economy was weak, but it also depended on time, materials, and equipment that employees siphoned from their official jobs to use in their private enterprises (in turn exacerbating problems with state production). At the same time, the contrasting forms of sociality, as well as the materiality of goods, of the first and second economies played a role in the ways public and private spheres were affectively delineated. As we'll see, acquiring goods in the official sphere was characterized by antagonistic forms of sociality, as citizens had to compete with one another for scarce goods and to endure encounters with representatives of the state, from hostile salesclerks to indifferent housing officials. In contrast, second-economy exchanges were based in personal social relations. Though these too were often antagonistic, they were ideologically framed by a kind of solidarity generated by shared efforts to circumvent state control and its mediation of material activity.

Similarly, the widespread association of certain goods with the state was made possible by their *difference* from those produced and circulated at home or in the semilegal second economy. Unlike the mass-produced goods of state production, second-economy goods were, of necessity, the things people could build, cook, or create at home or in small workshops to share with others, sell, or exchange. Factory workers regularly tried to make themselves special items at work on the sly (Haraszti 1978:138–46), but most goods produced for the second economy were not mass-produced. They tended to be things that did not require elaborate machinery or complex chemical processes like plastics. In addition to comestible goods like jams, spirits, and sausages, they consisted of durable goods made primarily of cloth, leather, wood, and wrought iron or, in the realm of house construction, mud, clay, stone, and slate. These goods and houses were often lionized as forms of self-production and sometimes identified as more authentically Hungarian. At the same time, when there was little alternative to them, they were seen as indicative of a dysfunctional modernity.

Despite the ways the second economy was often idealized, it produced its own alienation and invidious distinctions. It was maintained by social networks of obligation that entangled affective relationships with everyday provisioning. These complex systems of mutual obligation blurred the distinctions between intimate friendships and economic transactions in ways that may have been familiar, but at the same time made life difficult and instrumentalized personal relations (Sampson 1986; see also Pesmen 2000 for Russia). Steeped in modernizing rhetoric, urban citizens understood that these were holdovers from village life that were supposed to be alleviated by the freedoms of modern life and commodified divisions of labor. Engaging with the second-economy was a matter of necessity rather than choice. Even villagers who participated in systems of reciprocal exchange of labor in building homes (*kaláka*), as Endre Sík writes, did so not because of "its cheapness, pleasantness or efficiency, but the fact that there is no alternative to it" (Sík 1988:543). Nevertheless, when contrasted with the alienating process of consuming and provisioning through official channels, such private exchanges accentuated the tendency to interpret experience through perceived contrasts between an alienated public and an appropriated private sphere.

Citizen Consumers in the Soviet Bloc

With the rise of the citizen-consumer in the United States and Western Europe in the postwar period, capitalist states increasingly served as the mediator between commercial interests (manufacturing, retail, and advertising) and the "rights" of consumer-citizens (Cohen 1998, 2001). This mediating role became increasingly important with the growth of corporate structures and the disembedding of commerce from local social relationships (Carrier 1995; Polanyi 1944). In contrast, the socialist state in the same period took control of and centralized production and distribution. The highly bureaucratic, institutionalized state acted not only as a distributor of resources, as it can in capitalist welfare states, but was also the corporate entity or source for most mass-produced goods, determining their qualities, aesthetics, and prices. In addition, the state controlled distribution to state-managed retail establishments, where the staff members were also state employees.[5] National economic conditions were often conflated with an imposed morality for citizens, since the state had the power to determine what constituted legitimate material need and how such a need was to be fulfilled.[6] Despite the state's public promises to divert more resources from the needs of production to consumer needs, the centralized economic system remained structured around hoarding these resources, resulting in what Hungarian theorists Fehér, Heller, and Márkus (1983) called a "dictatorship of needs."

And yet the socialist state effectively invited the population to evaluate it in terms of the goods and environments the state sector could produce, and moreover, to regard them as signs of an economic prosperity to come and of the party's munificence and caring for its subjects. Though political dissent was suppressed, citizens were encouraged—through institutionalized venues for lodging complaints (*reklamálás*) (see also Fitzpatrick 1999:175–78 for the USSR and Zatlin 2007:ch. 7 for the GDR)—to protest things like manufacturing flaws. Indeed, the rhetoric of normative demandingness (*igény*) fostered such practices. While the plan itself was sacred and could not be questioned (Lampland 1995:

ch. 5), the human practices that made up its execution were fair targets, eliciting a constant stream of invective from everyday people about the shortcomings of state production and supply. Newspapers regularly published such criticisms.

Institutional Alienation and the Labor of Appropriation

The very commodities presented as evidence of an emergent socialist modernity were often exceedingly difficult for citizens to appropriate—not just in finding and buying them, but in putting them to use and integrating them into daily life. Anthropological approaches to the question of commodity alienation and appropriation are useful here as a heuristic to conceptualize how such relations might extend into the political.[7]

In approaches to mass production under conditions of (capitalist) modernity that build on the writings of Georg Simmel, the mass-produced object remains in its alienated commodity form and thus abstracted from social moorings until the moment of purchase or allocation, when its commensurability with the vast array of equivalent goods ends (Carrier 1995; Miller 1987, 1988). It then becomes singularized as a unique object, a material token of an abstract type, inserted into a particular context and generally associated with a specific person or social group (also Kopytoff 1986; see Miller 1987:190). Miller's work on consumption shows that this singularization is a kind of labor of appropriation, a socially/culturally inflected practice that transforms what was once a commodity into an inalienable possession (Miller 1987:191).

The labor of appropriation, however, can be initiated well in advance of the actual purchase or allocation, as James Carrier has shown. Advertising narratives in consumer catalogues or product placement in a store can provide singularizing "contexts" for goods, presenting each as one of a kind, with a unique history, origin, and even producer (Carrier 1990). Theorists using the framework of "alienation" and "appropriation" rarely acknowledge the affect implied by these terms. Carrier is no exception, but his work suggests the differences in degree to which consumers confront commodities as alienated in the first place. The insight that the work of appropriation can begin before purchase can be extended from advertising and media forms to the work of product designers, store layouts and displays, and the behaviors of salesclerks, real estate agents, and so forth, who "sell" through constructing and then naturalizing the unique "fit" between the product and the consumer. It should not be overlooked that much of this prepurchase appropriation can happen in noncommercial settings, such as when certain goods are singularized on the bodies or in the houses of our friends.

This framework only works for those things that can be taken up for cultural recognition as objects or which have qualities available for sense perception. Things like clothes, perfume, food, gadgets, and so on are things with potential for identification, prestige, for moral claims, as extensions of bodies or with identifiable pleasures or uses. Of these, dwellings have enormous potential for alienation depending upon the conditions under which people "live" in them, their social context, and the powers residents have over these spaces—powers, we can say, of "appropriation" (see for example Miller 1988).[8]

Mass-produced commodities are not, of course, a priori homogenizing. Indeed, the point of possessing a "branded" mass-produced commodity is that it is an authentic instantiation of the object known through mass media campaigns and disseminated widely. Hungarians acted on this power of mass-produced commodities when they created homemade versions of the goods they saw in the media but could not procure on the market.

Socialist Generic: The Brand of Socialism

Branding imbues products with social and cultural meanings and anchors them to existing values, places, and times. Even if not directly, a brand communicates something about the product's source, producer, or origins, through advertising and marketing but also through design (Moore 2003:334). In capitalist contexts, consumer research has shown that products, through their branding and design, can convey affective messages such as "caring" from the source company to the consumer. With this in mind, we can see the play between alienated, mass-produced goods on the one hand, and goods that are imbued with dense, cultural meanings on the other, in the opposition between *generic* and *branded* goods.

In capitalist markets, the generic brand—or no-name brand—consists of mass-produced basic goods with minimal packaging and label design and no advertising. A generic label simply identifies a product, conveying nothing more than its use value. The bar code, meanwhile, indexes an abstracted exchange value, an endlessly reproduced mass-market commodity. This labeling gives no information on the product's source or origins nor makes any qualifications about its particular qualities; it offers no contextualization of the item beyond its existence on the store shelf. And that setting, on a store shelf full of branded goods, is critical to the way generic brands acquire meaning and value. Consumers are aware that a substantial part of the price of a branded good often comes from the marketing of that good rather than the quality of the product. Moreover, state oversight ensures that even unbranded goods must adhere to product regulations governing safety and fitness for purpose. The thrifty shopper (Miller 1995) can then reason that in buying a generic good, he or she is paying for the product itself and not for the privilege of being manipulated by advertisers.

In state socialist contexts, this relationship was reversed. Modernist design ideology and practice assured that much of socialist retail space, signage, packaging, and even the design of goods were what we might call generic. Since housing was the good most obviously produced and allocated by the state, it became another commodity enveloped by a modern aesthetic. Moreover, this modern aesthetic deliberately blurred the distinction between residential, commercial, and institutional architecture, with the effect of making it all look institutional. The design of these materialities reinforced an understanding of the state as an impersonal and bureaucratic entity. In addition, by making residential housing look institutional, it contributed to the sense that the state's intention was to institutionalize citizens. This design not only worked to maintain the "alienated" form of mass-produced and commodified goods and buildings, but it reinforced citizens' alienation from the political regime.

Making Shopping "Socialist"

The socialist state attempted to control material consumption as a means of differentiating itself from capitalist consumerism. These efforts often dovetailed with political-economic considerations. Capitalism was characterized as producing exploitative modes of production, unequal distribution, competition, and misrepresentation—fomenting desire for products people did not need and wasting collective resources. Bananas acquired symbolic power and cachet for citizens of socialist countries, for example, because authorities deemed them an unnecessary luxury and so did not import them, whereas in Western Europe they seemed abundant and cheap. (Meanwhile, Cuban oranges were imported to support a "brother" socialist nation.)

Consumers were also unaware of the technical sophistication or expense necessary to make some products that otherwise seemed simple and basic. For example, scented soap required imported synthetic fragrance, but as one woman complained in 1979: "A bar of apple-scented soap costs between forty and eighty *forints* on the black market. We can manufacture soap ourselves, and we have apples aplenty. . . . So why is there no Hungarian apple soap?" (cited in Gerő and Pető 1999:224).

Defining an appropriate "socialist" mode of consumption was a topic of heated public debate in the 1960s and into the 1970s. Some pundits condemned new forms of consumption as "refrigerator socialism" and targeted women in particular for working just so they could buy a new furniture set. But party functionaries and professionals involved in commercial spheres were in the awkward position of having to apply ideology to practice. Finding the Soviet model wanting, they increasingly attempted to modify select Western trends for the socialist context. Advertising, storefronts and window displays, exhibitions, magazine spreads, and newspaper editorials bore signs of conflicting imperatives. On the one hand, they were to display socialist consumer products in the best possible light and to promote their tasteful use in order to modernize and civilize the populace. On the other, they were to discourage conspicuous consumption for social distinction, the undue influence of fashion, and waste (see György 1992:19–21).

The design, promotion, and display of consumer goods emphasized transparency and honesty in opposition to capitalist deceit and misrepresentation, echoing modernist avant-garde ideologies and aesthetics from the 1920s. Advertisements were supposed to educate consumers about newly available products and the use of new technologies, as well as to encourage them to raise their standards and become more modern. A print ad for clocks in Lakáskultúra, for example, emphasized how they would facilitate the rational ordering of time necessary for heightened productivity (see figure 4.1). It features images of modern-design clocks produced by the "Hungarian Clock Manufacturing" entity in a kitchen, on a bedside table, and on living room shelving, all furnished in the Socialist Modern style: "Clock in the (living) room! Clock in the kitchen! At all times, everything done on time, when one sees everywhere the exact time!" (Lakáskultúra 1967, 1:18).

The importance of transparency extended to shops and window displays. In contrast to so-called bourgeois preoccupation with façade and artifice, Socialist Modern forms were to be legible to the public through their unadorned simplicity. Instead of bearing the surname of the original owner or another proper name, state shops were designated by simple descriptives, in standardized block letters, differentiated only by number (figure 4.2). In every town in Hungary, shoe stores were designated by block type reading "Shoe Store" (Cipő Bolt), butcher shops as "Meat Store" (Húsbolt) and stationery shops by the acronym for "State Paper and Writing Implements Store" (ÁPISZ bolt). These resolutely literal names reinforced a sense of institutional standardization.

Window displays were often uniform in part simply because they were done by the same window designers working out of a central office, but the effect was to emphasize the degree of uniformity of the products on offer. The shoes displayed in the windows of state shoe stores were identical across the country, representing the complete selection of shoes available. Window displays in east European countries under socialism could be marvelously inventive with scarce resources, such as using foil candy wrappers to make decorations or thread to suspend clothing or objects. But understaffing just as often meant that products in the windows were visibly dusty and that displays were seldom changed. Goods in the stores were almost never framed by the elaborate packaging that became the norm in the commercial West, a practice that frames commodities as gifts and heightens the value of their source. Ironically, imported Western goods sold at state stores, such as Colgate and Palmolive toiletries, were packaged in cellophane-wrapped gift boxes and sold for higher prices, inflating perceptions of their value relative to socialist products.

Despite frequent attempts from above to improve customer service through legislation and establishing consumer rights, shopping remained fraught with tension. This aspect of the state socialist experience has been much described: the lines, the endless bureaucratic procedures, the hostility of retail staff, and the competition between consumers for limited stocks of goods. As in any retail setting,

Figure 4.1. Advertisement for modern clocks in *Lakáskultúra*, 1967.

Figure 4.2. On Dunaújváros's main avenue, the sign reads "Meat Shop," focusing on the product instead of the Hungarian word for the occupation of butcher (*hentes*). Photo by author, 1990.

sales personnel were the human face of the establishment, mediating between consumers, goods, and the sources of those goods. But instead of bridging the distance between mass-produced goods and potential purchasers in these stores, salesclerks actively discouraged appropriation in a number of ways. Customers were compelled to implore, cajole, or even bribe clerks into looking for and handing over desired items, whether bathing suits or blocks of cheese, in the right size, weight, and color. In self-service shops, salesclerks were often seated on a platform looking down on the hapless customer, emphasizing their position of power. As with other professions, many clerks used their positions to hoard coveted goods to release to favored customers or to barter with in the second economy. The result was a system that continued to reward forms of privilege rather than one that upheld socialist principles of equitable distribution. This "not normal" shopping experience itself (rather than the inability to procure a good [Merkel 1998:291–95]), created intense dissatisfaction with the regime and spilled over onto perceptions of socialist products.

Most consumer activity during the socialist period consisted in the exhausting task of daily provisioning, a burden borne largely by women. Since state butchers, produce shops, bakeries, and dry goods stores were separate, shopping involved standing in multiple lines, carrying bags from store to store, and then hauling the groceries home on foot or on crowded buses. At the same time, campaigns to produce a modern citizenry through housing and demanding consumption had fostered a population that expected pleasurable consumption. Sociologist Zygmunt Bauman wrote in the mid-1970s that the Western "*homo consumens*, brought up on the breath-taking raptures and nerve-breaking tensions of the capitalist market [would find] . . . little attraction in the paltry 'socialist' equivalent which offers the same tensions of endless commodity chase but little joy of acquisition" (1975:102–103). State socialism produced its own *homo consumens*, without perhaps the same raptures and tensions, but dissatisfied nonetheless with the failures of official state consumer culture to provide the excitement and aesthetic pleasure that are expected to come with some kinds of shopping. As a 1967 article in *Lakáskultúra* acknowledged, "Instead of the joy that comes with shopping" (*vásárlással járó öröm*), Hungarian customers encountered "problems, aggravations and unpleasantness" (*Lakáskultúra* 1967/3:10).

János Balatoni, a retired architectural draftsman, often recounted to me how in the 1980s, after Hungary had legalized a wide range of private enterprise, he would board a bus from Dunaújváros to Budapest for the day just to walk the "ring" (*körút*), the shopping street lined with window displays. He was bitterly conscious of the fact that he had spent more than thirty years of his life walking to and from work along the main street in Dunaújváros, called Steel Avenue (*Vasmű út*), with "nothing to look at." The city paper echoed his sentiments in a 1983 editorial, describing the twenty-minute walk from its newly completed "Peace" residential district to the center as deathly boring. "It's a different feeling to make this twenty-minute stroll past shops, places of entertainment and streets crowded with things to look at," the author points out, "than on a dead, garden-city side street, where even a dog barking counts as an event" (*Dunaújvárosi Hirlap*, April 1, 1983).[9]

Efforts to improve and distinguish products and retail settings did not necessarily benefit the state. New branded goods like Tisza shoes were popular, but their distinctive logos indexed a specific, unique site of production and the cultural values of that factory or workshop. Credit for their quality thus shifted from the state to the producer, in this case the Tisza shoe factory, which had a private, pre-socialist history.[10] In contrast, everything else remained in the realm of abstracted and generic "socialist production," easy to collapse with the bureaucratic state apparatus. Socialist brand-name sodas like Bambi and blue jeans like Trapper suffered by their constant comparison to the West. While appreciated, they were nonetheless understood to be imitations of Coca-Cola and Levi's—reproductions rather than "the real thing." This perception was reinforced when factories like the one that produced Bambi, with its expensive East German equipment, were repurposed to produce Pepsi-Cola after 1970, effectively displacing Bambi as the socialist brand (Adamik and Terdik 2008). Hungarian-made Trapper jeans suffered a similar fate in 1981 when the company manufacturing them acquired the license to make jeans under the British label Lee Cooper. (In the 1990s, it was precisely these socialist brands that came to be revalued as "authentic," unique and iconic of socialist everyday life.)

The fact that much of state production was identified with low-quality and generic goods was not lost on state retail concerns. With decentralization, store branding was sometimes used in an effort to distance new products from such associations. But as a 1980 television ad for the Skála department store demonstrates, this was a losing game. The ad opens with an inviting scene of an empty folding chair on the lawn of a summer cottage, set next to a small table with some kind of refreshing drink. A lanky man in shorts happily walks over and sits in the chair, which promptly collapses under him. As his face twists into resigned exasperation, large text superimposed on the screen clarifies: "This is NOT a Skála good!" (*Ez [NEM] Skála Aru!*) The ad tries to distance Skála from the assumed disappointments and aggravations of everyday engagement with other kinds of state production and their invisible, abstracted origins. The unintended effect of the ad, though, along with efforts to brand goods within the socialist production system, is to reinforce the status of generic goods as the true brand of socialism.

The official context for consumption also worked to maintain the alienated form of commodities. Even in Hungary, with its increased attention to consumer culture, little of the work of appropriation was done in advance of acquisition. Generic names, functional window displays, and institutional aesthetics of state stores did not frame mass-produced commodities as the wealth produced by and for collective labor. Retail staff, as the human face of official state consumption, exacerbated rather than mitigated the alienation arising from the impersonal exchange of money for object. Finally, the physical properties of state goods also contributed to this alienation by the ways they resisted appropriation *after* acquisition.

Material Properties of State Production

Although situated by the contexts of socialist retail spaces, mass media, and state moralizing discourses, the physical properties of state socialist consumer products and living environments played a visceral role in how they were experienced and evaluated, both relative to and independent of comparisons with those of the "West."[11] Negative evaluations were primary for durable, mass-produced goods, rather than foodstuffs and other perishables goods (see Caldwell 2002). The fresh bread produced by state bakeries, for example, came to be a symbol of socialist abundance, baked fresh daily and made of luxurious white instead of brown flour. The provenance of locally made foods was known, allowing them to escape the anonymous abstraction of other, mass-produced socialist goods. State regulations for foodstuffs throughout the socialist world standardized the content of food produced (for better or worse), but also maintained rigorous inspections for food safety (Jung 2009; Kravets and Örge 2010).

The most bitter and explicit criticisms were reserved for mass-produced housing, but first I look at the reception of smaller-scale commodities, such as clothes and furnishings. Party leaders, well aware of problems with product diversity and quality standards, worried about unfavorable comparisons with Western goods and the negative image of the socialist modernizing project such goods produced. Product quality had deteriorated to unprecedented lows in the early 1950s, when the object was to produce as much as possible for the least cost. Beginning in 1954, different state organs attempted different strategies to improve the quality of mass-produced goods and investigate flawed production, such as establishing quality control committees and councils. These entities had the power to make recommendations, create competitions, give out awards, investigate shoddy products, and attempt to supervise design and production (Ernyey 1993:104, 113, 126). But without hard budget incentives for firm managers, namely a crisis of revenue if goods were not sold, these initiatives were largely ineffective (Kornai 1992).

In Dunaújváros, the local paper reported in 1970 that the People's Quality Control committee (*Népi Ellenőrzési Bizottság*) had met to discuss problems confronting shoppers in the city (*Dunaújvárosi Hirlap*, Aug. 8, 1970). The report concludes that the regulations governing the "defense of the consumer" were only partially functioning, but it attempts to shift blame from the unitary state and the socialist economic system in general to factories, shippers, and retailers—all of whom were allegedly failing to carry out orders coming down from a benevolent regime. Investigators had found that for some things, like shoes, retailers were generally good about replacing a faulty pair or offering a refund. The exchange of more durable consumer goods, however, particularly furniture, was "often torturous for consumers with complaints."

The committee evaluated quality simply by measuring products against expectations for their ostensible function, durability, and craftsmanship. Shoes, the committee discovered, had not improved in quality but had become more expensive. In Shoe Store # 54, complaints had been lodged "against the quality of 1,200 pair of shoes, 500 of these rightfully so." Clothing seemed to have generated fewer problems, though the committee acknowledged that there were no published figures on the number of complaints. They conceded:

> It is a fact that quite a few of the "luxury" clothes available in Dunaújváros's "Modellház" [department store] have flaws. For example, the imported women's fake-fur coat called "Corál" from the Minta KTSZ starts shedding its artificial fur after a few wearings.... The Páva Women's Lingerie Factory's "Sheherezade" blouses shrink when washed.... Part of the problem is a lack of qualified sales personnel to inspect the clothes before the store accepts them, but also some items which require special handling don't come with instructions, so not even the shop girls can offer this information.

Complaints about furniture had increased:

> The Nagykanizsa furniture factory, once recognized as providing good quality products for commerce, recently shipped furniture that had flaws which only appeared after 2–3 months of use.... Cabinet doors warped... metal legs on the sofa beds fell off after a short time. A new furniture set arrived that is more expensive than the sought-after Vária wardrobe, and already has spots under the lacquer. The one-person sofa-bed of the [Olympia] furniture set is 135 (!) [sic] centimeters instead of 190. The investigation found that when a company discontinued a line because of quality flaws, it would bring the same product back into circulation under a different name, perhaps with some small change, and at a higher price.

Some goods of socialist production were noted for their quality and good design, such as the "sought-after Vária wardrobe," produced by the nationalized Lingel firm. Within COMECON, or the organization coordinating economic trade and development among the Soviet socialist states, member nations became known for prized goods they produced. East Germany, for example, was associated with, among other things, the quality of its toys, which were proudly displayed in the windows of the GDR cultural center in downtown Budapest. The Soviet Union produced several cameras of sturdy design. My Hungarian relatives made annual trips to Czechoslovakia for the higher-quality lingerie, linens, and glassware produced there. Commodities "made in Hungary" which were appreciated on an international market—like state-produced Ikarusz buses and Tungsram light bulbs, the historically renowned Zsolnay and Herendi porcelain, and the privately developed Rubik's cube—were the source of considerable national

Plate 1a. Cover for a 1972 book on summer and weekend cottages, illustrating the kind of modern design the authors advocated. Most cottages, however, were built as wooden A-frames, modified peasant houses, or simple structures (Callmeyer and Rojkó 1972).

Plate 1b. Advertisement for kitchen trays and the plastic they were made of, published in the state home décor magazine *Lakáskultúra* in 1968: "PLASTIC! Even if you jump on it, UNBREAKABLE!" (*Lakáskultúra* 1968, issue 6).

Plate 2a. Cover of *Lakáskultúra* in 1972, an example of widespread affection for old, weathered, and rounded objects for interior décor, including woven baskets, folk pitchers, and worn wooden boxes (*Lakáskultúra* 1972, issue 1).

Plate 2b. *Lakáskultúra* cover from 1983. An example of 1980s Organicist Modern, showing the dominance of linen whites and wood browns, with splashes of modern color in the purple rug and pillows. The room also includes a stereo, an antique oil painting, and painted folk plates above the stairs (*Lakáskultúra* 1983 (18)2).

Plate 3a. Interior of an apartment in a K-30 type panel construction building, reproduced thirty to forty thousand times in the country. The residents made their own furniture, including open shelving to divide the single room space into eating/sleeping areas. Posters of nature scenes like this one were a popular technique for bringing nature into the Socialist Modern apartment (*Lakáskultúra* 1983 (18)3: 18).

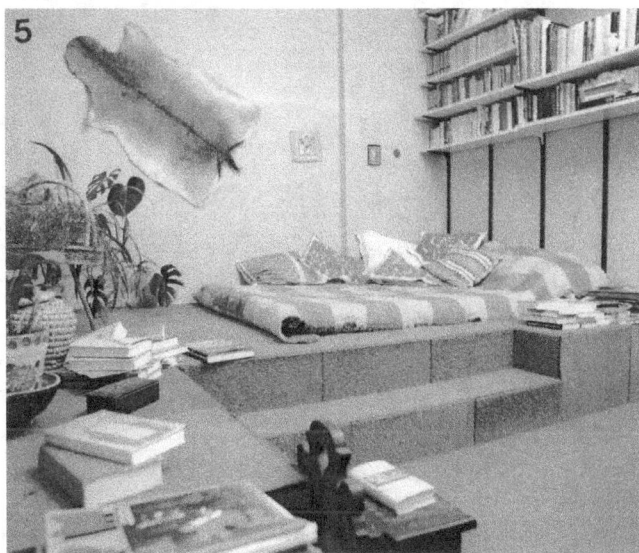

Plate 3b. Interior example of popular methods for mitigating the cold and boxy feel of concrete panel apartments in the 1970s and 1980s. Here the residents decorated with animal skins, warm colors, house plants, folk textiles and furniture, and a platform to create a resting/lounging space (*Lakáskultúra* 1984 (19)2: 15).

Plate 4. Typical high-rise building constructed of prefabricated concrete panels from the 1970s, but brightened by orange balconies. Photo by author, 1997.

Plate 5a. Magazine feature called "Happy Panel," showing new focus on bright colors for interiors after the fall of state socialism, as well as the continued preference for organic shapes and materials (*Tér és Rend: Lakberendezési Lap* 1996 (3)3).

Plate 5b. A panel concrete apartment interior in Dunaújváros, decorated with typical *polgári* (bourgeois) furnishings of inherited antiques, rugs, and art, that had not changed for decades. This décor gained renewed prestige among some sectors of the population in the 1990s. Photo by author.

Plate 6a. The steel gray and neon color of this industrial chic façade contrasts with the concrete gray of the apartment building that encloses it. Part of boutique row in Dunaújváros, 1997. Photo by author.

Plate 6b. The carved, wooden façade of a computer tech store on boutique row, set into a ground floor apartment of a concrete panel building. Visible above is the laundry hung out to dry on the balconies of the residential apartments. 1997. Photo by author.

Plate 7a. Dunaúyváros cityscape. Residential housing blocks line the city plateau, while a new road and street lights mark a developing neighborhood of family houses with bright red roofs in the valley below. 1998. Photo by author.

Plate 7b. Billboard for roofing tiles outside of the Dunaúyváros steel mill, reading " . . . in friendship with nature" and featuring the idealized image of single-family houses with red roofs, an image ubiquitous in the media in the 1990s. Photo by author.

Plate 8a. New house of whimsical, fairy-tale design, with rounded forms and "ice-cream" colors. Photo by author.

Plate 8b. New single-family house with thatched roof, stone walls, and other elements of Organicist architecture. Advertisement for house in *Szép Házak, Kész Házak* 1994(4).

pride.¹² Likewise, Helia-D, a face cream in distinctive black packaging developed in the 1980s, was hugely popular not just for local consumption but because it made an attractive gift for Western family members or acquaintances. It was a product that émigré Hungarian women, stereotyped for their haughty superiority, actually sought out in Hungary and took home. These commodities were claimed as "ours," as locally produced goods that would expand the nation's fame or reputation in the world. In the process, material goods and the people aligned with their production became "reciprocal agents of each other's value" (see Munn 1986). Goods desired by people known to be demanding reflected the discernment of the people who made them.

But many products simply failed to fulfill their promised function because they were produced out of inappropriate materials or were so poorly designed that they created intense aggravation.¹³ Sandals fell apart after one wearing because of poor quality glue. Milk was sold in flimsy plastic bags, impossible to pour without spilling. Even luxury objects held hidden frustrations, such as the Soviet-made, embossed silver cigarette case a friend once brandished in exasperation, manufactured too short to hold standard-size cigarettes. While in official discourse quantity was prioritized over quality by the aim of providing equitably for all, in practice the sacrifice of quality (which did not always result in a satisfactory quantity) was understood as reflecting the state's judgment of the quality of the people, who were supposed to be grateful for the substandard goods "thrown" at them.¹⁴

Poorly made products in capitalist settings affect the reputations of the companies that make them. In the state socialist context, flawed design and production were experienced in explicitly political terms. Consumers interpreted them as evidence of the regime's malicious intent, cheapness, negligence, or simple incompetence. Flaws in goods imported from a COMECON nation were seen as evidence of the failure of the Soviet system as a whole. The materiality of socialist currency itself was often seen as metonymic of devalued socialist production, especially in comparison with *valuta*, or "hard" currencies. Paper currency was often flimsy, worn, and tattered, and coins—especially the denominations of the forint and the aluminum *fillér*—were feather light, especially relative to the palpable weight of, for example, a deutschmark (see also Lemon 1998).¹⁵ The immensely popular satiric film *Kojak in Budapest* (Szalkai 1980) centered on this equation of dysfunctional objects with a dysfunctional socialist regime. The logic extended to goods that were positively valued: if they happened to break or were discovered to have flaws, the state, rather than the manufacturing entity governed by it, was blamed.¹⁶

In the realm of social distinction, the label "Made in Hungary" lacked cachet, something the state found difficult to overcome when it began limited production of higher-quality goods. The devaluing of Hungarian production in the eyes of an international community, moreover, was the cause of considerable bitterness at home and a basis for accusations that under socialism Hungary had lost its standards.

The lack of product choice, too, was seen as evidence of the state's "standardization" of its citizens—indeed, as evidence of the state's intolerance for human diversity. In capitalist contexts, product differentiation serves both to construct and to fulfill specific needs, and in the process it gives rise to new identities and social stratifications that depend on these specialized products for their existence. Hygiene products perhaps best illustrate this process, as Timothy Burke demonstrates in his history of colonization and commodification in Zimbabwe (1996). Mass-produced soaps not only replace locally made cleansers as signs of modernity and prestige, but differentiation between these soaps in strength, scent, and packaging produce and articulate distinctions between bodies—the sweat of men versus the perspiration of women, the skin of babies versus that of adults, and laboring bodies versus those of the leisure classes (Burke 1996). A deodorant packaged in pink and issued in feminine scents targets and produces a particular kind of consumer. It collapses the perceived distance between a standardized, mass-produced product and person (subjectively and physically), while retaining the sense of familiarity and compatibility with other products through standardization. Such tailoring can contribute to a sense of appropriation of a good *before* acquisition, appearing as something "made for me" (or for "us").

State socialist production, in contrast, was ideologically and pragmatically opposed to the targeting of individual needs. It focused on producing categories of objects and assumed that populations would adapt their consumption practices to the goods that were made available. A wonderful mockery of these principles appears in the German film *Goodbye Lenin!* (Becker 2003), in which an otherwise dedicated party functionary spends her days writing letters of complaint, deploying the rhetoric of efficiency and self-criticism to make her point. In one, she decries the overproduction of short, wide, and boxy shirts, but writes (sarcastically) that for the sake of socialist production, "in the future, we will endeavor to become ourselves shorter, stouter, and boxier!"

From the state's point of view, diversification was expensive, and standardized mass production better reflected principles of efficiency, rationality and meeting the needs of the collective. The centralization of furniture design, for example, meant that in the early 1960s, when the "contemporary style" was first publicized, just a few models of furniture were produced to serve the diverse needs of home, office, and factory for the entire country (Vadas 1992:179). The sense of official homogeneity was exacerbated by media rhetoric of statistics and abstraction in economic plans and in the constant barrage of reports on the numbers of, for example, television sets planned for, produced, or behind quota.

From the point of view of consumers, the homogenization of material products became equated with attempts to homogenize the people compelled to use them. Socialist citizens were supposed to conform to a Procrustean standard imposed from above. (Similar criticisms of homogenous, standardized, mass-produced consumer goods and housing emerged in the United States in the 1960s, at the height of Fordist production systems and the dominance of the International Style for capitalist architecture and public housing.) The fact that party elites and others with special privileges had access to other products and places to live only reinforced this perception. Their exceptional status was made visible by the diversity of goods they could appropriate and display against the backdrop provided by the rest of the population.

The state's tireless promotion of a Socialist Modern dictated that the populace restyle itself according to a state-sanctioned aesthetic. In the early twentieth century, modernist avant-garde movements in less-developed European nations like Italy and Hungary had sought to catch up with the "West" and enter a modern future, but by escaping a Western-dominated modernity's cycle of incessant change. In Hungary, a progressive cultural elite envisioned "an unconstrained future which escaped from the prison of the present" (Zentai 1999). In this, they mirrored the sentiments of the Soviet avant-garde, whose condemnation of capitalist modernization doubled as a "nationalistic reaction to the unbroken superiority of the West" and manifested itself in a desire "to flee from the oppression of modern time into an apocalyptic realm of timelessness" (Groys 1992:80). As a consequence, a timeless avant-garde style was to be immune to periodization. Instead, buildings and objects would be replaced with technologically superior ones before they could wear out. Panel buildings, I was often told, were only designed to last thirty to fifty years.

At the same time, Western fashions continued to be the measure of the "modern." Campaigns to make bourgeois decor old-fashioned and to encourage the adoption of the contemporary style were propelled in part by popular attention to Western European decorating trends. But the style that with its stripped-down utility was to have defeated fashion itself succumbed to fashion. While many state-produced goods, such as furnishings upholstered with a dark orange fabric, were considered fashionable from the 1960s to the mid-1970s, by the 1980s knowledge about shifting fashion trends in the West had rendered them out of date.[17] These state-produced goods constrained consumers in their ability to represent to themselves and others their full participation in a modern present. The early alignment of panel technology with Scandinavian design faded as it became associated with a Soviet-inspired and increasingly dated modernism.

By the 1970s, the state was making greater efforts to accommodate consumer tastes. A Hungarian Institute of Market Research was created to evaluate consumer needs and desires more systematically than the isolated efforts of the past (Hanson 1974:117–18), but it was difficult to put its findings into practice. Newly trained designers who were hired by factories soon found themselves in conflict with management, who had little incentive to produce new or improved designs (Vadas 1992). Economic reforms had greatly expanded the diversity of goods and services available, but the continuing presence of mass-produced goods marked by Socialist Generic design in everyday life—from shoes that did not quite fit to beds that were too short—remained a constant irritant with direct implications for political subjectivity.

Panel Apartment Buildings: Abstraction, Standardization, Ahistoricism

The socialist state's authoritarian presence in determining the material conditions of everyday life was nowhere more evident than in urban housing. The process of acquiring housing, as a state-produced commodity, was embedded in the alienating circumstances of impersonal exchange. Families were reduced by housing authorities to numbers on a seemingly endless waiting list, along with thousands of other supplicants. At the same time, they clearly understood housing to be their right and the failure of the state to provide housing to be a gross miscarriage of justice. The documentary-style, social realist filmmaker Béla Tarr captured the heartbreaking alienation of the process in the film *Family Nest* by depicting a long line of people standing for hours in an institutional hallway to get a few minutes' audience with a beleaguered and indifferent bureaucrat (Tarr 1979). They recount their stories—of children farmed out to be raised by other relatives for lack of housing, of marriages breaking up because of the crowding of three generations into a two-room flat, of a young wife and mother abused by her in-laws while her husband completes his military service—only to face a man who tells them there is nothing he can do for them: they must wait. Many waited upwards of fifteen years.

Those who did manage to secure apartments found the same impersonality embedded in the panel buildings (Figure 4.3). Official rhetoric that attempted to attribute progressive values of equality and egalitarianism to these building forms shaped the ways they were experienced. Since avant-garde modernist theory held that architecture was material base rather than representational superstructure, the building's form, stripped of all artifice, was to transparently reveal its function. As if this Adamic notion of signs (in which meaning arises transparently from the form) was not problematic enough, modernists also endowed such forms with the potential to transform human experience and social life. The design of a building was to effect this social engineering by iconic resemblance. Austere buildings visibly segmented into equal units indexed a materialized equality and would naturally produce egalitarian social relations among their residents—people joined in a collective of equal units.

Figure 4.3. New district of concrete panel construction (Sagvári) in Dunaújváros, 1970s. Photo by László Czakó.

The conceptual errors of this formulation were at least twofold. First, like all signs, icons are polysemous. Instead of signifying the importance of the collective and egalitarian social relations, these geometric, grid-like exteriors came to be "read" as authoritarian and dehumanizing, places from which to escape. Second, the design of the buildings into equal units materialized the state's disregard for differences among their occupants (physical needs, height, occupation, and so forth), as well as their social configurations (an elderly couple with grown children and their partners, a young couple with a baby and a grandparent, or a single adult), both among different households and within the same household over time. The inflexible designs and immovable walls made apartments difficult to personalize or to adjust to changing needs. The prefabricated concrete walls, panel residents often complained to me, were so hard that something as "simple as hanging a picture" required a power drill.

By the 1960s, state publications, acknowledging the limitations of panel construction, were framing the technology as the only way to end the housing shortages. But the influence of avant-garde theory and practice persisted in formulations that abstracted and standardized living space. City planners and party officials endlessly promised that a specific number of apartments would be built by the end of the year and would include so many shops, nurseries, and schools. New apartment designs were routinely discussed in terms of area, down to hundredths of a square meter. The local newspaper publicized the dimensions of apartments in the new C-T type of building to be erected in Dunaújváros and throughout the country (Figure 4.4): "Kitchen 6.05 m² with built-in cabinets; bathroom, 2.71 m²; WC 0.98 m²; smaller room 10.77 m²; foyer 6.2 m²" (*Dunaújvárosi Hírlap*, May 20, 1966). Some units were even described as designed for "2.5 persons." This detailed attention to size was partially a consequence of central planning: engineers attempting to save space and resources knew that their designs were being replicated in thousands of apartments. In the "one room plus three half-rooms" apartment I rented, two of the "half" rooms opened onto one another. When I asked János Balatoni, who had worked for years in the city's planning office, whether it was an "open plan" innovation, he chuckled before explaining: the design merely reflected the central planning office's desires to save that amount of wall section multiplied hundreds of times.

The state's top-down prescriptions for the allocation of space extended to hospitals, nurseries, schools, and movie theaters. Designs implicitly "relied on the assumption that the needs of citizens were largely uniform and hence standardizable, or that they could be made uniform" (Molnár 2005:118). This sense of abstraction was reinforced by the decontextualized representations of apartment complexes and buildings, pointedly drawn with no reference to the surrounding environment or personalization of space (see Figure 4.4).

The disorientation induced by these identical designs, with no landmarks or differentiating elements, became a standard trope for jokes and literature throughout the Eastern bloc. The best known is the Soviet comedy *Irony of Fate*, still shown on New Year's Eve in the former Soviet Union, where a drunken man is put on a plane by friends. Not realizing he has arrived in a different city, he goes "home" to his residential district, makes his way to his apartment, uses his key to enter it and lies down, only to be awakened by the real tenant, a woman who has found a strange man in her bed (Ryazanov 1975). The standardization of buildings, apartment size, and layout certainly allowed Hungarians living in them to develop a sense of solidarity, imagining themselves as sharing an experience with others who struggled to transform their allotted space into a modern, "comfortable" home. But this common experience also allowed for a collective resentment toward the state responsible for producing these spaces.

The positive association of panel construction with the improved political and economic conditions of the Kádár era quickly ebbed as it became apparent that panel apartment buildings were inferior in quality to those built in the Socialist Realist style. Public opinion of housing estates nationwide was negative by the early 1970s, with disillusion rising in relation to the massive expansion and deteriorating quality of housing over the decade (Bélley and Kulcsár 1980). In Du-

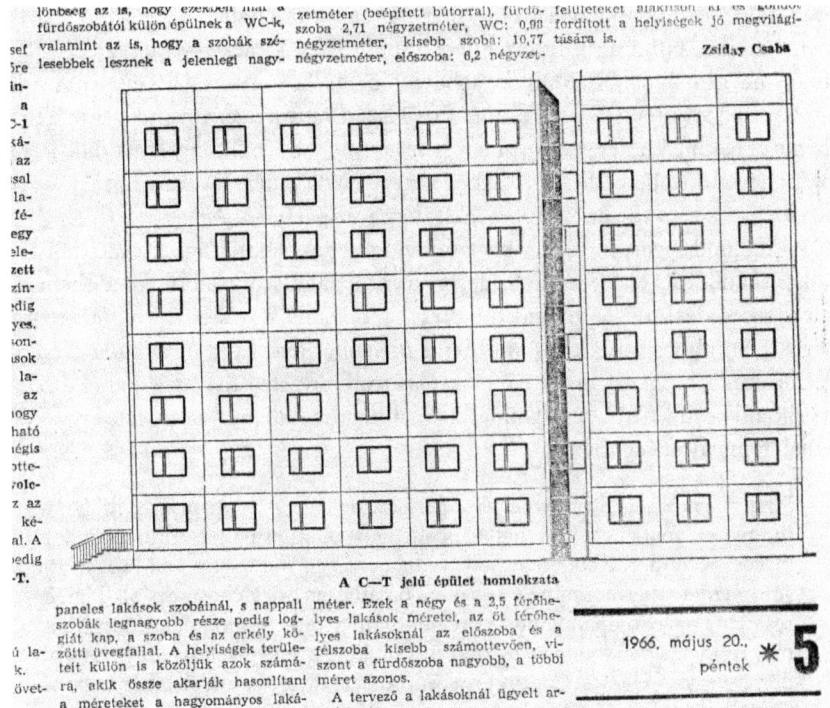

Figure 4.4. Drawing of the C-T Housing type of panel construction in the Dunaújváros newspaper, 1966. Courtesy of the *Dunaújvárosi Hírlap*.

naújváros, the quality of life in many existing city districts was substantially lowered through intensive fill-in development of the 1970s, as officials tried to save money by squeezing housing into green spaces within existing districts rather than building the infrastructure for new ones (Bánhelyi 1983:63–67). In the process, planners regularly violated prescribed density norms, leading to the progressive deterioration of residential districts. A report drafted by the head city planner in 1983 detailed this trend in the new town. In 1965, the prescribed density norm was 260 people per hectare, allowing for at least 21 square meters of green area per person. By 1975, the new Római city district averaged 423 people per hectare, and in some places 518. Three years later, the green space had shrunk to 1.73 square meters per person (Bánhelyi 1983:61–64). Even though the new town was surrounded by open fields, the Római district was one of the most densely populated in all of Europe—earning it the derogatory nickname of "Chicago."

The high density of the district was produced, in part, by the design of a set of buildings colloquially called the "fat houses" (*kövér házak*). The objective had been to fit the highest density of apartments into the smallest space (240 apartments in three buildings). The architect responsible was racked with regret by the time I met him in 1997. In his more sober moments, he portrayed his current work as planning for the city's future, but otherwise he returned again and again to the theme of having known, even as he was designing these buildings, that they were awful. He remembered being attacked for them at a public meeting in 1973, with no defense except the line, "But at least they are apartments!"[18]

By the mid-1970s, the experience of living in panel buildings as materialities rather than ideals had become widespread. Official discourse presented them as a less-than-ideal means to end the pressing housing shortage. Biting criticism of these buildings was a constant theme in venues from film to popular media. For example, a *Lakáskultúra* editor sarcastically insisted that new panel dwellers should be given a "Users' Guide," informing them of the "unexpected joys" of panel living awaiting them:

> First, the new renter or owner should know that their old furniture will not fit in the new apartment and that he or she must obtain smaller, multifunctional pieces. Second, the concrete walls radiate cold in the winter and heat in the summer. Furthermore, the walls don't breathe, as brick construction does, so residents have to open windows regularly to avoid running out of air. Many new residents don't know why they feel ill, but haven't been opening the windows every 3–6 hours. Continuous central heat dries the air, so it has to be artificially humidified. The electric outlets are limited in their power capacity, and so one shouldn't try doing the wiring oneself, since you can't know where the main is. There is only one place to run the cord for an outside television antenna, which can't be moved or the entire building's reception will be ruined. (Berényi 1976)

Members of the intelligentsia held panel buildings largely responsible for Hungarian social problems and malaise (see for example Fóti 1988; Konrád and Szelényi 1969). The general social alienation and isolation fostered by such built environments have been documented throughout the world. Originally these high-rise buildings were to be surrounded by green park, but in these densely populated areas, the remaining patches of grass were usually worn down to bare dirt. Exposed public spaces sported an occasional playground, ping-pong table, or bench but offered no sheltered spaces outside for residents to stop and chat and no central meeting spaces within buildings to congregate. Studies of Dunaújváros as well as in other parts of Hungary show that social contact among residents of these housing blocks was very low (Kántor 1996; Szirmai 1988; Valuch 2006). Residents complained about not knowing any neighbors other than those on the same floor, as enclosed stairwells and elevators transported them past other floors to their own. But there was also little occasion to meet neighbors from different buildings, as buildings faced outwards, rather than toward one another. Though panel dwellers had to put up with the intimate details about their neighbors on the other side of a shared concrete wall—when they went to the bathroom, what they watched on television, and whether they snored—they might never discover that person's identity. Inside the buildings, apartment doors made of PVC were painted institutional, monochromatic colors. Dark hallways, stairwells, and the small, cube-like elevators regularly reeked of urine. The elevators were plagued with mechanical problems, forcing people on their way home from work to hike up narrow staircases. These public spaces came to be seen as no-man's land and shaped idealizations of the private space across the threshold of an apartment door.

Despite full awareness of the problems with panel construction, Soviet states continued producing such buildings in volume through the mid-1980s. By the 1970s this technology was inexorably tied not to Scandinavian modernity but to a Soviet-inspired and an increasingly dated modernism. Nevertheless, for many people, their apartments felt like home. In Dunaújváros in the 1970s, a survey reported people to be fairly satisfied with their apartments and neighborhoods, especially if they understood themselves to be living among others whose social status corresponded to their own (Szirmai and Zelenay 1988). But the reaction to panel construction in general was overwhelmingly negative and politicized. The increasingly apparent uniformity of panel buildings, their rationalized abstraction of space, and their "substandard" quality were easily interpreted as measures of the state's low regard for those meant to inhabit them.

Western Goods, Normal "Systems"

From the 1960s on, increased exposure to foreign goods imported for their particularly desirable qualities only exacerbated negative evaluations of distinctly "socialist" things. Western consumer goods and images of Western lifestyles became constant reminders that socialism had still not caught up with the West. Images circulated through publications, television, and in Western movies, from Fellini's *La Dolce Vita* (1960), first shown in 1962, to fare that I myself saw in Hungary in the 1970s, such as *Hello, Dolly!* or *The Deer Hunter*. In addition to goods imported by the state and sold in specialty shops or in special packaging, relatives and friends abroad brought or sent Western consumer goods. Party officials, athletes, and other professionals who traveled regularly sometimes brought back such goods in their suitcases as a profitable, if illegal, sideline. Western tourists traveling to Hungary offered glimpses of foreign cars, clothing, cosmetics, and fashions.

Hungarians were also increasingly permitted to travel to the West and see for themselves. As elsewhere in the Soviet bloc, Hungarians talked of "going out" (*kimenni*) when visiting Western Europe or other capitalist states (even neighboring Austria) as opposed to "going over" (*átmenni*) to socialist states like Czechoslovakia. Their opportunities to sample what the West had to offer was severely

Figure 4.5. Wall of teenage girl's room in Dunaújváros in the late 1970s, decorated with jeans logos, advertising, teen magazine posters, and empty packaging of Western goods. Photo by author, 1990.

curtailed by the cash-strapped state's restrictions on the amount of hard currency they could obtain with Hungarian forints (which were not convertible in Western Europe). This policy had the unintended consequence of reinforcing Hungarian travelers' sense of inferiority as "Eastern bloc" citizens. If going by car, they had little choice but to camp and bring as much food with them as possible to minimize costs. Professional trips were no exception. A world-renowned chemist told me of going to a conference in Israel in the 1970s and being mortified when the whole group went to a restaurant: she ordered only an appetizer, but then the group decided to split the bill evenly, and she could not pay her share. The easing of visa restrictions to Austria in the 1980s allowed Hungarians to engage in forms of "shopping tourism," but the experience was often demoralizing (Chelcea 2002; Huseby-Darvas 2001; Wessely 2002). Moreover, the state condemned such trips, differentiating "good" cultural tourists from "speculators" (Dessewffy 2002).

The kinds of Western goods that made their way into the Soviet bloc included status-laden things one might expect, such as brand-name perfumes and blue jeans. But they also ranged from the practical, like Band-Aids and heavy-duty flashlights, to completely superfluous "fun or playful objects" like Smurfs (Hammer 2002:116). As in other Soviet bloc countries, many Western goods were prized as tangible materialities of a different world. The Croatian writer Slavenka Drakulic describes a doll she received from Italy as a child in just these terms, as "an icon, a message from another world, a fragment of one reality that pierced into the other like a shard of broken glass, making us suffer in some strange way" (1992:59). Western products intended for everyday use were often put on display; even the empty packaging—Coke cans, shampoo bottles, cigarette boxes—was pressed into service as decor (see Figure 4.5).

Daphne Berdahl points out the tremendous symbolic significance of these consumer items as evidence of Western connections and their use as social capital (Berdahl 1999b:124).[19] But people prized these objects as well for their intrinsic properties—bright colors, packaging, design, or craftsmanship—and what these properties must index about life "out there" (*odakint*). They were designed, it seemed, to make life easier, more comfortable, and pleasurable—even if these things also had the power to produce the "strange suffering" that Drakulic describes (1992). The humble Band-Aid, with its sterile packaging, skin-toned color, and user-friendly design perfectly embodies these qualities, when one compares it with the hassle of assembling scissors, gauze, and medical tape to bind a cut.

The state's moral censorship of certain Western commodities as decadent and corrupting inadvertently enhanced perceptions of these goods and the system that produced them. A bank administrator who was in her twenties in the mid-1960s vividly recalled to me her first sip of Coca-Cola. A boyfriend had managed to smuggle a bottle, with its distinctive shape, into the country, and he served tiny portions to friends in champagne glasses. They all thought they would experience some kind of hallucinogenic effect, but to their chagrin, nothing happened.[20]

That these select Western goods functioned as metonyms of another world can be attributed to a cosmology set up by the state itself and fed by propaganda efforts of Western intelligence agencies (Hixson 1997). The logic by which socialist material culture became emblematic of a unitary state's low regard for its citizens and failure of its economic system was extended to these Western goods. Their consumer-oriented design and properties were not just evidence of a better production system, but they served as icons of a more humane political and economic system, a place where living a "normal" life was possible. Thus, the opposition between state socialist and market democratic systems in the Hungarian context embedded politics in their respective products. Day-to-day encounters with a variety of goods and commercial spheres contributed to an incremental materialization of political subjectivity, just as it led to the politicization of materiality.

Within the Soviet bloc, the systematic export of higher-quality goods westward and lower quality goods eastward reinforced the unfortunate equation between the value of goods and the value of people. This dynamic was driven by socialist states' attempts to balance their trade deficits with the West by exporting those goods that might compete in capitalist markets. At the same time, the quality of exports headed east, especially to the Soviet Union, was determined by the prices the recipient nation was willing to pay, which barely covered low-quality production costs. These economic contingencies nonetheless reinforced perceptions of a population's standards for consumption, and Hungarians often prided themselves on their superior standards of consumption and production compared to their Eastern bloc neighbors (Nadkarni 2009:132 n.60).[21] Within all the Soviet bloc countries, however, many high-quality goods were reserved for export to the West and were consequently not available domestically except at expensive specialty stores, which often accepted only Western currency.[22] It is no wonder that by the 1980s many people were convinced that a market economy run by a democratic state would allow them to avail themselves of the consumer pleasures and attendant sense of value they had long imagined their Western counterparts enjoyed. (It is also no wonder, given the vastly different configurations of consumer capitalism, that this illusion was shattered almost immediately after 1989.)

Seen in its entirety, the material culture aligned with the official state sphere was far from alienated. People were able to appropriate the environment of artifacts around them, creating lifestyles and living conditions that were "far from the undifferentiated, homogenized, and uniform" of stereotype (Merkel 1998:284). They modified or transformed state products, from adding studs to a pair of jeans purchased at a state shop to transforming interiors of institutionally designed and allocated apartments into welcoming, domestic spaces. They produced their own commodities by reproducing clothes, interior décor, or forms of sociability seen in Western media (like keeping whiskey decanters in a cabinet), and devised a vast range of alternative strategies to obtain consumer goods of domestic and foreign origin. Throughout, these practices inculcated difference between the appropriated materialities of a private sphere and the alienated public space of the state.

Political subjectivities were shaped through affectively charged daily encounters with the state as materialized in retail settings, salesclerks, goods, and built environments, all seemingly working to obstruct attempts by citizens to make their own worlds. At the same time, the Socialist Generic brand identified the state as the abstract, unitary source behind flawed goods. This brand communicated this state as an entity that could only understand its citizens in abstract, standardized, and uniform terms—and as only worthy of the low-quality goods and living spaces the state production and distribution sector could produce. It was within this particular configuration of authoritarian politics and material worlds that Western goods became iconic of and acquired the power to project fantastic understandings of the "system" that produced them. The political logic of state socialist material culture generated an anti-socialist aesthetic, a set of values embedded in particular material forms and properties that opposed and counteracted the effects of state socialist materialities. The constitutive aesthetics of such practices is the subject of the next chapter.

5 Organicist Modern and Super-Natural Organicism

THE IDEAL OF modern, urban apartment living was, almost from the start, complemented by ownership of a summer cottage (*nyaraló*) or weekend getaway (*hétvégi ház*), sometimes called a *víkend ház*.[1] In the early 1960s, the state amended the "one-family, one-house" rule to allow additional ownership of a small, unheated cottage on a plot of land. Such cottages could not be used as a permanent home address and, unlike the primary residence, were subject to a small property tax. Members of Dunaújváros's professional class acquired tiny summer cottages by Lake Balaton or little weekend houses near the Danube, where Budapest's gentry used to have summer villas. Some had plumbing, others only an outhouse. Many working-class city dwellers bought vegetable plots further from the river as a source of extra cash or to supplement their household diets. These "hobby gardens" (*hobbi kert*) might have a tiny cottage on them, but just as often they had only a toolshed and some cooking utensils.

Numerous publications offered advice for cottage owners, and even *Lakáskultúra* featured sections on how to build and decorate these new spaces. As the jacket blurb on a book published in 1972 explains: "Urban living circumstances, increasing noise and smog, crowded environment, the effects of various 'stresses' make a person's desire for nature unavoidable. . . . It is necessary to fulfill the city dweller's most important aspiration: to escape from the city's everyday life into the natural environment" (Callmeyer and Rojkó 1972:201). This recreational and therapeutic appreciation of nature was a far cry from village life, and indeed, the land set aside for such structures was called a "resort area" (*üdülőterület*) and was zoned to prohibit the keeping of poultry and livestock. The cover illustration of the book on weekend houses (Plate 1a) epitomized this officially sanctioned ideal: a futuristic rectangle of concrete resembling a giant 1970s television, built on pylons to house the family car beneath.

It is no accident that this futuristic cottage is represented by an illustration rather than a photograph. The editors would have been hard pressed to find a real holiday cottage that resembled it.[2] The vernacular aesthetic that dominated cottage building and decorating was not complementary to modern urban materialities, as suggested by the illustration, but rose in opposition to them. It became an integral part of a widely shared aesthetic opposed to Socialist Generic, one which sought to restore the "natural" relationship of human beings to productive activity, to autonomy, and to national belonging. This Organicist Modern aesthetic, epitomized in natural materials and folk forms, was brought into urban apartments all over Hungary, deployed against an alienating Socialist Generic. It was not a return to a premodernist traditionalism of either peasant life or bourgeois materialities, but a way of generating a more "harmonious" modern lifestyle that fulfilled some of the dreams of a socialist modernity.

Because Organicist Modern emerged in a dynamic relationship with Socialist Modern—in harmony with some of its aspirations but opposed to a Socialist Generic—it spanned the last three decades of state socialism and continued to structure political dispositions in the 1990s. From the mid-1960s through the upheaval of socialist economic reforms in the 1980s and into the 1990s after the fall of state socialism, variations on this aesthetic became widespread across social strata, in both urban and rural areas. Just as the emergence of Socialist Generic was a shared phenomenon, an affection for Organicist Modern, especially for the home, also transcended social divisions. This value-saturated aesthetic regime shaped definitions of materialities that qualified as "normal," namely those in which particular qualities were aligned with anticommunist, national, and market economic sentiments. With the retreat of the welfare state in the 1990s, widespread disillusion with the lived experience of democratic politics and capitalism was offset by the promises that such Organicist materialities continued to hold out. Only now, such "natural" materials were increasingly to be found in the form of high-end, technologically enhanced commodities, commodities that transformed the do-it-yourself qualities of Organicist Modern into a Super-Natural Organicism.

Organicist Modern Out of Socialist Generic

In earlier years, private efforts to create modern interiors had largely aligned with the modernizing interests of the state. As a growing urban population moved into modernist apartments built under state auspices, many readily adopted the prescribed furnishing style. But by the time the OPEC oil crisis of 1973 was felt by state socialist economies, the credibility of a socialist modernity was waning (Vörös 1997). Experience of Socialist Modern materialities had rarely lived up to the ways they had been promoted in discourse, and even when it did, many people found that their lives were impoverished rather than improved by them. Utility furniture, when it was available, was indeed lightweight but also cheaply made, ill-conceived in design, and usually expensive rather than easily replaceable. Open-plan design, touted as both metaphor and physical embodiment of social equality and mobility, had been deployed not to expand living space and break down walls *between* rooms, but to crowd family members into the space of one small "multifunctional" room and atomize their activities.

By the 1980s, panel apartments had become paradigmatic spaces of a "future past"—that is, the dreams of a generation that is old or dead (Koselleck 1985). And yet the "abnormality" of socialist designs lay in part in their ostensible disassociation from specific times or places. As we have seen, modernist tastemakers disdained material goods that trapped or condensed time by collecting dust, inhibiting movement, or weighing down generations with the obligations of heirlooms. Modernism had no use for the concept of "patina," or the increase of an object's value through time and use. As things wore out, they were to have been discarded and replaced by better ones, produced with superior technology. Modernist materialities of plastic and concrete did not age well, nor could they be easily repaired. Thus the material world aligned with the state became increasingly broken and shabby.

These contradictions reinforced a growing disconnect between colloquial notions of "home" and the mass-produced housing in which urban dwellers now found themselves. In the city, the apartment was constructed as a private space offering sanctuary from the intrusive reach of the state. Apartment interiors were evaluated not for conformity to a contemporary style but for how well residents succeeded in making a visitor "forget that they were in a panel building" when they crossed the threshold into the heterotopic space of the home. This public/private opposition was reproduced in the distinctions made between the city apartment and the country cottage. The country cottage became an idealized, private space far away from the socialist city and the urban apartment.[3]

Central to the re-establishment of a more "natural" order was the restoration of traditional gendered hierarchies. City apartments were largely women's domains, as women generally continued to be responsible for all the household tasks even though they held down full-time jobs. Women were disproportionately affected by the rhetoric promoting the virtues of having high standards for one's material surroundings (*igény*). The order and cleanliness (*rend*) of the home were considered a direct reflection of a woman's character. At the same time, women were regularly criticized in the press for taking such standards too far and oppressing their menfolk.[4] Conversely, there was little for men to do in urban apartments besides tinker with electronic equipment or maintain the family car (if there was one), in part because residents were rarely allocated outside space for gardening or hobbies. Aside from the armchair in front of the television, apartments were spaces that excluded men or made their presence superfluous. Moreover, just as women were aligned in popular culture with the socialist state as engineers of their (often unwilling) emancipation from men (Gal and Kligman 2000a), women also became aligned with the image of the socialist city as a bureaucratic, rule-governed space.[5]

In contrast, the cottage became associated with masculine domestic activities and with a more earthy physicality (even though women worked, cooked, and cleaned at the cottage too). It was a private space where men could assume their rightful place as the head of household, and it was thus a space seen to restore a more "natural" relationship between the sexes. Men cooked meat stews in kettles on open fires and expended energies fixing up their cottages. Rigorous norms for order and cleanliness were relaxed, in part because the dirt of the country was considered healthier than urban dirt and pollution (Caldwell 2011; Pesmen 2000). Evenings were spent eating, drinking, and socializing. In warmer weather, some men used the cottages as a refuge from their wives and their cleaning activities as much as from the city.

The Materialities of Nature and Nation

The "natural" materialities of the rural cottage were brought into the city apartment in numerous ways, some of them mass-produced. In the 1970s, as the city grew and became increasingly dense with concrete, a vernacular Organicist Modern aesthetic evolved to transform this Socialist Generic (see Plates 2a–3b). Families strived to turn apartment interiors into heterotopic spaces that transported their residents into worlds far removed from the walls of concrete in which they were situated (see also Miller 1988). Popular decorating trends embraced organic shapes, so-called natural colors and materials, and aged or brightly colored folk artifacts as a way of breathing life, color, and character into what were increasingly seen as cold, gray, and uniform materialities. People put up floor-to-ceiling posters of nature scenes like mountaintops or forest glades to create the illusion of a fourth wall open to the wilderness (a trend that spread to the villages) (Plate 3a). Another popular trick was to put up wooden window frames, complete with curtains, on an interior wall. Rough linens, cottons and other natural fabrics were sought after, and sheepskins and furs were hung on walls or laid across sofa beds (Plate 3b). In the popular media, men were encouraged to give full expression to their do-it-yourself talents and woodworking skills, transforming apartments with modern but rustic furnishings, paneling, and cabinets. Wood was highly prized for its ability to humanize and warm the interiors of concrete panel apartments and also as a symbol of masculinity.[6] As the medium of masculine activity in the home, wood became iconic of a restored masculine presence in feminized urban apartments.

In the late 1960s, intellectuals in Budapest initiated a revival of interest in Hungarian material culture. Concerned about the erosion of an authentic Hungarian folk in the face of modernization, they began combing villages on the weekends to find old peasant artifacts like decorative pitchers and hand-painted plates to display in their urban apartments. Handcrafted objects made of clay, glass, natural textiles, leather, and wrought iron were qualitatively opposed to the homogenization of state socialist mass production (Figure 5.1, Plate 2a). This trend extended across social classes as a hobby in the 1970s, as urban women embroidered pillowcases, doilies, and runners with traditional Hungarian motifs. I was taught to embroider with colorful threads when I first went to Hungary as a child by my cousin,

Figure 5.1. Home décor of hand-painted plates with traditional motifs in a wooden display shelf. Photo by author, 1990.

a practicing lawyer. The peasantry had long been romanticized as the moral symbol of the nation and the repository of an authentic Hungarian culture, even if peasants themselves had often been stigmatized (Hofer 1991). But this revitalization of traditional material culture was made politically significant by the continuing presence of Soviet troops in the country. By the 1980s, the stakes of this trend rose with popular antagonism to a state policy that ignored the plight of ethnic Hungarian minorities in neighboring countries, particularly the roughly two million in Romanian Transylvania subject to Nicolae Ceausescu's persecution. The style became so popular that the state itself began to mass produce folk textiles and pottery, goods that were then bought in their commodified form by people in villages and by offspring of villagers in the city (*Dunaújvárosi Hírlap*, Jan. 6, 1970; S. Nagy 1987).

The growing fascination with ancient Hungarian tradition extended to other domains, as in peasant-inspired clothing fashionable among university students, who propelled the phenomenal rise in popularity of the folk Dance House movement in the 1980s (Taylor 2008). Sports arenas were filled for a week at a time with young folk dance troupes from all over the country and from minority Hungarian populations in neighboring countries. House revivals of Hungarian authentic folk dance attempted to reproduce a music played on ancient instruments to create "pure," primitive sounds thought to be unadulterated by the Hungarian "Gypsy" music played at weddings and in tourist restaurants. The most powerful example of this articulation of nature and folk culture with masculine materialities was the phenomenally popular rock opera *István the King* (*István, a király*) (Szörényi and Bródy 1984) in the genre of *Jesus Christ Superstar*. Although the story is of the victory in 1000 AD of the Christianizing king, St. Stephen (István), over paganism, the real hero of the opera is the pagan leader Koppány, who refuses to submit to a foreign God and rouses his followers in a deafening chorus around a midnight bonfire to sacrifice to the gods of nature. In contrast to the virile, bearded, and leather-clad Koppány, King István is portrayed as saintly and weak, doing the bidding of his German-speaking Christian mother. Given the tenor of the 1980s in Hungary, he is unequivocally aligned with a compromised Christianity and a feminized socialist state, both of which emasculate the Hungarian male.[7]

The impetus for incorporating nature into interiors stemmed not only from increasing disenchantment with Socialist Generic materialities but also from a growing awareness of the detrimental health effects of industrial pollution. In Dunaújváros, the steel mill emissions blanketed the city with a layer of soot each time the wind blew from the south. Once embraced as an engine of change, the mill was now regarded—especially by the middle stratum—as a blight. A "clean air movement" was forming in town as early as 1972 (*Dunaújvárosi Hírlap*, June 23, 1972). Cancer rates and the incidence of asthma among children were disproportionately high, and city dwellers accused the state of complicity in perpetuating this poisoning by setting the fine for polluting so low that the factory was happy to pay it rather than install expensive smokestack filters. As with low-quality products, the state was being materially indexed by artificial, man-made products and the industrial abuse of nature. By the time of the Chernobyl nuclear explosion in 1986 in neighboring Ukraine, Hungarian environmental activists—considered subversive by the government, along with those championing the poor—had already organized to oppose construction of the controversial Nagymaros dam on the Czechoslovak-Hungarian border (Harper 2006). While scholars cite Chernobyl as the event that shocked the Western world with the realization that experts did not have adequate control over societal "risks" (Beck 1987), for many Hungarians it simply confirmed that the Soviet Union and socialist government experts could not be trusted with the public welfare. Laura, who was a kindergarten teacher in her twenties at the time, remembers her father, a radiologist, coming home devastated after a secret briefing held several weeks after the explosion and telling her not to have any more children.

Replacing or covering up "man-made" materials with so-called natural materials was also consonant with the popular critique of the state's modernist project, privileging the material at the expense of the spiritual. Just as building a steel factory in the middle of a country with no iron ore was held up as a form of hubris, condemnations of communism centered on its godlike ambitions: of exerting total control over the future through central planning, insisting on human dominance over nature, and denying the existence of forces more powerful than human industry and scientific knowledge. Once seen as agents of liberation, manmade materials and industrial technologies were increasingly seen as agents of oppression. Such sentiments arose with and were inseparable from lived experience with synthetic materials like plastic and concrete, materials never encountered in "nature." Plastic is also the ultimate material of the mass-produced commodity, never experienced in the process of becoming but only in one of its many readymade forms (Barthes 1993). It is thus iconic of commodification, as Brad Weiss has shown, as "its easy convertibility of objects . . . alters the spatiotemporal connections between persons and things that are generated through work, cultivation, inheritance, affinity, and other generative activities" (Weiss 1992:549).

Moreover, concrete and plastic are often perceived as "cold" materials that arrest heat and thus interfere with the vital and temporal processes of transformation (cooking, fermenting, decaying, and fertilizing renewed growth) (cf. Weiss 1996:173–76). Popular focus on the qualities of synthetic materials like PVC plastic shifted from durability to their "unnatural" resistance to decomposition. Such man-made synthetic materialities in many ways mirrored the theory and practice of state socialism. In keeping with its relentless celebration of a timeless future, the socialist state was able to create fairly successful secular rituals for naming babies, for coming of age, and for weddings, but it could not figure out how to deal with nature's inevitable triumph, death. Socialist funerals disdained reference to an afterlife, focusing instead on remembrance of this-worldy achievements and sacrifice for the socialist collective (Black 2010; Betts 2008). Many people in Dunaújváros, including one of the new town's greatest patriots, chose to be buried in the village of their ancestors with a funeral presided over by a priest (Miskolczi 1980).

We can see such alignments of material properties or qualisigns in narratives about married couples moving into concrete apartment buildings, narratives that took on a strikingly formulaic character in the popular media, echoing and reinforcing popular discourses. A feature article in a 1983 *Lakáskultúra* epitomizes the genre. Titled "Would you believe it's a panel apartment?" it catalogues the herculean efforts of a young married couple (or, more accurately, the man) to completely transform their fifty-six square meters of space (Szűcs 1983b). The couple ripped out the new, standard-issue wallpaper and carpet and created most of the furnishings by hand. The wood-paneled kitchen cabinets they installed were complemented by bamboo matting covering the kitchen ceiling. They rescued and restored an old window frame, complete with shutters, from the demolition of a peasant house, installed it on an interior wall, added white curtains, and placed two geranium pots on the sill. Roughly hewn wooden posts supported a lean to canopy over their double bed. This redecoration was presented as having achieved the almost impossible goal of ridding the "panel room of its cube-like feeling" (1983b:18). The handmade décor was not a mode of resisting the commodity form as a priori alienated, but of individuating the uniformity of state socialist mass production. One of the couple's prize pieces, in fact, was a modern lamp with durable plastic shades they had purchased on their honeymoon in Western Europe (1983:19).

Throughout the 1980s, dark brown and off-white color schemes, from wall paint to household linens, dominated almost all the apartments featured in *Lakáskultúra* (Plate 2b). Brown was the qualisign of stained wood or leather, just as the off-white was supposed to evoke the qualities of natural textiles. The narratives accompanying this décor emphasized the intimacy, showiness, vitality, and "warmth" created by these particular materialities. The fact that the birth rate in Hungary had long been too low to maintain the population cannot be ignored in this partiality for materials that generated heat (and life) as well as intimate spaces for sexual relations. For example, a 1983 article on a tiny 24-square-meter (258-square-foot) studio apartment praises a young couple for finding the space to create an "intimate" corner for their bed (on a raised platform), and to accommodate their "passion" for collecting antique things. Such vital life forces are generated by wood floors, dark wood shelving and cabinetry (all made by the young man), antlers and animal skins, and the "linen textile that radiates warmth" on the walls surrounding the dining nook (Varga 1983).

These narratives illustrate the dynamic relationships between the sensory experience of material properties, affective sentiments, and discourse. By bringing wood, animal skins, natural textiles, and stones into the house, urban Hungarians transformed apartments that had been configured as sterile and cold into "homes." Such attachments to homey environments were inseparable from affective alienation from the existing political order. As we will see, they also generated an attraction to a free market, democratic system, including expectations for the "normal," more "natural" life that many people believed would be made possible by such a system.

Architectural Organicism

These transformations to modern furnishings paralleled similar developments elsewhere in the Soviet bloc as well as in Western countries where the state had propagated modern design—Sweden in particular (Löfgren 1994).[8] Yet the potency of the vernacular aesthetic was peculiar to the Hungarian configuration of politics and materialities. More formal articulations of this vernacular style emerged among some professional architects in the 1960s, who despite their differences became loosely unified under the label of a Hungarian Organicist school with roots in the Hungarian Art Nouveau or "Secession" (Szecesszió) movement of the early twentieth century.[9] While some of these architects only wished to modify Socialist Modern, others rejected outright what they saw as a dehumanizing architecture aligned with the "domination of bureaucrats and the building industry over architectural creativity" (Ferkai 1998:290). This informal, marginalized group advocated a site-specific architecture that "grew out of Hungarian tradition, used skilled rural tradesmen like wood-carvers, and reconnected people with a naturalist spirituality" (Heathcote 2006). Although popular exposure to these architects and their designs was fairly limited until the 1980s (Crowley 1993b:88–89), these developments can be seen as part of the emergence of a wider vernacular aesthetic.

By the late 1970s, the work of the organicist school's two main proponents, György Csete and Imre Makovecz, had become influential both within and outside the official architectural profession. Csete understood organic to mean "something rooted deeply in the soul of native tradition" and rejected any kind of angularity in composition in order to create buildings as shelters or sanctuaries (Ferkai 1998:290). A local Dunaújváros sculptor commissioned Csete to design a house and studio for him in the old village district of Pentele (*Dunaújvárosi Hírlap*, Aug. 30, 1983). Built in the early 1980s, the house was octagonal in plan and entirely encased by the roof, challenging the classical modernist cube, in which there is no visible mark of shelter. Imre Makovecz drew on vernacular forms and folk art (as influenced by Rudolf Steiner), but extended their range beyond Hungarian traditions to include anatomical, Celtic, and Far Eastern motifs, considering them "memories of the same collective subconscious" (Figure 5.2). He understood his architecture to be a "defensive magic against all impersonal powers" such as communism (and, after 1990, corporate capitalism) (Ferkai 1998:291; Heathcote 1997). This Organicist aesthetic, in all its variations, was an overdetermined response to the materialities of Socialist Generic and their alignment with the bureaucratic state.

From early on, professional architects, even those firmly committed to modernism, had attempted to ameliorate the relentless uniformity of panel architecture. Dunaújváros city planner Tibor Weiner had promoted such modifications as far back as 1960, when he joined with others to suggest painting panel buildings with bright colors in "modern" asymmetrical patterns. His efforts met with mocking editorials in the local newspaper (*Sztálinvárosi Hírlap*, May 1960). This politicization of panel building aesthetics continued for two decades. While an orthodox modernist faction attempted to teach people to appreciate the aesthetics of the buildings in their unadorned simplicity, directing their attention to the "interesting play of light and shadow" made by their shapes (*Dunaújvárosi Hírlap*, Feb. 1,

Figure 5.2. Makovecz chapel at Siófok, 1986–1990. Web image from 2010. Photo used with permission by the Imre Makovecz Foundation.

1972), other pundits praised the "interesting novelty" (*érdekes újdonság*) of a building on which one vertical row of apartments had been painted red, not just the balconies (*Dunaújvárosi Hírlap*, June 6, 1975).

In 1975, a group of young architects from the southwestern city of Pécs became widely known for their controversial attempt to "decorate" and "humanize" panel buildings by painting abstracted versions of red tulip motifs on the blank firewalls of ten-story buildings and by designating otherwise unmarked entrances with a playful, rounded concrete entryway. Powerful members of the architectural professions condemned these undertakings as both aesthetically and politically heretical, accusing the group of echoing the Secessionist style's use of the tulip as a symbol of the Magyar people at the turn of the century (Ferkai 1998:290; see also Major and Osskó 1981 for the "tulip debate"). The stormy debate that followed pushed these architects into adopting a traditionalist position in opposition to modernism, reflecting a long-standing intellectual polarization between an urban, cosmopolitan faction that identified with Europe and a more nationalistic, populist faction centered in the values of the countryside (Molnár 2005). After the tulip incident, the group was deprived of its license and had to disband, but not before many of its ideas for panel exteriors had been put into effect (Ferkai 1998:290). By the 1980s, the power of modernist orthodoxies had waned, though a discernible divide remained between those architects promoting new configurations of modernist forms and those abandoning them entirely.

1980s: Socialist Market Reforms and the End of Socialist Modern

Socialist-Style Neoliberalism

Hungary's semilegal second economy and economic reforms had contributed to rising standards of living, but the socialist good life was also being subsidized by massive foreign debt. Continuing obligations to COMECON and deteriorating terms of trade precipitated by the global oil crisis caused economic growth to slow and then reverse. By the late 1970s, Hungary's burgeoning hard-currency debt was in the billions of dollars, exceeding a year's worth of exports. To maintain the country's creditworthiness, the party was forced to implement unpopular price hikes for consumer goods, raising food prices by 25 percent while real wages fell by almost 4 percent (Révész 1990: 100, 104). An estimated 30 percent of the population without access to second-economy goods or income was becoming pauperized, with urban families and female-headed households hit particularly hard (Haney 2002:166).

The economic reforms of the 1980s were extensive. The socialist state legalized small, family-owned-and-operated private companies, and in 1985 it extended legal status to much larger for-profit firms, including cooperatives within state-owned companies that were allowed to operate on company premises after regular working hours. Hungary's already extensive economic ties and trade relations with the Western world increased in 1982, when it formally joined the International Monetary Fund, driven by its need for convertible currency and better rates on loans. The IMF's influence on the direction of reforms is well-documented. The state introduced such market mechanisms as inflation, limited unemployment, and taxation and continued to scale back subsidies for food, utilities, family support, and the like, but with greater rigor (Haney 2002:169). Even though the state had been withdrawing from the housing sector for two decades, by 1988 the drain on the state budget of various housing subsidies came to 80 billion Hungarian forints (HUF) annually. The Communist parliament took action, raising rents on state-owned flats by 25 to 30 percent and retroactively terminating favorable building loans of 3 percent—making loans suddenly unaffordable for many just moving into houses they had newly built.

Hungarians of the professional classes by-and-large experienced the decade as a time of increasing economic freedoms, including opportunities for private profit and greater access to desirable consumer goods. In the mid-1980s, travel restrictions to Austria were lifted and many traveled there to work or for shopping trips. At the same time, rising prices and shrinking subsidies meant that standards of living for many people could only be maintained by taking on second and third jobs in the second economy, exacerbating the hectic pace of everyday life. More families slid into poverty. From 1985, the socialist state began instituting new criteria for state assistance. Instead of redistributing collective wealth to all citizens as participants in a national workforce, the state sought to wean workers from the expectation that the state would provide work or benefits through guaranteed employment, offering instead to retrain and provide unemployment benefits. These benefits, however, failed to put recipients above subsistence level (Haney 2002:181–83). Social services began to classify populations by income and level of material deprivation, thus constituting new class divides by "inventing the needy" as a social category (Haney 2002:176).

Socialist Revival of Class

These profound shifts in political economy were accompanied by corresponding discourses about social classes and the material worlds associated with them. Socialist Generic materialities were aligned with the proletariat, a class increasingly associated with an unnatural form of government as well as with characteristics of dependency and lack of initiative (chapter 6). Socialist values were downplayed in official discourse, and the state's ideological commitment to the working class faltered. At the Hungarian Socialist Worker's Party Congress of 1985, aging party secretary János Kádár insisted in a televised address that Hungary remained a socialist society where the exploitative classes had been eradicated. "Yes, classes still exist," he acknowledged to the audience of party members in their professional suits, "but they are all working classes, and there are no irreconcilable conflicts between them" (Magyar Szocialista Munkáspárt Kongresszusa 1985).[10] The party officially recognized that a small-scale entrepreneurial stratum would "continue to contribute for some time to the life of socialist society," as it began to discipline the working classes with the threat of unemployment.

This decade of economic crisis and neoliberal reform coincided with a new fascination among historians, urban intellectuals, and dissident writers with a historic *polgár,* or bourgeois-citizenry. This was the very group that had been presented as cultural producers, as possessing the ability to acquire and appreciate Old World interiors and antique objects while maintaining a critical distance from these materialities as symbols of capitalist class hierarchies or inherited status. For everyone else, *Lakáskultúra* and newspaper articles had promoted the practice of mixing artifacts from the past into modern décor. The rise of Organicist Modern as a dominant trend did not exclude such old and finely crafted pieces—indeed, their age and materials (lace, wool textiles, carved wood, oil paintings, ceramics, and porcelain) were generally in harmony with natural and folk materialities. The class provenance of these objects was rarely discussed. They were referred to simply as old or antique (*régiség*).

These intellectuals and cultural producers began to reconnect these materialities with the lifestyles and civic consciousness of a presocialist bourgeois class by the late 1970s. Even though antique materialities in Hungary were the remains of both a bourgeoisie and a gentry, their interest focused on the bourgeoisie because it had constituted the antithesis for state socialist theory, politics, and aesthetics. Particularly attractive for these intellectuals was the notion of a bourgeois private sphere, or a protected space allowing for interiority, domesticity, and the cultivation of the self, in contrast to a socialist society where politics pervaded all aspects of life. While the nationalist-populists agitated for a return of a patriarchal family structure and women's confinement to the domestic sphere, the liberal opposition, influenced by the theories of Habermas and other writers on civil society, saw in the second economy a potential parallel to the bourgeois private-public sphere of industry and commerce, producing autonomous and independent citizens (see also Hankiss 1989). For writers such as György Konrád (1984), such a private sphere was to remain free of politics. Central to this "antipolitical" civil society was the value of "home and free time . . . the spatial and temporal dimension of civic independence," where one's artificial state persona is not identical with one's true self and "respect for money and property have not undermined other values in the moral consciousness" (Konrád 1984:197–202).

This veneration of an urban bourgeoisie was grounded in its material trappings and taste. Where a modernist avant-garde had once set itself up in opposition to the pretensions and artifice of a bourgeoisie, now the remains of bourgeois materialities seemed to embody a realm of beauty and civilized values in contrast to the genericist aesthetics of the state and the ostensible duplicity of life under communism. Among a cultured intelligentsia, identifying oneself as part of the "bourgeoisie" strangely became a form of resistance. Iván Szelényi, with some irony, noted in the late 1980s the attraction to the "beautiful homes of bourgeois intellectuals, where people sipped afternoon tea from fine china in living rooms full of antique furniture, conversing about Proust and Mahler," their "autonomy" and "irony and humor (so badly lacking among party intellectuals), their loyalty to friends (in contrast to the party loyalty of Communists, who, in principle, should always have been ready to betray personal friends for 'the cause'), their unshakable good aesthetic sense (in contrast to the horrors of Socialist Realism)" (Szelényi et al. 1988:52).

As economic reforms of the 1980s took hold, some intellectuals hoped that the descendants of a historic *polgár* or at least their cultural traces would revive latent political and cultural dispositions as much as economic practices (as with the German *Bürger*). For others, the search for a Hungarian bourgeoisie was motivated by a desire to reveal traces of an autonomous capitalist spirit in peasant-workers or second-economy entrepreneurs. Here the notion of *polgárosodás* (embourgeoisement) was used to mean eradicating mentalities of entitlement and dependence on the state, reforming slack work habits, and fostering risk taking, economic autonomy, and entrepreneurial activities, as well as civic responsibility (Szelényi et al. 1988:22). The kind of historic middle class associated with this sociopolitical ideal was to become a powerful cultural force in the political landscape of the postsocialist 1990s.

The Demise of Socialist Modern

With the state's rapid divestment and decentralization of responsibility for residential housing in the 1980s, the age of panel construction finally came to an end. In Dunaújváros, the last district of panel buildings was erected early in the decade. This district included buildings of varied heights, more moderate sizes, and some adorned with modular entryway façades painted bright yellow. The city and the steel factory both experimented with new ways to use panel technology, building single-family homes from panels as well as a complex of terraced panel apartments that cascaded down a hillside, complete with garages and hefty price tags. The steel factory built two-story townhouse-style developments for its workers, moving away from panel architecture altogether. By the end of the decade, it was building larger duplexes in postmodern designs for its management. City planning authorities attempted to mitigate the austere modernism of public spaces with rounded planters, wooden park benches and other modes of breaking up undifferentiated, rectilinear spaces. The legalization of small businesses was most visible in the many kiosks that emerged alongside the roads between panel high rises, and by the late 1980s, shopkeepers in more densely populated areas were permitted to rent ground-floor apartments and convert them into small stores

Organicist Modern and Super-Natural Organicism | 153

Figure 5.3. Late 1980s, cooperative, self-built housing development in Dunaújváros.

with neon signs. Residents said they appreciated these lights not only for their color but also because they provided illumination at night and distinctive landmarks in the otherwise generic cityscape. The same effect was created by advertising for such things as state-sponsored homeowner's insurance that appeared on the blank firewalls of taller panel buildings.

In the city, social stratification continued to align with the quality and location of housing. The centrally located brick buildings of the Stalin era, with their enclosed courtyards, remained more highly valued for their location and quality materials. The city council encouraged young couples to build loft apartments in the attic spaces of these buildings. Panel buildings were ranked according to their location, height of the building, and the density of settlement—the lower the better. For the first time, the garden city district's image began improving as higher-status professionals had new houses built there. In the late 1980s, more city dwellers, with hopes for second-economy incomes, began to build houses for themselves in nearby villages. A new development in town epitomized this change in direction. A private architectural firm in conjunction with the steel mill received permission to build eighty-eight Austrian-style family houses with red tiled roofs, whitewashed walls, flower boxes, wooden balconies, and shingles, all laid out along winding brick streets with decorative lampposts (Figure 5.3). These were a combination of self-build and condominium properties, in which the city subsidized some of the infrastructure but future owners were to build most of their own units and contribute to the financing of water mains and other utilities (Pecz 1996:36–38).[11] The development was completed in the early 1990s and was unquestioningly considered a "normal" and postsocialist environment. It was to be the last housing development in the town.

1990s: The Fall of State Socialism and the Affective Power of Organicist Materialities

In 1988, János Kádár was ousted by his own party after thirty years in power. Although the Communist Party had controlled the political process throughout the economic reforms of the 1980s, by the end of the decade it had begun to introduce choice between Communist candidates who endorsed substantively different agendas. Public demonstrations over environmental abuses and the plight of Hungarian minorities in Romania grew increasingly bold. In June of 1989, various opposition groups joined to organize the reburial of Imre Nagy, the Communist Party leader executed for his role in the revolution of 1956. The Communist Party joined the ceremony, hoping to align themselves with the martyred leader and so avoid being tarred as his executioners. More than one hundred thousand people turned out for the occasion and cheered when student leader Viktor Orbán boldly called for the departure of Soviet troops from the country. In September, Hungarian border guards began allowing vacationing East Germans into Austria without a visa, precipitating an exodus of East Germans to the West through Hungary. The Hungarian Socialist Workers' Party formally dissolved itself in October 1989, a few weeks before the fall of the Berlin Wall. A faction of the party was resurrected as the Hungarian Socialist Party—with "worker" dropped from its name.

The peaceful "system change" of 1989–1990 was carried out through cooperation between the opposition and the former Communist Party *nomenklatura*. With the exodus of Soviet troops, the first democratically elected government, the Hungarian Democratic Forum (MDF) came to power on a platform of jubilant Hungarian nationalism and took up the cause of Magyar minorities in neighboring countries. Although there had been no purging of Communist Party officials after the fall of state socialism, the policies and reforms carried out by the new state were guided by an opposition to communism *in absentia* (see Gal 1994). The success of second-economy endeavors combined with the inefficiencies and sometimes outright absurdities wrought by centralized economic control had convinced much of the population that shifting to a decentralized, market economy would usher in a Western-style prosperity—maybe not immediately, but fairly quickly (see also Bodnár 1998:508–11; Lampland 1995).[12] In contrast to the unnatural experiments of state socialism, the "natural" Organicist Modern materialities produced at home or in the second economy reinforced the legitimacy of market exchange, competition, self-interest, and a degree of social inequality.

These dispositions greatly influenced the direction of sweeping institutional reforms, most of which sought to undo the legacy of the socialist state.

As in other nation-states in the region, the re-establishment of private property in Hungary was considered central to the political legitimacy of the new order. This position was bolstered by international actors such as the IMF and the World Bank, which made the privatization of state firms and retraction of state benefits a condition for granting the country crucial loans. The institution of private property was linked to the emergence of a healthy middle class, itself a concept "influenced by teleological ideas of 'transformation,'" as anthropologist Michal Buchowski noted for the region, that "played an ideological role in the building of the new liberal political and ideological order" (2008:49). As we will see in chapter 6, the type of middle class that would emerge was far from clear, while the marketing of a wide range of furnishing styles provided tangible evidence that there were many possibilities for such a class. But in political rhetoric, scholarly discourse, and the media, the dominant focus was on the revival of a historic Hungarian *polgár* or bourgeois citizenry—a focus that included a now widespread appreciation for antiques and the other material trappings of such a class.

The Organicist school of architecture moved out of its marginalized position to become the official design ideology of the newly independent Hungarian nation-state as well as a popular design style for new houses (Figure 5.4). Imre Makovecz was chosen to represent the country at the International Exposition in Seville in 1992, and his pavilion could not have been more diametrically opposed to Socialist Modern. Inverting the modernist paradigm of a roofless cube, his structure was almost entirely enveloped by a slate roof and constructed of all "natural" materials. No two of the wooden joints were of the same size, and no mechanical tools were used by the traditional craftsmen who assembled it. In contrast to modernism's focus on the future arising out of a tabula rasa, Makovecz centered his pavilion around a denuded tree, its roots exposed under a glass floor to represent the nation's grounding in the past as it extended into the future (Eke n.d.).

Throughout the country, newly autonomous local city councils attempted to disguise the Socialist Genericism of formerly socialist civic squares by adding peaked roofs to block-like modernist buildings and painting them pastel colors. Some towns replaced concrete bus stops with shelters made of carved wood, modeled on traditional Transylvanian gates. In Dunaújváros, as we saw in chapter 1, Organicism was a dominant theme in early attempts to transform the urban landscape from the twisted marble arch of ancient Hungarian design commissioned by the village elders to the new Roman Catholic cathedral and Calvinist church, both designed by Organicist school architects. In Tiszaújváros, another socialist new town built to support the chemical industry, the large and empty town square had been dominated by a box-like town hall and a 1970s-era department store in the shape of a faded blue rectangle. The town council tried to mitigate the austere

156 | Politics in Color and Concrete

Figure 5.4. Makovecz-inspired house in Tiszaújváros, 1996. Photo by author, 1996.

effect of the square by depositing an undulating wall of ochre-colored stones onto the pavement and adorning it with fir trees, iron lampposts, and wooden benches (Figure 5.5).

City authorities were joined in these efforts by private commercial interests driven by new imperatives to "attract" people, commerce, and capital. Storefronts and interiors of new, privatized spaces like bars, cafes, and theater lobbies became canvases for all sorts of fantastic tableaus, made possible in part through the wider selection of materials and building technologies available. Dunaújváros's boutique row collected an assortment of these styles, from elaborate, retro-industrial chic to sleek, postmodern spaces fragmented with mirrored shards and futuristic furnishings (Plate 6a). Organicism here too extended its range. A computer technology shop counterintuitively rejected a high-tech design in favor of wrapping its façade with layered curves of warm-toned wood (Plate 6b). A new *kozmetika* or beauty salon was built into a spacious loft apartment, where beams painted purple crisscrossed the ceiling, arched wooden doors were set with rose-colored contoured glass and opened onto triangular-shaped rooms, all floored with gleaming white ceramic tile. The owner proudly showed me around. It was a space, she hoped, "of fantasy." As these examples have illustrated, Organicist Modern aesthetics were being extended and transformed by the globalizing marketplace to

Figure 5.5. New, undulating stone wall, shrubbery, and cast-iron bench added to a Socialist Generic town square. Photo by author, 1996.

constitute a more exclusive, commodified and professionalized Super-Natural Organicism.

Transformative Materialities and Sentiments of Liberation

By the mid-1990s, popular critiques of state socialism were muted by widespread disillusion with capitalism and democracy. As we'll see in chapter 6, lived experience of austerity measures, unemployment, radical income inequalities, and failing medical, educational and transportation systems led many to mourn aspects of state socialism and the security it had offered. In the 1994 elections, the nationalist MDF party was ousted for its dismal handling of the system change, and the reformed Socialist Party was elected or "restored" to power, depending on one's perspective. Hungarian political life was again polarized along the enduring divide between urbanists and populists. This time, it took the rancorous form of those supporting the Socialists and their coalition partner the Free Democrats (SZDSZ), a socially progressive but fiscally neoliberal party, and those committed to a nationalist opposition, now incarnated by the Party of Young Democrats (FIDESZ) led by Viktor Orbán, who won the elections of 1998. Although both sides claimed to defend the interests of the nation and the welfare of their respective constituents, neither could reverse the tide of privatization and welfare-state reform.

Even so, political dispositions continued to be generated by the enduring presence of Socialist Generic materialities, as panel apartments dominated skylines and housed more than a quarter of the population (and a much higher percentage in cities). Hungarians of diverse ages and incomes were compelled by affective desires and social pressures to transform their homes, even those within concrete panel buildings, to align with what they hoped would be a new, more natural order.[13] Proponents of neoliberal economics, environmentalists, and protectionist nationalists all defined their politics in some way by opposition to a state socialism aligned with crumbling concrete. The discrediting of the state socialist system is thus impossible to disentangle from antipathies toward materialities aligned with the socialist state.[14]

We cannot see such aesthetic transformations to the material environment as passive reflections of political change; rather, they actively contributed to the generation of new political ideologies. In the media and in popular discourse, glowing descriptions of transformed home décor were often in the same idiom used to describe Hungary's "release" from Soviet domination and its political and economic transformation from socialist state to an "open society" and "free market" regime. In some respects, these alignments were not new. The rectilinear forms and mass-produced uniformity of concrete housing estates had been for years aligned with closed borders, the restrictions of the planned economy, and the limited means of expression associated with an authoritarian state. When city dwellers enlarged windows, tore down dividing walls between rooms, or moved out of panel buildings altogether, they were of course doing what they could to enlarge and open their living space. But in the postsocialist 1990s, they regularly explained their motives for transforming their living spaces with expressions such as "To escape from right angles!" or "Breaking free of standardized cubes!" as if channeling Hungary's release from the confining authority of communism. In a context where people had regularly spoken of being "walled off" or "walled in" from the rest of the world (Hixson 1997:231), such expressions linked the embodied experience of socialist living spaces iconically to the equally embodied, affective experience of citizenship in a closed country.[15]

My interlocutors in Dunaújváros shared in the rhetoric of interior décor magazines that aligned rectilinear angularity with metaphors of incarceration, regularly publishing articles with titles such as "Breaking out of a rule-bound order." Correspondingly, breaking out of stifling apartments was somatized by continued reference to breathing. Károly, the unmarried owner of a door and window workshop, proudly showed me his renovated apartment in Dunaújváros, with walls removed between the front and interior rooms, cork flooring, and an American kitchen where the balcony had once been. Standing in the center of this space, he spread his arms wide and exclaimed: "Here I can breathe!" Referring to open-plan kitchens as American, as Károly did, had both political and cultural resonances. Before 1989, such kitchens had been known as "open kitchens" in the official press. Although *Lakáskultúra* had been featuring such kitchens since the late 1960s, until the late 1980s they were prohibited by formal building codes.[16] While "American" was often used to contrast crass materialism and historical naiveté with more refined, "European" sensibilities, it also stood in for a perceived contrast between an American laissez-faire social order and the rigidity of Central European norms for propriety. The open "American" kitchen removes the formal artifice of separating the place of dining from the place where food is prepared, bringing into view the transformation of nature into culture. The legacy of Socialist Modern discourse had been to link the notion of "openness" with qualia of an open space indexing physical relaxation. This relaxed informality was physiologically expressed by exhaling. But the phrase "freedom to breathe" continued to be used, primarily by men, in describing their feelings of suffocation in urban apartments and the need to be outside to breathe in the fresh air of the countryside, whether at the cottage—now a place that could legally be winterized—or moving to a detached family house.

Between the late 1960s and the 1990s, people had lost faith in rhetoric that attempted to convince the populace that it was possible—with sufficient energy, labor, and creative thought—to transform tiny apartments into transcendent, heterotopic private spheres. Instead, a different kind of rhetoric filled a host of new interior (and exterior) design publications. Home renovations were described as enabling an escape from the unhealthy mixing of public and private life, of finally inhabiting dwellings where demands (*igények*) were no longer compromised. In a typical example from the newly privatized *Lakáskultúra*, a new homeowner is asked whether he and his family had grown out of their old place. The answer: "Yes, it was very small, we didn't fit," replies the man. "Agnes and I ran our advertising studio out of a corner. The constant mixing of our family and business lives became increasingly difficult to bear.... I love the space because it is of such human-scale (*emberléptékű*). There are places one can always retreat, like the office, the bedroom, the children's room. And the rest is open all in one, the kitchen, dining room and living room. No one is shut out or left out" (Lukovits 1995:78). Here is the realization of the fantasy open plan that broke down divisions between cooking, eating, and socializing areas along with their social divisions of labor. At the same time, this plan also allowed for private rooms set aside for particular activities, like work, sleep and sex, or containing material clutter. Privacy from the outside world continued to be maintained by curtains, shutters, and a new kind of opaque, convex glass pane for doors.[17]

Panel apartments were increasingly referred to in these terms, as not fit for human habitation or as not being scaled for humans. A factory manager was asked by a reporter why he had moved to a house in a fairly inaccessible village. "We lived in a 1 ½ room panel," he answered. "Need I say more? Here there is space, a workshop, and air" (Rist 1996:24–25). This was not simply the euphemistic rhetoric of the upwardly mobile: I heard such expressions from people of various ages and social statuses. A retired seamstress named Anikó insisted to me that every day for twenty years, she'd chanted to herself, "Out of here! Out of here!" as she climbed the stairs with heavy groceries to her eighth-story panel apartment (the elevator was always broken). She and her husband had managed to move to an older, unfinished house in the village, where they kept a vegetable garden. Though she complained of having to return to the city by bus to supply her grown children with produce, she felt she'd become "more calm and peaceful."[18]

The preference for "natural" materials and organic shapes continued unabated, but often with new, commodified forms (Plate 7b). Furnishings and building materials that had been produced and made available in the second economy were supplanted by mass-produced and imported commodities available for cash. Bamboo furniture had become an accessible and affordable way to furnish. Indoor fountains bubbling over stones became a popular novelty in Dunaújváros, as they were thought to humidify the parched air of panel apartments and provide soothing sounds. Feng Shui books and practitioners helped people living in rectilinear urban housing counteract perceived negative forces with fountains like these as well as with mirrors and other objects said to channel energies. Older "natural" materialities like sheepskins and homemade carpentry were edged out by new commodities such as German leather furniture, Porotherm housing bricks, Bramac roofing tiles, and environmentally friendly heating systems. While many of the huge, picture-window-size posters of nature disappeared, people signaled their affinity with a natural order by extending the range of wood furnishings and replacing linoleum with ceramic tile crafted to have the qualities of enduring materialities like flagstone, marble, granite, and slate. These products were widely advertised as "natural" materials, but ads made sure to index their superiority as nature that had been transformed by modern technologies into "super-natural" materials.

These new materialities and appropriations of "Eastern" techniques to create a more harmonious order recapitulated critiques of the modernist project, often overlapping with nationalist, environmental, and religious concerns. A conservative magazine for house builders called *Family House* (*Családi Ház*) regularly combined these themes. Pitched to the widest range of people involved in house building, it was subtitled "The magazine for builders, contractors, architects, entrepreneurs and dreamers." One article condemned the rectilinear as contrary to nature, not just in buildings but in the design of gardens.

We almost never find square, rectangular or pyramid forms and the straight lines of right angles in nature.... [Mankind] created corners, straight lines, flat planes... a process accelerated in the 20th C by the Bauhaus and other modern architectural schools.... Today, the reaction has set in... breaking the spell, the enchantment of the angular. A new architectural romanticism has rediscovered the circle, the cylinder, the ellipsis and curved forms in general. [These] turn their back on *the rigid cubes and artificial, inhumane* worlds opposed to the natural/human environment (my emphasis) (Hódi Tóth 1997:61–62).

The writer echoes the eighteenth-century landscape architect William Kent, who coined the romantic mantra that "nature abhors a straight line" (Ingold 2007). The attack on the rectilinear here is not an indictment of an ordering aesthetic such as *rend*. Instead, it is an indictment of an ideology that tried to suppress rather than *shape* a natural world, including the ambition to engineer human nature through the medium of an imposed built environment.

Condemnation of an "unnatural" rectilinear was matched by the celebration of rounded forms, asymmetry, and eclecticism in form and color—qualities considered necessary for human beings to flourish, allowing for creativity, imagination, and such things as the "Freedom of Improvisation" (the title of one interior design feature).[19] A retired schoolteacher, struggling to live on her small pension as the state progressively withdrew social benefits, nonetheless admired the colorful new houses we passed on a bus ride. She related with pride how she too had introduced playful elements to the interior of her small apartment and the pleasure she got from replacing the solid wall dividing her sleeping area from the living room with one of glass bricks that allowed natural light to shine through. In *Lakáskultúra,* the new owners of a loft apartment mused about their redesigned home. The husband reflected that he had grown "more and more pleased with the irregularly shaped, well-proportioned space, and the possibility of using the eaves of the roof for creating tucked away, intimate places" (Rubóczki 1996).

The importance of a masculine presence in home interiors and exteriors continued apace, in both materials and in discourse. For example, an engineer in Dunaújváros described the pink shade of his newly built house as the color of "red meat."[20] But nationalist sentiments and their materialization had become divisive. The outbreak of civil war in neighboring Yugoslavia in 1990 had rapidly defused the romanticism for doctrines of national self-determination in the West. Liberal-minded, urban professionals who identified with cosmopolitanism were sensitive to charges that Hungarian nationalism was a form of irredentism and thus opposed to European values. Over time, many turned against the nationalist design of the Organicist architects, though not away from new commodities touting their natural and organic materialities. Many of the new lower and middle classes came to deeply resent the preferential economic treatment Romanian Hungarian immigrants received from the state at a moment when they themselves felt in need of assistance. In many apartments, hand-painted folk pitchers and embroidered pillowcases quietly disappeared, reframed as acceptable for the cottage but inappropriate for an urban setting.

If the Organicist designs by Makovecz had a somber tone, recalling Magyar pagan traditions and spirituality, there was a more whimsical style, influenced by the Austrian artist and architect Friedensreich Hundertwasser, that evoked descriptions such as "fairytale" (*mese*), "magical" (*varázslatos*), and "enchanted" (*elbűvölő*) for houses and interiors. Such houses tended to have radically asymmetrical and even "melting" elements to their façades and were often painted in natural tones of green, brown, dark yellow, and orange (colors that had been preferred by villagers for the more modern "square house"). One example, a house in a nearby suburbanizing village, resembled a squat, irregularly shaped mushroom, with wooden doors and an undulating shingled roof that mimicked the forms of thatch (see Figure 7.6 in chapter 7).

Even though they bore the mark of having been designed by a professionally trained and therefore expensive architect, such houses were viewed differently from new houses built with turrets and grand entryways, which were often criticized as the pretensions of the *nouveaux riches*. The Hobbit-like earthiness and merry, childlike qualities of these Organicist designs generally inspired expressions of delight. A 1998 feature titled "Fairytale House in Dabas" describes how the "enchanted" interior greets the guest with a rich play of colors, forms, and ideas (Czeglédi 1998). The interviewer praises its "extravagance, the influence of Hundertwasser; that it is farcical, harlequinesque and flies in the face of bourgeois taste." Meanwhile, the owner insists that he had the house designed to "establish a home that diverges from the customary pattern, and yet is still functional." He emphasizes how "it serves its dwellers with spiritual comfort," something "more important than function" (Czeglédi 1998:40). By evoking the intimacy associated with family privacy and the playful leisure of childhood, these interiors starkly opposed the publicity of state socialist architecture, with its austere functionalism and lack of space for intimate relations or spiritual growth. Play, fantasy, and color served as an explicit rejection of Socialist Modern's valorization of efficient functionality and adult productivity, responsibility, and sacrifice (see Plate 5a).[21]

Finally, postsocialist renovations articulated with the valorization of individualism and autonomy. People bemoaned growing social inequalities, but they insisted on the human need for expressing creative difference and for providing an outlet for healthy, "natural" competitive impulses, echoing home journal titles such as "Not from a Mold, with Color!" For city dwellers still stuck in panel construction apartments, magazines continued to promise ways to create an "Oasis in the Panel Vastness" or "Enchantment in 64 m^2," both titles from 1997 issues of a new home décor journal called *Beautiful Home* (*SzépLAK*) that targeted the large population living in panel apartments. Like a modernist city, absolutely different from everything around it, the renovated apartment transports its inhabitants into a transformed world. In so doing, it defines the outside world as a monochrome, oppressive, and polluting public through its heterotopic materialities. As one journalist wrote in describing a female engineer and single mother's apartment, one that had been "whimsically furnished with a comfortable mix of modern furniture and antiques": "Is this truly in a panel residential estate? . . . This apartment is different. From the moment I step in, I forget the panel masses" (Lukovits 1996:42).

This anti-socialist aesthetics was not a form of conscious political expression through consumption but a response to a materially debased modernist aesthetic experienced as imposed by an oppressive regime. As Habermas has remarked, one of state socialism's most troubling legacies was that the state misused progressive ideas for its legitimacy and so discredited them (cited in Veenis 1999:109). As in other socialist regimes, the reaction to state material culture in Hungary embraced values opposing those of socialist ideology: individualism, self-realization, competitiveness, pleasure, family privacy, and intimacy. The socialist state, no matter how idealized in hindsight, was in the 1990s still associated with a material culture experienced as degrading to citizens and as evidence of the state's profound misunderstanding of human nature. This legacy promulgated desires for materialities that seemed in harmony with capitalist understandings of human nature and at the same time allowed for individuated shelters from capitalism's harsh demands—arenas of play, comfort and rejuvenation, and a transcendent permanence.

In the following chapters, I explore how shifting property regimes were experienced by households and the confusion they created about an emerging social order—one that did not conform to most people's expectations. Socialist Modern and its transformation into Organicist Modern had been an aesthetic shift shared by much of the population across social divisions. But the changes of the 1990s incorporated a plethora of housing and decorating styles, promoting individuality and diversity, but also a sharper divisiveness between social groups. In this melee, an anti-socialist, Super-Natural Organicist aesthetic became a powerful mode of legitimating emerging income inequalities and social stratifications, as members of an aspiring middle class transformed their domestic material worlds in accordance with this high-standard but distinctly Hungarian aesthetic.

6 Unstable Landscapes of Property, Morality, and Status

EARLY IN THIS book, I recounted an incident in which a university student from Dunaújváros nodded out the window of our bus at a silver car speeding by and remarked, "If everyone had a car like that, that would be normal!" In one breath, this young man summed up a complex mixture of expectation and disappointment. As with widespread invocations of a counterfactual "normal" in Hungary, he expressed the socialist middle strata's frustrated expectations for the kind of life they had assumed would be ushered in by democracy and a free market. Simultaneously, he delineated places and kinds of behavior in Hungary that conformed to such expectations. His insistence that "everyone" was entitled to a car like that also highlighted the fact that most people were still sitting on the bus. At the same time, these people could see that others—often inexplicably—enjoyed not only "normal" material goods and environments but far more lavish ones. Just as disturbing was the emergence of a visible homeless population as well as the regular sight of impoverished pensioners selling small, straggly bouquets of daisies on street corners.

As I got to know residents better, we would return to some of the same places they had first shown off to me as signs of the Europeanization of the country, but this time to complain about emerging social hierarchies and to try to make sense of them. Organicist Modern had been one manifestation of discontent with state socialism, a phenomenon that also became a national, popular aesthetic, symbolizing a sense of unity across social divides. But the end of the unitary state combined with the rise of acrimonious politics and new social stratifications had shattered what was left of such solidarity, even if it had only been defined in negative terms. Now, new property regimes and the incursion of global economic forces were generating the second great redistribution of wealth in Hungary in less than half a century. While politicians, intellectuals, and other elites discussed the fate of the former socialist middle strata and sought anxiously for signs of a new *polgári* middle class, many Hungarians were contending with an unstable landscape of shifting material and moral worlds: new forms of property, loss of taken-for-granted benefits, and new and bewildering ways to make and lose money, not to mention changing understandings of money itself (Verdery 1996:168–203).

As elsewhere in the region, an alarming and pervasive discourse held that the population was being divided into winners and losers. This discourse critiqued a new system that seemed to be rewarding undeserving members of society—unprincipled entrepreneurs and "parachuting communist" opportunists—while punishing hard-working and law-abiding "normal" citizens. Its power came in part from how it was aligned with the socialist-era discourse that pitted a morally inclusive "us" against the "them" of party bureaucrats and elites of the unitary state (Ries 1997:19). But its crude dichotomization of society vastly oversimplified much more complex distributions of tragedy and fortune; it also obscured how people tried to evaluate the sudden poverty and prosperity of others and manage their relationships with friends and family as their economic circumstances diverged. One enduring principle, however, that had been promoted and transformed during socialist times was to evaluate people according to their associated materialities, or their "standards" (*igények*). Thus Hungarians continued to attend closely to the qualities of goods and to equate certain materialities with human value and dignity as they were connected to wider sociopolitical and economic systems.

Existential Insecurities

The first decade of the system change was experienced as a cataclysm that destabilized conventional understandings of how things worked, what one needed to do to prosper in the world, and who would benefit from the new order (cf. Patico 2008). State socialist rule had also been plagued with uncertainties generated by an unpredictable and often punitive bureaucratic state, and the 1980s had introduced greater economic insecurity and new social stratifications. But the uncertainties of the 1990s were of a different order. Existential insecurities rapidly replaced an initial euphoria.[1]

Instead of ushering in Western-style economic prosperity, the system change intensified economic insecurities. Hungary's unique experience with limited decentralization and entrepreneurship certainly helped it become the highest recipient of foreign investment in the region by the mid-1990s, but its entry into a globalizing market was beset by the structural disadvantages shared by many of the former Soviet satellites. Because it had been deeply interdependent with the official state-run sector, the second economy failed to provide the cushion of an established, privatized sector that experts had predicted. In the 1990s, state-owned and cooperative assets still made up 75 to 80 percent of the economy's working capital; citizens still enjoyed employment securities, if not the guarantees they'd once had; and a wide range of social security benefits were still in place. Since a majority of trade had been channeled through COMECON, the economy was devastated by its collapse. It was further undermined by a crippling foreign debt, crisis in the privatizing state sector, and the general economic disarray created by the collapse of the state-led economy and a laissez-faire approach to introducing market mechanisms.

In retrospect, the particular moment of my fieldwork marked a nadir in the Hungarian postsocialist economy and in a collective sense of well-being. After four bitter years of life in an "emerging democracy," Hungarian voters in 1994 had rejected the incumbent nationalist party (MDF) and brought back to power, this time through free elections, the Hungarian Socialist Party (MSZP). The reformed Socialists had campaigned on an image of experienced leadership and promoted the perception that they would slow the progress of economic reform and restore social benefits. Instead, with the guidance of its neoliberal coalition partner, the Free Democrats (SZDSZ), the Socialist Party implemented "shock therapy" reforms under pressure from the IMF and European Union to reduce Hungary's foreign debt and slash expenditures. Called the Bokros Package, after the finance minister, these reforms included austerity measures that devalued the currency, levied temporary extra duties on imports, and instituted steep price hikes (up to 60 percent). These austerity policies were experienced as a betrayal not just of the working classes, but of all those people who had once been part of a socialist middle strata and expected to constitute the new middle classes. Four years later, in 1998, the socialists were replaced by a party touting both its national and its "civic" credentials, the party of the Young Democrats (FIDESZ) who began calling themselves "the Hungarian *Polgár* Party."

One of the most painful and unanticipated effects of the regime change was to erode or eliminate many of the benefits of living in a socialist state that had come to be regarded as rights. State subsidies for food, shelter, heat, child care, transportation, health care, sports, education, films, books, and cultural life had once been extended to the entire population (in theory) as basic amenities necessary for a modern, civilized populace and for the common good. Thus, with the withdrawal of state subsidies, not only had everything become more expensive, but more things had to be paid for out of fixed incomes.

Rising food prices quickly took their toll on how often people could socialize with friends, as they could no longer afford to uphold norms of generosity in hosting. The shock of having to pay for utilities—sometimes a high percentage of a monthly wage—transformed the experience of the home as a physical space. People had to learn to conserve electricity and heat in their own apartments, adjusting themselves to the cold in spaces that had often been overheated in the past. Instead of the abundance many had expected of democracy and capitalism, these new and visceral deprivations were felt even by those who were relatively well off.

The landscape was also being fragmented by the emergence of privatized venues alongside those the state had once provided for a modern, socialist citizenry. This process was exacerbated by the erosion of quality of public spaces, facilities, and services with the loss of state subsidies. In Dunaújváros, people talked about how parks and flower beds used to be so well-tended and how buses had run on time. The public workout gym at the Workers Cultural Center had been converted to a boutique gym for pay. The Olympic-size pool remained, but it had considerably raised its entry prices. While those better off were attracted to new private facilities and services, others were being priced out of once fairly well-maintained swimming pools, public transportation, and medical facilities. As with neoliberal reforms elsewhere in the world, public services were becoming aligned with an underclass (Guano 2002).

Dramatic evidence of a rapidly shifting social structure combined with general upheaval heightened anxiety over the long-term consequences of present action or inaction. Should one buy one's privatizing apartment? Quit one's job to join a friend in a new venture? Sell or keep compensation coupons (see below)? Without a sense of continuity with the past, people voiced their uncertainty over where actions taken today would lead tomorrow.

How long this "moment" was to last and how long it would take before conditions became stable (or, alternatively, ossified) was far from clear. This dilemma was particularly difficult in a milieu where indecision and the inability to act decisively, especially for men, was considered a weakness of character. Some managed to avoid the humility of seeking financial advice from family or friends by turning to popular genres of prognostication like horoscopes—indeed, horoscopes in the 1990s offered far more advice on financial matters than on romance (Fehérváry 2007). Others became vulnerable to various forms of fraud, like pyramid schemes, that preyed on their pre-1989 utopian expectations of a market economy (Verdery 1996). More and more people turned to the plethora of emerging religious, spiritual, and alternative health venues, from the Mormon Church to tarot and iris reading.

Anxiety over economic decisions was conjoined with those of status, a predicament that sociologist Iván Szelényi called "status anxiety." In this "attempt to find one's place in the new, capitalist system of inequality, the stakes are nothing less than that the position acquired *now* will determine their family's fate in the future" (Szelényi, cited in Dessewffy 1998).[2] Károly, a reluctant workshop owner, voiced these concerns somewhat dramatically: "People sense that this moment will decide who will be not rich and poor, but slaves on one hand and slave-owners on the other."

People reacted to these unstable conditions in very different ways. For Géza, an engineer in his late forties, the regime change presented opportunities in the factory that were a continuation of the hybrid private-state (KGST) engineering work he had done in the 1980s. An outgoing, energetic person, he envisioned himself freed of restrictions that had constrained him in the past, and he persisted in the face of numerous setbacks to gain control over his area of a small, newly privatized firm subcontracting to the steel mill. But the regime change overwhelmed his wife Margit, who was a lawyer. When the company she worked for was privatized, she was forced to resign after refusing to comply with what she felt were unethical requests by a superior. As a lawyer, she could have started her own practice, but as she and Géza often repeated, she wasn't by nature an entrepreneur or "the type of person to go after clients." She was immediately rehired as a prosecutor in a neighboring city, but still continued a rigorous schedule of further education for job security, and—like so many others in the country—she collected Coca-Cola bottle caps in the hopes of winning its sweepstakes. As she explained to me one day (while checking under her bottle top): "It never occurred to me before that one day I might starve, or lose the roof above my head." While capitalism brought with it new opportunities, the institution of private property had not created a closer relationship between people and objects, but had introduced the possibility of losing everything (Miller 1987:75, after Simmel 1978:304).

Making Private Property and Property Owners

At the time of the system change, there was never any question that the main means of restoring Hungary to an independent, democratic, and capitalist nation-state would be the restoration of private property. The moral correctness of private property, however, was also linked to the restoration of the country as a Christian nation-state. A front-page editorial in the Dunaújváros newspaper in 1997, decrying the rise of petty theft and apartment break-ins, invoked the name of Hungary's patron saint, proclaiming, "St. Stephen made Christianity the law of the land, but also sanctified the law of property" (*Dunaújvárosi Hírlap*, Aug. 25, 1997). The morality inhering in private property was explained to me one day by an elderly leader of the village of Pentele. "Property is necessary to be moral," György Nagy said as we sat on the veranda of his comfortable peasant house drinking homemade apricot nectar, with the smells of pigs, dogs, and flowers gently alternating around us. Though he had been the head of the collective farm for many years, he condemned collective ownership in the terms widely attributed to Soviet party secretary Gorbachev, namely that "collective property is no one's property." Nagy pointed out to me a multistory house down the street that had been built with separate apartments by an extended family in the 1970s and was now in a state of disrepair. Because no single family possessed it, no one felt the sting of shame for its appearance, nor did they feel that investment in the building would stay with their family unit. Collective ownership, even within one extended family, he insisted, confused the representational purpose and thus "ownership" of the building's maintenance. Spaces said to be "for everyone" were claimed by no one.

For the new state, however, re-establishing capitalist private property (and with it the propertied classes) was not a straightforward matter. This was in part because of the hybrid forms of property that had arisen during the Kádár era and in part because of the difficulty of finding legitimate "owners" to whom to assign state property (Hann 1990:100). A logical first step in atoning for the sins of the communist regime seemed to be to compensate former owners (or their descendants) for property that an illegitimate socialist state had confiscated over four decades or to restore property to its "rightful owners." But just as elsewhere in the former Soviet bloc, compensation schemes managed to anger more of the population than they succeeded in appeasing. Those compensated were often bitter for the meager amount they were awarded, but they were also unhappy with badly run auctions and the inequities and corruption in the distribution process (see also Altshuler 2001; Chelcea 2001; Verdery 2003). The women working at the understaffed Land Registry office, responsible for validating compensation claims, understood these complaints. They saw the injustice of basing compensation solely on property violations and failing to recognize other forms of "loss" suffered for more than forty years. A local sociologist explained to me that professionals had worked for suppressed salaries their entire lives, salaries justified by state subsidies for everything from utilities to vacation packages and guaranteed pensions. In the new era, their meager pensions had not been adjusted to compensate for the loss of those subsidies. As the engineering draftsman János Balatoni quipped, "We worked for low salaries because we were building the country for ourselves. Now, the new regime is selling off the people's property but we aren't seeing a forint of it!" Here he repurposed the much-ridiculed slogan of the Stalin era, "The country is yours! You are building it for yourselves!" to underscore how a population whose lives had been dictated by the socialist system were now being disenfranchised by a capitalist one.

For the new Hungarian government, selling off or privatizing larger, state-owned concerns for which there was no presocialist "rightful owner" was a different kind of problem—especially if any of these assets were to remain in Hungarian hands rather than be sold off to foreign companies. Since socialist citizens had been severely restricted in the amount of capital they could amass, few had enough capital to proffer even a down payment. The instability of financial institutions was a further obstacle, preventing the new regime from doing much more than rapidly divesting itself of state-owned property. But property that had been built up by the socialist state also needed property owners. Some of the larger state firms were privatized by passing out company shares to employees, though usually their stake was so small they had little negotiating power. Thus the state and lending institutions came up with other novel ways of creating private owners without economic capital.

Former party bureaucrats or managers of state firms enjoyed considerable advantages in this privatization process, particularly those who had been involved in business dealings with the West or who could use their existing connections to the state financial sector to borrow the capital they needed (Róna-Tas 1997:215–17) (but see Szelényi et al. 1998:120–21). Derogatively referred to as "parachuting communists" or "pink entrepreneurs," these former party members had the connections in place to position them ideally as managers and directors of the new company, this time also as shareholders. Since they had no property of their own, they used the company itself as collateral for the loan. While this is common practice in capitalist countries like the United States, to many Hungarians it appeared to be yet another "not normal" aspect of the transition made possible by the former communist system. Moreover, these former elites were themselves the experts who helped to determine what the company was worth in the first place, vastly under- or overestimating the company's value depending on their goals. Much of what remained was transferred to local governing councils as part of a larger project of radically decentralizing government.[3]

The ideologically loaded task of privatizing state-owned housing usually fell to local governments. In the absence of any established system of mortgage lending, they instigated various schemes by which residents could buy their apartments. In the early 1990s, people still living in state-owned apartments rushed to buy them, usually according to the terms of a 1969 privatization decree by which renters could become owners by paying monthly installments that were so low they barely covered maintenance on the building.[4] In Dunaújváros, where the state still owned a relatively high percentage of housing compared to other cities (in 1986, it administered almost half of the 22,000 dwellings in the city), only 1,853 apartments were left in city-council ownership by 1995. Even urban professionals like Margít and Géza, who had lived in state-owned apartments for their entire lives, suddenly felt the pressure to gather their savings, borrow from friends and relatives, and sell off family heirlooms to raise the capital for a down payment. In Western media accounts of privatization, this behavior was presented as a natural response to the opportunity to become property owners (they neglected to mention that this opportunity had been available for many people since 1969). A more accurate accounting would be that policy changes between 1989 and 1991, combined with perceptions of a life to come under a Western, capitalist order, created persuasive incentives for people to become the full owners of apartments they had considered as "theirs" under the state socialist system.[5]

The privatization of apartments in buildings created unwieldy ownership structures and new sources of conflict for residents living within them. Most state-constructed housing operated under cooperative or condominium forms of ownership and were occupied by both owners and renters. Instead of housing a group of people who had all agreed in advance to the conditions under which they would own part of a property, newly privatized buildings combined people of diverse economic and social circumstances, with equally divergent attitudes toward joint maintenance expenses.[6] Especially in the poorly insulated panel buildings, the skyrocketing cost of utilities complicated already strained relationships among residents. Most buildings had only a central meter for water and heat for the entire building, making it impossible to identify the culprit for a high bill. Stories abounded of residents of largely privatized buildings trying to force out the few remaining residents still in state-owned apartments, who were often behind on house payments. Some of these housing collectives, whose buildings were preferentially located, were able to generate revenue for building repairs and maintenance by renting out ground-floor space to shops—like those on Boutique Row—or by selling advertising space on the roof or firewalls. Others, however, were forced to rely entirely on fees extracted from already strapped residents, with the result that many buildings fell into disrepair.[7]

When the "one family, one house" restriction was abandoned in 1989, it created in one stroke the conditions for a real estate market, allowing for new possibilities for commodifying the home. The privately owned home was also placed in the new realm of potential investment, since the owner could resell or rent at market prices immediately after purchase. Privately owned apartments could also be used for collateral against small loans. At the property records office, a young clerk named Gita said that more and more people were coming in for their "property ownership" papers, so they could leverage their apartment against debts. She noted that this had once been a cause for profound shame but was now becoming commonplace. This practice increased the alienability and insecurity of the home as property.

Despite its new fungibility, "real estate" was still by far the most popular form of saving across the country (*Népszabadság*, June 6, 1996). While a detached family house with garden was becoming the preferred investment, buying one's apartment was also seen as a way to regain the security once provided by state rentals (*Ingatlanpiac*, May 28, 1996). Almost everyone who was able to raise the funds did so. While many intellectuals and urban professionals began to bank their savings and invest in "value paper" (*értékpapír*, or stocks and bonds), most others continued to keep their savings in cash at home or sank them into the materiality of the home itself. In this era of economic insecurity, storing one's wealth in articles of substance seemed far less risky than investing in new stocks. An architect, for example, showed me her savings bonds, printed out on flimsy computer paper. "I'm cashing them in to buy something solid," she said, gripping the wooden arms of her chair for emphasis. Commercial advertisements for the durability and quality of construction materials recycled a phrase associated with people who had thrown themselves into the project of building a house: "If once you build . . ." ("*Ha már egyszer építkezik . . .*"). The concluding part of the phrase is left unspoken: one "builds to last" (Plate 7b). As in many parts of the world, family property became central to the project of transcending the insecurities of the new order (Miller 1994:133–44; Shevchenko 2009:89).

Contingent Fortunes and Shady Commerce

The compensation system reinforced widespread sentiment that system change had arbitrarily produced winners and losers. Although the ability of the former *nomenklatura* to maintain their elite standing was exaggerated (Szelényi et al. 1998:120), many people were dismayed to see that former Communist Party elites were positioned favorably in the "exit to capitalism" rather than being ousted along with the political system they had served. Much good fortune also seemed to be based on contingency. Compensation coupons were awarded to those whose families had lost property forty years before or to employees of state firms worthy of privatization, but not to others, like the university sociologist. Some people entered the 1990s with marketable skills, such as knowledge of English or computer programming, while others, from Russian teachers to secretaries with no computer skills, were quickly let go. Professionals in their twenties and early thirties had the best chances for employment with multinational corporations; those in their forties and fifties were considered dispensable, too steeped in "Communist" methods and mentalities to "retrain."[8] And yet even such people were better off than most pensioners and unskilled workers, a group in which Roma were overrepresented, who were most affected by privatization of state companies. These groups were considered the disorderly poor and were blamed for their predicament.[9]

In a society where people had been limited in the amount of capital they could acquire and where financial practices like stock market trading or vague occupations such as "consulting" were unknown, sudden prosperity was viewed with suspicion. A general dismay with and distrust of rapid accumulation of wealth that had no visible origin in hard work or material production, along with a long-standing rural hostility toward involvement in trade, were common throughout the region.[10] The furor made over the new villa of the Socialist Party prime minister at the time, Gyula Horn, illustrates the point. Because of his very public career as a politician both before and after 1989, which never commanded a particularly high salary, people saw the house as both proof of graft and a symbolic refutation of the ideology he had once stood for.

Occupations and identities having to do with commerce had never been highly regarded in presocialist Hungary, and communist ideology had attempted to reinforce such suspicions. In the hostile economic climate of the 1990s, people assumed that those doing well must be breaking the rules: cheating on taxes beyond what would be acceptable, committing fraud in the privatization process, taking advantage of the many loopholes (*kis kapuk*) created by the upheaval in the legal system, exploiting workers, and even having ties to organized crime. At the same time, it was widely acknowledged that the state's lack of support for small businesses and taxation policies meant that, to survive, even legitimate businesses were forced to engage in shady activities (see also Bodnár 1998:503). As many men were fond of saying, "In this world, it's impossible to be honest and survive."

Evaluating Wealth

No longer subject to censorship, attempts to identify emerging capitalist classes became a national pastime in the 1990s. Social scientists researched consumption habits, income distribution, civic consciousness, and activities. Business-oriented newspaper articles and seminars anxiously attempted to identify the new "heroes of enterprise"—entrepreneurs, bankers, financiers—who might provide "role models for the restructuring of the economy" (Marosán 1994:72). While the composition of a new middle class was of widespread concern (as I discuss later in this chapter), new elites were also singled out by social scientists who hoped to understand the magnitude of social change and the types of people who defined success in the emerging postsocialist world.[11] Media representations that dealt with transforming social hierarchies and displayed images of dramatic new material worlds were touchstones in this time of economic, social, and political upheaval.

In Dunaújváros, legitimate means of accruing wealth and appropriate behavior for those who prospered were topics of constant discussion. In these discussions, people gained information, tried out new positions for the sake of argument, and in the process re-evaluated their opinions. As elsewhere in the country, the new elite were the subject of intense scrutiny by the rest of the population. People regularly referred with resentment to "the upper 10,000," or the population of new super-elites (the top one-tenth of one percent in a country of ten million). In a revealing television program, a handful of wealthy Hungarians were interviewed in the search for a positive model for elite behavior (MTV2, April 18, 1997). Featured were an entrepreneur, a banker, a young CEO, and an opera singer. All but the opera singer justified their occupations in a market economy to Hungarians who objected to them, but they then went on to talk about the need for a propertied stratum with business morals, civic consciousness, and restraint in conspicuous consumption. The show used characters from the TV show *Dallas*, which aired for the first time in Hungary in 1990, to provide negative models of "new rich in track suits," who dressed with an informality inappropriate to a moneyed elite.[12] It then turned to examples of Hungarian nobility and moneyed aristocracy as models who—unlike contemporary Hungarians—had grown up with wealth. These included the American Hungarian heir to the Zwack liquor empire; the Hungarian-speaking octogenarian heir to the Habsburg monarchy, Otto; and a historic figure, the Hungarian aristocrat Count István Bethlen, who had lived a "restrained" lifestyle. The interviews indexed the wealth of the individuals profiled through shots of their material worlds: marble-columned bank corridors, the gilded opera hall, luxury apartments, and cars (MTV2, April 18, 1997).

The city's intelligentsia and professional classes predictably chastised the new rich (*újgazdag*) for their lack of taste, attempting to police the boundaries and social codes legitimating their own social prestige. The cultural center's former director, Irén, disparaged the newly wealthy businessmen and factory directors, the ones who wore "track suits" to her training sessions on how to behave at buffet luncheons. Houses with even a minor extravagance like a fountain or goldfish pond might provoke the observation, "They have money, but lack sense!" Such remarks invoked European bourgeois values, reinforced during state socialism, whereby disposable income should be spent on cultivating the self through books, travel, and high culture rather than on superficial exteriors. I became used to hearing people in Dunaújváros make sweeping generalizations about the illegitimate occupations of people they saw driving fancy cars, sporting the latest cell phone, or flashing a designer watch: "They're all crooks and thieves." Although many such accusations were unsubstantiated, when people said "Mafia! Drug dealers!" they were referring to a known underworld presence.

At the same time, there was more ambiguity about new displays of wealth than there was in Russia at the time. There, the *nouveau riche* were called "New Russians" as "an epithet of difference . . . people somehow alien from the unmarked, 'ordinary' Russian crowd," and who did not lay much store by Soviet principles, such as "the value of honest labor, of supporting the *kollektiv*, of respect for the working masses, of high-minded personal frugality, and above all, the production of goods for the benefit of society as a whole" (Humphrey 1997:86–87). In Hungary, there were no "New Hungarians," as variations of such a lifestyle were considered normal for a legitimate middle class in the context of a European nation-state.

In Dunaújváros, with its working-class base, more flamboyant styles were also associated with over-the-top celebrity culture, one in which entertainment, money, and fame combined to overwhelm traditional notions of class and legitimacy. Moreover, though residents often spoke in derogatory tones about a particular rich person and some moral compromise that person had made to come by wealth, they were quick to add, "But I wouldn't turn it down if it was offered to me!" Such caveats were common as people of all ages qualified their anger at new income discrepancies and marked their distance from socialist ideologies of egalitarianism (see also Rivkin-Fish 2009 for Russia).

Occupations dealing with business and money matters were also gaining in prestige and legitimacy. English terms such as *biznisz* (business) and *menedzser* (manager) had been taken up and transcribed into Hungarian. For a younger generation, getting a job with a corporation that would put a "car under your rear end," especially a multinational corporation—even as an ornamental (*dekoratív*) receptionist—was considered a coup. The relatively new category of "entrepreneur" (*vállalkozó*) or "businessman" (*biznisze mber*) also had an ambiguous status in this re-evaluation of private wealth. For younger generations, it often held the glamour of the new, Western-style, postsocialist world, with the allure of autonomy and promise of material prosperity combined with the thrill of risk and danger, especially as an occupation for men (see Pine 2012). The signs that some entrepreneurs had underworld connections seemed to be part of the appeal, embodied in the new breed of aggressive young men with closely cropped hair, driving expensive cars. Indeed, a certain kind of criminality could even be heroic, especially if it undermined the authority of despised banking institutions and a corrupt police (Nadkarni 2000). For others, entrepreneurs were "cultural heroes," new model citizens of a capitalist nation-state (Vörös 1998). The label was further complicated by the vast differences among types of people involved in private business, the scale of their enterprises, and the transparency of their accumulation. A former local handball star I had known as a teenager had become a recruiter for a mafia trafficking in exotic dancers sent to the West, and he drove around town in his white Mercedes with German plates. A mother-and-daughter business, meanwhile, went bankrupt selling crocheted sweaters from a kiosk. Both, however, understood themselves as entrepreneurs.

Throughout the socialist period, official rhetoric had denounced landlords, property owners, and capitalists as equally guilty of exploitation, but such connotations were shifting as these categories were repopulated. Erzsi had been granted a tiny quantity of shares when the engineering company she worked for was privatized. Instead of selling them off (for a pittance) as most of her colleagues had done, she'd held onto them. It was her way of offsetting her increasingly marginalized and impoverished status in the postsocialist order and connecting, however tenuously, to her parents' former *polgár* status. As she mischievously joked one day after a shareholder meeting: "It's a good feeling being a stockholder!" (*részvénytulajdonos*). Károly, in contrast, frequently lamented his new status as a "property owner." He had reluctantly assumed 50 percent ownership of a privatizing window and door-making workshop in exchange for managing it—and thereby keeping his job. But he was being eaten up by the stress involved. He'd had to take on personal debts to finance its development, including mortgaging his family's beloved summer cottage at Lake Balaton, and he was worried about losing it. By referring to himself as a property owner, he sarcastically referenced categories such as "capitalist" or "factory owner," fully aware of their former pejorative meanings but also aware that people now assumed them to come with power and privilege—and so vastly misunderstood his situation.

Passing through the town, acquaintances would draw my attention to the brightly painted new houses with their red-tiled roofs scattered among the older buildings in Pentele or the district of houses self-built during socialism. Most people classified the visibly prosperous as either members of the former political or technocratic elite or as entrepreneurs of various types and legalities. They could point out the house of the factory finance manager, the house of the factory production director, and the house of the local "Carpet King," but they rarely made blanket condemnations of the vast income disparities these homes symbolized. Instead, they focused on the means by which the wealth had been generated and the mode by which the personhood of the owners had been transformed. With the exception of the well-liked mayor, sometimes criticized for his new Audi, there was significant overlap between local politicians, entrepreneurs, and former communist factory directors.

People in Dunaújváros often insisted that nothing had changed since 1990 except that the factory elite used to be "communists" but now they were "capitalists." An elderly man I met at the bus stop identified himself as a *"proli őslakó,"* meaning an industrial worker who had come to build the city in the 1950s. He had been able to move his family into an urban apartment ten years after he'd arrived, and eventually had a garden plot in a nearby village, signs that he had achieved the middle strata standard of living. "Nothing has changed," he said, noting that the proletariat always got screwed by higher-ups.

This man was referring specifically to the continuities of management in the steel factory. Calling themselves "Steel XXI" (*Acél XXI Kft.*), a group of twenty-one former Communist Party officials and factory directors formed a management group that maneuvered its way into an official contract with the state—at that point run by the reform Socialist Party allied with the neoliberal Free Democrats—to run the company as pseudo-CEOs for a number of years and collecting formidable "success fees" (*sikerdíj*) for their efforts. Feelings were mixed about this development. On the one hand, indigenous direction was preferable to foreign takeover, which could have resulted in massive layoffs. Steel 21, while profiting handsomely by their deal, nonetheless continued to reinvest company profits and attempted to transform the factory into a viable postcommunist enterprise. On the other hand, general long-standing resentment of a well-paid managerial class that didn't seem to do any of the real work carried over to these directors and was exacerbated by the behavior of some of its members.

The factory directors were vilified as cheaters in the new capitalist game, prospering without risk to themselves but by their access to state (and therefore ostensibly "public") capital and connections. They were also seen to have opportunistically betrayed the ethics of the system they had once served. But the resentment they provoked came as much from their transformations in lifestyle and bearing as from their business practices. One director nicknamed Johnny (Dzsony) was well-known in town for his extramarital dalliances and also because his lavish house in Pentele was reportedly packed with Western goods, including groceries. The problem was not the Western provenance of the goods themselves, but the lack of discrimination among them and the naked display of status, since everyone knew that equally good if not better foodstuffs could be found in Hungary for a fraction of the price. Another director provoked ire not because he was using factory workers to build his new villa—a holdover practice from state socialism—but because his wife wouldn't let the workers use the bathroom. Differences in status hierarchy and even their expression in higher material standards of living were acceptable. What was shocking was the crass and explicit way in which workers were no longer being treated as human equals.

One day, I was driven past the row of factory directors' houses in Pentele by a man who had been a skilled worker in the factory for more than thirty years. When I had first met him and his family, they had driven me by this section of town to show me a "normal" neighborhood, one that they presumed compared favorably to what I knew in the United States. But this time around, he focused on the larger social shifts epitomized by these new residences: "For years we were all called 'comrade,'" he said, gesturing at eye level to emphasize egalitarian, face-to-face relations. "Now those guys sit in their offices, and when you go to see them, they shake their finger: 'No more 'comrade.' I am now 'Sir' to you!" A retired factory foreman named Gábor also expressed bitterness at emerging hierarchies and their expression in income disparities. He also had favored the greater egalitarianism of the workplace, and he now framed it as wise business practice; listening to the men on the factory floor helped him decide what had to be done. "I always talked to people using the [informal] *tegezés* form," he said, "even if they were uncomfortable reciprocating. My door was always open. . . . In the 1950s and 1960s, the salary ratio of director to worker was three to one, then gradually rose to about twenty to one, but now it is more like fifty to one."[13] He echoed the sentiments of several other men I'd spoken to who had worked in higher positions in the city and the steel factory: "Of course I think directors should make more money than workers, but they must deserve it!" The income differences of the socialist period, he suggested, were reasonable given differences in skill and responsibility, but signs of mutual respect affirmed the underlying equality between managers and workers as people. The sheer scale of capitalist income discrepancies was distorting this principle.

In contrast to the directors, who were widely seen as a cabal, most people I met considered Sulák, the "Carpet King," to have made it big through shrewd but legal business tactics and saw him as an example of a real capitalist, a self-made millionaire. At first, friends gave embarrassed laughs as we passed by his large, lemon yellow house, saying "Oh Sulák, *sumák*" (meaning "shyster"). Positioned conspicuously at the foot of the hill leading up to the town center, the house had few windows but featured a large garage door made of reinforced metal and a high wall surrounding the property. Sulák and his house represented the new rich in the classic sense, someone uneducated and, according to the journalist Marta, who had once interviewed him, quite crude. However, I was often corrected if I mentioned Sulák as an example of a new category of morally suspect entrepreneur. A working-class couple who had risen to good positions in the factory explained that Sulák was a "true capitalist" (*igazi kapitalista*). "There are very few of these in Hungary, who worked hard for their wealth," they said. "Of course he probably cheats on his taxes and has stolen, but he didn't injure people with it and he didn't use up a large company's fortune." A woman of gentry background agreed: Sulák, she claimed, was a smart guy who saw the writing on the wall in the late 1980s and got rich through clever business practices. "He is respectable," she said, "because people can see how he makes his money, saw him grow not overnight but gradually." Sulák with all his money remained a local yokel. If he was a bit of a laughingstock, he was not pretending to be someone he was not.

Few people in town openly claimed to come from noble (*úri*) or gentry (*dzsentry*) stock in Dunaújváros. An exception was one of the town's first real estate agents and a local politician for the socially progressive but neoliberal party, the

Free Democrats. He described himself at our first meeting through reference to his noble lineage—along with his astrological sign—while sitting in his family house in the Garden City district, one he had bought finished and was in the process of renovating. Busy making a fortune with several local pharmacies, this man attempted to distinguish himself from the ranks of the new rich by fashioning himself as a patron of the arts and champion of the disenfranchised. At the same time, he talked openly of using his connections to have the road in front of his house paved.

Postsocialist Status: Joining the New Middle Classes or Escaping the Stigma of the Proletariat?

While politicians and journalists were debating the characteristics of a new, bourgeois middle class, the dynamics of social status in everyday life were highly unstable. Discussions and representations of a new middle class were important, but people experienced the public arena in the 1990s as fraught with antagonistic status positioning, a positioning that was structured by opposition to a stigmatized proletariat and Socialist Generic materialities. So while people often aligned themselves with the moral high ground of the new regime's losers or created a solidarity of suffering in their interpersonal interactions, they also struggled to mark themselves as successful participants in a transforming society.[14]

As in the past, personal appearance and material order signaled moral character and respectability, but people were adjusting to the rapid influx of new materialities in a time of significant shifts in the social, political, and economic contexts in which such materialities obtained their meaning (Sampson 1994:11). The equation between a person's self-respect and his or her exacting standards (*igény*) for material appearance and belongings was an easy fit with capitalist commercial logics—indeed, one that capitalism was much more likely to satisfy.

Marta, the Dunaújváros reporter introduced in chapter 1, was ashamed because her salary didn't allow her to dress or travel in a "normal" manner, one that would be *reprezentatív* or indicative of the status accorded to her profession. She worried that people whispered that she was *igénytelen,* or lax and even lazy in caring for her materialities—though she ran every day to keep her weight down, made sure her daughter practiced the piano, and scrubbed the kitchen floor every night. She even toyed with the notion of working as a high-class prostitute on the side since it would at least, or so she had heard, provide her with the income she needed to restore her dignity. She was, by her own admission, obsessively jealous of a fat woman who pulled up to the grocery store by her apartment every weekend in a car, loaded up the trunk, and drove off to her husband and their family house in the countryside.

Certain qualities only possible through consumption were particularly effective at communicating postsocialist success in Dunaújváros, such as driving a car not made in the former Soviet sphere or sporting the orange-tinged glow that came from visiting a tanning salon. In the 1990s, Eastern Europeans rapidly outpaced the Euro-American West in cell phone purchases and use. A new cell phone was a device that both symbolized and made possible participation in a capitalist, European present. Even in the late socialist period, the landline telephone had remained a scarce good and a considerable sign of prestige. But in the 1990s, the cell phone's cutting-edge technology, absolutely coeval with Western European technology, and the public evidence it provided of one's membership in a network of cell phone owners, catapulted it to the apex of goods signaling belonging in a new order. A friend from a well-known theater family had plenty of cultural capital but very little money in those days. The cell phone he only half-jokingly displayed when we went out for coffee looked real and could ring if he pushed a button, but that was the limit of its technological reach.

People were acutely conscious of the growing power of such status symbols to inspire respectful treatment for no other reason than that they communicated wealth or connection to well-being. A common lament was "Now, only money matters." It referred to the way money had displaced older, less visible markers of status, such as cultured speech and bearing or educational attainment. It also indexed the loss of other forms of reciprocity, such as those required by the second economy and their reduction to the calculus of money. Older generations despaired at the erosion of respect for the elderly. One Saturday, I went on a drive with Ildikó (Ildi), an economist in her mid-thirties who worked as an assistant director at the steel mill, and her seven-year-old son, András. At about 1 PM, we stopped by a restaurant in an old castle ruin for lunch. The waitress claimed that she couldn't bring us anything at all for an hour, since they were serving a wedding party upstairs. Ildi stormed out, convinced that if she'd had her cell phone out or if we'd spoken English, they would have been able to produce at least a sandwich. "They saw two women and a kid," she said, "and that was that. I hate this Hungarian snobbism!" In the next locale, she had her phone out on the table, and we were served without incident.

Stories circulated of respectable persons who had not (or could not) adapt to this new alignment of material signs and status, and who had been treated in ways unthinkable during socialism. A sociologist in Budapest related how one day he was stuck in traffic in his beat-up Skoda (the Czechoslovakian car), late for a meeting, and a mafioso-looking guy with a shaved head jumped out of the large imported car behind him and started yelling in a fury, "You stupid *peasant (Te bunkó paraszt)*! If you don't get out of the way I'll blow your head off!" As this episode makes clear, as much as folk culture had been romanticized, the term *"paraszt"* or peasant was still often used as an epithet to index rural backwardness. The Dunaújváros city planner, for example, called elderly city dwellers "peasants" under her breath because they had no interest in giving up their garden plots to make way for family houses. The label was becoming equated with outdated socialist commodities and ignorance of postsocialist status markers.

The stakes for aligning oneself as a participant in a postsocialist order were heightened by the frightening fate of the proletariat and its alignment with a failed socialism. The urban proletariat, derogatively referred to as *proli*, had become almost the lowest stratum of society, barely above the new category of homeless *(hajléktalan)*.[15] The proletariat had been so compromised by its association with communism that in Hungary's first "free" democratic elections (1990), not a single party on the ballot aligned itself with the country's sizable working-class population. As the director of a film about urban youth, Gabor Dettre, noted, "During communism there was some dignity in coming from the lower classes. But after communism everything was taken from these families. After 1989, Hungary tried to become what it used to be—a nation of gentry. The working classes really started to feel deprived" (Nadler 1995). When the Socialist Party enjoyed a comeback in 1994, they capitalized on the mistaken perception that they would restore social benefits. But this did not ameliorate the proletariat's position in Hungarian social life. Referring to the Socialist's landslide victory, an older, returned émigré lamented that "the people are stupid . . . proletarianized by communism."

The bodies of those considered *proli* became isomorphic with their related materialities, arousing the visceral disgust being generated by the shabby materials and sterile environments of Socialist Generic. Cigarette-smoking, malnourished, prematurely aged people who swept the streets were called *"proli."* But this was also what Anikó, a young woman with *polgári* pretensions, called a young couple in jean jackets on a Saturday morning at the farmer's market, whose baby had spit out its pacifier: "Look at those *proli*, they'll probably pick it off the ground and put it back in his mouth!" *Proli* were white Hungarians who were considered to be uneducated, dirty, and unable to maintain themselves in an orderly way. This maligned category overlapped with but was distinct from the racial/ethnic category of "gypsy" *(cigány)* or Roma. Both were stigmatized by their failure to live up to mainstream norms for their material appearance and environments, lacking a sense of *rend* or orderliness and having inadequate standards *(igénytelen)* for these materialities—a clear sign, it was assumed, of an insufficient work ethic.

The negative associations "respectable" Hungarians made with the proletariat were compounded by the awareness that the West had stereotyped socialist citizens as a working class aligned with shabby material goods. This phenomenon was particularly apparent in the reunited Germany in the manner in which West Germans (Wessies) described their eastern counterparts (Ossies). Daphne Berdahl captured such evaluations in her ethnography carried out in the early 1990s (Berdahl 1999:167). "Ossies could be identified by their pale faces, oily hair, poor dental work, washed-out formless jeans, generic gray shoes, and acrylic shopping bags. They smelled of body odor, cheap perfume, or [as one Wessi informed her], 'that peculiar disinfectant.'"[16] Here, human bodies become inscribed with the material qualities of an abnormal modernism, of sterile bodies whose bad teeth are the ultimate indexes of poverty and decay. Their value as workers and as bodily substances has become aligned with inert, mass-produced, generic commodities made out of artificial instead of authentic, living, "natural" materials. Thus the qualities of the goods become reciprocally aligned with the value of the labor that made them. No longer blamed upon an oppressive state that dominated workers, the shoddy quality of state socialist commodities was equated with the quality of a socialist working class and their inherently "undemanding" *(igénytelen)* nature. Kata, the owner of the cosmetics salon with purple ceiling beams, said, "I can't blame the European Union for not letting us in: Hungary's huge *proli* stratum drags down the country." At the same time, a local commissioner defended Dunaújváros to me in an interview, lauding the high standards Hungarians in general had for their material environments compared to what he had seen of the United States on television—of inner cities and underpasses full of graffiti and garbage, clear signs of an *igénytelen* people.

Occasionally, someone would mourn the devaluing of the working classes or would refer to them positively using the term "working class" *(munkásosztály)*. In Dunaújváros, some people used proli as a way to critique the new market society: "Socialism was good for *proli* kids," Ildikó's husband Tamás reminded me. "They all got to go on vacation to Balaton—not just the rich kids." Not surprisingly, such comments came almost exclusively from people who were from the lower classes and had prospered during socialism.

Family, Friends, and Diverging Fortunes

Status conflicts in an anonymous public sphere were unsettling, but perhaps more so were the seismic shifts in long-standing relationships with acquaintances, friends, and even family wrought by diverging fortunes. In the fall of 1997, I joined a team doing surveys on the city put together by the local technical college's sociology department, and I was able to explore five different city districts and conduct interviews with people living in them. One day I accompanied Ágnes, a local insurance agent in her forties who was making extra money doing door-to-door surveys. When knocking on doors in the Pentele village district, we happened on an old classmate of hers. The house was a modern duplex her family had built in the 1980s when the construction ban in Pentele was finally lifted. This woman had been able to hold onto the house despite the sudden rise in interest rates on building loans in 1988. She was aware that Ágnes's family had not been so fortunate and had been forced to sell the house they had built in a nearby village. She positioned herself in the moral middle of her former social circle, below some old friends but above others, by reflecting on how her socializing patterns had changed with changes in material circumstances. She admitted she no longer visited some friends because they now lived in surroundings so upscale she felt she "didn't fit in there." Others she no longer saw because "they couldn't even offer a cup of coffee," the minimum gesture of hospitality, and these encounters were humiliating for them.[17]

This particular conversation was unusual, as people were rarely willing to talk openly about these situations; but with Agnes, this woman wanted to commiserate in the solidarity-building register of losers, discussing the shocking increases in the price of bread, heating, and public transportation, all the while sitting in her modest but modern and spacious family house. At the same time, her self-positioning was consonant with an almost universal characteristic of middle-class culture, namely positioning oneself between high and low.[18] Her task was complicated by the quandary that she was talking to someone who was on the borders of what had once been a stable, socialist middle stratum.

Ildikó, the economist, was a winner by all objective standards—a working-class kid who did well academically and had earned several degrees. Level-headed and self-confident, she was rapidly moving up in the steel factory's management hierarchy. But she struggled to internalize her shifting status, a process made more difficult by the contradictory position she often found herself in with her family and friends. She had begun treating herself to luxury goods she'd been exposed to on her business trips: nicer wine, imported chocolate, Chinese food, prepackaged steak. Her new passion was horseback riding; she described her contact with horses as transforming, the first thing she felt she had done for herself rather than to fulfill the expectations of others. Although her husband Tamás in his good-humored way indulged these whims, he found them difficult to understand. Not only was he ten years her senior and had grown up in a large village family of Schwab (therefore "frugal") decent, but he worked as a driver for the steel mill's professional athletic teams. Ildikó had tried to take friends and family to the fancy Chinese restaurant in town—a place reserved for the upper echelons of steel factory personnel and justified by the need for a *reprezentatív* place to take foreign clients. But her friends were often uncomfortable in these surroundings with the strange fare and extravagant prices.

The *Polgár* and Other Kinds of Middle Classes

The use of the term "middle class" (*középosztály*) was new in political discourse, but what it referred to was often vague. Much political rhetoric and scholarly research focused on Hungary's historic *polgár* or bourgeois citizenry as the quintessential "middle class."[19] But the term was sometimes interchangeable with the socialist "middle strata" (*középréteg*), the population that many had assumed would transform into the new middle classes. It could also refer to the model of the Euro-American postwar middle classes, composed of gainfully employed families and defined by respectable consumption rather than heritage. These heterogeneous models for the middle classes were a favored topic in the popular media, becoming a staple in decorating magazines.

The turn-of-the-century and interwar Hungarian *polgár* were regularly featured in national newspapers on either side of the political spectrum in the 1990s. Articles about the lifestyles, values, and character of this social group were accompanied by memorable black and white photographs of families dressed for outings in their horseless carriages, posing in spacious apartments or airy sitting rooms, or enjoying Sunday afternoon meals in the garden. The heightened significance of this *polgár* category stemmed in part from how it had been developed as part of an oppositional discourse in the late 1970s, as discussed in chapter 5. As Judit Bodnár has noted, "the ideological attack on the bourgeoisie effectively made anything 'bourgeois' an element of a desirable past" (Bodnár 2007:142). While some urban intellectuals focused on the Jewish/German industrial classes and their intermarriage with the gentry, in more conservative publications the role of these "foreign" elements was often downplayed or omitted altogether, focusing on the predominantly Magyar population of civil servants. This "class" was understood to embody an ideal combination of civic consciousness and loyalty to the nation-state, along with entrepreneurial energy. As such, people used it to endorse different political and economic positions, claiming these policies would help such a class to flourish.[20]

Outside of political discourse, *polgár* took on the features of a lifestyle or mode of behavior rather than a class. As an adjective, *polgári* was also a way to reference norms for propriety and citizenship. For example, a radio talk show host joked with a caller: "Are you really a true *polgár*? You never stole apples from a neighbor's tree?" Some welcomed this trend, even though this new attention to etiquette seldom conformed to old standards of usage. A women's magazine described the appropriate *polgári* customs for couples on Valentine's Day—itself a post-1989 commercial import.

The return of the *polgár* to class politics reversed the fortunes of *polgári* furnishings, long devalued as second-hand and old-fashioned in relation to the prestige of the new and modern—especially among self-ascribed, urban intellectuals. At a party held at a writer's Budapest apartment, I watched with astonishment as a young man performed a frankly erotic caress of an inlaid Biedermeier wardrobe. The popularity of such patina-dense artifacts was bolstered by international demand for the relatively inexpensive heirloom antique furnishings to be found in Hungary. *Polgári* interiors were often featured as a privileged form of home décor, albeit one that the decorating industry was doing its best to detach from inherited cultural capital. Its narratives focused instead on the acquisition and explicit construction of the lifestyle, where any person of taste might have recognized objects of value that had been cast aside by others before it became popular to do so. A man who had discovered a Biedermeier chair covered in grime in a warehouse was one such person, as was a woman from a working-class family who recognized a Persian rug being used as a foot rag. In both cases, these people restored these objects to their former luster through loving labor. Although such taste did not have to be inherited, it nonetheless aligned the qualities of the owner with those of the object. An antique piece, an interior decorator explained in a weekly economics magazine, "carries with it its own aura. Somehow it is good to be near it. . . . Such an object elevates the prestige of its owner: first, it provides witness that [the owner] does not struggle with financial difficulties, secondly, the object's soul/intellectuality (*szellemisége*) inevitably carries over onto its owner—at least at first glance" (Kőrősi and Tomán 1996:110).[21]

In Dunaújváros, my inquiries into embourgeoisement (*polgárosodás*) were met with a shrug of the shoulders or sighs of exaggerated despair. My respondents—many of whom considered themselves to be *polgár*—claimed there had never been a *polgár* stratum of any consequence in the "city of the proletariat," and the few who chose to stay were technical professionals, not a cultured intelligentsia (*humán értelmiség*). Laura's mother, who had been an elementary school teacher for decades, remarked on how she truly understood this when she moved back to her home town of Kecskemét, a historic city in the middle of the country. In Dunaújváros, she claimed, people were rude on the street, and children addressed her with the familiar "you" form (*te*). In Kecskemét, people were more "civilized": a man offered to carry her suitcase, people greeted one another in the street, and children addressed their elders with respect. She experienced displays of deference based on age and gender as desirable forms of sociality in contrast to the new town's ideological imposition of "egalitarian" norms of address that felt antagonistic.

People who understood themselves to be of *polgári* status, as during the state socialist era, were fairly recognizable by their material culture, dress, and general habitus. A popular pastime was to take an after-dinner stroll along the high embankment above the Danube. The town's older *polgár* could be easily distinguished by their hats, by their more formal clothing, and even by their gait from most of the other walkers in their track suits and jeans. They were mostly known to one another, as members of the local intelligentsia or as having a *gimnázium* or liberal arts high school education (as opposed to technical school training). They rarely situated themselves explicitly in a class hierarchy but suggested their status using other markers of distinction: by the ways they would refer to other classes or manners associated with them, or by mentioning a story that included a parent's or grandparent's occupation, residence, education, wit, self-discipline, and prized possessions.

Others in Dunaújváros were far more ambivalent about the new salience of a Hungarian bourgeoisie. The celebration of this historic class implied the privileging of those who could claim some form of *polgár* ancestry and thus the restoration of a form of social stratification that had been delegitimized for forty years.

The new town had been a place where people who displayed *polgár* manners had often been accused of "putting on airs" (*játssza az eszét*).[22] Some proponents of *polgári* behavior were nonetheless irked when people who had never before been considered *polgár* performed affectations of higher status. *Polgári* was used here in much the same way as *úri* (noble) was used, indexing good manners and respectability, and it thus echoed the historically blurred boundaries in Hungary between bourgeois and gentry culture. Such manners had always implied a privileged upbringing, but *úri* was also used to poke fun at someone for putting on airs. One day I asked Erzsi, whose father had been an agricultural scientist (and thus a *polgár*) what she thought of a coworker I knew. "Oh István," she replied. "He plays at being the 'noble boy' (*úri fiú*), but he's not a bad guy."

The material culture called *polgári* was similarly regarded with ambivalence if not outright disdain as old-fashioned. Dunaújváros had no antique shops and, unlike larger cities in the country, no demand for them. This had less to do with associations with a petty bourgeoisie, as I discuss in chapter 7, than with the continuing importance of displaying one's participation in a capitalist modernity. There were exceptions, however. Kata and her husband, both of whose parents had come from villages and had risen to middle-strata status in the new town, had acquired some antique pieces for their loft apartment before they decided to embrace the new trend of renovating a peasant house in *polgári* mode. For that project, they had begun to collect authentic folk furniture and rustic peasant tools to display.[23] A professor at the technical college, when he heard of my interest in furnishing, insisted on taking me to his new panel apartment in the city center. Its three rooms were packed with oversized, carved antique furniture, oil paintings, porcelain vases, and statuettes, all inherited from a distant uncle. He admitted that his children complained that their apartment was unlivable and more like a cluttered, dusty museum than a home—echoing the rhetoric of Socialist Modern.

Despite the salience of a *polgár* or bourgeois-citizenry in political discourse, other models and materialities for middle-class life abounded. Throughout the country, contemporary models of middle-class life to be found in Western Europe or the United States were far more appealing. Such consumer-based middle classes were salient for their continuities with the former middle strata's legitimacy based on modern respectability. New styles of home furnishings, modern and traditional, made material a wide variety of middle-class lifestyles that fell into neither the styles of a European bourgeoisie nor those marked as more lavish and luxurious—such as the restored interiors of the remnants of an aristocracy. Some of the new "traditional" styles, such as American, gingham-checked country furnishings or Shaker and other styles referred to as *puritán* were not readily available in Hungary; others, such as those featuring modern and comfortable couches, were widely advertised, in higher-priced German and Italian leather versions, or in more affordable print fabrics. A high-tech, modern, and masculine décor was also popular for urban professionals, as were furnishings bought at IKEA, an imported sort of Super-Natural Organicism considered expensive by Hungarian standards of the time.

The history of capitalism and class formation in the United States was also referred to as a way to understand the unforeseen consequences of the capitalism emerging in Hungary after 1989. Most Hungarians were familiar with the (mythical) American model of middle classes based not only on television but also on travel abroad and books in translation, many of which focused on the late nineteenth to middle twentieth centuries. One of these paperback bestsellers, first brought to my attention by a young convert to Mormonism, was called *Millions out of Nothing*. It catalogued the exploits and often indigent backgrounds of early industrial millionaires. By an author named E. A. Jameson, this book was first published in Hungarian in 1920 (Jameson 1993)!

Anna, a divorced woman in her forties working at the city museum, sought me out to discuss American values and culture. Her interest was sparked in part by her conversion to Seventh-day Adventism and its practice of an unmediated, self-reliant reading of the Bible. Weber's *The Protestant Ethic and the Spirit of Capitalism* (published in Hungarian in 1982) had explained much to her about a Western attitude and its role in what Americans and Europeans had been able to achieve, particularly the quality of "hope" and a belief in God's help. When I grumbled offhand about postsocialist materialism, she mentioned Daniel J. Boorstin's book *The Americans*, translated into Hungarian in 1991. "Americans are beyond concern with material appearances," she believed, "because they went to America in 1620 with the conviction of their Puritan ethic, and built up that land and fought for their freedom, unencumbered by an aristocratic code." She had found this ethic so compelling that she'd taken up quilting as a distinctly American, productive practice.

A number of people mentioned Boorstin's book to me. Ildikó and Tamás, with no *polgár* in their backgrounds and no interest in religion, had also read the book, but they were interested in only the top three of the nine layers of American society it presents: first, old-name inherited wealth like the Rockefellers; second, those with some inherited wealth as startup capital but self-made through wits and good fortune, like Bill Gates; and finally, the CEO types who made millions without risking their own capital. In this model of American social life—from the early industrialists to the Ewing family—class status or family background seemed less relevant than ambition and hard work (and perhaps unscrupulous behavior) in reaching the status of comfortable middle class, or, as in the book on millionaires, to get rich.

From *Neighbors* to *Family, Inc.*

Two of the most popular state-produced television shows in the 1990s gave their rapt audiences contrasting visions of middle class experience.[24] *Neighbors* (*Szomszédok*)

Unstable Landscapes | 187

was first aired in the late 1980s. In the postsocialist 1990s, its story lines shifted to address the experiences and shattered expectations of the former socialist middle stratum. It opened with a panoramic shot of gray, panel concrete buildings in Budapest at dusk. The second, called *Family, Inc.* (*Família KFT*) aired in 1991, and was written as a Western-style sitcom featuring a new kind of Hungarian middle-class entrepreneur. Its opening shot was of a two-story family house painted moss green on a sunny street in the historic and touristy town of Eger.

Most of my neighbors in a panel building in Dunaújváros watched *Neighbors* religiously. It remained the most popular Hungarian show on state television until it ended in the late 1990s, occasionally topping the Western favorites E.R. and *Dallas* in prime-time ratings (*Népszabadság*, April 8, 1997).[25] The show depicted people who were struggling to maintain their respectable status and thus dignity after the system change: doctors, educators, and bureaucrats still employed by the state, service sector workers and struggling entrepreneurs, the elderly and retired, and young couples still living with parents. It included no alcoholics, prostitutes, or gangsters from the burgeoning criminal world. Its characters were portrayed as adhering to values that they perceived to belong to a gentler past—even as they tried to fit into the harsh realities of a new market-driven order. In one episode, a man sits by his old computer, which is frustrating his attempts to connect with the wider world via the Internet—a practice that echoed earlier attempts to connect to the outside world by listening to Radio Free Europe. Yet he is unwilling to take on the moral burden of a loan to pay for a new machine. In another, an elderly couple, wanting to renovate their apartment, argue over whether or not to have the painting done "without receipts" and thus avoid the 25 percent tax. When they finally renovate, the wife exclaims, "This will be our apartment's system change!"

The weekly show *Family, Inc.* (*Família KFT*), in contrast, depicted the antics of a family that was enjoying the financial and material well-being of a postsocialist order—one indexed as much by its carefree tone (accompanied by laugh track) as its material displays. This show too was enormously popular, watched by more than a quarter of the population by 1996 (*Budapest Business Journal*, Aug. 5, 1996). It seemed to appeal particularly to younger generations with its lighthearted irreverence and utter avoidance of moral or ethical dilemmas—much like the playful irreverence and antimoralizing of a Super-Natural Organicist aesthetics. Notably, the show was financed through corporate sponsorships, and product placements were regularly worked into the scripts. Its characters prospered through entrepreneurial endeavors, worked hard but not too hard, and lived the postsocialist good life: they had new cars, wore nice clothes, bought furniture and other consumer goods, and took vacations. Little if any reference was made to the socialist era. The location shots provided the "normal" backdrops of renovated historic streets and modern shopping areas the equal of any in Western Europe. One of the family-owned businesses was a café, the quintessential privatized public space of 1990s capitalism. In contrast to *Neighbors*, with its communal implications, the sitcom name *Family, Inc.* invoked the paradigmatic social and economic units of bourgeois capitalism: the family and the incorporated business. Little if any mention was made of the family's background or connection to a historic bourgeoisie, despite the setting of the show in one of the most historically significant towns in the country.

The producer of *Family, Inc.*, György Gat, had also been involved in the production of *Neighbors*. In a 1996 interview, he underscored the contrast between the two shows. "*Neighbors*," he said, "is like a soap opera. Not funny, but making a statement about Hungarian reality. I'm not interested in that [anymore].... I want to have a good life, I want to have my cars, I want to eat well" (*Budapest Business Journal*, Aug. 5, 1996). To present its narrative of legitimate, postsocialist success, the show had to crop out of the frame disagreeable realities like panel apartment buildings and run-down health facilities, erasing evidence of the socialist past. The show realized a version of the fantasy that had been generated during the last decade of the socialist period, namely that the end of Communist Party rule would provide the economic and political conditions necessary for normal life and personhood. In constructing images of a postsocialist Hungarian middle class aligned with modern, fashionable, and technologically sophisticated material worlds, it offered Hungarians a vision of a modern Hungary they could be proud of, but one that had to literally cut out all that didn't fit.[26]

By the late 1990s, the overt discourse of "winners and losers" was waning as social positions were beginning to stabilize. As we will see in the following chapters, for Dunaújváros's new middle classes the most important criterion for attaining new middle-class status was not in proving one's ancestral connection to a historic Hungarian bourgeoisie, but in the ability to move out of the socialist city altogether, to a newly built, autonomous family house in suburbanizing neighborhoods. But in a world where people were sliding into destitution, even people critical of the new order or those who continued to adhere to values of moral substance over material display, like the characters in *Neighbors*, were compelled to distance themselves from the regime's losers. Worries about Hungary's place in an international order were reflected in emerging conceptions of the domestic social order, as parts of the population were identified with a First World citizenry, while others were being branded as an underclass that dragged the country down.

7 The New Family House and the New Middle Class

An Unlikely Suburb

In Dunaújváros, the old village sector of Pentele, once run down and neglected, quickly became one of the most prestigious places in town to live. With its newly paved or cobbled streets, renovated Catholic church and manor house, and recently opened private bakery, it was the only part of town that could be transformed into a piece of (presocialist) historic Hungary. The city's emerging elites had the connections and finances to buy scarce land here or in the gentrifying Garden City district on which to build their new, eye-catching houses. The breathtaking material difference of these houses from the gray, concrete buildings making up the socialist norm in town aligned them with illegitimate wealth rather than with respectable middle-class status (Plate 7a).

But there was another controversial transformation to the landscape around the new town, one that was emerging throughout the country: small but growing neighborhoods of new, detached family houses on the outskirts of nearby villages (Figures 7.1, 7.3, 7.5, and 7.6). Often painted bright white or in the "ice cream colors" (*fagylalt színű*) of lemon yellow, apricot, raspberry, pistachio green, and chocolate brown, they also stood out, but here against a rural backdrop of unpainted or soot-stained houses with faded gray and brown roofs. Newly available construction materials, technologies, and labor contributed to their distinctive appearance.[1] Unsurprisingly, the eclectic architectural designs of new houses in Hungary in the 1990s, to varying degrees, were material condemnations of the straight-line and the rectilinear form. In subtle or dramatic fashion, these new houses incorporated organic, rounded, and often playful forms into their façades, including undulating roofs, convex mirrored glass, round columns, and arched windows. They also made prominent use of "natural" materials, such as wood, stone, and even reed thatch (Plates 8a and 8b). But these houses also marked their difference from their rural peasant or working-class neighbors through the material forms of the house and the new, leisure lifestyles they represented. Their cultivated lawns, gazebos, and rock gardens made them anathema to the rural peasantry, for whom the multiuse garage, productive garden, or livestock pen indexed a work ethic essential for respectability (Lampland 1995:316–23), but also to an older generation of city dwellers with weekend gardens, who were driven to tend, pick, and preserve whatever grew on their plots.

These houses were being called *kertes családi ház*, or "family house with a garden," a term that carried with it associations with the respectable, bourgeois culture of the presocialist era.² Commercial images of idyllic houses with red-tiled roofs nestled among green hills were used to advertise everything from building materials and home insurance to the grand prize in product-related raffles and the lottery, conveying a much-desired security and prosperity. Even personal ads tried to play on the value of the "family house with garden," as men in possession of some kind of detached house tried to attract significantly younger women as mates, even if it was only a "square house" built in the 1960s. And indeed, such a pitch was likely to work. A socialist-era house with a garden was being seen in a new light, especially when compared to a cramped panel apartment with no outdoor space. Raymond Williams has shown how, in times of change, the relative merits of the country and the city often become re-evaluated (Williams 1973). In Hungary, after four decades of urbanization policies and the denigration of rural areas, the countryside was being regenerated in discourse and through infrastructural transformations.

The local city planner insisted to me in 1996 that "of course" everyone in the city with the means to do so was moving out to the proverbial family house with garden. Sharing the sentiments of many during this period, she assumed the emergence of such housing was a natural development of capitalism and a sign that Hungary belonged in Europe—but also that these houses were part of long-term Hungarian practices and values. For outside observers, the houses seemed to fit the dominant narrative of suburbanization as the housing form best suited to the emerging middle classes. The overpowering image of oppressive urban public housing being replaced by private, detached homes reinforced conventional understandings of a transition from state socialism to market capitalism, whereby the socialist welfare and the collective values it stood for would be replaced by neoliberal regimes based on self-governing, autonomous subjects.

The ideological power of this new, suburban house form came as much from its symbolic opposition to the built environment of state socialism as from idealizations of Western models. In the simple aesthetic code of the postsocialist era, the values assigned to these two housing forms during state socialism were inverted. Housing estates were being equated with the past, with discredited ideals of collectivism, and with a denigrated urban proletariat, despite the preponderance of the former middle stratum still living in them. Indeed, social scientists and journalists published articles expressing concern about the inevitable "ghettoization" of the panel apartment city districts, making up one-quarter of Hungary's housing stock (Földházi 1989; Ladányi and Szelényi 1997). In contrast, the detached family house was acquiring new value in opposition to the values claimed for socialist architecture, namely as evidence of the autonomy, property rights, and prestige of a new, capitalist middle class (cf. Miller 1984 for England).

Family House and Middle Class | 191

Figure 7.1. New family house with an extravagant tower in an emerging suburbanizing village near Dunaújváros. This village attracted the most new house builders in part because of its location, on the Budapest side of the new town, and also because the village laid out roads and promised utilities. Photo by author, 1996.

The growing valorization of this suburban house form also brought with it the final demise of a socialist-era vision for a just social order. The keys to individual housing units were once presented as access to an inclusive paradise, even though they had become the keys to lock the rest of the world out of a family's private domain. By the 1990s, the adage that a "man's home is his castle" had become the unquestioned ideal. This new order was understood to be naturally competitive and the new middle class exclusionary. The suburban family house as a detached and autonomous form, as well as its high quality and durable materialities, became isomorphic with the qualities of the family it sheltered. Far from merely symbolizing a new middle class, the house and its echoes of Organicist Modern materialities legitimated and actively constituted its shape and character. The billboard for Bramac roofing tiles in Plate 7b, placed on the edge of the steel mill grounds, epitomizes this ideal. With polluting smokestacks visible behind it, the billboard features red-roofed houses in a verdant agricultural and mountainous terrain and reads "in friendship with nature" across the top. Below, the line "If once you build . . ." is placed next to a set of dark red tiles tied up like a gift, with the rest of the well-known expression left for the viewer to fill in: "you build to last forever." For Hungarians, the sentiment expressed was that if you threw yourself into the once-in-a-lifetime endeavor of building a house, you didn't skimp on quality but invested all you had to build the best house possible.

The Trouble With the Suburban Family House in Hungary

This reversal could not "undo" overnight what had taken decades to establish. The urban apartment had long been privileged in discourse over the detached, family house, but more significantly, the state's investment in infrastructures had generated embodied and enduring perceptions of the superiority of city over country. In Budapest, this kind of suburbanization had begun in the late 1980s and took off in the 1990s (see Valuch 2004:550), but in Dunaújváros such building had been reserved for the city elite and only as their weekend cottages. For many of the town's professionals, educators, civil servants, and skilled workers, the family house carried with it lingering associations with rural backwardness. Even though most of the houses built in the 1970s and 1980s were fully modernized and many were bigger and of better quality than urban apartments, they were still aligned with the lifestyles of families doing agricultural work and perhaps manufacturing for the second economy (Figure 7.2). This urban middle strata continued to equate a modern, civilized lifestyle with an urban apartment paired with a country cottage. While many Hungarians were well aware of suburban middle-class culture elsewhere, this housing form and the conditions for its existence had not yet been constructed locally—the utilities and paved roads, the commercial services in semirural areas, the widespread ownership of private cars. The very notion of a "middle class" that commuted from suburban areas had to be created in a context where such commuting workers had always been lowly peasant-workers arriving on buses from villages.

Unlike the United States, Western Europe, and other places in the world, the Hungarian state in the 1990s did not have the resources to provide private commercial developers with incentives in the form of infrastructure, financing, or other subsidies for residential construction, especially in provincial towns.[3] Thus most of these new "suburban" neighborhoods were being built, as in the socialist period, house by house—each one the private project of an individual or family. Prospective homeowners did not consume a ready-made dwelling designed by a professional, but crafted their houses by combining material resources, human contacts, and labor that both drew upon and innovated architectural styles. The resulting house, in size, location, and style, was the deliberate expression of what the family could manage of their collective desires.

House building was something considered appropriate for a family (that is, only heterosexual couples with or expecting children). Divorced people, single mothers, and single men understood themselves to be excluded from the family house, both as a social norm and as a practical possibility—even though the media often featured exceptions, such as the Olympic kayak champion lauded in the na-

Figure 7.2. Older peasant houses on the right, with tile and thatched roofs, and outhouses. On the left, modern self-built houses from the 1980s. Several streets over a new, suburbanizing neighborhood was emerging. Photo by author, 1998.

tional "Women's Magazine" (*Nők Lapja*), a single woman who had built a lovely house for herself. The window frame business owner Károly, for example, had the means, connections, and expertise to build a house for himself but hadn't done so. Instead, he had bought a panel apartment on the plateau overlooking the Danube River, and he showed it to me as it was being renovated with corkboard floors and an American kitchen. "It's not a family house," he acknowledged, "but it's perfect for a bachelor, and maybe alright for awhile if I get married and have a child." Implicit in his statement was that he no longer considered such an apartment adequate for a family.

Prospective house builders or even buyers were further stymied by economic conditions, which for builders were worse than they had been for decades. Mortgages were nonexistent. Until the 2000s, housing loans from the National Bank (OTP) were difficult to obtain, even at interest rates of 28 to 32 percent, and were capped at HUF 1.5 million—nowhere near enough to buy or build anything. With the exception of new family grants, the government had frozen support for new house building. The price of building materials was skyrocketing. As prospective house builders tried to offset escalating prices, they would buy bricks far in advance of the day they might actually use them. Stacks of building blocks covered

Figure 7.3. New houses under construction in suburbanizing village near Dunaújváros. The house shown has the mark of professional labor and sports a trendy thatched roof. Next door, a family is building a "square house," a much simpler form of construction, and park their Trabant out front. These house forms and cars exemplify the gulf between new suburban residents. Photo by author, 1997.

in plastic sheeting proliferated on building sites. The only financial incentive for building a house in this period was that newly autonomous rural districts, in the hopes of repopulating villages, offered plots of land inexpensively and promised (eventually) to pave roads and to provide running water and electricity. But for a significant proportion of Dunaújváros's former middle stratum, a family house of any kind was simply out of reach.

New house builders of the early to mid-1990s were early innovators willing to take the risk of trying to establish a suburban house form in rural areas dominated by peasant or working-class self-built housing, and where few prewar villa housing existed. Laura and Zoltán were paradigmatic of this kind of new entrepreneurial middle class who marked their difference from their neighbors by eschewing a productive garden and planting only flowers alongside a few herbs. "I've done enough hoeing in my life!" Laura said, referring to the long weekends she had spent down the road at their weekend cottage hoeing and weeding and then preserving the fruits and vegetables for household consumption.

Changes in modes of production were also creating new systems of distinction between house builders still using forms of *kaláka*, the rural system of labor exchange, and those using commodified contract services (Figure 7.3). These differences were materialized in the resulting structures and also in different kinds of neighborhood relations. *Kaláka* was on the decline as stonemasons, electricians, and plumbers were able to command high prices on an open market and neighbors and friends were less willing to lend their services. This form of building was being supplanted by a "self-powered" (*önerő*) or a hybrid market mode of construction (Hegedűs 1992), which continued to rely on the labor of immediate family and friends but also used hired labor far more extensively. "Self-powered," as the term implies, rarely involved entering into the complicated system of community debts and obligations of *kaláka*. For young working-class couples, lack of local ties often precluded reciprocal exchanges of labor, and they ended up doing most of it themselves. For new middle-class house builders, paying cash for the labor of hired hands was a way of avoiding the hassles and burdens of such reciprocal obligations. A popular practice was to employ illegal migrant Romanian Hungarian workers who were rumored to be far cheaper and who worked harder than lazy and spoiled Hungarian day laborers (the working classes).

Because such building methods used more skilled labor and could take advantage of new building materials and technologies, they produced the distinctive look of the prototypical new family house. Such family houses were in turn distinguished from the elaborate villa housing that was entirely contracted to professionals. Political cartoons often revealed the disconnect between older and newer forms of building. The one in Figure 7.4, from the local paper, shows a couple in professional dress building a house of cards while hired workmen build a villa next door. While the couple's plot of land is ringed by a rickety fence, the new villa already has a decorative privacy wall.

Negotiating a Family House

Despite all of these obstacles, by the mid- to late 1990s, anyone aspiring to new middle-class status had to face the often contentious question of whether or not to build a family house and, if so, what form the house would take. During my

Figure 7.4. Political cartoon, "Builders: this is all we can manage," October 26, 1996. Reprinted courtesy of the *Dunaújvárosi Hírlap*.

extended stay in Dunaújváros and shortly thereafter, three families I had gotten to know well moved from panel apartments in the city to houses in one of the nearby villages. Comparing the differences and similarities between these married couples in class background, resources, and self-positioning in the new order provides us with a window onto the many factors at play in the establishment of the family house form as a constitutive force in the production of a new middle-class status in Hungary. As we will see, the forms and materialities of the house itself limited who could enter the ranks of this new middle class, but they also became central to how these families negotiated the transformation of self that was necessitated by this radical transformation of their living space. After all, as the slogan so often used during state socialism continued to trumpet, "Show me your home, and I'll tell you who you are!" This new home not only positioned them in a shifting order but contributed to how that order was being conceptualized and materially constituted. As in the past, such ideal homes become a window onto the wider order being imagined (Wright 1981).

Laura and Zoltán were recently married entrepreneurs in their mid-thirties in the mid-1990s (second marriages for both). Laura's parents had lived and socialized with other families who worked in professional positions at the hospital. Her mother had grown up in a provincial town, the daughter of a fairly well-to-do Catholic shoemaker, while her father's parents had both been doctors. Her grandmother had been the first female to get a medical degree in a family of Jewish physicians, and she converted to Calvinism when she married Laura's grandfather. Laura's status as the daughter of a doctor was enhanced by her mother's skills as a seamstress who made sure her only child was always distinguished from Socialist Generic fashions. After high school, she married a rising star of the local semiprofessional soccer team and had a daughter, Virág, but tensions in the marriage arose in the 1980s as her husband was sidelined by injury. He was able to find lucrative work in the semilegal high-rise construction industry in Austria, but when that work ended he refused to accept the low-paying employment available to him in the town. Their marriage ended shortly before the regime change, precipitated by the success of Laura's English-language school. She had taken advantage of economic reforms in the late 1980s that allowed small businesses, and she capitalized on the credibility she had gained from a trip she had taken to the United States in her early twenties.

Her second husband, Zoltán, was involved in a variety of entrepreneurial activities, first running a village disco bar and then opening a secondhand "Western" goods store. The latter was supplied by Austrian Roma who picked through Viennese dumpsters to salvage things wealthy Austrians threw away but that many Hungarians would associate with high quality despite their previous use. He had a background in restaurant management, following in his father's footsteps. Although his father's family was proud of their respectable status, they had no claims to a *polgár* (bourgeois-citizen) background and were instead examples of proper (*rendes*) provincial people who attained middle-stratum status during the socialist period.

Margit and Géza were professionals in their mid-forties at the time of the regime change and were therefore part of the generation that had to fight to remain relevant in the new order, having worked in the socialist system for more than two decades. Although shy, Margit had graduated at the top of her law school class and returned to Dunaújváros to work as an assistant to the local prosecutor. She and

Géza married in the early 1970s, ostensibly after their parents had pushed them together as a marriage between "good families." They had a son, Péter, who was in his late teens and struggling to get into the university.

Finally, Ildikó and Tamás were from working-class and peasant families respectively. Ildikó had grown up in the city, the exceptionally bright daughter of unskilled workers. Hers was a success story of socialist opportunity policies. "My university stipend was more than my parent's salary," she once told me. When she had a son at age twenty-six, she used part of her three-year state maternity leave to get another degree in business economics. From a job teaching at the local technical college, she took a well-paying position at the steel mill and was in the process of moving up rapidly when I met her, in her early thirties. Tamás's parents had come to the new town in the 1950s from villages in the region to work in industry and live in a modern city apartment. They had recently moved back to a farmstead after thirty years living in a spic-and-span urban apartment, yearning for the life of the land. Then in his forties, Tamás had been an outstanding student and leader of the local Communist Youth chapter—which had become a legal cover for a more-or-less independent and depoliticized youth organization. In contrast to Ildikó's blossoming career, Tamás's job as chauffeur for the factory was being terminated, which fostered anxieties at home. As he said, "Nothing is certain in this world!"

While all three married couples earned well above the average wage in Dunaújváros at the time, ostensibly about HUF 30,000, or $150.00 per month, trying to rank them in terms of their financial status is an almost impossible task. Ildikó, with her high-ranking position at the steel mill, likely earned the highest salary of the group, one boosted by job perks such as a car, travel, bonuses, and interest-free loans. Her husband, Tamás, probably earned the least. Géza and Margit were also salaried employees whose combined incomes compared to Ildikó's, and they also got benefits through their workplace. Margit, for example, was partially paid in travel expenses for her many vacation trips that her company then wrote off as a business expense.[4] Géza worked tirelessly to gain control over part of his company, which eventually increased his earnings substantially. At the time he was taking on private jobs on the side. As private entrepreneurs, Laura and Zoltán's incomes were the most insecure. Laura's language school provided a steady but modest income, while Zoltán's many ventures in the hospitality industry were boom and bust depending upon whether he was paid by vendors or stolen from by employees. He eventually struck gold by accident, becoming a middle man transporting medical cleaning products.

The new possibility of a suburban family house with a garden became a test of marital relationships. The decisions these couples made about this house form became a way through which they negotiated changes to their status within a larger, shifting landscape of social prestige, respectability, and well-being. Their ability (perceived and actual) to obtain such a house became a way in which they actively produced such identities, while they legitimated their new status in their selection of the kind of house they eventually came to live in, its interior divisions, and its material aesthetics. What became clear is that for this new and often beleaguered "middle class" in Dunaújváros, the importance of a *polgár* ancestry to middle-class status faded and indeed paled in comparison with the importance attached to positioning oneself as a newly made middle class. This new middle class was forged in the market capitalist conditions of the postsocialist era and demonstrated its legitimacy through the consumption of high-quality materials and living environments made both "moral" and "Hungarian" by their alignment with a Super-Natural Organicism.

Material Entrepreneurs: Building a House

For Laura, living in a family house with a garden had been a long-standing dream. Laura's childhood home had been a relatively spacious two-room apartment (53 square meters or 500 square feet). In a brick building constructed to house the doctors who worked at the hospital down the street, it had a foyer, a main room with a balcony, one bedroom, a kitchen large enough for a small table and chairs, a bathroom, and separate toilet. As was customary in "good families," the bedroom had been Laura's domain growing up, and every square inch of it was organized; even the objects in her drawers were stored in separate boxes. Her parents slept on a pullout couch in the main room, and every morning they had stowed the bedding in cabinets to restore the room to its daytime use. In the early 1980s, when Laura married her high school boyfriend, they traded places with her grandmother, moving into her smaller one-bedroom panel apartment while she moved in with her son, Laura's now-divorced father. In 1983, the young couple's daughter Virág was born and as a baby was given the bedroom. Laura and her husband slept in the main room on a double bed covered with a sheepskin throw. A bookcase divided this sleeping nook from the small sitting area furnished with the complete Biedermeier set inherited from her grandmother (tea table, upholstered chairs and settee, bookshelves, and grand, embellished wardrobe). The marriage fell apart right before the system change, and Laura remarried in 1993.

With the help of Zoltán, Laura embarked upon the building of a family house in 1994, on the fringes of a nearby village, just up the road from where her family had a small A-frame weekend cottage overlooking the Danube. It was the first new house at the edge of fields of wheat and corn that had been designated as a new area for house building by the local village council. During the three long years it took to build the house, she lived in a state of constant agitation, bursting with anticipation of "escaping from the city" (*menekülni a városból*) where she had lived her whole life. In 1994, she walked me through the empty spaces of the half-built rooms of her "dream house," pointing out who and what would be where, how she imagined each room when it was finished, and the personal details built into the house's design. Set back in a large, enclosed garden, the house featured cathedral ceilings with an exposed second floor and three finished bedrooms. When finished, it would have an American kitchen that opened onto the large living room. The two girls (Zoltán had a nine-year-old daughter) would each have a room, sharing a large bathroom. The upstairs had space to build an extra apartment, and they imagined one of the girls might want to return there someday with her family, or perhaps one of their elderly parents would move in with them. Laura was particularly pleased with the separate laundry and sewing rooms. The two-car garage had extra space for storage. The difference between her old apartment and the new family house was extraordinary. Looking out the window frame of the (small) master bedroom, she joked that she would be able to wake up in the morning and laugh at the city in the distance, a cloud of industrial smoke beyond an expanse of farmland.

For Laura and Zoltán, the sense of opportunity offered by the system change had been a cornerstone of their new marriage, and building a family house was integral to their plan for the future—a place they could raise their two children, entertain friends, and eventually care for their parents. They imagined it to be an appropriate material setting for two entrepreneurs in a newly European nation-state, and they pored over new house and interior design magazines for ideas. Considering themselves members of a new *polgár,* entrepreneurial class, they retrospectively attributed the failure of their previous marriages to differences in social class, differences made manifest in their spouse's less demanding expectations (*igények*) and their inability to muster the drive necessary for achieving these materialities.

Polgári *Disdain*

Resistance to the family house in the 1990s was part of a more general resistance to challenges to an older way of life, particularly by those who had the most to lose by the erosion of such things as education or profession as markers of respectability. An older generation of educated professionals like Margit and Géza, nearing forty or older at the time of the regime change—often with grown children—put up the most resistance to these new expectations and to incorporating changing conditions into their familiar value systems. For example, when Kata, the thirty-something owner of the beauty salon, sold her spacious loft apartment in the center of town to a factory director, her mother Irén, who had been director of the city's cultural center, was furious. Kata and her husband had decided to renovate and modernize an old peasant house "in bourgeois style," as new housing publications called it, but the mother insisted they had been "taken in by a fad." Even more upsetting to her was that they had stooped to rent another apartment while the house was being renovated, as she associated renting from another person with the degradation and shame of not living autonomously, in one's own home. From the mother's perspective, Kata and her husband had achieved an absolute ideal in the loft apartment, not only four times the size of the standard apartments below it, but in the same building as her parents and her grandmother. Having herself moved to Dunaújváros from a village, she could not fathom why anyone would want to move "back."

Similarly, my interview with a sociologist named Éva at the local junior college suddenly turned personal when her disparaging comments about the family house as a new status symbol provoked a colleague sitting nearby, whose family had just finished building one. Éva was a confirmed intellectual, adhering to the white-collar ideal of an urban apartment (where she lived with her husband, dog, and cat) and a weekend cottage, "because everyone should have a place that is green." Her colleague Mária had just moved to a house after living most of her life in Dunaújváros apartments. Mária insisted, indignantly, that a "family house" was about much more than status, and that status was only important if the exterior was emphasized. People wanted them because they liked to work in the garden, to breathe better air, to have more space for the family. I mentioned an article I'd read discussing the detrimental effects of suburbanization on women in the 1980s, who usually bore the brunt of fewer services, a larger house to clean, and infrequent bus access to the city, since men usually claimed the only car. Éva chimed in, "and there's no telephone, one is completely isolated." For Mária, this was all too much, a failure to recognize conditions that had changed dramatically: "Of course there's a phone, and everything else besides!"

Later and in private, Eva had more to say on the matter. Her comments revealed the underlying shifts away from the ideal of urban living central to the socialist project, but also to an older bourgeois (*polgári*) value system. She explained that her colleague was "the property-owning type . . . who lives to work on her house and garden." She contrasted this type of person with people like herself, who preferred living in an urban apartment during the week and using the weekends to do a little gardening at her cottage. Urban life for her was equated with a desirable and morally imbued sociality. As she put it, "I like social life, to visit friends for a quick coffee, or to pop downstairs to go shopping. I would feel isolated in a family house." Lest this be mistaken for an adherence to socialist values, however, she continued with modest pride, "My parents were a bit bohemian (*bohém*). We lived in a house with fruit trees and lilacs, but we didn't weed and hoe" (*nem kapáltunk*). As with Laura, insisting on her distance from hoeing was still a relevant status marker, and in her case marked her parents as part of a prewar middle class removed from the peasantry and from rural garden plots. While Éva did admit to freezing produce from their weekend garden, she confirmed her status as an intellectual who engaged in the time-consuming activity of reading: "I don't have time for more than that."

Margit and Géza probably could have financed the building of a family house in 1990, but it never occurred to them. Instead they gathered their resources and sold some inherited antiques to buy their state-allocated panel apartment. They quickly sold this apartment to buy a slightly larger one on the fourth floor of a ten-story panel building along the main avenue in "a good part of town, despite the noise." Before they moved in, they had the entire apartment renovated, particularly focusing on upgrading and beautifying the bathroom with ceramic tiles and gleaming fixtures. Just as *Lakáskultúra* had long promoted, their modern furniture and high-tech entertainment coexisted with *polgári* furnishings and art inherited from Margit's family. Margit had gotten rid of most of their painted plates and other folk decor, but a few of the pillows she had carefully embroidered remained. Géza had always been up on the latest high-tech gadgets and owned all those within his economic reach: stereo and video equipment, calculators, pens, phones. In the mid-1990s, their eighteen-year-old son Péter had a computer with a scanner and a modem connection, but Géza was just getting started with his laptop. His new Suzuki was his pride and joy, in the "forest-green" color so popular at the time. A wiry, cheerful man, he was cutting back on his two-pack a day smoking habit.

By contrast, the only thing that animated Margit was discussion of her travels out of the country. Otherwise, she was a stream of complaints about her poor health and the other "not normal" conditions many women in the region had to contend with: the horrors of her bus commute (getting up at 5 AM to wait in the freezing cold to catch the crowded 6 AM bus), the indignities she had to suffer at work, dissatisfaction with her hairdresser, and her domestic duties caring for her "boys" and now also her ailing parents. When talk turned to travel, she was transformed into a lively interlocutor, full of enthusiasm and wonder. She went to Western Europe often, but she'd also been to Bangkok several times, to China, to the United States twice, to Mexico, to Egypt. She particularly loved London, where, she claimed, "people are civilized and decent." She came back to her life in Hungary and existed, it seemed, only for the day she could leave again. Géza, who had a phobia of flying, rarely accompanied her on these trips.

For a time, both had been disdainful of conservative rhetoric that framed family houses as regenerating the extended family and presocialist values and instead regarded them as symbols of the nouveau riche. Their three-room, 80-square-meter (860-square-foot) apartment was larger than the average family house, Géza repeatedly noted, and had plenty of room for them and Péter. But at other times he insisted that it was only "natural" for people to want more space after living in such confined apartments for so long. He also repeated the mantra that it was "unnatural" for humans to live more than two stories above ground. Both Géza and Margit believed the resurgence of popularity in the extended-family house would be short-lived. After all, few couples got along well enough with their in-laws to live in nearby apartments without conflict, much less under the same roof. The generational divide had just become too great. One of the reasons for their own move had been to put a little distance between them and Margit's parents. They were still close enough to look in on them, but her mother could no longer "pop over in her bathrobe."

When Géza began taking a more active interest in another place to live, Margit continued in her opposition, understanding well that the burdens of a house in the village—its isolation, lack of services, and spotty public transportation—would fall on the woman's shoulders. It would also mean an even longer commute for her and far more housework. More importantly, she could not assimilate the "family house" into her identity as a member of an urban, *polgár* intelligentsia. "Even if we could afford it," she argued, "we don't need the space of a family house now that Péter is grown." As a compromise solution, Géza looked into an apartment in one of the terraced buildings of the 1980s. These were the same size as their place but included a large outdoor, rooftop patio and the luxury of a garage. They also cost four to five million HUF ($30,000–35,000), paid in full at time of purchase. By the time he could arrange for credit through contacts at the steel mill, the place was sold, but he kept looking and hoping. Their son encouraged him, desperately hoping to move to a family house and maligning their panel building at every opportunity. Echoing common complaints, he argued with his mother about the dark, suffocating stairwell, the "disgusting" elevator that was often out of order, and the horrible feeling of coming home and having the hall lights, on self-timers, go out before he'd reached their door.

Margit had long ago given up on seeing Hungary, but especially Dunaújváros, as a place to realize her dreams. In the mid-1990s, when acquaintances began to build and move to family houses, she had little incentive to change her forms of distinction or shift her desires. A member of the generation that had been "cheated by history," she felt too old to take advantage of the opportunities of the system change, to learn new languages and new ways of doing things, but too young to retire. Adhering to her *polgári* values, she preferred to spend her income on travel. Even though Hungary was now ostensibly poised to join Europe, she saw little sign of a "civilized and decent" life in her own surroundings. Travel was her way of partaking in a lifestyle she had long understood would have been hers as a lawyer if she had lived in a European country. Like many Hungarian professionals during the socialist era, her national identity was bound up with a sense that she would have prospered if she had been rooted elsewhere. If Laura and Zoltán were attempting to position themselves thoroughly within a potential Hungarian middle-class society, she chose to disassociate herself from a "second-class" Hungarian social order. Géza, in contrast, was sociable, and because he worked in the steel mill, he figured he knew half the city, at least by face. He began to understand that living in a qualitatively different kind of material environment was now possible within Hungary itself. Although he didn't articulate it this way, his desires to build a family house were also about wanting to participate in an emerging local, as well as Hungarian, social order.

Out of Reach

For Ildikó ("Ildi"), in her early thirties when I met her, moving to a family house became a central preoccupation. The panel apartment she and her husband owned was relatively new and large, with two small bedrooms allowing them the luxury of a "French bed." (They had bought the apartment in 1984, right after the government increased "entry" prices.) It was always clean and neat, resembling some of the more impersonal modern interiors pictured in ads and magazines, with no idiosyncratic objects or mementos. Tamás had installed white tiles in the hallway, and they'd furnished the main room with a black wall unit holding books and the television, a sofa and armchairs in black and gray with lilac accents, plants by the balcony window, and the tinkling sounds of a decorative fountain to moisturize the air. Their nine-year-old, András, had his own small room with television and computer. Ildi often talked about how she'd like to transform the apartment, attracted to the idea of installing wooden beams in the panel apartment kitchen to give it a more rustic look.

While on some occasions Ildi was quite happy with her modern, urban apartment, she increasingly echoed widespread discourses in voicing her longings to move to the "peace and quiet" of the countryside, to "escape the panel masses" she found so claustrophobic. Her explorations of other ways of living was changing her experience of her apartment, making it feel more cramped and "unfriendly." She dreamed of a house outside of the city, where András could have a dog and they could go outside, where they had more space, and where she could have rustic furniture and snuggle up to a traditional, closed ceramic fireplace (*cserépkályha*). On weekends, she took me with András to visit school friends with houses in their new Hungarian-made Suzuki, or on drives in her company car around new housing sectors "so that when the time comes, I'll know what I want!"

We often toured the village nearest to Dunaújváros en route to Budapest (Rácalmás), which had already become a destination for house builders in the late 1980s and in the 1990s was quick to lay out plots, scrape dirt roads between them, and set up posts for electricity lines. These roads were lined with new houses in various states of completion and of various shapes and sizes, including a few of asymmetrically modern designs, some inspired by Austrian farmhouses, and many with clear signs of Organicism. We drove by her pediatrician friend's house, which cost HUF 7.5 million (five times the price of a one-bedroom apartment in Dunaújváros at the time), but Ildi insisted that not just the wealthy were building houses there. One of her schoolmates got the "fortune" (*vagyon*) necessary for building by doing dangerous transport work in Albania, while other families took out what for her seemed huge loans of two to three million forints and had to pay back the equivalent of an average month's salary just on interest. Repeating the oft-heard litany about house building, she continued, "Then they sacrifice everything to build, do as much as they can themselves, never go on vacation, never buy anything else. And then once it's built they have to buy furniture, and by the end, they've often destroyed the marriage."

Ildi's bucolic dream of a family house was not shared by her husband. Tamás's extended family had all lived in villages, and he wanted nothing to do with the labor, the flies, and the smells he associated with rural living. He preferred to spend his free time at home watching sports on television. While he was on good terms with his parents, he declined to accompany us when we visited them at their peasant house, with its outhouse, summer kitchen, vineyard, and carefully raked garden plot, as well as the menagerie of dogs, pigs, chickens, ducks, and rabbits. "They're crazy," he said. "They have a modern apartment here in the city where they lived for years, but they prefer being out there living in uncivilized conditions." On weekends, he spent his time coaching youth basketball teams and driving factory-sponsored professional teams to competitions in Germany and Austria. Neither his salary nor his labor were going to help Ildi realize her house. He cautioned me once about thinking that all the new houses around were indicative of a more widespread prosperity. Despite Ildi's excellent position, which he judged to be about fiftieth in the factory of ten thousand people in rank and salary, he assumed a new family house was out of reach even to someone of Ildi's rank.

Ildi, however, was coming to see herself as part of an emerging, professional middle class in a modern, European Hungary. Her new position entailed regular travel to France and England, and the first time we met for English-Hungarian language exchange, she showed me photos of a trip to Amsterdam, where she'd admired the interior decor with its antique furniture: "People there live with and value those beautiful, old things," she said, echoing the sentiments of *Lakáskultúra* articles on *polgári* interiors. "I'd love to furnish my home with antiques, but we can't afford them. Besides, they aren't appropriate for panel apartments. . . . In truth, we can't afford to express our standards and tastes (*igények*)." These trips abroad and experiments with new forms of consumption, however, were transforming her demands (*igények*) for standards of living—exactly the process that early socialist ideologues used to encourage the working classes to become more bold in their demands and expectations. Her superiors and colleagues at the steel mill were all moving to family houses, and over the next few years, she became determined that one day she would live in one too.

Unfulfilled Expectations

The new house builders of the early 1990s, like Laura and Zoltán, represented a vanguard with a vision for middle-class life in Hungary that they set out to fulfill. Laura was able to ignore the prevailing stereotypes of house builders to create the kind of living space she associated with the normal and dignified kind of life the end of state socialism would make possible. She also assumed she would take her rightful place in a world that rewarded entrepreneurial autonomy and enterprise, and she was empowered by the social status she had always enjoyed as the daughter of a doctor of *polgári* background. Nonetheless, things had not gone exactly as planned.

Building the house had been an enormous project, but a typical one. They financed it by borrowing from relatives and by using Laura's mother's small apartment as collateral on loans with high interest rates. Laura had sold the apartment she had inherited from her grandmother for capital and had asked her father to move into his girlfriend's tiny apartment so that her family could live in his two-room apartment during the construction period. Zoltán in particular spent much of his time scouring the country for discounted materials, using connections for supplies and skilled labor and counting heavily on family and friends for financial and physical assistance. Sinking all their income and hours of labor into the house, they deferred family holidays abroad and shared the use of an old and unreliable—though foreign-made—car.

When I arrived in early 1996 for fieldwork, they were all still crammed in the city apartment, construction considerably slowed by financial troubles. Laura's English-language school was going well, but Zoltán's disco bar and used clothing store were not. They finally moved into the unfinished but livable space that summer. In contrast to the pattern of the 1970s and 1980s, when new house exteriors were often left unfinished, they had prioritized painting the house exterior a sunflower yellow and installing a goldfish pond. Meanwhile, the indoor stairway to the loft and the ceramic fireplace were still missing. The main floors were finished in a mottled, moss green ceramic tile, with a counter dividing the kitchen from the living area clad completely in ochre and olive tiles. The raised living area floor was of wood and was framed by wood paneling on the cathedral ceiling. Laura set up an indoor cactus garden in the open, windowed entryway.[5] They were too busy to have the house "dedication" party they had planned—in fact they were often too busy to see anyone. The girls loved their rooms, but Laura's thirteen-year-old daughter, Virág, disliked the commute to the city and being so far from her friends. Parents and friends who had been welcome to drop by and help while they were building and finishing the house were now often treated as intruders to the family's new domestic privacy—a situation that would eventually explode in family quarrels.

In the autumn, I visited Laura in her new house. She told joking anecdotes about how the family had shouted at each other across the space when they first moved in. Out the window the wind and rain blew across the fields, backlit by the sun setting in the distance. The house finally looked lived in, curtains in the polished windows, furnished and decorated with crystal vases and brass teapots, with plants covering the unfinished concrete of the loft. The living room, however, was furnished with two modern, comfortable, fabric-covered couches in earth-tone patterns. Zoltán had banished Laura's antique Biedermeier furniture set upstairs and out of sight. Both fully identified with an ambitious, risk-taking, and hard-working middle-class who they expected would occupy a place of privilege in the new capitalist order. Laura's antique furniture communicated an old-fashioned and inherited status. Their newly purchased furniture, while far less valuable, communicated their success in a postsocialist present.

Laura and Zoltán relished the reactions they got from friends to their new house, especially those living in Western Europe or North America. One Hungarian American gushed over their achievement, calling the house a "*Kúria*," the term for country estates of the old nobility. An old buddy in a white Mercedes stopped by for a chat. They all chuckled together when this friend recounted his reference to the TV show *Dallas* as he'd come up the walkway: "We're here to see the Ewing family!" The following summer, a Hungarian German friend came with his wife for a small party. The house and garden were immaculate, and we all sat outside on the patio under umbrellas and had drinks. Laura and Zoltán's male relatives joked about "this damn house," telling competing stories of the labor they'd contributed and how Zoltán "conveniently" disappeared at the most opportune moments. Meanwhile, Zoltán told the friend from Munich how much he had been thinking of him while he worked on the lawn, anticipating his reaction: "I wondered how you would see this, how much it's developed since last year."

In contrast, they were often taken aback by negative reactions from local friends and acquaintances. While some appreciated the house, for others it became an object of contempt, competition, or resentment. An architect from Budapest felt the house, manicured lawn, and goldfish pond were in bad taste. Kata, who had sold her spacious loft apartment to renovate a peasant house, was an old friend of Laura's, and she told me that she simply couldn't bring herself to visit them at their new house. Laura noted her absence with chagrin. I was told by others that the house, with its impressive two-story facade, gave the impression that they were "full of money" (*tele vannak pénzzel*). Local friends and colleagues with economic ties to the couple invariably came away from a visit to the house feeling resentful and cheated. Zoltán had hired a workman because his wife worked in Laura's language school. This woman was someone Laura trusted and with whom she hoped to foster a good working relationship, in part by paying her well. Things soured after Laura invited them out to see the house. The man failed to finish the work and Zoltán suspected him of using their materials on other jobs. Instead of being grateful for her compensation, the woman too had become dissatisfied. Her new suspicion that Laura was "rich" and had been sinking the school's profits into a house of incomprehensible proportions had transformed her interpretation of their relationship.

In fact, Laura and Zoltán had been able to pull together the house only by using all the resources at their disposal, and they only had to pay a fraction of the cost of building a new house in Budapest, especially one designed by a professional. But this strategy had created its own tensions. They lost the friendship of Károly when Laura talked him into providing windows and doors from his framing business for the new house at a cut rate in exchange for some English-language lessons. Károly and Laura had known one another since childhood, as their parents had been colleagues at the hospital. When the windows he gave them leaked, they demanded new ones. Károly, angry at being manipulated into working for a dubious exchange, expressed the sentiment of many when he accused Laura of pretensions to a status beyond her means—of having demands far above what she could afford: "I can show you some houses," he said to me again and again, "big ones, luxury ones, owned by people with the money to maintain them!"

But there was more to this dispute than Laura's pretensions. The new meanings and materialities of the house were at odds with the older reciprocity practices Laura and Zoltán employed to realize it. These practices of exchange were common when people expected to reciprocate labor and resources, and when they pilfered resources from the state firms where they worked. But after the collapse of socialism, especially in the case of people building more extravagant homes, such practices came to be considered exploitative. They took advantage of old friendships, they used up extended family resources, and they hired cheap but illegal laborers—all in a climate where occasions for reciprocity had disappeared. It was unlikely that Károly would ever take advantage of his free language lessons, but more importantly, since he now owned the firm, providing new doors and windows at "cut rates" was not at the expense of an impersonal, boundless state, but was coming directly out of his own pocket.

New Middle-Class Materialities

Despite all the troubles with the family house, by the end of the decade both Margit and Géza and Ildikó and Tamás had moved into such houses. How can we explain this shift, beyond the particular marital negotiations of one spouse giving way to the other's desires? The years of my main fieldwork (1996–1998) were a period in which those who had rejected the "family house with garden" as an ideal form for a Hungarian middle class were gradually brought around to the idea. These were people with perspectives as different as Margit's, with her urban *polgár* identity, and Tamás's, who was unwilling to make the move "back" to the village existence his family had escaped decades before. The process of moving from panel apartments to family houses was not experienced as simple compliance to the demands of status, but as motivated by transcendent goals—for family and for self, part of an endeavor to create the much idealized conditions for a livable, respectable and normal life. It was also propelled by the deteriorating conditions in the city and the emergence of a new kind of "suburban" way of life in these villages.

The Family House and Middle-Class Status

By the late 1990s, potential house builders had enough examples of this new housing form to judge which forms and aesthetics were successful and which were not, as small neighborhoods of such houses had emerged in most of the villages within twenty kilometers of the town. It was also becoming clearer which neighborhoods were attracting people who would be Dunaújváros's new middle classes and which areas were being populated by self-builders who lacked other alternatives. Laura, for example, had chosen the site for her house in the early 1990s, but the location did not turn out to be in an area favored by other house builders of a new middle class. It was among plots set aside for young couples who were struggling to build themselves smaller houses of basic design through pronatalist building grants, laboring evenings and weekends at the building site (Figure 7.5). Instead of the middle-class suburban milieu they had envisioned, Laura and her family had to contend with the hostile stares of their new neighbors and eventually gave up trying to establish relations with them. They had built their house with the faith that Hungary would claim its place in a European order without the encumbrance of socialism, and they assumed they would be able to inhabit what they considered a lifestyle commensurate with those enjoyed by middle-class entrepreneurs elsewhere in Europe. They felt betrayed by the new regime for the many difficulties they had encountered in realizing their dream house.[6]

The transformation in attitudes and perceptions of the suburban house was assisted by Organicist discourses that revalued the countryside in opposition to the socialist city. The new suburban house form was drawing on numerous continuities with older semiurban housing forms. This was not just in discourse but in selective appropriation of their materialities, and all in opposition to the qualities of Socialist Generic. The very term "family house with a garden" harked back to the interwar middle-class ideal, drawing on powerful images in the popular media of the bourgeois family enjoying a meal in the peaceful garden on a summer afternoon.

With their enclosed gardens, gazebos, and green lawns, new suburban houses also took on the values once reserved for the cottage, which contrasted the fresh air and the calming effects of being in nature with the pollution and hectic pace of modern city life (see also Caldwell 2011). In Dunaújváros in particular, with its high rates of childhood asthma attributed to pollution from the steel mill, family

Figure 7.5. A new house built in the modest "square house" form typical of village self-build construction practices in the 1960s and 1970s, but painted light yellow and with new, middle-class landscaping instead of a productive garden. Photo by author, 2004.

houses in the country could be crafted as healthier places to raise children and in general more conducive to a balanced family life. Providing a healthy place for childhood figured prominently in Laura's and Ildikó's articulated desires and later justifications for a family house. Likewise, one of Margit's objections to moving to a family house had been that their son was almost grown and therefore past the age when he would have benefited.

If the weekend cottage presented itself as an obvious precursor to the new middle-class house, the role of the socialist-era, self-built, rural family house was more complicated. Conservative proponents of the family house continued to draw on associations with the autonomy and economic independence of houses built by families themselves, even though the political economy of building houses had been fundamentally transformed. As we have seen, a populist intelligentsia had looked to provincial peasant entrepreneurs to become a model for the new entrepreneurial classes. Many of these writers lauded the human capacities mobilized by the privately owned materialities of a family house and its garden. Sándor Kopátsy, for example, was an economist and regular contributor to the new magazine *Family House* (*Családi Ház*). Kopátsy listed the idealized virtues of houses built through *kaláka* just as it was declining as a mode of house building:

> First: Nothing brought together the extended family, the circle of friends, more than mutual building (*kaláka*).

Second: There was no better school for polytechnic capabilities than constructing your own utilities. Many hundreds of thousands learned this way to plaster, to install, and repair electricity and plumbing.
Third: Nothing brought as much self-confidence as the finished house and its further beautification. A house with a garden promotes the development of everyday feelings of success and happiness. The need to fix something, the first ripe fruit, the most beautiful rose on the block—these make the residents better, more optimistic. (Kopátsy 1993:52)

This housing form, Kopátsy implies, inculcated a sense of self-sufficiency and pride in seeing the fruits of one's labor on one's own property. Moreover, the values of familial autonomy reside in a privately owned house with normalized, European character: "We won't be truly European if we are accepted into the European Union, but only when most families can say, 'My house is my castle'" (Kopátsy 1993:52). But early populist advocates of the family house like Kopátsy failed to recognize that *kaláka* was fast becoming obsolete. A new kind of house builder had no interest in cultivating produce on their property, nor in using their own labor to build their house. Even though many builders continued to expect financial assistance and free labor from their extended family, they wanted to avoid the onerous obligations of community building exchange as much as possible. Not surprisingly, these early supporters of the family house were opposed to many of the neoliberal policies introduced after the regime change, policies promoted with appeals to the values of autonomy and self-sufficiency.

The private sphere of the home had been idealized as an island of family privacy from the socialist state—whether in the form of an urban apartment or a rural family house. But the very term "family house" indexed its association with wholesome, heteronormative married life with more than one child, in contrast to the socialist apartment. Socialist-era apartments had long been criticized for destroying the extended family, while small kitchens discouraged practices like family meals where everyone can sit down at once (generating jokes about having to pull stomachs in and use only a spoon). Echoing the rhetoric of anti-socialist Organicism, the material environment of the family house was also supposed to generate divisions of labor and inculcate healthy gender subjectivities. City apartments had been blamed for eliminating the adult male's role and space in the home, and it was assumed that masculine identity would be bolstered not just by the "natural" environment and building projects that the weekend cottage had once provided, but also by the autonomy of a detached house.

It was also becoming harder to deny that the new family house provided the possibility of realizing widespread ideals for a normal life fostered during the state socialist period but made untenable by the design and cramped spaces of socialist apartments. The new housing form included the expansion of the open plan into spaces allowing people to "breathe" and at the same time the individualizing divisions of use-designated spaces. It also accommodated new desires for spaces associated with modern lifestyles in the West, such as a dedicated master bedroom fostering healthy marital relations, bathrooms liberated from drying laundry, and most of all a large room open to the kitchen in which the entire family could gather. These spaces also allowed for new forms of hospitality that encouraged reciprocation, and inviting friends and neighbors for barbecues and drinks on the patio became common practice. Finally, as with the villas of the new economic elite (Czeglédy 1998) these houses and their gardens also fulfilled the spatial and representational requirements of business socializing. They were "distinguishing" or *reprezentatív* spaces for the people that lived in them, tangible evidence of their prosperity and success in the new order.

Organicist Legitimacy

Despite the diversity in the appearance of new houses, most of them had extended qualities of Organicist Modern from interiors to exteriors, helping to construct them as both respectable and distinctly Hungarian. Unlike postmodern forms in the West that featured fragmentation and renewed attention to façade, these housing forms reflected the particular disenchantments generated by the materialities of a state socialist modernity. As we saw in the examples above, house builders carefully chose among the variety of new house forms and design elements within their reach, positioning themselves as part of this new, exclusive middle class, and yet marking their modesty and virtue.

The affective appeal of the Organicist aesthetics of new houses often placed them beyond reproach, even though they were evidence of growing social inequalities. Indeed, the moral superiority inherent in a preference for "natural" materials reflected a continued critique of the modernist project, including its artificial (and ineffectual) attempts to eradicate social stratification. The socialist-era correspondence between qualities of materials and of people merged seamlessly with new, commercial rhetoric that equated the qualities of commodities with the qualities of people. The fundamental difference was that in the new order the state was no longer responsible for extending "livable" worlds to the working population. Instead, the market economy would only extend "quality" materialities to those able to pay the price, thus merging the many beneficial properties of "quality" materials with the prestige of calculable expense.[7]

We saw in previous chapters how an urban proletariat was increasingly aligned with the worst of Socialist Generic materialities. But the emerging middle class also differentiated itself from that other marginalized population, the peasantry, long associated with good, natural, and healthy dirt as well as imbecilic backwardness. The Organicism of new suburban houses was not framed as a "return to nature," but as an advance to a "super" natural state. Advertisements for roofing tiles epitomized this formulation, as in one listing the "ingredients" of roof-

Figure 7.6. New house with arched wooden doors and red tile roof echoing the curves of thatched roofs. Photo by author, 1997.

ing tiles: "Air, Earth and Fire . . . nature that creates" (*Családi ház* 1997/1). While these materials index their difference from the uncooked "nature" of peasantry, they are also transformed by powerful technologies into high-quality commodities for "demanding" consumers. The thatched roofs of new "bourgeois" peasant houses, for example, are chemically treated to make them flame-retardant and water-resistant. Italian tiles designed to look like the rough-hewn stones of castle floors or the terra cotta of Roman baths are manufactured with the latest pressure-resistant technology. In comparison to a material like plastic, which has no visible origin in nature, materials that look and feel like slate—in other words, that have the qualia of slate—index a natural origin, never mind that we can point out the constructedness of this categorization.

High-quality roofing tiles and other high-end home building products conveyed the moral superiority of being in harmony with nature rather than dominating it. At the same time, as the customer reviews of Bramac roofing tiles reveal, home builders made much of the tile's high quality and long-lasting durability as part of a moral project to protect future generations and to build prosperity in a house of material permanence. The expense of these commodities indexes their quality as well as the quality of those who can afford them. In this way, the high-quality materialities of suburban family houses legitimate the people sheltered

Figure 7.7. Advertisement for a business selling (and displaying) a high-tech thatched roof. Image courtesy of Szabolcs Varga.

within them as part of a respectable Hungarian middle class. Their embrace of the powers of a natural order, which includes a free market as much as it does a natural life cycle, produces them as moral persons. As such, they become deserving of the material worlds in which nature is enhanced and controlled and which may indeed help them and their children live longer, healthier lives.

Buying a "Finished" House

By the end of 1997, Ildi had brought Tamás around to the idea of a house. With the help of a no-interest loan from the factory, they bought a "finished house" (*készház*) in a less-prestigious village, south of Dunaújváros and on the end of a street of houses built in the 1980s. On the other side were old peasant houses, some with thatched roofs and mud walls, with fowl pens and vegetable gardens. Even though it was not the house Ildi had hoped for, it was a few streets away from the area of new houses where she had first developed a passion for horseback riding. It had been achieved with minimal strain on their finances and relationships and was a place where her close friends and family could be comfortable. Given the imbalance in their professional status, the house was not incongruent with Tamás's background. Never having had even the "weekend cottage" of the socialist middle stratum growing up, nor the garden plot of peasant-workers, Ildi fully engaged with the well-being promised by life in the country: nature, fresh air, peace and quiet. She made sure they got several dogs and a cat to provide András, now ten years old, with the "healthy" country experience, even though he was usually glued to the computer screen. They painted the exterior a moss green and completely refurbished the interior—including the addition of a ceramic fireplace to provide the warmth and the "homey" feeling she craved. At about 120 square meters (1,300 square feet) the house was twice as big as their apartment had been, and it had an American kitchen with a white-tiled floor open to a raised, carpeted living room with a large television.

Within a year, they had become acquainted with the neighbors. Ildi had her hair cut in one woman's home hair salon, and she started having her clothes made by another. András had developed a network of friends on the street to play computer games with. Even Tamás was reluctantly pleased, despite the flies and outdoor work, and began to spend more time at home. He'd spent a summer building a car port around the back of the house that replaced the vegetable garden. Over the next few years, they refurbished the basement garage and installed an automatic gate, fully transforming the yard from productive garden to leisure space. While the ground floor remained their living space, they refinished the enormous attic into an all-purpose room with a heavy wood dining table, oversized television, sleeping area for guests, workout area, and mosaic-tiled bathroom complete with a wooden "Finnish" sauna. Except to occasionally use the sauna, the only time Ildi went up to use this new space was to iron. The cost of their renovations easily outstripped what it would have cost them to build a new place. Nonetheless, for both, the form of their house provoked few anxieties about overstepping their class status, as very few of their renovations were visible from outside. The only public evidence of Ildi's ample salary was her new Volvo parked in the driveway.

Having a House Built

Two years after I'd left in 1998, Margit wrote me an e-mail, beginning very much in character: "I won't reproach you [for not writing]; one has to accept the laws of today's world, and we too are very busy . . ." She continued, though, with a surprise: "We are trying to buy a plot of land in Rácalmás. . . . I would like to spend my elderly years in a family house. . . . The construction is uncertain, because we don't have the money for it, but if we can solve the problem of the start-up capital, then we will get a bit of money from selling our current apartment. We'll sell the Trabant too and a few other things. There are many problems, but it is helpful that Géza is so understanding, and supportive of me during my frequent illness-related depressions." In December 2000, on a quick visit, they took me out on a foggy evening to see their half-finished house. Géza was barely able to contain his excitement. Margit was also clearly pleased, dismissing now the difficulties of the additional commute. She spoke with quiet pride of how their son Péter had shown a new "responsibility," sleeping out at the site to keep robbers from taking materials, and applying himself as never before to his studies. And also of her husband, who, she said, had demonstrated an energy she had never thought possible in completing the project, supervising all aspects of the construction himself, and using his expertise as an engineer to make sure it was of the highest standards (*igények*).

The design and mode of production of the house had been part of what enabled Margit to make this transformation, allowing her horizon of the possible to expand. Although they still had to be involved in building the house, the process was not the *kaláka* mode of production of the past—an anti-intellectual, uncultured, and materialist pursuit. The new house was built entirely by professionals, incorporating the latest technology and state-of-the-art conveniences. Géza explained how he'd gone to other building sites of houses being built privately (*maszek*) to find the best and cheapest labor, and then he'd supervised them throughout. Everything was of top quality and the latest technology, including the widely advertised Porotherm building blocks, heated floors, and even a state-of-the-art central vacuum cleaning system that Géza insisted was American. Moreover, it shared an Organicist aesthetic with many of the houses in similar, new "suburbanizing" areas. Painted a dark pink that Géza called the color of red meat, it was a single-story house with a red-tiled roof and a deep overhang made of finely fitted and stained wood. It was surrounded by a large lawn with garden furniture on a patio, all enclosed by a high gate.

For both Géza and Margit, the design of the house epitomized quality and restraint: at 200 square meters (2,150 square feet), it was more than double the size of their old apartment, but because it was one story it was not visibly large from the outside. The design, they both emphasized, was practical, with a room entirely for storage, a one-car garage, a laundry room, two baths, a master bedroom and two additional bedrooms, one reserved for Péter, who by this point was off at college in Budapest. The interior was spacious and well-appointed, but they described it in terms of comfort, warmth, and privacy. The front area was floored entirely in ceramic tile that looked like white marble, and it included an American kitchen open onto a large dining room and recessed living room with large picture windows on three sides. While Margit considered it the kind of house that a lawyer in London would be delighted with, it was important to her that it eschewed obvious signs of "luxury" and made minor concessions to her requirements for modesty and practicality. For example, it had no fireplace: "Who would clean it?" she asked. The large, luxurious bathroom was a combination of one Margit had seen in a London hotel room and a "Mediterranean" one featured in *Lakáskultúra*. It had a large walk-in shower but no tub: "In this busy world, who has time to take baths?" Margit's inherited *polgári* furnishings and art objects, which had been accorded prominent places in her urban apartment, were now relegated to a room with the door closed. They were replaced in the open living area by German leather sofas and a modern coffee table made of a slab of granite. The display case and shelves around it were used for the many artifacts she'd brought back from her world travels, such as a carved stone statue from Bali placed on a lace doily.

When I visited a few years later, Margit showed me around the growing neighborhood of similar, distinctly "suburban" houses. Their neighbors included the star of the city's professional women's handball team, a former Communist Party secretary, and a truck driver. Margit commented that this was where Dunaújváros's middle class was moving, pointedly using the term *középosztály* (middle class) rather than *polgár*. When I objected that this area was hardly for the average Hungarian, she conceded: "Yes, unfortunately in Hungary the middle class is very small." As for her neighbors, she was only dissatisfied with two, making judgments about the residents based on the form of their houses rather than on their professions. One had an oval-shaped roof that had apparently collapsed several times, a sign of the homeowner's irresponsibility and desire for extravagance beyond his abilities. The other had small statues of cherubs and fountains in the bricked-in front yard—a sure sign for her that the family was Roma.

In most of my communication with her up until that point, Margit had emphasized the financial and physical sacrifices they made for this house, all justified through the focus on their son. But her last remark about the Hungarian middle class that included the professional athlete next door was a telling one. In moving to such a neighborhood, she had begun to think that what she regarded as a "normal" world would be possible for her in Hungary. She was also understanding herself as part of a different kind of class structure, one in which such distinctions as *polgári* values would continue to play a role but would not be the only game in town.

Moral Materialities and History

In these narratives, the forms and materialities of this new "suburban" family house facilitated its acceptance as a sign of middle-class distinction and as a new form of respectability. These forms also helped middle-class aspirants negotiate the radical transformation of their material environments and the accompanying implications for the kind of person they were now becoming. This was done in part by establishing continuity with familiar values and their alignments with particular materialities, even as the qualities of these materialities were being deployed in new ways. As we've seen, the new house form had managed to draw on the anti-socialist values of both the cottage and the self-built house of the worker-entrepreneur.

At the same time, the distinct materialities of this house established its distance from its rural precedents as a new suburban middle-class form with its modern comforts, bright colors, and leisure landscaping. Ildi and Tamás's entire house disguised extravagances like the indoor Finnish sauna within its modest exterior. But for the other two families, particular interior elements were significant in establishing the legitimacy of these houses as moral spaces for their residents, inscribing them as hard-working citizens deserving of such materialities. The laundry and sewing rooms in Laura's house not only enabled the family to use the rest of the living space "normally" without having to circumnavigate clothing hung to dry, but they embedded Laura's domestic contributions into the structure of the house itself. Similarly, Margit's pointed decision to do without a bathtub in her otherwise lavish bathroom and the importance Géza placed on their high-tech, energy-saving water heater were similar features that produced them as moral citizens capable of practicing self-restraint. At the same time, the high quality of their materialities and the ways they articulated a concern for living a normal, natural existence came at considerable expense. Like expensive, new hybrid cars in the United States, they inscribed their owners as concerned with the natural environment and as high-quality, high-status people.

Meanwhile, *polgári* furnishings in Dunaújváros had lost whatever aura they once had for embodying an idealized bourgeois sensibility. The criteria for middle-class membership had become far more challenging. The home environment was to express individual eclecticism and imagination and at the same time elegant good taste through the myriad and ever-changing possibilities of modern lifestyle consumption.

While the material requirements for the imagined standards of living of "First World" middle-class citizens have shaped the emergence of middle-class culture in Hungary, the incorporation of such standards was neither immediate nor unchallenged. The suburban family house in Hungary is not a form of enduring cultural value. It acquired new value in the 1990s by virtue of its opposition to the materialities of state socialist architecture, but also to the ideologies claimed for that architecture. The family house, positioned in opposition to the collective, artificial uniformity and forced egalitarianism of socialism and the working classes, now appears as the embodiment of the "natural" values of capitalism. Even though urban apartment blocks continue to house a wide spectrum of Hungarian society, including many who claim middle-class status, the new family house has successfully been aligned with the weekend cottage, contrasting the calming effects of nature with hectic effects of modern city life. It also appropriated the idealized qualities of autonomy and independence associated with the self-built family house of the rural entrepreneur, but was distinguished from them by the aesthetics of a Super-Natural Organicism. It thus appears to be both continuous and inevitable, coalescing into one form two values forged in opposition to state socialism: the romanticization of nature and the idealization of the private sphere. The gradual triumph of this form has transformed local systems of value just as the form itself developed according to the aesthetic specificities of the Hungarian context. A socialist-era middle stratum has been gradually displaced, not by a historic bourgeois middle class or its culture, but by a new, entrepreneurial, and professional middle class. In the process, the material form of the new family house has not only redefined the conditions for belonging to the ranks of respectable society, but has been instrumental in constituting and legitimating an emerging middle class.

8 Heterotopias of the Normal in Private Worlds

In 1997, I met a local journalist who wrote for the steel mill newspaper. When I explained my research to her, she immediately understood it to be about the relationship between one's living space and one's sense of self in the world. She referred me to an article she had written on a new local handyman business that specialized in refurbishing panel apartments. I reproduce the first part of it here, as it gives articulate form to narratives and expressions in regular circulation during the late 1990s in Dunaújváros, a narrative that will feel familiar to the reader of this book. It is a narrative of recent history and of the expectations for and disappointments in the system change. It is also a narrative about the resilience of the idea that transformations to one's home can produce transcendent transformations to one's life. And finally, it is a narrative that hints more broadly at the emerging relationship between one's private home life and the wider sociopolitical and economic order. The title of the article? "My home, my castle!" (Kozma 1995).

> There was a time when we used the summer vacation for rest. The entire family retreated, if nowhere else, then to Balaton Széplak [the steel mill's resort for workers at Lake Balaton called "Beautiful Dwelling"]. When the second economy picked up, everyone used their free time for working, and with the diligence of bees, tried to create better circumstances for themselves. A "real estate" phenomenon began, and family house belts developed. Standards (*igények*) arose which exceeded the panel apartment's "complete comforts" [namely]: a green belt, a little garden, and the expression: "I don't want to hear my neighbor's snoring." The system change paralyzed this kind of change in quality, this progressive movement.
>
> In the past, building a house was never a cakewalk and many failed—if not materially, then by sacrificing the marriage. Now, the practice of putting up a house through *kaláka* has almost completely ceased, and slowly, its meaning is also being lost in common knowledge. Today, only a very few are able—using a new word—"to finance" (*megfinanszírozni*) a life space fitting their standards (*igények*).
>
> And the majority? The majority these days doesn't even think of changing their furniture ... they look at the colorful brochures (IKEA, Tutto Mobili, Michelfelt) and try to be satisfied with the good old "French bed" in their bedroom. In place of a new kitchen, they buy a few rows of tiles, change the linoleum floor and cover the old, built-in cabinets with self-sticking wallpaper. Men with clever hands will sometimes wallpaper, paint, plaster, and even make

do-it-yourself furnishings (*barkácsolni*). For those who can't, the old furnishings stay, and they have committed themselves to a lifetime of the wall-unit closet, the two sofa beds, and the coffee table.

Burned out desires and people, petrified relations. What can be done?! ... Those who still have some spirit tear down walls, open up rooms, or divide them. It is no longer forbidden, and most apartments are now in private ownership: just the grounding wall must stay as is! "Difference" attracts, something special, "let mine not be the same as the neighbor's." Breaking out of the grayness, the habitual, the panel masses. If I can't do it on the outside, then at least let me enchant from the inside, so that my individuality can be seen. I don't want mass housing, I want a home, a real one, where not just my body, but my spirit can rest! My house, my castle! ...

[With such changes...] we can make peace with the world, with ourselves, knowing that we don't have to look, helplessly, at others'—perhaps visible—well-being. Even within the panel walls we can create for ourselves a little island ... one that can mirror our dreams.

—Erzsébet Kozma (1995)

The anxieties and desires Kozma expresses here are familiar. There is the obligatory alignment with the "moral losers" of the system change, the population of the socialist middle stratum who in retrospect realize that even though life was difficult during state socialism, the last few decades were a time of steady "progress" in standards of living. For many in Dunaújváros's broad middle stratum, the regime change "paralyzed" this progress rather than producing the smoothly running system promised by the properties of Western material goods, a system that was supposed to create the conditions for a "normal" life. While Kozma notes the importance of creating something special and reflecting difference, the well-being sought here is not simply one of invidious distinction. It is one of transcendent transformation in and through the realm of the material, of a yearning to "break out" of the gray confines of a socialist-era materiality and the constraints this gray implied. "Difference" is a mark of visible personhood, rising above the anonymity of the crowd and the reductive abstractions of socialist citizenship. As Robert Foster has noted, after Levi-Strauss: "Social life requires difference and distinction; these are the qualifications that motivate exchange, alliance and communication" (Foster 2009:10). Its importance is nothing less than the struggle for social recognition over the namelessness of death.

By availing oneself of this helpful renovation service, Kozma implies, even residents of panel estate apartments can transform their aging Socialist Modern furnishings, the "wall-unit closet, two sofa beds and the coffee table." Such renovations are necessary to create the spaces for a normal life, spaces meeting their standards and thus constructing (as well as mirroring) their sense of self-value. This service offers the hope that people left behind in panel apartments won't have to stand by helplessly, watching the well-being of others while they themselves remain trapped by the materialities of a now-dead state socialism and its "petrified" social relations. As they had for years, such transformations promised to rejuvenate one's "burned out desires" with life-giving, sensuous materialities.

But above all, this passage is about the restorative powers of that dwelling called "home" and the shelter it offers from an outside world, and at the same time how it constructs that outside world. The qualities of such private domestic spheres, so often called "islands," "oases," or fortified "castles," produced them as shelters from the hassles, dangers, and anxieties of the outside world.[1] Such tropes of withdrawal and isolation from a public sphere envisioned in overwhelmingly hostile terms are entirely in keeping with socialist-era formulations. They particularly invoke continuity with socialist-era inscriptions of domestic space as a sacralized sphere beyond the reach of an intrusive state and of shelter from a "not normal" world. In the 1990s, however, the heterotopic inscription of homes through Organicist Modern shifted from an opposition to a unitary state to the display of Super-Natural Organicist commodities as a mark of middle-class distinction. The ideal home became described in terms of fantasy and escape as much as a rejuvenating, "natural" hearth. Similarly, formulations of private and public were undergoing subtle transformations calibrated with new expectations for "normal" life, transformations that again drew upon the distinctions of gender. These shifting conceptions of public and private had implications for the transformation of Hungarian society and the production of "normal" personhood.

Postsocialist configurations of public and private spheres were influenced by idealized conceptions of bourgeois, Western European orderings of the social, political, and economic world. Hopes were high in the first years after 1989 that without the disrupting interventions of the centralizing state, an orderly, civilized, and more "natural" relationship between private and public spheres would develop—in short, Hungarian citizens could finally enjoy the conditions of a normal existence. This ideal included cleansing the private domestic sphere of the economic activities that had become part of family life with the second economy. For many, it also meant restoring idealized gender relations of male breadwinner and housewife and the corollary restoration of traditional gendering to public and private, domestic spheres. Indeed, in Dunaújváros women whose husbands made enough money to allow them to stay home enjoyed a certain prestige and were generally envied by other women who "had" to work.

Significantly, it was to the new democratic state that the aspiring middle classes turned to usher in this more "natural" order in the early 1990s, an expectation fostered by the first democratically elected government and its promises to place the country on a path of embourgeoisement. Such optimistic expectations for the state were short-lived. Once reviled as the enemy of the private, autonomous family, the state was now thought of in terms of abandonment and betrayal. As we have seen, the new state was divesting itself of responsibility for employment, housing, and other provisions that improved the general welfare. It was thus "abandoning" the majority of the population whose livelihood had been undergirded by state companies. It was also "betraying" ostensibly hard-working middle-class people through high taxation and by failing to legislate an orderly market economic sphere conducive to the prosperity of an entrepreneurial *polgár* middle class. Despite the general disdain for state socialism, the new state was being judged by standards for public order set by the old state, proving itself ineffectual in curbing the avaricious machinations of those citizens willing to overturn traditional norms of economic conduct and exploit the loopholes of a nascent capitalist legal system. In the late 1990s, citizens disillusioned with the new regime could still hold out hope that Hungary's problems stemmed in part from the country's continuing divide from Europe. In the meantime, they had to contend with what seemed like signs of Hungarian system dysfunction: squabbling political parties, corruption scandals, an ineffective justice system, financial instability, and a sensationalist media. If Hungary was ever admitted to the European Union, many believed, then Western Europe's civilizing influence would allow the conditions for a "normal" life to develop. (It was only after admittance to the EU in 2004 that Hungarians began to blame the EU for its problems, coming to align the EU with the Soviet Union as an external, rule-governed power intervening in Hungarian autonomy.)

Men, Women, and Wild Capitalism

As a corollary to falling expectations for such an ordered nation-state, narratives abounded in the 1990s speculating on how long it would take for Hungary to "catch up" with Western levels of order, lawfulness, and standards of living. Common estimates were between ten and thirty years. When pressed, most people would reflect thoughtfully and with nuance on the economic and legal situation. But in everyday conversation they regularly resorted to two related explanations for the continuing lack of normalcy in Hungarian social, economic, and political life. First was the conviction that the continuing presence of "not normal" systems, conditions, people, and habits from state socialism were interfering with the establishment of a "normal" present, and thus with the workings of the new institutions of democracy and capitalism. Just as had happened four decades earlier during the socialist attempt to transform society, fault for failure rarely lay with the institution of transformation (e.g., the planned city, the socialist building campaign) but with people and material environments. Particular kinds of Hungarians and the intractable materialities of state socialism were to blame.

A second, equally powerful narrative dramatized Hungary in the 1990s through hyperbolic comparisons to mythical eras in the teleological development of democratic capitalism and nation-states, rather than a form of neoliberal capitalism specific to the 1990s. These were the stages of history socialism had tried to "leap over" or speed through with planned industrialization. One such era was Dickensian England, the dog-eat-dog world of cruel industrialists and exploited masses, known from communist-era history texts as well as from Dickens, but just as much taken from images from a popular BBC television series that dealt with a nineteenth-century shipping family, the Onedin Line.[2] More commonly invoked, however, were two eras from American history as envisioned by Hollywood: the Chicago of the 1930s, when gangsters ruled the city, and the American "Wild West" of lawless gunmen pitted against upstanding citizens courageously building new lives on the frontier. It was the "wild" of the Wild West, recontextualized within Marxist stages of historical materialism, that produced the paradigmatic expression for the postsocialist 1990s: the "era of wild capitalism" (*vadkapitalizmus korszaka*).[3]

Scholars have written of the striking masculine imagery and material qualities prevalent in the fledgling postsocialist democracies (cf. Einhorn 1993). Éva Federmayer wrote that "the two key metaphors of the dominant discourse in Hungary [in the 1990s] are *kemény* (hard), even '*kőkemény*' (rock hard) on the one hand, and *lágy* (soft) on the other. 'Hard' signifies the brave new world of capitalism and phallocentric competitiveness, while 'soft' denotes the renounced 'goulash communism'" (Federmeyer 1997:247). This imagery continued in the 2000s. Gal and Kligman wrote that "despite the proliferation of female small-scale entrepreneurs, it is men more than women who are increasingly associated with the idealized and even romanticized private, the dynamic, capitalist sector of the economy. Indeed, the aggressiveness, initiative, and competition that are identified with the market are becoming new representative forms of masculinity" (Gal and Kligman 2000a:59).

Postsocialist economic and political conditions were increasingly seen as demanding a new type of person and moral code. They were conditions necessitating masculine characteristics—but these were important for both men and women. One night after a movie, Laura, Zoltán, and I stopped for a drink at the most upscale new pub in town, a Western-themed place named "Geronimo" that had been tacked onto the side of the deteriorating local movie theater. I knew that the owner had used his wife's legally obtained income in her graphic design company, where my roommate worked, to finance the extravagant wrought iron stools we were sitting on. I grumbled that the wife had used the pub to justify not giving her own employees a raise in three years, among them, Zoltán's own stepsister. But he had no sympathy for his sister, gender aside. "It's a hard world. If someone asks me for a raise, I'd also say 'no.' If they don't pursue it, well then, 'Fuck you!'" [in English]. "If they're not willing to stand up for themselves, then it's their own fault."

Similar sentiments surfaced most poignantly in how some of the aspiring middle class felt they had to prepare their children for survival in "this world."

Some traits were continuous with the past, such as being neat and clean, polite, and well-appointed (*rendes*), as well as being diligent and purposeful in one's activities. The ability to land on one's feet and to find one's place in the world also continued in importance, though now the stakes had risen considerably. Other qualities, however, echoed neoliberal capitalist rhetoric such as "flexibility" and "risk taking." In a relatively unchanged imbalance, the criteria for girls was often harsher than for boys, as parents tried to prepare daughters for the difficult burdens of the "double shift" awaiting adult, married women (of full-time employment paired with full responsibility for domestic duties). Changes were afoot here too, as girls were aggressively groomed to employ their feminine charms not only to manipulate men, but in marketable ways as well. It had become clear that attractive young women (*dekoratív*) stood a far better chance of landing a corporate job in a high-visibility position, such as receptionist or secretary, and the classified advertisements were explicit on this point, specifying that women over thirty need not apply.

The norms of being "demanding" (*igényes*) of one's materialities, both of one's environment and one's person, had now been taken to an entirely different level. To get positions like these, it was not enough to be competent and to be presentably groomed, something that any "body" could achieve, at least in theory. Now, entire groups of people were being excluded for things they could not change—because they were too old or too unattractive. The socialist ideology that inequalities are bred into people by a system that dictates they accept their station in a hierarchy, and corollary attempts to train the lower classes to be more "demanding" (or to demand more), is here not so much reversed as transformed. In this world, it is not enough to be born into privilege to make one's way in the world, but to be born with the physical and mental characteristics to succeed. Like the American ideology of pulling oneself up by one's bootstraps, this formulation obscures the ways class privilege magnifies any "natural talents" and compensates for weaknesses, just as class disenfranchisement magnifies disadvantages and suppresses inherent gifts.

Some parents took this imperative to secure the futures of their children even further. Kata, the beauty salon owner and wife of the hospital director, insisted that her eleven-year-old daughter would learn several languages so that her future did not depend on her physical attributes: "This way, if she lost an arm, she could still support herself." A working-class father, the signs of alcoholism on his prematurely aged face, told me about how he was raising his daughter. "This world is hard (*kemény*)," he said, "not like before. You can't count on people to take care of you. . . . I'm not instigating a Spartan order, but I want her to learn a team sport, not something soft like tennis. Tennis takes skill and strength, but with team sports, where one has to struggle, you learn about combat." Many social scientists and feminist scholars observed alarming trends in employment patterns after the fall of socialism showing that women were being inordinately affected by a postsocialist economy.⁴ Even in Hungary, where the high percentage of women in the service sector led to better rates of employment, women in rural communities were often thrown back on the power of their fathers and fathers-in-law with the decline in state employment (Thelen 2003). Nonetheless, instead of being relegated to a domestic sphere, I found that girls were being prepared for the new demands of postsocialist economic survival.

In these accounts, it is no longer an oppressive state that forces people to retreat to the "normal" domestic spaces of the home, but the merciless world of postsocialist Hungarian laissez-faire market economy and the kinds of people it produces. For example, László, a man in his mid-thirties who occasionally traveled to Germany for semilegal work, felt he had seen what a "normal life" might look like. It consisted of things like going grocery shopping after work in a supermarket and not having to worry too much about the cost of food. In Hungary, he felt people were now preoccupied with themselves and had become more intolerant. "Hungarians," he told me, "are unprincipled, made of flimsy stuff (*gyarló*). If they get into a position of wealth or power, they walk right over their friends or acquaintances from the past, not acknowledging anyone who helped them. They then take whatever they can get from their position."

Zoltán voiced similar sentiments one day as we were sitting outside their new house on a beautiful summer afternoon. The goldfish pond and flowerbeds had a settled look, and the rapidly growing fir trees planted around the perimeter were turning it into an enclosed, sheltered space. He fondled the springy turf with pride, wondering (half-seriously) whether to send photos of his lawn to an English gardening magazine. I had mentioned my troubles with fieldwork, finding people to be guarded, and he responded with characteristic vehemence:

> With tough economic times, people are reduced to indigence (*rászorultak*). They close themselves off, become embittered . . . they have no sense of tolerance and don't give others right-of-way. In such circumstances, they look down on those who are poorer than them, lower than them, but if someone has so much as a glass of water more, they want to rip their throats out!

He sighed, then, looking around at his serene surroundings:

> When people don't have a peaceful, secure home (*békés, biztonságos otthon*), a car and enough money in their pocket to get a fill-up without anxiety, to take a vacation . . . they become bitter. It is a necessity to have a home, an island for themselves, where there is peace.

It was common in Hungary in the 1990s, as Zoltán did, to illustrate this "lack of tolerance" with the evocative scenario of Hungarian roadways, where status, power, and their relationship to socialism were distilled in vehicles ranging from the tiny East German Trabant to the largest, most powerful West German Mercedes (Berdahl 1999a). Knowing the material composition of the Trabant helps to illuminate the magnitude of this imbalance. Produced in East Germany from the early 1960s to 1991 with almost no changes to its design, the Trabant body was made of Duroplast, a kind of plastic containing resin and strengthened by cotton waste from the Soviet Union. Its two-stroke, two-cylinder engine was sufficient to propel the light body, and it carried up to four adults. It had decent fuel economy but puffed out high levels of hydrocarbons and carbon monoxide. The materialities of a soft and ineffective but polluting socialism being overrun by a hard and effective capitalism were viscerally experienced on the road, as Hungarians traveling in socialist-era cars had to submit to the principle of "might makes right" when foreign cars powered past them on two-lane highways.

The pervasive positioning of the postsocialist economic sphere as an almost mythically masculine place of struggle was often collapsed with characterizations of Hungarian society itself in its "natural" state. As we have seen, during state socialism, stealing resources and time from the state to give to one's family was considered entirely ethical. Moreover, as Martha Lampland has shown, villagers felt it was only human nature to work for oneself and one's family first, and they scoffed at state socialist attempts to get citizens to think in terms of an abstract "collective wealth," especially when their experience was that those who profited the most from this system did little of the work (Lampland 1995:271). Without the artificial interference of the socialist state, however, society reverted to its "natural" Hobbesian state of every man for himself, particularly since the socialist state had attempted to destroy local senses of community, cooperation, and empathy.

The loss of state interference was felt as more than simply the loss of economic security. Particularly the middle-aged and elderly recognized that even though worker brigade activities and collective workdays were coercive and "stupid," they had brought people together. One woman, a banking administrator in her fifties, recalled to me how her women's brigade had a great time each December fabricating a journal of their activities for the year. She missed this sense of community, even though one source of their solidarity was an opposition to the "ridiculousness" (*hülyeség*) of such ideologically driven tasks. Others missed the activities once provided by the steel mill and other local firms, such as chartered buses to theater performances in Budapest and intramural sports for adults. Although people generally agreed that firms needed to focus on generating a profit, they felt the loss of the social role such institutions had once provided.

Widespread concerns for the state of Hungarian society were reflected in a sermon I attended in the Catholic church in Pentele. I had been invited by Júszi, the rosy-cheeked, sturdy wife of the former head of the agricultural collective who had explained to me the sacrality of private property (chapter 6). The priest encouraged the parishioners to demonstrate more "solidarity, togetherness, readiness to help," citing the Mir space shuttle and how the astronauts understood that "We are all one family." With no room to be individualistic and selfish, they had to cooperate. Similarly, in Christianity, he emphasized, "We love God and Jesus Christ, but we love the church too, the church community, community itself."

What is striking about these dramatic visions of chaos and social disorder, about the loss of community and empathy, is that young and middle-aged men voiced them with the most passion. Their wives and girlfriends listened to their depictions, then injected tempering words. For example, when Zoltán insisted that a "fuck you" attitude was the only way to survive in this world, Laura nodded, but then added that it was nonetheless important to maintain some kind of honor and decency (*becsületesség, illendőség*). Zoltán conceded this point with a shrug—noting that they (really she) had raised teacher salaries at her language school even though they couldn't raise fees. Similarly, when László was complaining about the lack of normal conditions in Hungary and the malicious behavior of his neighbors, his wife Zsuzsa tried to remind him that such things happen everywhere. "One has to accept what is here, now," she explained. "OK, so everything doesn't go as you would like, but if you wait until everything goes normally, you will go crazy."

In these conversations, women's accounts of the economic private sphere tended to be less apocalyptic than that of their partners. Laura often talked about future plans at the language school. Zsuzsa, who was about thirty and worked at the land registry office, took correspondence courses for a degree in accounting and liked to take trips to see the country's many castles. Her husband joked that she liked them because she could imagine herself as a princess. She felt the postsocialist world with its expanded borders was full of opportunity and couldn't understand the behavior of some of her male colleagues, who stayed on in low-paying jobs in the feminized bureaucracy. "If I were a young, unattached man," she said, "I'd be seeking my fortune abroad."[5] These women complained about abnormal conditions and compared their lifestyles unfavorably to the idealized lives of Western women, but they refrained from dividing their worlds into a moral private and an amoral public.

The gendered construction of self was here too aligned with ideologies of public and private. In Hungary, as we have seen, women, with identities partially anchored in their domestic duties, actively constructed order (*rend*) on a daily basis. Their ties and responsibilities to their families took precedence over nonfamily, "public" matters, even if part of these included providing for their children financially (Kovács and Váradi 2000:183). In contrast, men tended to feel their sense of self tied to their participation in the economic and political life of their communities, including a responsibility for public order, though they were no less invested in the home as a "private" and autonomous space. But there is more to the story. In a continuation of sorts with state socialist patterns, while female partners often engaged in more regular, legal activities—albeit often low-paying—their male partners pursued higher risk, often illegal and irregular endeavors, which also promised more spectacular monetary rewards.[6] Indeed, a number of men who had worked for good pay (at illegal or dangerous jobs) in Western Europe refused to work for low wages at home. This had been the case for Laura's first husband, who had worked as a high-rise, semilegal construction worker in Austria. He had gotten used to being well compensated for his labor and so refused to work for a pittance at home.

The saying, "In this world, one simply can't do business honestly and survive" usually referred to minor infractions of the law, such as not giving receipts. It was not uncommon for men to be associated with semilegal, even criminal activities, from using questionably obtained financing to smuggling goods. Their imaginings of the postsocialist world may have accurately reflected their subjective experience, but it also allowed them to position themselves as long-suffering heroes, doing what had to be done (given the circumstances) for the sake of their families.[7] These imaginings are shaped by notions of a traditional, bourgeois patriarchal family, much as Habermas described it, where the raw pursuit of economic self-interest in the private sphere must be offset by a separate, protected domestic realm, with a wife/mother at its center, a sphere that redeems the head of household through the humane morality governing it (Habermas 1989).

And yet while women were positioned at the center of the domestic sphere, they continued to work, often making as much as or more than their male partner over the course of a year. They were also engaged in more socially active occupations—running service-oriented businesses such as language schools or beauty salons, selling insurance or health supplements, even working in the government bureaucracy. Female entrepreneurs, in my experience, were more likely to talk about what they did not in terms of profit but, as a Chinese supplement saleswoman put it, in terms of the importance of "believing in what you are selling/offering." Surprisingly, some of the husbands of these women began doing a bit more of the domestic labor (though they rarely admitted it and tended to limit their involvement to cooking and grocery shopping rather than laundry and cleaning). Their masculinity no longer compromised by an emasculating state, it became less important for these men and their partners to define their gender roles entirely through a rigid domestic division of labor. Similarly, men saw their wives as economic partners rather than as compulsory employees of the bureaucratic state, once aligned against men (see Freeman 2011 for a similar experience in Barbados).

Abnormalities of Daily Life: Making "Not Normal" People

Despite these differences, men and women alike complained bitterly of having to endure the continuing abnormalities in everyday life, abnormalities that were generally tied to difficulties with transportation, provisioning, and living spaces, as well as the "not normal" people one had to deal with in public space. These difficulties were linked to the many obligations one had to family. Many people continued to share Margit's assumption that people in London, for instance, lived a more "normal" life, one free of the hassles, conflict, and exhausting pace (*rohangálás*) that permeated Hungarian existence. Such a life of civility, efficiency, and order was also a life conducive to the existence of a different kind of person, imagined to be calm and dignified. This fantasy of civilized personhood was the antinomy of the type of person thought to be necessary for survival in Hungary, someone characterized by grasping at things and situations in a panicked, spastic way (*kapkodás*). Women in particular commiserated over their impossible schedules, late buses, insolent store clerks, and never-ending run-ins with bureaucracies. Even horoscopes assumed that the typical Hungarian reader was stressed out and overworked and consequently was someone who would act or react in haste—who would allow emotions of panic, anger, perceived slight, or despair to govern their behavior (see Fehérváry 2007).

Anikó, the frail seamstress who had just moved from a panel apartment to an unfinished house in a nearby village, stopped in one day when I was visiting Margit to deliver a message. She was out of breath and said she couldn't stay as she had lots to do before catching the bus back home. Her shoulders were hurting from carrying the bags of vegetables her daughter had asked her to bring in from her new garden. As she hurried off to her son's new loft apartment, she mentioned that he complained that everyone but his parents had been to see it. "It would be normal to be happy for them, because they are happy," she said, but then grumbled about her exhausting life. "It's terrible that a person has to run around this much, this never-ending rushing around (*rohangálás*). The family is large, everyone presses for help, and I want to help them, especially my daughter with her two small children. But everyone needs help." On another day, Laura stopped by unexpectedly about six months after moving into her new house, at her wits end. She'd had enough of this hectic life, she said on the verge of tears, and was determined to change her priorities. She had given up her car to pay for the house and hadn't taken a vacation outside of Hungary for years. Now, she insisted, the family would take a break and go to Italy, even if it meant waiting for a year or two to finish the upstairs banister and the fireplace. As these examples illustrate, moving to an unfinished family house did little in practice to ease the burdens of a stressful life.

The discourse of *rohangálás* was not new to the 1990s, but had been used to characterize life in the 1970s and 1980s as well. In the 1960s and 1970s, the division between the hectic workweek and leisure time weekends was often glamorized in publications as an aspect of modernity, one that was spatialized through the contrast of a modern urban apartment for the workweek and the rustic rural cottage for the weekends. During the late socialist period, people attributed the difficulties of daily life to the inefficiency and corruption of the socialist state, but also to the sense that the Kafkaesque state bureaucracy intentionally erected obstacles to control as well as to wear down the populace (Berdahl 1999b; Verdery 1991, 1996). Nonetheless, as Berdahl writes for the GDR, as much as people bridled at bureaucratic procedures and state intrusions into their personal lives, they believed there was some administrative necessity for these obstacles, however ill-intentioned (Berdahl 1999b). After 1989, the collapse of the state was accompanied by the confirmation that many of these daily hassles were the product of nothing more than an obstructive socialist state. Margit, for example, was dismayed rather than pleased to discover that I had only had to fill out one form at the Dunaújváros post office to send an overseas package in 1997. The years of carefully filling out multiple forms had convinced her of their inherent necessity for the workings of the postal system. I could almost see in her face the painful recognition that years of her life had been wasted in overcoming similarly pointless bureaucratic tasks.

In the 1990s, middle-class aspirants saw every such difficulty as the legacy of the socialist system and the kinds of people it created. Géza complained that he still had to arrive at the steel mill for his engineering job at 6 AM with the shift workers. This was a socialist-era policy to underscore parity between white- and blue-collar workers, but one that he saw as pointlessly making everyone suffer because some people's jobs required it. "I'm not objecting to the insecurity and the risk" (of post-1989 capitalism), he said. "I just want a more normal, a more humane, order! The simple things that smooth the day's progress."

As we've seen, Hungarians had a sense that "not normal" conditions forced otherwise decent people to behave unethically. Indeed, achieving "normal" standards of living was necessary in order to live an ethical, spiritually meaningful life, particularly in providing conditions for harmonious relationships with one's family. As Ildikó confided to me, "it's not normal that I don't want to go see my sister. But I feel so claustrophobic in her small apartment!"

"Peace and Quiet" and the Idealized Family

Equations of upscale private spheres with transcendence are familiar from middle-class constructions of these worlds in advertising, movies, and other mass media in Western Europe and in the United States. Marianne Gullestad writes that "peace and quiet" constitutes a central cultural category in Norway, and perhaps throughout Scandinavia, expressing the value of "personal wholeness and integrity . . . [which are] easily threatened by the perceived fragmentation of modern social life" (Gullestad 1992:143). This state of being is tied to the modern material world and the divisions of life between work and leisure, public and private, city and country. Formulations of leisure time and its settings in the family house or in "nature" at the family cottage are conducive to an inner state of calm and control, as well as to an absence of conflict in one's social and personal relationships (Gullestad 1992:143–45). These are opposed to the rush and bother of everyday life, situated on the street and in the city: errands, paid work, and a lack of freedom in organization of time and activities.

While these resonate with long-standing Hungarian dichotomies, there are also telling differences. In Hungary, "peace and calm" (*békesség és nyugalom*) are not spoken of as easily achievable states of being, but as ideals achieved through great struggle or captured in rare, fleeting moments. Furthermore, what Gullestad offers as the implicit philosophy of life, humanity and action in Norway evoked by such terms as "peace and quiet" (1992:147), hardly reflects Hungarian ideals for self and social relations. For most Norwegians, Gullestad maintains, good social relations between people demands maintenance of a certain distance that should not be violated and thus control of the self; this distance allows the other to be "whole, balanced and safe by ... avoiding open personal conflicts" (1992:147). For most Hungarians I knew in Dunaújváros, such behavior characterizes the stereotypically reserved northern European who in some contexts might be described as civilized but in others as cold or unfeeling. Extending such social distance to family members "to keep peace in the house" would be anathema to many people. Moreover, in certain situations, loss of control continues to be an appropriate response, particularly for men. Many men and women exhibited a high tolerance for open verbal conflict. I regularly found myself caught in the middle of these arguments, whether between family members or between my landlord, the neighbors, and the repair man. Though I found them to be unsettling, I came to realize that in the highly opinionated shouting, people were listening to one another. Nonetheless, these disputes, particularly between family members, often escalated into lengthy periods where those involved stopped speaking to each other altogether.

Hungarian middle-class aspirations for peace and calm, for harmonious family relations, seem to reflect fantasies of more civilized ways of life unlikely to be realized, or even appreciated, in practice. Identical surveys conducted in Dunaújváros in 1977 and in 1992 asked respondents to prioritize their life goals and desires. Respondents overwhelmingly ranked "family" first, followed closely by "having a peaceful, orderly, calm life." Third in importance was having some dimension of faith or spirituality in their lives. A distant fourth through seventh were "freedom from obligations," "success," "work," and "respect." Whatever respondents felt about their own family relations, they fully believed in family as a transcendent value of the highest order and knew it to be the morally correct response to the question. It may have also been crucial for identity. As Olga Shevchenko found in postsocialist Russia (2009:9, 90–96), when other aspects of identity such as one's profession are shifting and unmoored, one's identity within a family is what is secure and inviolate.

In an ideal world, "family" should be inseparable from "peace, order and calm," but as the survey showed in distinguishing the two, family was also recognized as the source of financial, emotional, and physical obligations and suffering. As one oft-repeated expression put it, "Without family, there would be no need for medicine!" In the postsocialist order, however, reliance on the family for material support continued apace and in many circumstances increased (Pine 1996; Thelen 2003; Shevchenko 2009). During the socialist period, the state encouraged the upwardly mobile aspiration of parents to sacrifice for their children neverendingly, and this expectation continued among an aspiring middle class. Not only did my middle-aged informants make sure their children would have apartments of their own when they were older, but I repeatedly saw them continue to invoke this obligation from their own aging parents. A plant nursery worker in her mid-twenties I knew from the women's soccer team used a common expression to explain her decision to put off getting married and having a kid: "First, I want to see a bit of the world, make some money," she said, "and after that it can be: 'Everything for the child.'"

When a Normal Home Is a Heterotopia

The insistence on the normalcy of what in Hungary counted as a high standard of living was also an insistence on the modesty and morality of such standards, and it arose from an understanding that Western middle-class lifestyles were far more than luxuries. As we have seen, they were essential conditions for the development of harmonious family relations and for becoming the kind of person one wished to be. Such utopian imaginings were a staple of socialist ideology. For East Germans, the West gradually seemed to materialize all the unfulfilled promises of the socialist utopia once it became clear that the "beautiful life" used by socialist ideology to justify years of hardship and toil was never going to be realized (Veenis 1999:95–98). In other words, socialism had conjured expectations for a utopian world that it was never able to produce, but over time, such a utopian system seemed to have come into existence in the West.

The correspondence between "normal" material conditions and the possibility of being a normal person was also linked to long-standing ideals for a presocialist bourgeois mode of life, one reinforced by state-socialist-era publications attempting to raise the cultural level of the population. Despite the preponderance of entire families living in tiny apartments, *Lakáskultúra* contributed to the importance placed on giving a child its own space and of recreating public and private, frontstage and backstage areas. Recall that while writers recognized the "unfortunate small size" of mass-produced apartments, they nonetheless insisted that creating a livable and practical home "doesn't depend on the number of meters" but on "some compromise and rational thinking" (*Lakáskultúra* 1976[xi]1). In postsocialist interior design magazines, particularly those geared toward the one-quarter of the Hungarian population still living in panel construction apartments (2.5 million people), the time and effort put into rearrangements of small spaces, the ingenious solutions for insoluble problems, continued to take up a significant amount of space. *SzépLak* (Beautiful Home), a new home décor magazine that targeted panel apartment dwellers, encouraged its readers to spend what little money they had on transforming their apartments into "Enchantment in 67m^2" or "Panel Luxury."

The perception in the 1990s of a continued abnormalcy in service, bureaucratic, and social spheres reinforced among citizens the desires to focus time and energy on creating spheres of normalcy in spaces within their control. This furthered the inclination fostered during the socialist period to invest emotionally and financially in the domestic private sphere and remain detached from civic life. As we saw in Dunaújváros, the growing presence of new, postsocialist spaces sharply contrasted with and transformed the significance of the older spaces around them, creating disjunctures in temporal and spatial experience (chapter 1). In Hungary after socialism, private domestic spaces were envisioned as having the potential to be the ultimate heterotopic space, complete with the power to envelop and transform their inhabitants. They appeared to be places where an idealized "normal" life could transpire, contained within but isolated from the "not normal" world surrounding them. As Foucault observed, heterotopias often result from attempts to create spaces that are "irreducibly 'other' and perfect in contrast to the messiness around them; they are spaces not of illusion, but of compensation" (Foucault 1986:27). As such, they are predicated on a sharp division between spaces, the heterotopic space being a kind of all-encompassing "interior" creating its own reality within a problematic context.

The ideal of a free-standing family house with a garden (*kertes családi ház*) exemplified an anti-socialist heterotopia. These new houses became spaces in which families could try to create the normal conditions missing from the wider socioeconomic and political order. They were also residential forms that constituted the relationship of citizens to this new order. On the one hand, such detached buildings could be seen as the paradigmatic form for a newly independent middle class of a newly independent nation-state, as autonomous people within a nation-state made up of self-directed citizens. This new housing ideal was a clear rejection of the alienating "collectivist" experience of socialist apartment buildings and the failure of this residential form to create a harmonious society. At the same time, these new houses came to be islands or fortified castles that shut out this new order when it failed to conform to expectations for normalcy. Instead of being incorporated into or producing a new, middle-class society, these houses were often understood as spaces of secession from this "not normal" Hungary. The private thus became reconfigured as a refuge, not from the all-intrusive socialist state, but from the "not normal" world of postsocialist neoliberal capitalism. The players in this postsocialist "external" world included a now weak and ineffective state, but one that was no longer figured as "unitary." Instead, it was aligned with a succession of political parties standing in for the interests of fragments of the Hungarian population. The state was no longer an entity against which the Hungarian "people" could imagine themselves to be unified, but one that divided the population against one another into vociferously opposed political factions.

Residents of apartment buildings also had the potential for heterotopic separation, as described in the opening passages of this chapter in which a panel apartment can become an enchanted island. The objective continued to be to "forget" the wider social context of the personalized space of an apartment, both the materialities of mass housing and the presence of one's neighbors. Just as apartments and family houses could be restorative places for body and spirit, specific spaces within them also had restorative powers. Kitchens and bathrooms were singled out for transformation by residents, a trend reflected in special issues of home improvement/interior decor publications and trends elsewhere. Within the idealized spaces of interiors, new American kitchens and luxury bathrooms could be seen as nested heterotopias, sites of particular potency for condensing "the modern" with their concentration of advanced household technology and hygienic standards. At the same time, they became key sites for differentiation from a dated socialist modernity. New kitchens and bathrooms were spaces in the home where antisocialist values (for family and individual growth) were most powerfully opposed to the "unnatural" and impersonal intentions of Socialist Modern design. Hidden within interiors, new kitchens and bathrooms were less revealing about local status concerns than they were about how people wanted to transform themselves via the material into part of an idealized reference group and system of values. With their high-tech, hygienic, and high-standard qualities, these spaces were not only "normal" enclaves within a "not normal" context. They generated utopian imaginings of "modern" lifestyles beyond Hungary's borders. Through the experience of material worlds understood to be equivalent to those of First World citizens, people could imagine themselves as belonging to this global middle class and thus as fully realized human beings. In a "real home," not just the body, but the spirit can rest.

The state socialist kitchen, as we've seen, became one of the most reviled and ridiculed features of state planning, coming to symbolize socialism's detrimental effects on the Hungarian family as it effectively prevented (as was intended by many modernist planners) simultaneous seating of an extended family for dinner. Such kitchens continued to be considered "not normal," another example of state socialism's "unnatural" social policies. Cramped and cluttered socialist-era bathrooms, with clothes drying overhead, likewise suffered from modernist assumptions that laundry would be done in a common space in the building. These bathrooms and water closets had little to do with notions of privacy or the cultivation of the individual body and self. They were spaces for the functional fulfillment of waste elimination, hygiene, and a number of other household tasks. Nonetheless, we can recall that bathrooms were singled out in state publications like *Lakáskultúra* as places to judge the modern respectability of a family, and already in the 1970s as places worthy of beautification.

The upgraded kitchen, with new tile, cabinets, lighting, and modern appliances, indexed equivalence with Western material standards. This index was made explicit by an advertisement for a home-improvement loan, placed under a photo of a typical socialist-era kitchen, pots crammed into tiny cabinets: "Our fridge is Swedish, our coffee maker is German. Why can't our kitchen be American?" (see Figure 8.1).[8]

The American kitchen was prized in part for "opening" the space between kitchen and living area, allowing the mother/wife to be engaged with the family while she cooked, even if this meant watching television. In this way, the "normalization" of the American kitchen has implications for family life and shifting uses of food as a mediator of family relationships. As a Dunaújváros sociologist explained, cooking for loved ones is a primary mode of communicating affection and respect (Kántor 1996:30; see also Miller 1998). In a 1998 *Lakáskultúra*, an editor reiterated the common derision of the modernist/socialist design of the "future kitchen" based on the notion that the kitchen would eventually lose its importance in the house as the woman shed her role as housewife and most dining would take place outside of the home. She asserts, instead, that "humanity has been kitchen-loving since ancient times" in emphasizing the importance of this site for family relationships. Opposing the kitchen to the conditions characterizing the outside world, she describes it as a "place where one doesn't have to be harried and nervous ... [where one can] speak earnestly while engaged in tasting and sipping. That is why ... the center of family life ... will always be the kitchen" (1998/6:3).

If American kitchens appear beneficial for the family life of the modern middle class, then luxurious bathrooms promise to be spaces for self-indulgence and even rejuvenation for the spirit. In showrooms and magazines, theme bathrooms (from terra cotta Roman to country style) reinforce a message of self-improving leisure with props like soft towels draped casually over the tub, soaps, a book, candles, a champagne glass. In Dunaújváros, people drew from these images to create approximations in their own homes as space, finances, and ingenuity allowed. The bath had become a place fantasized as an escape from the sights, sounds, and smells of the outside world, but also the turmoil of family life. In some popular publications and commercial advertisements, it was framed as a ritual space for healing through the powers of water, meditation, and solitude. In others, it was a space of luxurious self-pampering and attention to appearance, for men and women alike, through mirrors and the paraphernalia required for preening.

Figure 8.1. Advertisement for bank loan using an image of a typical socialist-era kitchen: "Our fridge is Swedish, our coffee maker is German. Why can't our kitchen be American? 10 different options for apartment renovation credit." Reprinted with permission from Erste Bank, 2001.

While publicity for new baths helped construct desire for these heterotopic spaces as places to recover from the stresses of everyday life, expressions of longing were mixed with an ambivalence missing from similar expressions for new kitchens. As we saw with Margit and Géza's bathroom, the individualism and leisure implied by new bathrooms violated cultural norms equating respectability with constant productive labor or activity (Lampland 1995:315–21). Thus, while their bathroom was a centerpiece of their new suburban house, they made it with no bathtub. In Laura and Zoltán's house, the children used the full bathroom—decorated with sea shells—while Laura joked about Zoltán's struggles with the soap in their small shower stall. Perhaps Ildikó and Tamás most fully realized the heterotopic ideal, one reflecting their marriage, in the Finnish-style wood sauna they shared on weekends.

There is a structural equivalence to the properties of heterotopic spaces in the postsocialist era and the properties of Western commodities during state socialism. Select Western commodities gained their powers through their very disjuncture from the socialist context, "displayed" as metonyms of a system in opposition to state socialism and its politically saturated material culture (chapter 4). Similarly, postsocialist heterotopic spaces gained their power precisely through their disjuncture from local conditions and from their ability to simulate belonging to the "normal" economic, political, and social systems believed to exist elsewhere. These promises were embedded in the very qualities of their materiality, in an aesthetics constructed in ideological opposition to an "unnatural" socialism and thus reflecting respect for "natural" human needs and desires.

While state socialist regimes were known for their inability to produce abundant consumer goods and high standards of living, it was nonetheless under these very regimes that mass consumer society and modern consumer subjectivities emerged—and with them an attentiveness to the qualities of material goods and environments that were equated with human value. Reinforcing rather than contradicting widespread temporal and moralizing discourses of modernization, the socialist state prioritized the material project of becoming modern over other modes of attaining social respectability and modern personhood. Home furnishing practices in postsocialist Hungary were often attempts to create a kind of transcendent life that had long been imagined was being lived elsewhere. While throughout the socialist period Hungarians attempted to construct their homes as islands of privacy and normalcy, in the postsocialist period they began to imagine themselves to be in touch with a wider world through the Internet, international bank cards, and a lifestyle associated with high-quality material goods—thus bypassing the "not normal" world of their immediate surroundings and the people inhabiting them. American kitchens and renovated bathrooms operate on this same structural principle. They epitomize attempts to create heterotopias of normalcy within a "not normal" local world and yet, with their high-tech hygiene and postmodern decor, incorporate Hungarians into an imagined world and lifestyle beyond Hungary's borders. Ironically, it is precisely local technological and governmental conditions in Hungary that allow for these fantasies of displacement. As we have seen, achievement of such "normal" material worlds will never end the search for a "normal" life, nor will it allow Hungarians to "make peace with the world, with ourselves."

Epilogue

THE FORMER SOCIALIST "new town" of Dunaújváros managed to weather most of the challenges of the 2000s, primarily because of the steel mill's continuing viability. Many of the city's panel construction apartment buildings have been given facelifts of colored insulation several inches thick—an expensive process paid in equal parts by European Union funding, the local government, and contributions by residents. Now, instead of the masses of gray-white buildings that once rose like a cliff face from the city plateau, visitors to the city are greeted by a motley array of ice cream colors, as buildings are differentiated by pistachio greens, apricot oranges, chocolate browns. In town, the grand hotel built in the early 1950s has reopened. Renovated and painted a light yellow and white, its shades are similar to many of the other renovated classical Socialist Realist buildings that line the main avenue. An Internet café and restaurant now spill out onto the once-bare square in front of the still-dilapidated movie theater. To the delight of many teenagers, McDonald's finally arrived in town in the mid-2000s, putting the city on the map as a place recognized by this multinational corporation. Positioned conspicuously at the foot of the avenue leading up to the city from the village, its colorful play structure and golden arches compete with the arches of the cathedral just up the hill. But the boutique row that had been such a vibrant pedestrian corridor in the 1990s has fallen on hard times with the opening of several big-box stores like Tesco, Aldi, and several new shopping malls nearby. Other local businesses have also faltered, unable to compete. As one retired schoolteacher related, "I would rather buy from my old butcher, but I can't afford it! His prices are double those at Aldi."

The city's population peaked in 1986 at 62,000, but in subsequent years declined steadily, dropping to 57,000 in the 1990s. In the 2000s, the decline was more precipitous, down to 48,000 in 2011. Young people were seeking work elsewhere and the aspiring middle classes continued to move to suburbanizing areas nearby, while the elderly were dying off. Nonetheless, urban apartments retained their value and prices were still determined by location and quality of building. There had never been enough housing to begin with, so the population decline merely reduced crowding in existing buildings. Although the steel mill, Dunaferr, never cut the workforce in half as threatened, wages had also not risen significantly, keeping most workers and their families in city apartments. The suburban neighborhoods of villages grew slowly but steadily. The areas around all of my informants' new houses have filled in with people of fairly diverse levels of prosperity. Depending upon their fortunes and resources, families built their own homes or hired outside labor or building firms. Housing developers still avoided the region, even though a new highway now connected Dunaújváros to Budapest, cutting commuting time by as much as half and making the trip far safer for those who could pay the toll.

For my closest interlocutors in Dunaújváros, the 2000s brought more upheaval but also a greater sense of adjustment to a status quo. Some of my older acquaintances were widowed or died, while others have managed to carve out lives for themselves through family interdependencies and odd jobs. Many suffer from a litany of health problems. Of the children of the aspiring middle-class couples I knew in the city, many are floundering, unable to get decent and steady employment. Others find themselves working impossibly long hours in their professions. Already in their late twenties and early thirties, all of these now-grown children have put off having families of their own. Their parents, meanwhile, continue to live in the houses they moved into in the 1990s and the early 2000s. In every case, parents made sure to provide their children with small apartments in Budapest rather than in Dunaújváros.

Despite the city's attempts to diversify, Dunaújváros remained a factory town. The steel factory still employed eight thousand workers by the end of 2010, even after downsizing and restructuring. The factory's fate mirrored the progress of privatization in much of the country, as more and more of Hungary's assets were removed from local control and incorporated into the global economy. Until 2003, the steel mill remained in state hands and became a political football because of its symbolic associations with state socialism and ties to the Socialist Party. As recounted in chapter 6, during the Socialist Party's four years in power in the mid-1990s, a consortium of local factory managers and politicians who called themselves Steel XXI won a state contract to direct the company. At the time, this shift caused resentment in the town, as these managers, who were well-known locally, built nice houses and drove around in Audis and BMWs. By the mid-2000s, however, many employees of the factory were nostalgic for such local bosses. During its four years in power (1998–2002), the conservative nationalist party, FIDESZ, managed to oust Steel XXI in a dispute over "success fees" (*sikerdíj*), or bonuses, and initiate negotiations for the factory's privatization. By 2004, the year Hungary officially joined the European Union, Dunaferr found itself under the control of the integrated holding company ISD (Industrialny Soyuz Donbass). Registered in Switzerland, ISD was in fact owned by the Ukrainian oligarch Sergey Taruta, one of the richest men in the world, and two partners. Specializing in mining and metal enterprises, ISD already owned three Ukrainian steel companies and one Czech company when it added Dunaferr to its roster. Unlike the local directors who had personal connections to the town, the Ukrainian owners controlled the company from afar. Lower-level managers at Dunaferr complained that "the Ukrainians know no laws," telling of tapped phone lines and thugs hired to keep state safety inspectors from doing rounds at the factory. By 2010, the economic crisis had forced Taruta and his partners to sell off controlling interests in ISD to the Russian company Carbofer, with the participation of the Russian Development Bank, Vnesheconombank. Dunaferr, the local paper noted ironically, was once again being controlled by Russians.

By the time Hungary was admitted to the European Union in 2004, much of the population had become disillusioned with the promises it once held and were concerned about the costs membership might exact on the country. Although longings for a "normal" life remained, people were increasingly skeptical that Western Europe in the 2000s was still to be regarded as a paragon of such a normal world. Long before the economic crisis began in 2008, Europe's reputation was tarnished with news of corruption scandals, cases of widespread food contamination, and state failures to prevent the weak and elderly from dying in heat waves. People spoke of how the forces of globalization, the seemingly endless political corruption, and the ineptitude of the state had made old standards of civilized and orderly normalcy impossible, even in those places that may once have fostered it. For Géza, this recognition freed him from long-held expectations that business in postsocialist Hungary should be conducted according to principles of transparency, fairness, and honor. By the mid-2000s, his endeavors had become more successful once he had fully embraced "that this is how business is done everywhere."

Such disillusion only reinforced the conviction that people had to try to create spheres of normality for themselves in spaces within their control. Many families who had successfully transitioned to the new middle classes have been successful in this endeavor—enjoying more space, appliances that work, the ease of driving to a supermarket instead of carrying groceries by bus. Many of my interlocutors had again taken up some of the do-it-yourself activities they had once considered part of their "not normal" lives. No longer burdened by having to build houses, forage for consumer goods, or make their own clothing and furniture, people embraced these practices as pleasurable and productive activities to do in their free time, and yielding unique products superior to those available in stores. On one visit in October 2010, everywhere I went women proudly showed me their well-stocked pantries of self-canned fruit compotes, jams, tomatoes, and peppers. Men had formed social clubs for making their own spiced sausages and pálinka, only now experimenting with unusual flavors and packaging them with their own printed home-brand labels. Several men had become wine connoisseurs, actively participating in judging Hungary's burgeoning number of private vineyards. And provincial cities attempted to attract tourists and the business of locals by sponsoring such things as paprika or *kolbász* (sausage) festivals. These practices were all understood to be ways of reproducing things and with them people that were uniquely Hungarian in a register that accorded with contemporary, international gustatory practices.

As with the other countries in the region, Hungary had been required to adopt wholesale the voluminous policies, treaties, and legislation of the European Union (the *acquis communautaire*), incorporating it into national law and enforcing it. Hungarian citizens were asked in a referendum to vote on whether or not to join the EU, but like other candidate countries from Eastern Europe, had no say in negotiating the terms of accession. Moreover, membership in the EU did not include membership in the Eurozone. Hungary's currency remains the forint until it is able to meet the financial criteria dictated by the EU, something that may never happen.

A number of high-profile incidents such as the Hungarian paprika scandal (where deregulation and free trade resulted in the contamination of that iconic Hungarian export, red paprika, with toxic bacteria [Gille 2009]) seemed to confirm some of Hungarians' greatest fears about the EU. Nevertheless, it seemed for a time that other benefits of membership besides EU financial assistance might accrue to the Hungarian population. Among these was the new possibility of obtaining housing mortgages, as the state began to allow commercial banks to offer cheaper, long-term loans for housing, thus making the real estate market much more mobile. All three of the families discussed in chapter 7 took advantage of these loans to buy apartments for their grown children. Since these loans were primarily made in Swiss francs, however, the economic crisis of 2008 left thousands of people, including those in Dunaújváros, holding highly inflated foreign currency debts (Bodnár and Molnár 2010:797). By the early 2010s, the Hungarian economy was the weakest in the region, in part because it had been the least insulated from the global economy from years of privatization to foreign-owned capital and radical state decentralization.

Politically, the increasingly tangible influence of the European Union on domestic issues and finances worked to the advantage of socially conservative, nationalist parties—especially in the eastern half of the country, where poverty has been most dire. The ruling Socialist Party's numerous gaffes, one of which incited violent protest in the streets of Budapest soon after the party was re-elected in 2006, led to its resounding defeat in 2010 at the hands of the right-of-center party FIDESZ and its charismatic leader, Viktor Orbán. Even Dunaújváros, which had always voted with the Socialist Party, turned against them in this election cycle, more out of deep hostility to the Socialist Party's technocratic and elitist leaders than because of FIDESZ's claims that the Communists had never truly been ousted from power. The defeat of the Socialists also made room for the rise of the far-right party, Jobbik, campaigning on a platform that explicitly aligned Hungary's former loss of sovereignty to the Soviet Union with its current financial and bureaucratic domination by the European Union and foreign capital. Its answer was to take back Hungary from these foreigners, particularly Jews, and also to rid the country of crime by ending EU-mandated protections for Roma (gypsy) minorities and reinstating gypsy crime units on police forces. While FIDESZ distanced itself from Jobbik's open attacks on Roma and Jews, it often echoed its rhetoric pitting a beleaguered Hungary fighting for its autonomy against the power of foreign multinational corporations and the cultural and financial dictates of the EU. This rhetoric has been backed by state directives limiting the interest that banks can charge, levying significant windfall taxes on the privatized retail, energy, telecommunications, and financial sectors, and refusing to bow to EU pressures to comply with its economic and legal conditions for new loans. Given that more than half of state revenue currently comes from EU funding, it remains to be seen what comes of FIDESZ's calls for economic self-determination. In the meantime, the Orbán government's increasingly blatant institutionalization of one-party power and curbs on media freedoms have exposed the EU's lack of effective sanctions for member states unwilling to play by their rules.

The rise of the far right has been accelerated by its creative use of the latest Internet and social networking sites, but long-term attachments to anti-socialist, Organicist materialities and their imbedded ideologies have provided fertile ground for such politics. In the 1990s, these materialities helped to constitute Hungarians as a moral and civilized European middle class and Hungary as a "normal" European country. In the 2000s, disillusionment with the European Union shifted the salience of these same materialities, as they instead confirmed Hungarian identity as both grounded in ancient Hungary and at the same time up to date and sophisticated in production and consumption of quality and design. With its victory in 2010, FIDESZ appointed the Organicist architect Imre Makovecz (1923–2011) as head of the Hungarian Academy of Arts with the agenda of promoting only those artists who represented the nation in a positive light. The conflation of the EU with state socialism has been possible in part because of aesthetic resonances with impersonal and homogenizing domination from afar, only this time deployed to unite both wealthy Hungarians and those who have most keenly felt the effects of the European Union's deregulation and lack of economic protection.

Hungary's predicament bears out Zygmunt Bauman's prescient warning of 1991. The collapse of communism, and with it the long-standing dream of modernity, left a world in which there was little alternative to a Western-style capitalism and, moreover, one in which talk of collective welfare or regulation of the market had lost credibility. The dangers, Bauman noted, included the fact that "freedom" defined solely by the market is woefully inadequate as an anchor for identity and therefore "tends to be accompanied by the renaissance of the self-same irrationalities that grandiose projects of modernity wished to eradicate" (Bauman 1991:44).

Notes

Preface

1. He later published a semiautobiographical account of his prison years, documenting systematic abuse and torture of political prisoners and providing information about the trials and executions of hundreds of people at the hands of the Stalinist state—information until then unavailable (Fehérváry 1978). See Fehérváry 1989 for English version.
2. A conflict thus arose between returned émigrés and residents over who could claim authentic "Hungarian" status. Voices in the émigré community insinuated that forty years of state socialism had warped the national character of those who had stayed behind, while residents denied Hungarian status to those who had abandoned the country and had not experienced state socialism (Huseby-Darvas 2003).

Introduction

1. Bíró 1990; Iordanova 2003; Milosz 1990.
2. Anders Aman relates similar encounters during research for his book (1992). The city's engineers, architects, and even the chief city planner avoided living in it. Even the city's greatest local patriot in the 1970s asked to be buried—not in Dunaújváros—but in the village of his ancestors (Miskolczi 1980).
3. Hungary's population in 1995 hovered around the ten million mark, although the birthrate had dropped below the percentage necessary to maintain the population.
4. I refer to the ideological aims of the Communist Party as "communist," but to the political and economic states of the Soviet bloc as "socialist" and so follow the terminology used by these regimes. Theoretically, when socialist states reached the stage of communism, the state would "wither away."
5. I use the term "materiality" to include the role of the material in meaning, but at the same time to move beyond "material culture," or the realm of culturally recognized objects (objects recognized by subjects). The term "materiality" can include the potential qualities of what we can recognize as material properties (see discussion below on Peircean qualisigns), but also material processes and effects (of affecting and being affected). For the purposes of this book, a crucial aspect of the term "materiality" is the role of the material in producing affective responses in human beings that may or may not become part of conscious awareness. In so doing, I am exploring the place of the material in the affective life of people and of a nation. (My thanks to Jason Pine for this phrasing.) See in particular Miller 1987, 2005; Tilley 2007; Ingold 2007; Latour 1999; Peirce 1955; Munn 1986; Keane 1997, 2003; Hull 2012; Gell 1998; Hall 1969; Brown 2001; Massumi 2002; Norman 2004; Verbeek 2005.
6. See Weiss (2012) and Manning and Meneley (2008) on relating particular materialized aesthetics or totalities to cosmologies.

7. For a synthesized analysis of four of these five periods, see Fehérváry 2012. Socialist Realism was the official term for the state-sanctioned art and architecture of the Stalinist period. I use the term Socialist Modern to index a material aesthetic, one similar to what Susan Reid calls Khrushchev Modern for the Soviet Union (Reid 2006); I do not use it to mean a socialist version of modernity, as do Pence and Betts for East Germany (Pence and Betts 2008). Socialist Generic, Organicist Modern, and Super-Natural Organicism are my terms, though Organicist Modern is drawn from a combination of Socialist Modern and the Hungarian Organicist school of architecture.

8. I use the terms "material worlds" (instead of "space" or "built environment") to emphasize the experienced materiality of the home as an inhabited place complete with furnishings and decor, degree of cleanliness and upkeep, smells and sounds, pets and plants, the felt presence of other inhabitants (even in their absence), and awareness of an external context. Material worlds are conceptually bounded places. See Nancy Munn's use of "lived space" and "space-time" (e.g. 1971; Munn 1986, 1994, 2004); or Henri Lefebvre's division of socially produced space into dialectically interrelated "spatial practice" (space produced by a particular society), "representations of space" (space as conceptualized), and "representational space" (lived space) (1991:38–39). See also Brad Weiss on "lived worlds" as the "oriented space and time that emerges through the process of inhabiting a world. . . . Sociocultural activity is continuously making and unmaking dimensions of this lived world" (1996:7).

9. Castillo 1992; Castillo 2000; Dowling 1999; French and Hamilton 1979; Kotkin 1995; Miliutin 1974; Miskolczi 1980.

10. Kristen Ross (1996) makes a slightly different argument for the role of modernist materials and modernization programs in postcolonial France.

11. The shifting technologies of consumer goods also play a role in dictating practice (Latour 1992), including how standards of comfort are normalized (Shove 2003).

12. Scholarship on this topic covers a wide range of disciplines. See, for example, Gell 1998; Norman 2004; Attfield 2000; Forty 1986; Verbeek 2005. Some excellent research is in corporate ownership.

13. Unlike a Saussurean semiotics, where the relationship of signifier and signified is divorced from materiality, a Peircean semiotics allows us to think about the suggestive or resonant nature of our sensory experience with materialities. See, in particular, the work of Nancy Munn (1986); see also Hull 2012, Keane 2003, 2006; Lemon 2011; Manning and Meneley 2008; Manning 2012; Daniel 1987.

14. Such materialities extend to properties that are not available to sensory perception but become ascribed to materials through a combination of phenomenological experience and cultural evaluation—such as when suspicions about the chemical properties of concrete combine with perceptions of its coldness to create evaluations that it is "unhealthy" (see Meneley 2008).

15. See Irvine and Gal 2000; Lemon 2011; Manning and Meneley 2008.

16. For example, Orvar Löfgren and Bob Foster describe in different ways how a nation might cohere as a concept through the myriad ways it is in fact "material" (Foster 2002; Löfgren 1993).

17. A number of collections on the home in industrialized settings diverge from the structural and symbolic approaches of the past and also see the home/house as more than simply expressions of the identities and values of its inhabitants. See, for example, volumes by Birdwell-Pheasant and Lawrence-Zuñiga (1999); Chapman and Hockey (1999); Cieraad (1999); Miller (2001); Ravetz and Turkington (1995); Wright (1985). In 2004, a journal was established called *Home Cultures*.

18. Leora Auslander demonstrates differences in national attachments of an interwar Jewish bourgeoisie in Germany and France through an analysis of interior décor (1996; see also

Auslander 2002). See also Richard Wilk (1999) on the class aspirations and entitlements embedded in the La-Z-Boy recliner in the United States, and Richard Sennett on the radiating social effects of the "comforts" of modern life (Sennett 1996).

19. Scholarship on the Soviet Union cannot be applied unproblematically to Eastern European socialism and vice versa. First, state socialism in Eastern Europe began thirty years later, and it began with the last gasp of Stalinism rather than with Bolshevism. What Yurchak calls "late socialism" in the Soviet Union coincides with almost the entire socialist period in Eastern Europe. Second, communism in Eastern Europe was inextricably tied to the Soviet empire, a country that most Eastern European populations regarded with ambivalence, at best.

20. Anthropological accounts of official consumer culture have focused on the tension between the state's promises to deliver a modern "good life" and its ability or willingness to do so. They draw on short but influential passages by Katherine Verdery (1996:26–29) and John Borneman (1991:17–18), both of which describe a scarcity that produces frustrated desires. Verdery writes of the "politicization of consumption," where "even as the regimes prevented people from consuming by not making goods available, they insisted that under socialism the standard of living would constantly improve. . . . The system's organization exacerbated consumer desire further by frustrating it and thereby making it the focus of effort, resistance, and discontent" (1996:28).

21. For Marx, we become alienated from the objects of our production under the conditions of capitalism, as we often do not "own" the means of production (that is, the materials and machines used to make objects). Moreover, we forfeit our ownership over our own labor when we sell it for a wage and thus forgo the self-making qualities of those things we have produced, which become commodities that stand over and against us, products of our own labor that we now have to buy back. Under Soviet socialism, workers had little power over means of production.

22. Mauss argued that when we give and receive, we enter into a relationship—though not necessarily one governed by affection—and that commodity exchange in its purest form does away with such relationships. The use of money, which as an abstraction can make anything commensurable with anything else, not only erodes prohibitions on buying and selling things once considered beyond price but also makes social relationships between exchange partners unnecessary (Mauss 2000).

23. In her account of "normalization" in Czechoslovakia, Paulina Bren (2010) analyzes the post-1968 regime's role in fostering political indifference by encouraging citizens to concentrate on improving their private lives and re-establishing "peace and calm." She draws on Lauren Berlant's critique of this "inward turn" to an idealized private sphere and creature comforts, acknowledging the problems that arise for any political system when the population is disengaged from politics.

24. Gal and Kligman 2000a; Goven 1993; see also Kideckel 1993 for Romania; Konrád 1984.

25. There is an extensive literature on the private and public in socialist Eastern Europe, its relationship to the informal economy, and its production of an us/them divide. See, among others, Creed 1998; Gal and Kligman 2000; Jowitt 1992:287–94; Konrád 1984; Sampson 1987; Verdery 1996; Wedel 1986. For the ramifications of the us/them divide for ethnic groups and nationalism, see Verdery 1996:92–97. Hungarians I was in contact with in the 1980s and 1990s did not use the term "public" in everyday conversation. Instead, they marked the private sphere or a private life (*magánélet*) or of a private economic sector (*magánszektor*, or *maszek* for short), as separate from everything else (spheres of the state, politics, workplace, and so forth).

26. Manning writes of the politics generated by the disappearance of the "unitary state" in Georgia (2007b). See also Erik Mueggler on how the communist state was experienced as an external entity in rural China (2001).

27. Lampland 1995; Sampson 1985/86; Verdery 1996; Wedel 1986.
28. For elaborations of this position, see Bockman and Eyal 2002; Gille 2010; Lemon 2008; Verdery 1996; Chari and Verdery 2009.
29. For histories of the Hungary economy in the socialist period, see Berend 1990; Berend and Ránki 1985; Róna-Tas 1997; and Révész 1990. For an analysis of state socialist economies in general, see Kornai 1992 and Verdery 1991, 1996.
30. The following statistics are drawn from the Hungarian Central Statistical Office annual publications, Központi Statisztikai Hivatal 1995 and 1997.
31. For recent ethnographies exploring transforming or emerging configurations of middle-class cultures in globalizing economies, see Foster 2002; Freeman 2000; Guano 2004; Liechty 2003; Mazzarella 2003; O'Dougherty 2002; Owensby 1999; and Patico 2008.
32. See Judy Farquhar (2002:5–6) and Nancy Munn (2004:2) on the use of popular culture artifacts as evidence.
33. Susan Gal has argued (1991:454) that critics of state socialist political rhetoric are proponents of linguistic ideologies that hold Western democratic political language as somehow direct and truthful in contrast to the "indirect" rhetoric of state socialism, with its use of metaphors, decentering, allegory, suppressed premises, and myth. She shows that the real issue is not the discourse per se but "rather what social groups have control of them and how exclusive that control is."

1. Normal Life in the Former Socialist City

1. Several new glossy magazines reflected the importance of a presocialist as well as postsocialist "Hungarian" material culture. One featured restored Hungarian castles, gentry estates, and bourgeois villas as well as antiques (*Szalon*), while others were geared to large-scale engineering and architectural projects in Hungary (*Magyar Építészet* and *Atrium*).
2. See Creed 1998:1–3 for Bulgaria; Altshuler 2001 for the Czech Republic; Galbraith 2001 for Poland; Rausing 1998 for Estonia; Stukuls 1997 and 1999 for Latvia; Greenberg 2011 for Serbia; Búriková 2004 for Slovakia. In societies with more distant prospects for "joining Europe," references to a normal world often took on a more abstract character (see for example Pesmen for Russia (1999; 2000) and Watson 1999 for Georgia. For a discussion of the dual uses of "normal" during state socialism in Poland, see Wedel 1986:151–52.
3. In brochures, publicity films, and books, the city and factory had long attempted to ground the city in a deeper history, namely the ruins of a Roman military settlement (180–260 AD), Intercisa. It had been discovered while digging the foundation for one of the newer panel-construction city sectors (Római).
4. The Dunaferr Dunaí Vasmű Rt was the fifth largest corporation in Hungary in 1995, employing 10,500 employees (Dunn & Bradstreet 1996).
5. This attitude has continued to dominate local identities. For example, in 2008, the city refused to host a "retro" May 1st parade organized by a businessman and apparently sanctioned by the (at the time) ruling MSZP or Socialist Party (Balogh 2008).
6. Dr. Attila Kiss, interview, September 3, 1997.
7. See Brian Schwegler on "Europe Place" in which a Slovak-Hungarian border town attempted to Europeanize itself through a shopping center constructed in the various styles indicative of European nations (Schwegler 2002).
8. In this way, Hungarians I knew in the 1990s were unlike some Russians, Czechs, and Poles, who at times referred to a maligned status quo—such as corruption, shoddy products,

or the need for constant dissembling to get things done—as "normal" and even "ours" with or without irony (Altshuler 2001; Pesmen 1999, 2000; Wedel 1986).

9. Ákos Róna-Tás explains such bitterness by remarking that "losses and gains are calculated in comparison to the state of the developed West . . . even those whose economic situation has improved and who stand on the upper level of the economic hierarchy of their society perceive their own position as inferior" (1996:41).

10. Acute attention to how the Western media represents Hungary continues to be a mainstay of Hungarian media, particularly during such moments as the Olympics (when Hungarians tend to win a high number of medals), but also more routinely. For example, the largest national paper *Népszabadság* has had a weekly section on international reporting on Hungary titled "How They View Us." As with other small countries, such concerns in Hungary are not just about national pride, but reflect an understanding of the potential economic and political consequences for how the country is regarded in the world. See Andy Graan for an elaboration of the importance of national "image" in Macedonia (Graan 2010).

11. Daina Stukuls (1997:131–34) and Sigrid Rausing (1998:190) make similar arguments about political and quotidian rhetoric of normalcy in post-Soviet Latvia and Estonia respectively. In Hungary as well, in political rhetoric, "normal" refers both to the West as a standard, but also to a precommunist, "democratic" period in national history.

12. This work ethic is evidently widely shared despite regional variation. Lampland, Stewart and others draw on Fél and Hofer 1969; Bell 1984; Erdei 1941; Hann 1980; and Hollos and Maday 1983. See also Huseby-Darvas for the persistence of these values among American Hungarians in Michigan (2003).

13. As in English, the concept of order thus expands to the social world and to disciplinary regimes. *Rend* can refer to the order of social classes and states, such as a bourgeois citizen order (*polgári rend*) or a gentry system of values (*tiszti értékrend*). Shared linguistic roots do not necessarily indicate shared meanings, but it is striking how many words related to directing, organizing, policing, and systems have *rend* as a root (*rendező, rendezés, rendfenntartás, rendszer*).

14. Unlike Western youth at the time, who objected in general to authority and bourgeois norms, Hungarian youth were also disillusioned by the moral compromises they felt their parents' generation had made to the socialist state in exchange for material comforts.

15. My thanks to Eva Huseby-Darvas for this example. See also S. Nagy (1987:107–109) for accounts of unused luxury living rooms and baths in rural and suburban households during the 1970s and 1980s.

2. Socialist Realism in the Socialist City

1. "New towns" in Eastern Europe included Stalinstadt (Eisenhuttenstadt) in the German Democratic Republic (GDR), Nova-Ostrava in Czechoslovakia, the expanded city of Dimitrovo (Pernik) in Bulgaria, Huneadora in Romania, and in Poland, Tychy and Sztálinváros's "sister city" Nowa Huta. See Kotkin (1995) on the Soviet prototype.

2. Between 1945 and 1960, the Soviet Union extracted an estimated $23.2 billion from the east European countries, an amount greater than the aid the United States handed out through the Marshall Plan (Borhi 2004:139).

3. Socialist Realism has been called "an impossible aesthetic" (Robin 1992), because it demanded that art refer to the "reality" of the socialist future as if it already existed. But in fact this practice had much in common with what Michael Schudson has called "capitalist realism"

or commercial advertising in the West: both depicted a social and material world that was recognizable but at the same time ideal and aspirational (Schudson 1986:210–18). The difference lay in Socialist Realism's monopoly over representation and in the stakes involved during Stalinism: making the "wrong" kind of art work, public statement, or architectural form could be life-threatening.

4. These also provided updates on the current party line so that professionals could maintain a politically correct vocabulary well into the 1980s (Lampland 1987:85).

5. Exhibit (1994): *Where do we live?* Intercisa Museum, Dunaújváros.

6. An idealization of muscular and healthy bodies was common throughout the modernizing world. See Hobsbawm 1978 for socialist iconography, Aman 1992 for Eastern Europe, Mosse 1985 for Germany, and Frykman 1993 for Sweden.

7. For my knowledge of the early history of Sztálinváros, I am indebted to Miklós Miskolczi, a native of the city, long-time reporter for the local paper, chronicler of city history (Miskolczi 1975, 1980), and subsequently the editor of a national women's magazine, *Kiskegyed*. Also invaluable was the help of Viktória Szirmai (interview 1997), a sociologist specializing in Hungary's planned cities, and her work (Szirmai 1988, 1998; Szirmai and Zelenay 1988) and as Viktória Angyal (1976).

8. Magyar Filmintézet, Budapest.

9. See in particular *Sztálinváros* by András Sándor (1951).

10. In the Soviet Union, the great industrial projects of the early 1930s were celebrated as the triumph of human labor and will over the elemental forces of nature. In the building of the Belomor Canal, former enemies of Soviet society were to be transformed by their labor, cleansed of impurities by discipline and exertion, to become true citizens. The forced labor camps were thus considered "humane and socially hygienic," curing prisoners of philistinism and individualism and "breathing new life into them" (Carleton 1994:993–95).

11. The attempts to oppose these styles through aesthetic minutiae could verge on the absurd, as Greg Castillo shows: Kurt Liebknecht, then the head of the East German Architecture Academy, insisted in 1952 that *vertical* window banding was a socialist characteristic while *horizontal* banding was a capitalist one (Castillo 2000).

12. Exhibition: Hól Elünk? (Where do we live?) 1994. Intercisa Museum, Dunaújváros, Hungary.

13. Weiner was at the Dessau Bauhaus until it was forced out of Germany. In 1931, he accompanied a group of German architects led by Hannes Meyer to the Soviet Union to take part in the planning of the new socialist town of Omsk.

14. For a more extensive treatment of the modernist origins of Socialist cities, see Szczepanski 1993, Fehérváry 1995, and Castillo 2000 and 2010.

15. Thirty-two thousand copies of the brochure were printed. An abridged version of the brochure, *Sztálinváros: The Building of Our First Socialist City* (*Sztálinváros Elsö Szocialista Városépítészetünk*), was reproduced in Miskolczi 1980:158–59.

16. An English-language publication from the mid-1960s describes the steel town with its smokestacks as having "something of the appearance of a health resort" (Halász 1965:13). Echoing modernist utopian rhetoric, it claims that the city was planned as "a large scale urban settlement of organic growth, satisfying the demands of modern man for comfort, hygiene, education and in its appearance" (1965:15).

17. Already in 1951, the country had to restore a rationing system, as consumer goods and housing were in critical shortage and the standard of living had dropped (Miskolczi 1980:69).

18. Nationwide, new housing construction had not kept up with the rapidly expanding urban populations and lagged far behind Western European numbers (Aman 1992; Hoensch

1988). More than three hundred thousand people had left villages and agricultural pursuits to join the ranks of industrial workers, but less than half the dwellings called for in the five-year plan had been built (Róna-Tas 1997:49). In this period in Sztálinváros, there were 503 people per one hundred apartments of one or two rooms each, coming to three to five people per room (Bánkuti 1958:19).

    19. Interview, Zoltán Csizmadia. More than a few prisoners got reprieves from executions or sentences of hard labor to work in prison-run planning or engineering offices.

    20. Interview, Budapest, 2004. This couple mentioned that in the 1950s, professors who transferred from their comfortable homes near the Austrian border to work in a new university in the industrial city of Miskolc were housed in villas confiscated by the state.

3. Socialist Modern and the Production of Demanding Citizens

    1. See Buchli 1997, Gerchuk 2000:82–89, and Reid 1997 and 2006 for the Soviet Union; Crowley 1993a for Poland; Stade 1993, Castillo 2000, Betts 2008, and Veenis 1999 for East German versions; and Löfgren 1994 for the Swedish incarnation promoted as one of the primary models for Hungarian unit furniture.

    2. The infrastructure for high-density areas is more complex and expensive than for houses, despite being concentrated in a smaller area. The cost of producing, transporting, and creating the steel structures for concrete panels was not cheaper than traditional brick-and-mortar building techniques and was more difficult to maintain. Moreover, residents could not contribute to such large-scale construction nor help with structural improvements as they could with single-family homes, where they ended up taking on most of the burden (Róna-Tas 1997: 110; Stretton 1978:195–97).

    3. See Buchli 1997; Crowley 1993b; Gerchuk 2000; Reid 1997; and Stade 1993. I am grateful to David Crowley for confirmation of this perspective, based on research he conducted among design professionals in the early 1990s (personal communication, December 2003).

    4. In Hungarian, the expression "good life" is "*édes élet*," reflecting aspirations to the modern standards of living emerging in postwar Europe. As far as I can tell, the expression gained wider currency in Hungary after the opening of the Fellini film *La Dolce Vita* in 1962.

    5. Központi Statisztikai Hivatal (Hungarian Central Statistical Office), www.népszámlálás .hu/hun/kötetek/11/tables/load1_3.html.

    6. The interest in utility furniture was widespread in postwar Europe and the United States (Vadas 1992:161). In wartime Britain, it was at first legally mandated (Attfield 1999). This furniture design had been featured in the late 1940s at the Milan Triennial and at the Museum of Modern Art in New York (Szalai 1997). Unfortunately, when production of the standard design began again in Hungary in the 1960s, "it fell miles short of the high aspirations of its original advocates" (Ernyey 1993:100).

    7. Victor Buchli describes a similar assault on dust and dirt by the Bolsheviks in the 1920s, a rhetoric that added the specter of microbes (Buchli 1999:52–53).

    8. In work predating Bourdieu's *Distinction* (1979), Ágnes Losonczi (1977) argued that an individual's environment, and thus class position, structures the relationship between "needs" and "activity." Peasants, skilled workers, and professionals regard "activity" or work as fulfilling and having a value in itself, while unskilled workers see work as inescapable rather than as a choice. Workers' thrifty attitude toward material resources arises from the basic constraints governing their lives. At the same time, cheerfulness in social contact is valued highly, reflecting the importance of class solidarity absent in other groups (Ferge 1979:313–16).

9. Many cultural producers believed that encouraging such modern consumer consciousness would help to reduce shortages of consumer goods. Of the Soviet bloc nations, Hungary in particular recognized the consumer's "determining influence" early on (Reid and Crowley 2000:11). The language of *igényes* allowed writers for such venues as *Lakáskultúra* to goad state sectors in charge of production. Design professionals argued that "exacting consumers" were key to the development of the service and production sectors of the planned economy, "bringing new forms of production into being and insisting on more customer-friendly service" (*Lakáskultúra* 1967/3:18–19). These efforts met with little success, however, as they contradicted the state production sector's primary objectives of fulfilling plan quotas.

10. This behavior was not true for some in the highest echelon of party leadership, such as János Kádár himself. In Dunaújváros, Ferenc Szabó, the steel mill director from 1972 to 1991 and therefore one of the most powerful men in the country, adhered to status markers within the range of those accessible to the population: he lived in a centrally located apartment and had a modest country cottage on the Danube in a prestigious location.

11. Buchli writes of a similar shift from much earlier in Soviet history, from a belief that objects spoke class truths about their owners (denotative) to a much more contextualized interpretation allowing for ownership of such goods as long as it was with the appropriate consciousness (Buchli 1999:55–62).

12. Following interwar sociologist Ferenc Erdei, S. Nagy divides Hungarian society into parallel rural and urban social structures, each identifiable by a particular interior. Rural society included the feudal-peasant, the bourgeois-peasant, the village petty bourgeoisie, the village poor and the village intelligentsia. Urban society included the urban poor, the traditional urban worker, the urban petty bourgeoisie, the urban bourgeoisie, and the urban intelligentsia (S. Nagy 1987:104–10). These older classifications were more or less intact but had been altered by fashions as well as by new housing forms, such as the modern square village house and the housing estate (S. Nagy 1987:359–560).

13. In Hungary, according to a 1958 publication, the desired amount of space was 9 square meters per person (following the Soviet example), but the average was still 7.2 square meters. The total size of an average dwelling at the time was about 40 square meters total with 26.6 square meters of living space—or 286 square feet (Bánkuti 1958:92).

14. The Firenze included a section of drawers, totaling 0.7 cubic meters; display shelving, about 6.4 meters in length, with space for a television, radio, a light, figurines, and the like; a double-doored closet with room for approximately twenty hangers; a folding-down "bar" or liquor cabinet; a book shelf three meters long; and lower storage compartments of 6 square meters for bedding (*Lakáskultúra* 1976/3:2).

15. In the 1970s, housing authorities introduced the "half room" (defined as under 6 square meters or 64 square feet) to provide a sleeping alcove. In the panel apartment I rented, the half room was furnished with a "French bed" that so crowded the room that only one side of the built-in closet was accessible.

16. The earliest such plan I could find, in *Családi Ház Mintaterve* (1956), included modern conveniences such as indoor bathing facilities, electricity, and even gas cooking, while using minimal building materials and eliminating "wasted" space such as a large attic. The 1956 plan is for a single-room house, while a 1983 book features many designs of three-room houses (*Családi Házak* 1983). A 1974 order specified a maximum of 140 square meters for houses (and 80 square meters for weekend cottages). By 1982–1983, the state finally removed restrictions on size (*Családi Házak* 1983:20).

17. "*Mutasd meg a lakásod, s megmondom ki vagy!*" See Torday 1979 and numerous features by this name in *Lakáskultúra*. See Oláh 1970 for the expression as applied to gardens.

4. Socialist Generic and the Branding of State Socialism

1. These reforms considerably decentralized decision making, giving directors of state enterprises the authority to set prices on products, to seek out new supply sources, and to dispose of residual income (Hanley 2000:156).

2. Verdery (1996:26–29) and John Borneman (1991:17–18) both provide short but influential descriptions of how state-instigated desires were thwarted by scarcity, making consumption the focus of effort, resistance, and discontent.

3. Supplies of foodstuffs, consumer goods, and housing varied enormously from region to region, as well as at different times. In Romania, the relative consumer prosperity of the early 1970s was followed by a decade of terrible deprivation.

4. In such a model, the buyer becomes an unimportant variable, compelled to purchase whatever is produced (Kornai 1992). What is lost in this view is not simply the effect of consumer practices on the economy, but what happens when citizens' worlds are forcibly structured by the materiality of that production.

5. My use of terms taken from capitalist contexts to describe state socialist consumer culture (commodities, employees, managers, retail establishments, corporate entities, branding) is also meant to dislodge the actual experience of state socialist material culture from its ideological claims.

6. The Kádár leadership rigorously maintained the moralizing distinction between real needs and "false" needs until the bitter end (Dessewffy 2002:52).

7. My use of this opposition refers to affective experience, and so differs from the Marxist definition of alienation that focuses on the experience of producers working in conditions structured by capitalist property relations, where they are by definition alienated from the goods of their production because they no longer own their labor (even if they don't realize it).

8. One only has to think of the vast differences between prison cells, homeless shelters, dormitory rooms, urban rentals, state-allocated public housing, self-built homes, and suburban mansions and of the different positions people occupy within that space, such as homeowner, domestic servant, middle-class teenager, and housewife.

9. This problem was not limited to the Soviet bloc, as critics in the United States also advocated for the importance of vibrant streetscapes (Jacobs). In socialist Hungary, however, the state was again blamed for denying human pleasures. (My thanks to Erika Buky for this point.)

10. Nationalized as a state factory in 1949, Tisza acquired its brand status in the early 1970s and garnered international recognition for its shoes, including an Adidas line of soccer cleats. Tiszas never reached Adidas status, I was told by people who had been teens in the 1970s and 1980s, but were elevated by the association.

11. By "state socialist consumer products," I mean goods of Hungarian state manufacture as well as imports from COMECON member nations, namely the states who were part of a council of mutual economic assistance for the Soviet sphere. "Western" goods, by contrast, refers to goods produced for the consumption of citizens in Western capitalist nations but not necessarily produced in the West. In fact, the often multisited origins of products consumed in the West ironically included goods made in socialist bloc countries for export.

12. Maya Nadkarni describes Hungarians in the 1990s as "longing to be . . . recognized as preexisting rather than potential members of the European cultural and historic community," a process linked to goods of Hungarian production. As she writes, these "frustrations . . . were . . . exemplified by the Rubik's cube . . . a toy which in the early 1980s found its way into nearly every Western household just as it did within Hungary, but was rarely recognized as a specifically Hungarian invention. It thus failed to export the Hungarian self-image as a nation

whose scientific skill and creativity was on par with that of more affluent countries, even as it demonstrated that its products could indeed provoke reciprocal consumer desire" (Nadkarni 2010:207).

13. Dale Pesmen writes that in Russia in the early 1990s, products seemed to have had everything good stolen out of them before and during manufacturing, something blamed on Soviet perestroika (Pesmen 2000:45, 147).

14. This expression of disdain for state production was common throughout the region.

15. The Polish zloty was reputed to float in water. Brian Porter-Szűcs, personal communication.

16. My thanks to Susan Gal for this insight. Brands with a good reputation can withstand bad products (for a time), as users will interpret a flawed item as an anomaly.

17. Testimony to the sheer volume of furniture produced in this era in this dark orange color, usually with an abstract or plaid print, could be found throughout the 1990s on the sidewalks of Budapest during the semiannual *lomtalanítás,* or city junk removal.

18. I later learned that this man had renovated and modernized a traditional peasant house for himself in the countryside in the 1980s. Although this was common practice for architects in Hungary, it was also consistent with modernist architects in the West, who designed housing estates for the poor but built detached houses for themselves in the suburbs (Miller 1984).

19. Anthropologists providing insight to this widespread practice include John Borneman (1991) for East Germany, Gerald Creed (2002) for Bulgaria, and Dale Pesmen (2000) and Alexei Yurchak (2006) for Soviet Russia.

20. The Hungarian film *Csinibaba* (Tímár 1997), set in 1962, lampoons such perceptions in a scene in which teenagers admiring American cigarettes argue over whether they contain cocaine or opium (see Fehérváry 2006).

21. A man who had worked in a canning factory during the 1980s related to anthropologist Maya Nadkarni that he was told to take "better care of the products for internal consumption than of those scheduled to be exported east to the USSR." "At stake here," she observes, "was not only the obvious resistance to what many perceived as Russian occupation but also the perception that unlike Hungarians, people in the former Soviet Union would 'consume anything'" (Nadkarni 2009:132 n.60).

22. An example from my own experience was a choice brand of Polish ham, only available in Poland in the *Pewex,* or hard-currency shop.

5. Organicist Modern and Super-Natural Organicism

1. These weekend houses were sometimes called a *víkend.* Ownership of a rural cottage or "dacha" became common for urbanites throughout Eastern Europe (see Bren 2002; Caldwell 2011; Lovell 2002). In presocialist Hungary, the tradition of a summer house was reserved for the wealthier urban, middle classes and elites. The landed nobility lived on country estates, and instead might own a winter place in the city. Middle-class families in towns were more likely to have a small vineyard with a cellar and a press house.

2. The decade 1965–1975 was the boom period of vacation house building, as 80 percent of the 220,000–250,000 built between 1960 and 1980 were constructed then (Hegedűs and Manchin 1987:252).

3. Most scholars agree that the cottage became an integral site for the production of political subjectivities during state socialism, but also that the state sanctioned cottage culture for the sake of political stability. As Paulina Bren (2002) argues for Czechoslovakia, the cottage (*chata*) kept people occupied and stationary, out of the cities where mass gatherings tended to

take place. Moreover, cottage culture was a socially conservative force, reinforcing not only family hierarchies but also concepts of property and regard for a distinct kind of respectability (Bren 2002).

4. An article from the local paper exemplifies the genre, describing a composite figure of a woman who drives her husband crazy with her *"pedáns"* order, constantly nagging him as if he were a child. The journalist implies she cares about nothing so much as having everything cleaned, ironed, waxed, and polished (*Dunaújvárosi Hírlap*, Dec. 5, 1960).

5. In divorce cases with children, women were usually awarded the apartment and primary custody of the child.

6. See Adam Drazin (2001) for the same phenomenon in socialist Romania. Frances Pine writes that even though Gorale villagers in highland Poland now live in brick houses, the beneficial qualities of old wooden houses are remembered. "Wood is necessary for health, the villagers say, and a wooden house breathes and keeps people well" (Pine 1996:447).

7. Considered the most popular Hungarian musical of all time, *István, a Király* was also made into a film and a bestselling album, still popular today in Hungary and among Hungarian minorities in Romania and Slovakia.

8. In Sweden, modernist architecture and furnishing styles promoted for use in new housing estates were also moderated with peasant artifacts. A popular preference for natural, more "homey" materials domesticated the institutional aesthetic of high modernism and came to define a Swedish modern style, which became part of the national identity and a major export (Löfgren 1994).

9. In the late nineteenth century, Hungarian architects attempted to develop a unique Hungarian style of modern architecture by adopting principles from Art Nouveau. They created the Secession (Szecesszió) style, where Hungarian folk motifs like tulips and bees replaced the exotic and literary symbols of Art Nouveau in Western Europe, such as orchids and Medusa's heads (Crowley 1993b:8). The foremost innovator of this style was Ödön Lechner.

10. 13th Congress of the Hungarian Socialist Workers' Party, as reported by the BBC, broadcast April 8, 1985. See video clip titled "Kádár János beszéde MSZMP XIII. Kongresszusa 1985. Március" at www.youtube.com/watch?v=kwevlvPB0SQ.

11. The city administration said about the new plan in 1984: "In our socialist city's housing plan, private house building has been taking an ever greater role . . . especially the construction of up-to-date garden sectors, and, as long as [this practice] is appropriate to the settlement's requirements and within the parameters of a unified organization, this is a trend we encourage!" *Lakásépítők Magazinja* 1984(2):52.

12. Martha Lampland (1995) has shown how collective farm members' experiences with socialist technocratic organization as opposed to their own second-economy activities were another realm in which the free market was seen to reward hard work and valorize autonomy.

13. In 1990s urban Hungary, the socialist "nostalgia" movement was limited to popular cultural references signifying insider knowledge (often ironic) and tourist venues (Nadkarni 2002).

14. Serbian architect Srdjan Jovanovic Weiss founded the Normal Architecture Office, in part to provoke such associations by proposing the rebuilding of socialist common spaces such as people's stadiums in Socialist Modern styles—as explicit reminders of the values lost with the rejection of such architecture (Weiss 2006). He harbors no hope that people will actually revalue the architecture itself (Weiss 2009).

15. But compare this architectural response to communism with Serbian Turbo-Folk Architecture, forged in the nexus of postsocialist wartime experience and rejection by the European Union (Weiss 2006).

16. This openness was made possible by technological innovations like central ventilation systems that evacuated cooking odors so they didn't permeate furnishings.

17. Thanks to Zsuzsa Gille for this reminder.

18. See Martha Lampland, though, on how women in village contexts also suffered from stress and "nerves" from the burdens of keeping family afloat (1995:293 n. 16).

19. Compare with the Comaroff's depiction of how missionaries in Botswana promoted rectilinear housing forms against the Tswana's rounded houses to inculcate proper notions of private property and gender relationships (Comaroff and Comaroff 1992).

20. See also Gerald Creed on the exaggerated use of "masculine" materials in Bulgarian mummers' costumes in response to the marginalization of men in rural communities created by postsocialist unemployment (Creed 2011).

21. Xiaobing Tang writes of middle-class fashioning in 1990s China, where the reification of interiority and difference contrasts with the socialist state's moralizing discourses. Material pursuits generated *vitality* in a fusing of "objects, desire, money and action" when compared to the debasement of conscience and "purity" by ideological coercion (Tang 1998:532, 535).

6. Unstable Landscapes of Property, Morality, and Status

1. See Bunce and Csanádi (1993:273), who argue that uncertainty should be the point of departure for analyzing postcommunism. Compared to Russia during this period (Shevchenko 2009), however, Hungary in the 1990s did not experience chronic crisis. Some segments of the population were devastated, but the currency remained fairly stable and unemployment figures were lower and more fragmented.

2. Social scientists from both Central and Western Europe made similar observations in the early 1990s about the effects of rapidly changing status, loss of moral codes, and the uncertainty of "who will be poor tomorrow and who rich," pathologized by social psychologist Šiklová as "collective postcommunist schizophrenia" (1993:737). See also Claus Offe (1993:674–75). Others mourned the loss of second-economy networks, noting that the market "removes the need for particularistic reciprocity," "a conversion which cut through families, destroyed social ties and reciprocities, and was all the more brutal in its sudden transparency" (Kolankiewicz 1994:151).

3. In 1990 and 1991, decentralizing laws passed much control from the national government to local governments, called *Önkormányzatok*, or "self-governments," including giving municipalities ownership of previously state-owned apartments, with the burden of their upkeep, for use for revenue and social welfare.

4. The 1969 decree gave tenants in buildings of fewer then twelve units the right to buy their apartment, provided at least 75 percent of their cotenants participated. The decree provided strict regulations for payment schemes as well as a guideline for setting prices. In the 1990s, prices were set at mid-1980s prices, or about 15 percent of the estimated market value. If paid outright, the price was discounted another 40 percent. Otherwise, the tenant paid 10 percent of sale price in cash, and the remainder monthly over thirty years at a 3 percent fixed interest rate (inflation in the early 1990s hovered around 30 percent). The new owner could resell or rent at market prices immediately after purchase, or use it for office or retail space without reporting changes (Alter and Németh 1993).

In late 1994, the local paper warned Dunaújváros tenants that they had the right to buy their apartments at these rates until March 31, 1995. After that, they could only buy if the local government was willing to sell. Current occupants continued to have the first right to buy, but at less favorable terms, though they could still pay with compensation coupons (*Dunaújvárosi Hírlap*, Nov. 11, 1994).

5. As discussed in the introduction, the meanings of "private property" fostered in the socialist era were usually at odds with Western European norms of the full alienability of property rights (see also Verdery 1996:299).

6. The number of condo-type buildings or *társasházak* rose from 10,000 to about 75,000, a development necessitated by the privatization of 500,000 apartments (*Népszabadság* Jan. 23, 1997:32).

7. A 1992 law allowed formerly state-run apartment condominium associations to create their own foundational rules and also to allow individual buildings within the larger association to step out of it and set up their own. Apartment associations like those in Dunaújváros had been vast operations but were reduced to an administrative core, with all other duties farmed out to subcontractors. New laws passed in 1992 and 1997 were designed to clarify the licensing process and legislate questions regarding everyday operation—for example, lowering the number of required signatures from the almost impossible consensus of 100 percent to a simple majority needed to make repairs, sell a unit, or take out a building loan. The 1997 law in particular attempted to encourage private real estate developers to invest in building residential housing.

8. Boyer discusses such attitudes among journalists in a re-united Germany (Boyer 2001).

9. See Róna-Tas 1996 for a sociological breakdown of losers in postsocialist Hungary.

10. See Altshuler 2001 for the Czech Republic; Berdahl 1999 for East Germany; Lampland 1995 and Róna-Tas 1996 for Hungary; Rausing 1998 for Estonia; Humphrey 1997, Pesmen 2000, and Ries 1997 for Russia; Verdery 1995 and Sampson 1994 for Romania.

11. See Agócs and Agócs 1993; Szelényi 1998; Róna-Tas 1996; and Marosán 1994 for Hungary; and Sampson 1994:14–15 for Hungary and Romania.

12. Hungarians had known about *Dallas* while it was airing in the west (1978 to 1991), but it was first shown on Hungarian Television (MTV) from 1990 to 1997.

13. The ratio at the time in the United States was over 300 to 1.

14. During the 2000s, the notion of a moral "loser" gave way in popular speech and the media to the notion of a "born loser" (*született lúzer*) or someone who by disposition was destined to be a failure.

15. Social scientists used the term to refer to urban, unskilled labor who were in dead-end career trajectories of the state socialist period (Szelényi et al. 1988).

16. In an incredible example of the continuing stigmatization of socialist Eastern Europe, a Norwegian artist "recreated" the "scent of communism" for an exhibit on extinct and exotic smells—one described as "the smell of gray, of worn concrete, a light perfume of drab industrial stench, a hint of smoke and stale air" (Burr 2009).

17. See also Shryock (2004). Even though these conditions were not as extreme as those in civil-war- and earthquake-torn Armenia, Stephanie Platz's observations about the loss of social contact when people cannot perform hospitality requirements still ring true (Platz 1996).

18. Middle-class culture is structured by claims to be both national and modern, and also by positioning itself as morally superior to both a profligate and promiscuous elite and an uncivilized and undeserving poor (Frykman 1987; Liechty 2003:61–86).

19. Scholarship on the historic *polgár* had been underway in the late 1970s and 1980s (see chapter 5), but in the early 1990s the topic was a focus of intellectual activity (see for example Gerő 1993; Gyáni 1991; Hanák 1992; Sasfi 1993; Somogyi 1991).

20. For example, in the mid-1990s the dominant opposition party to the Socialists appended its name, FIDESZ, to include *polgár*, combining the meanings of citizen and bourgeois.

21. The editor of *Lakáskultúra* warned in 1993 that while this style was again in fashion after the old regime's antibourgeois attitude, one had to be "careful not to get buried in the nostal-

gia for the old . . . but maintain an individual eclecticism" and not forget that "the people sitting around the old polgár dining table are of the late-20th century." As a voice of mass consumption, he was in the business of removing restrictions on anyone's ability to appropriate them. He also seems concerned that the socialist era's reframing of the value of antiques, original works of art, handcrafted rugs, and so forth might be lost.

22. Signs of *polgár* status in Dunaújváros could also misfire elsewhere, such as wearing fur coats and hats in the metropolitan city of Budapest—where it marked one as old-fashioned or even petty bourgeois (*kispolgári*).

23. Peasant artifacts were the preferential decor for the trend of modernizing old peasant houses with state-of-the art conveniences and expensive thatched roofs. In these settings, carved wooden furniture, iron farming tools, and folk decor—if "authentic"—were entirely appropriate. There they functioned as status symbols for the aspiring middle classes far enough removed from village life to romanticize Hungarian "folk" culture and to bask in the prestige of "cultural preservation."

24. These shows were broadcast on the Hungarian national television channel, *Magyar Televízió*, and were sometimes used by the state to educate the public on certain issues, such as whether or not the nation should join NATO. A third show was called *Kisváros*, or "Small Town," and was the rural equivalent of *Neighbors* but about people in a small town plagued with New World corruption and crime, centered on a valiant local police department.

25. Unlike *Dallas*, the series E.R. ran concurrently with its showing in the United States.

26. Both series ended in 1999. *Family, Inc.* could not compete with Western competitors on cable, but *Neighbors* has been rebroadcast a number of times since, suggesting that its themes still resonate with the considerable population that identifies with middle-class respectability but continues to live in panel construction apartments.

7. The New Family House and the New Middle Class

1. Many houses built during the socialist era were stuccoed but left unpainted, and people explained that paint had been expensive and of low quality. The more modern "square houses" of the 1960s and 1970s had once been painted a dark yellow with bands of green or rust brown, but their façades had faded or become soot-stained in the intervening years. Houses built in the 1980s were marked by their white paint and style, usually with steeply pitched roofs with the second story built into the attic (see Figure 7.2).

2. Remnants of turn-of-the-century bourgeois villa culture gave larger cities some of their character, but the interwar period had also produced districts made up of the middle class "family house with garden," primarily in Budapest and its surrounding fringes. In provincial towns, office workers, artisans, and skilled workers making up a lower middle class often lived in modest versions of such a house (Kósa 2000:187). But many people in the 1970s and 1980s had also referred to newly built houses with this phrase, distinguishing them from a peasant house.

3. In the United States, the rapid expansion of the postwar suburbs was a direct result of state incentives and infrastructural investment. The state's preference for detached housing spread over vast expanses came in part from fears of possible nuclear attack on densely populated urban centers (May 1988). Soviet-style development, in contrast, had been driven by desires for urbanization.

4. In a form of continuity from state-socialist-era practices, Margit's compensation as a lawyer came in part from "benefits" like a trip to Bangkok. Certain travel agencies were willing to falsify the place of travel on the receipt, making a pleasure trip look like a trip to a legal

convention. The firm she works for can then deduct this amount as a business expense, while passing on the "benefit" to Margit as untaxed income. Margit also used some destinations, such as Thailand, as shopping trips for goods for her family that would have been many times more expensive if bought in Hungary.

5. A few years later, they added a footing of stones around the base of the house exterior, emulating a neighboring house designed by an Organicist school architect.

6. At one point, Zoltán claimed, "I could have built this house much more cheaply and easily in the 1980s." He attributed his financial miscalculations and the difficulties they had had in completing the house to state incompetence and corrupt and inefficient banking practices. But his defensive boast was also a misrecognition of how building practices had changed and how his and Laura's expectations for a house had risen.

7. Compare with Michele Rivkin-Fish's argument that Russians who paid for private services like heath care (rather than taking advantage of "public" services) were admired and considered to be of quality character, even by people working in those institutions, since they "valued" high-quality care (2009).

8. Heterotopias of the Normal in Private Worlds

1. In the Hungarian version of "A man's home is his castle" (*Az én házam, az én váram*), the word for "fortified castle" (*vár*) is used rather than that of a castle-palace (*kastély*).

2. This British series *The Onedin Line* first aired in the 1970s and was on a second run in the mid-1990s. It chronicled the rise of a shipping magnate family in Liverpool. The sympathetically portrayed main character, James Onedin, worships profit, prioritizing his business interests over his own comforts, his family, or charity. He tries to hide rare moments of tenderness by disguising them with profit motives, as when he asks his wife to come along on a trip with him in order to save him housekeeping expenses.

3. These narratives of exaggeration often came up in the context of political corruption, of financial scandals involving privatizing state companies or banks, of rising crime rates and mafia coupled with an ineffectual and corrupt police force—all contributing to a generalized sense that Hungarian society had descended into lawlessness and disorder.

4. Einhorn 1993; Funk and Mueller 1993; Gal and Kligman 2000b.

5. Women in Poland demonstrated similar expectations and disappointment in their "passive" menfolk (Marody and Giza-Poleszczuk 2000).

6. Entrepreneurial endeavors allow men to pursue much-desired autonomy, raising the stakes for success or failure (cf. Konrád 1984; Lampland 1995). Though they continue to blame state policies for their difficulties, in the new "natural" market order, such failure is internalized (cf. Gal and Kligman 2000).

7. Also relevant here is the romanticized image of the bandit-like criminal as social hero in Hungary, discussed in chapter 6.

8. A billboard I saw in 2004 for Italian tiles played on concerns with loss of Hungarianness in such transformations: "*Magyar Konyha, Olasz Stílusban*" (Hungarian kitchen/cuisine, in Italian style).

Bibliography

Newspapers and Design Journals Referenced

Az Otthon: lakáskultúra, kert, szabadidő. Budapest: Pallas, 1989–present.
Budapest Business Journal: Business news that works. Budapest: European City Business Journals, 1992–present.
Családi ház: Építkezők, építtetők, építészek, vállalkozók és reménykedők lapja. Budapest: CSH 2000 Építészeti Kft., 1998–present.
Családi ház mintaterve. 1956. Budapest: Budapest Főváros Tanácsa V.B.
Családi házak. A magánlakásépítés ajánlott tervei. Budapest: ÉTK (Építésügyi Tájékoztatási Központ), 1983.
Dunaújvárosi Hírlap: regionális napilap. Hírlap Press Kft., 1996–present.
Dunaújvárosi Hírlap: az MSZMP Városi Bizottsága és a Városi Tanács lapja. Székesfehérvár: Fejér Megye Hírlap Lapkiadó, 1961–1990.
Lakásépítők Magazinja. ÉVM Magánlakásépítés fejlesztése Célprogram Bizottság támogatásáva. Budapest: Műszaki Kvk., 1964–1989.
Lakáskultúra. Belkereskedelmi Minisztérium Lakberendezési Bizottsága. Budapest: Közgazdasági és Jogi K., 1964–1993.
———. Axel-Springer, Budapest Kft., 1994–present.
Magyar Nemzet, Budapest: Nemzet Lap- és Könyvkiadó Kft., 1938–present.
Népszabadság. Budapest: Népszabadság Zrt., 1957–present.
Szép Házak, Készházak. Budapest: Vogl Elemér, 1992–present.
SzépLAK: Lakberendezés, Ökológia, Környezetkultúra. Budapest: Domopress Bt., 1996–present.
Sztálinvárosi Hírlap, az MSZMP Városi Elnökségének és a Városi Tanács Végrehajtóbizottságának lapja, 1957–1961.
Tér és Rend: Lakberéndezési Lap. Budapest: Tér és Rend Kiadó Kft., 1995–2001.

Books, Articles, Films, and Websites

Adamik, Zsolt, and Roland Terdik. 2008. "És már Bambi is kapható." Stradolju website, e-pub date: July 20, 2008.
Agócs, Péter, and Sándor Agócs. 1993. "The Change Was But an Unfulfilled Promise": Agriculture and the Rural Population in Post-communist Hungary. *East European Politics & Societies* 8(1): 32–57.
Alter, Zoltán, and Gábor Németh. 1993. Privatization of Apartments in Budapest. *Heti Privinfo* 1: 21–23.
Altshuler, David. 2001. Anchors of Identity: Property, Morality, and Difference in Czech Society. Department of Anthropology, University of Chicago.
Aman, Anders. 1992. *Architecture and Ideology in Eastern Europe during the Stalin Era:*

An Aspect of Cold War History. Boston: Architectural History Foundation and the Massachusetts Institute of Technology.
Angyal, Viktória. 1976. Szociológiai hipotézisek egy történeti monográfia apropójából. *Szociológia* 1: 153–58.
Atkinson, Paul. 2006. Do It Yourself: Democracy and Design. *Journal of Design History* 19(1): 1–10.
Attfield, Judy. 1997. Design as a Practice of Modernity: A Case for the Study of the Coffee Table in the Mid-century Domestic Interior. *Journal of Material Culture* 2(3): 267–89.
———. 1999. Bringing Modernity Home: Open Plan in the British Domestic Interior. In *At Home: An Anthropology of Domestic Space*, ed. I. Cieraad, 73–82. Syracuse, N.Y.: Syracuse University Press.
———. 2007. *Bringing Modernity Home: Writings on Popular Design and Material Culture*. Manchester: Manchester University Press.
Auslander, Leora. 1996. *Taste and Power: Furnishing Modern France*. Berkeley: University of California Press.
———. 2002. Jewish Taste? Jews and the Aesthetics of Everyday Life in Paris and Berlin, 1933–1942. In *Histories of Leisure*, ed. R. Koshar. Oxford: Berg Press.
———. 2005. Beyond Words. *American Historical Review* (October): 1015–45.
Bakos, Ferenc. 1994. *Dictionary for Foreign Words and Expressions (Idegen szavak és kifejezések kéziszótára)*. Budapest: Akadémiai Kiadó.
Balogh, Éva. 2008. Hungarian Retro. *Hungarian Spectrum*. http://esbalogh.typepad.com/hungarianspectrum/2008/05/hungarian-retro.html. Accessed May 25, 2008.
Balogh, János. 1985. Az igény. *Lakáskultúra* 20(7): 7.
Balogh, Sándor, Gizella Föglein, and Sándor Szakács, eds. 1986. *Nehéz esztendők krónikája, 1949–1953: dokumentumok*. Budapest: Gondolat.
Bánhelyi, Károly. 1983. *Részletes rendezési terv. Dunaújváros, Hungary*. Dunaújváros, Hungary: Tervező Iroda.
Bánkuti, Gábor, ed. 1958. *A lakás*. Budapest: Közgazdasági és Jogi Könyvkiadó.
Bars, Sári. 1963. Modern lakás, modern bútor: A lakásberendezés új művészete. *Dunaújvárosi Hírlap*, December 6, 1963.
Barthes, Roland. 1993 [1957]. Plastic. In *Mythologies*, 97–99. New York: Vintage Books.
Bauman, Zygmunt. 1975. *Socialism: The Active Utopia*. New York: Holmes & Meier Publishers.
———. 1991. Living Without an Alternative. *The Political Quarterly* 62(1): 35–44.
Beck, Ulrich. 1987. The Anthropological Shock: Chernobyl and the Contours of the Risk Society. *Berkeley Journal of Sociology* 32: 153–65.
Becker, Wolfgang, dir. 2003. *Goodbye Lenin!* 121 min. Germany.
Bell, Peter D. 1984. *Peasants in Socialist Transition: Life in a Collectivized Hungarian Village*. Berkeley: University of California Press.
Bélley, László, and László Kulcsár. 1980. Közéleti viszonyok az új lakótelepeken. In *Tanulmányok az életmódról*, ed. M. Szántó. Budapest: Gondolat Könyvkiadó.
Berdahl, Daphne. 1999a. "(N)Ostalgie" for the Present: Memory, Longing, and East German Things. *Ethnos* 64(2): 192–211.
———. 1999b. *Where the World Ended: Re-Unification and Identity in the German Borderland*. Los Angeles: University of California Press.

Berend, Ivan. 1990. *The Hungarian Economic Reforms 1953–1988*. Cambridge, Mass.: Cambridge University Press.
Berend, Ivan T., and György Ránki. 1985. *The Hungarian Economy in the Twentieth Century*. New York: St. Martin's Press.
Berényi, János. 1976. Szekrényfalak: uniformizál vagy öltöztet? *Lakáskultúra* 11(3): 3–5.
Betts, Paul. 2008. Building Socialism at Home: The Case of East German Interiors. In *Socialist Modern: East German Everyday Culture and Politics*, ed. K. Pence and P. Betts, 96–132. Ann Arbor: University of Michigan Press.
Birdwell-Pheasant, Donna, and Denise Lawrence-Zuñiga. 1999. Introduction. In *House Life: Space, Place and Family in Europe*, ed. D. Birdwell-Pheasant and D. Lawrence-Zuñiga, 1–38. Oxford: Berg Publishers.
Bíró, Yvette. 1990. Landscape after Battle: Films from the Other Europe. *Daedalus: Journal of the American Academy of Arts and Sciences* 199(1): 161–82.
Black, Monica. 2010. *Death in Berlin: From Weimar to Divided Germany*. Cambridge: Cambridge University Press.
Bockman, Johanna, and Gil Eyal. 2002. Eastern Europe as a Laboratory for Economic Knowledge: The Transnational Roots of Neoliberalism. *American Journal of Sociology* 108(2): 310–52.
Bodnár, Judit. 1998. Assembling the Square: Social Transformation in Public Space and the Broken Mirage of the Second Economy in Postsocialist Budapest. *Slavic Review* 57(3): 489–515.
———. 2007. Becoming Bourgeois: (Postsocialist) Utopias of Isolation and Civilization. In *Evil Paradises: Dreamworlds of Neoliberalism*, ed. M. Davis and D. B. Monk, 140–51. New York: The New Press.
Bodnár, Judit, and Virág Molnár. 2010. Reconfiguring Private and Public: State, Capital and New Housing Developments in Berlin and Budapest. *Urban Studies* 47(4): 789–812.
Borhi, László. 2004. *Hungary in the Cold War, 1945–1956*. Budapest: Central European University Press.
Borneman, John. 1991. *After the Wall: East Meets West in the New Berlin*. New York: Basic Books.
Böröcz, József. 1993. Simulating the Great Transformation: Property Change under Prolonged Informality in Hungary. *European Journal of Sociology* XXXIV(1 (May)): 81–107.
Bourdieu, Pierre. 1977. *Outline of a Theory of Practice*. Cambridge: Cambridge University Press.
———. 1984 [1979]. *Distinction: A Social Critique of the Judgement of Taste*. Translated by R. Nice. Cambridge, Mass.: Harvard University Press.
Boyer, Dominic. 2001. Media Markets, Mediating Labors, and the Branding of East German Culture at Super Illu. *Social Text* 19(3): 9–33.
Bren, Paulina. 2002. Weekend Getaways: The Chata, The Tramp, and the Politics of Private Life in Post-1968 Czechoslovakia. In *Socialist Spaces: Sites of Everyday Life in the Eastern Bloc*, ed. D. Crowley and S. E. Reid, 123–40. Oxford: Berg Press.
———. 2010. *The Greengrocer and His TV: The Culture of Communism after the 1968 Prague Spring*. Ithaca, N.Y.: Cornell University Press.
Brown, Bill. 2001. Thing Theory. *Critical Inquiry* 28(Autumn): 1–22.

Buchli, Victor. 1997. Khrushchev, Modernism, and the Fight against *Petit-bourgeois* Consciousness in the Soviet Home. *Journal of Design History* 10(2): 161–76.
———. 1999. *An Archaeology of Socialism*. Oxford: Berg.
Buchowski, Michal. 2008. The Enigma of the Middle Class: A Case Study of Entrepreneurs in Poland. In *Changing Economies and Changing Identities in Postsocialist Eastern Europe*, ed. I. W. Schroder and A. Vonderau, 47–74. Berlin: LIT Verlag.
Bunce, Valerie, and Mária Csanádi. 1993. Uncertainty in the Transition: Post Communism in Hungary. *East European Politics and Societies* 7: 240–75.
Burawoy, Michael, with Janos Lukács. 1992. *The Radiant Past. Ideology and Reality in Hungary's Road to Capitalism*. Chicago: University of Chicago Press.
Búriková, Zuzana. 2004. Consuming Socialism: Domesticated Socialist Shops in the Slovak Village. In *Thinking Together. Proceedings of the IWM Junior Fellows' Conference, Winter 2003*, ed. A. Cashin and J. Jirsa. Vienna: IWM Junior Visiting Fellows' Conferences.
Burke, Timothy. 1996. *Lifebuoy Men, Luxe Women: Commodification, Consumption and Cleanliness in Modern Zimbabwe*. Durham, N.C.: Duke University Press.
Burr, Chandler. 2009. Whole Lot of Non-Scents: What Do the Sun, An Atomic Blast and Communism Smell Like? *New York Times Style Magazine*, Women's Fashion special edition. February 19, 2009, 110.
Caldwell, Melissa L. 2002. The Taste of Nationalism: Food Politics in Postsocialist Moscow. *Ethnos* 67(3): 295–319.
———, ed. 2009. *Food and Everyday Life in the Postsocialist World*. Indianapolis: Indiana University Press.
———. 2011. *Dacha Idylls: Living Organically in Russia's Countryside*. Berkeley: University of California Press.
Callmeyer, Ferenc, and Ervin Rojkó. 1972. *Hétvégi házak—nyaralók*. Budapest: Műszaki Könyvkiadó.
Carleton, Greg. 1994. Genre in Socialist Realism. *Slavic Review* 53(4): 992–1009.
Carrier, James. 1990. The Symbolism of Possession in Commodity Advertising. *Man: Journal of the Royal Anthropological Institute* 25: 693–705.
———. 1995. *Gifts and Commodities: Exchange and Western Capitalism Since 1700*. London: Routledge.
Castillo, Greg. 1992. Cities of the Stalinist Empire. In *Forms of Dominance: On the Architecture and Urbanism of the Colonial Enterprise*, ed. N. Alsayyad, 261–87. Brookfield: Aldershot.
———. 2000. Constructing the Cold War: Architecture, Urbanism and the Cultural Division of Germany, 1945–1957. PhD diss., University of California.
———. 2010. *Cold War on the Home Front: The Soft Power of Midcentury Design*. Minneapolis: University of Minnesota Press.
Chakrabarty, Dipesh. 2000. *Provincializing Europe: Postcolonial Thought and Historical Difference*. Princeton, N.J.: Princeton University Press.
Chapman, Tony, and Jenny Hockey, eds. 1999. *Ideal Homes? Social Change and Domestic Life*. London: Routledge.
Chari, Sharad, and Katherine Verdery. 2009. Thinking between the Posts: Postcolonialism, Postsocialism, and Ethnography after the Cold War. *Comparative Studies in Society and History* 51(1): 6–34.

Chelcea, Liviu. 2002. The Culture of Shortage During State-Socialism: Consumption Practices in a Romanian Village in the 1980s. *Cultural Studies* 16(1): 16–43.
Cieraad, Irene, ed. 1999. *At Home: An Anthropology of Domestic Space*, Syracuse, N.Y.: Syracuse University Press.
Cohen, Lizabeth. 1998. The New Deal State and the Making of Citizen Consumers. In *Getting and Spending: European and American Consumer Societies in the Twentieth Century*, ed. S. S. et al. Cambridge: Cambridge University Press.
———. 2001. Citizens and Consumers in the US in the Century of Mass Consumption. In *The Politics of Consumption: Material Culture and Citizenship in Europe and America*, ed. M. Daunton and M. Hilton. Oxford: Berg Press.
Collier, Stephen J. 2011. *Post-Soviet Social: Neoliberalism, Social Modernity, Biopolitics*. Princeton, N.J.: Princeton University Press.
Comaroff, Jean, and John L. Comaroff. 2000. Millennial Capitalism: First Thoughts on a Second Coming. *Public Culture* 12(2): 291–343.
Comaroff, John L., and Jean Comaroff. 1992. Homemade Hegemony. In *Ethnography and the Historical Imagination*, 265–95. Boulder, Colo.: Westview Press.
Cornelius, Deborah S. 2011. *Hungary in World War II: Caught in the Cauldron*. New York: Fordham University Press.
Creed, Gerald. 1998. *Domesticating Revolution: From Socialist Reform to Ambivalent Transition in a Bulgarian Village*. University Park: The Pennsylvania State University Press.
———. 2002. (Consumer) Paradise Lost: Capitalist Dynamics and Disenchantment in Rural Bulgaria. *Anthropology of East Europe Review* 20(2): 119–25.
———. 2010. Strange Bedfellows: Socialist Nostalgia and Neoliberalism in Bulgaria. In *Post-Communist Nostalgia*, ed. M. Todorova and Z. Gille, 29–45. Oxford: Berghahn Books.
———. 2011. *Masquerade and Postsocialism: Ritual and Cultural Dispossession in Bulgaria*. Bloomington and Indianapolis: Indiana University Press.
Crowley, David. 1993a. Building the World Anew: Design in the People's Republic of Poland. In *Design and Culture in Poland and Hungary: 1890–1990. A Tempus 'Design for Industry: East/West Europe' Reader*, ed. D. Crowley, 50–59. Brighton: University of Brighton.
———. 1993b. Organic Architecture. In *Design and Culture in Poland and Hungary: 1890–1990. A Tempus 'Design for Industry: East/West Europe' Reader*, ed. D. Crowley, 88–91. Brighton: University of Brighton.
Crowley, David, and Susan E. Reid. 2000. Style and Socialism: Modernity and Material Culture in Post-War Eastern Europe. In *Style and Socialism: Modernity and Material Culture in Post-War Eastern Europe*, ed. S. E. Reid and D. Crowley, 1–24. Oxford: Berg.
Czeglédi, Cecília. 1998. Meseház Dabasban: A rögtönzés szabadsága. *Lakáskultúra* 33(6): 38–44.
Czeglédy, André P. 1998. Villas of Wealth: A Historical Perspective on New Residences in Post-Socialist Hungary. *City and Society* 10(1): 245–68.
Daniel, E. Valentine. 1987. *Fluid Signs: Being a Person the Tamil Way*. Berkeley: University of California Press.
Dessewffy, Tibor. 1998. Az elkeseredettség másik oldala. (Embitteredness: The other side of the story.) *Népszabadság*, November 14, 1998.

———. 2002. Speculators and Travelers: The Political Construction of the Tourist in the Kádár Regime. *Cultural Studies* 16(1): 44–62.
Djilas, Milovan. 1957. *The New Class: An Analysis of the Communist System.* New York: Praeger.
Douglas, Mary. 1970. *Purity and Danger: An Analysis of Concepts of Pollution and Taboo.* New York: Penguin Books, Ltd.
Dowling, Timothy C. 1999. Stalinstadt/Eisenhüttenstadt: A Model for (Socialist) Life in the German Democratic Republic, 1950–1968, PhD diss., Tulane University.
Drakulic, Slavenka, 1992. *How We Survived Communism and Even Laughed.* New York: Harper Perennial.
Drazin, Adam, 2001. A Man Will Get Furnished: Wood and Domesticity in Urban Romania. In *Home Possessions,* ed. D. Miller, 173–99. Oxford: Berg.
Dunham, Vera S. 1990 [1976]. *In Stalin's Time: Middle-Class Values in Soviet Fiction.* Cambridge: Cambridge University Press.
Dunn & Bradstreet, Hungaria KFT. 1996. Top 100 Companies. *The Wall Street Journal, Central European Economic Review:* 18.
Einhorn, Barbara. 1993. *Cinderella Goes to Market: Citizenship, Gender and Women's Movements in East Central Europe.* New York: Verso Books.
Eke, Zsolt. n.d. Gems of Timber Architecture—Pavilions of Expos: Hungarian Pavilion in Sevilla and Swiss Pavilion in Hannover. http://hej.sze.hu/ARC/ARC-060517-A/arc060517a.pdf.
Elias, Norbert. 1978. *The History of Manners. The Civilizing Process.* New York: Pantheon.
Erdei, Ferenc. 1941. *A magyar paraszttársadalom.* Budapest: Franklin Társulat.
Ernyey, Gyula. 1993. *Made in Hungary: The Best of 150 Years in Industrial Design.* Budapest: Rubik Innovation Foundation.
Fabian, Johannes. 1983. *Time and the Other: How Anthropology Makes its Object.* New York: Columbia University Press.
Farquhar, Judith. 2002. *Appetites: Food and Sex in Postsocialist China.* Durham, N.C.: Duke University Press.
Federmeyer, Éva. 1997. Black Mother and Cyborg Existence: Reading Octavia Butler from Hungary. In *Women and Men in East-European Transition,* ed. M. Fleischmidt, 247–58. Cluj: Babes Bolyai University.
Fehér, Ferenc, Ágnes Heller, and György Márkus. 1983. *Dictatorship over Needs.* New York: St. Martin's Press.
Fehérváry, István. 1989. *The Long Road to Revolution: The Hungarian Gulag 1945–1956.* Santa Fe, N.M.: Pro Libertate.
Fehérváry, Krisztina. 1995. Building the New Socialist City: Modernism and Modernization in Stalinist Hungary. MA thesis, University of Chicago.
———. 2006. Innocence Lost: Cinematic Representations of 1960s Consumption for 1990s Hungary. *East Europe* 24(2): 54–61.
———. 2007. Hungarian Horoscopes as a Genre of Postsocialist Transformation. *Social Identities* 13(5): 561–76.
———. 2012. From Socialist Modern to Super-Natural Organicism: Cosmological Transformations through Home Décor. *Cultural Anthropology* 27(4): 615–40.
Fél, Edit, and Tamás Hofer. 1969. *Proper Peasants: Traditional Life in a Hungarian Village.* Chicago: Aldine Publishing Company.

Ferge, Zsuzsa. 1979. *A Society in the Making: Hungarian Social and Societal Policy 1945–75*. White Plains, N.Y.: M. E. Sharpe, Inc.
Ferguson, James. 2002. Of Mimicry and Membership: Africans and the 'New World Society.' *Cultural Anthropology* 17(4): 551–69.
Ferkai, András. 1998. Hungarian Architecture in the Postwar Years. In *The Architecture of Historic Hungary*, ed. D. Wiebenson and J. Sisa, 277–97. Cambridge, Mass.: The MIT Press.
Finn, H. M. R., and A. P. Finn. 1964. *The Planahome Book of House Plans*. Richmond, Surrey: Planahome.
Fitzpatrick, Sheila. 1992. *The Cultural Front: Power and Culture in Revolutionary Russia*. Ithaca, N.Y.: Cornell University Press.
———. 1999. *Everyday Stalinism: Ordinary Life in Extraordinary Times: Soviet Russia in the 1930s*. New York: Oxford University Press.
———. 2000. Introduction to Part III: Consumption and Civilization. In *Stalinism: New Directions*, ed. S. Fitzpatrick, 177–81. London: Routledge.
Földházi, Erzsébet. 1989. Lakótelep vagy Gettó? A miskolci csökkentett komfortfokozatú lakótelep tervének sajtóvisszhangja a napilapokban. *Szociológia* 2: 207–19.
Forty, Adrian. 1986. *Objects of Desire: Design and Society Since 1750*. London: Thames and Hudson.
Foster, George. 1965. Peasant Society and the Image of Limited Good. *American Ethnologist* 67(2): 293–315.
Foster, Robert. 2002. *Materializing the Nation: Commodities, Consumption and Media in Papau New Guinea*. Bloomington: Indiana University Press.
———. 2009. Things to Do With Brands. Paper presented at the annual meetings of the American Anthropological Association, Philadelphia, Pa.
Fóti, Péter. 1988. *Röpirat a lakáshelyzetről*. Budapest: Magvető.
Foucault, Michel. 1986. Texts/Contexts. Of Other Spaces. *Diacritics* 16(1): 22–27.
Fowkes, Reuben. 2002. The Role of Monumental Sculpture in the Construction of Socialist Space in Stalinist Hungary. In *Socialist Spaces: Sites of Everyday Life in the Eastern Bloc*, ed. D. Crowley and S. E. Reid, 65–84. Oxford: Berg Press.
Freeman, Carla. 2000. *High Tech and High Heels in the Global Economy: Women, Work and Pink-Collar Identities in the Caribbean*. Durham, N.C.: Duke University Press.
———. 2011. Neoliberal Respectability: Entrepreneurial Marriage, Affective Labor, and a New Caribbean Middle Class. In *The Global Middle Classes*, ed. R. Heiman, C. Freeman, and M. Leichty. Santa Fe, N.M.: School for Advanced Research, SAR Press.
French, R. A., and F. E. Ian Hamilton, eds. 1979. *The Socialist City: Spatial Structure and Urban Policy*. New York: John Wiley & Sons.
Frykman, Jonas. 1987. Clean and Proper: Body and Soul Through Peasant and Bourgeois Eyes. In *Culture Builders: A Historical Anthropology of Middle-Class Life*, ed. J. Frykman and O. Löfgren. New Brunswick, N.J.: Rutgers University Press.
———. 1993. Becoming the Perfect Swede: Modernity, Body Politics, and National Processes in Twentieth-Century Sweden. *Ethnos* 58(3–4): 259–74.
Funk, Nanette, and Magda Mueller. 1993. *Gender Politics and Post-Communism: Reflections from Eastern Europe and the Former Soviet Union*. New York/London: Routledge.

Gal, Susan. 1991. Bartok's Funeral: Representations of Europe in Hungarian Political Rhetoric. *American Ethnologist* 18(3): 440–58.

———. 1993. Diversity and Contestation in Linguistic Ideologies: German Speakers in Hungary. *Language in Society* 22: 337–59.

———. 1994. Gender in the Post-Socialist Transition: The Abortion Debate in Hungary. *East European Politics and Societies* 8(2): 256–86.

———. 2002. A Semiotics of the Public/Private Distinction. *Differences: A Journal of Feminist Cultural Studies* 13(1): 77–95.

Gal, Susan, and Gail Kligman. 2000a. *The Politics of Gender After Socialism: A Comparative-Historical Essay*. Princeton, N.J.: Princeton University Press.

———, eds. 2000b. *Reproducing Gender: Politics, Publics, and Everyday Life after Socialism*. Princeton, N.J.: Princeton University Press.

Galbraith, Marysia. 2001. 'We Just Want to Live Normally': Intersecting Discourses of 'Public' and 'Private' in Poland. Annual Meeting of the American Anthropological Association. Washington D.C.

Garner, Philippe. 2008. *Sixties Design*. Köln: Taschen GmbH.

Gáti, Charles. 1986. *Hungary and the Soviet Bloc*. Durham, N.C.: Duke University Press.

Gell, Alfred. 1998. *Art and Agency: An Anthropological Theory*. Oxford: Clarendon Press.

Gerchuk, Iurii. 2000. The Aesthetics of Everyday Life in the Khrushchev Thaw in the USSR (1954–64). In *Style and Socialism: Modernity and Material Culture in Post-War Eastern Europe*, ed. S. E. Reid and D. Crowley, 81–99. Oxford: Berg.

Gerő, András. 1993. *Magyar polgárosodás*. Budapest: Atlantisz.

Gerő, András, and Iván Pető. 1999. *Unfinished Socialism: Pictures from the Kádár Era*. Budapest: Central European University Press.

Ghodsee, Kristen. 2005. *The Red Riviera: Gender, Tourism, and Postsocialism on the Black Sea*. Durham, N.C.: Duke University Press.

Gille, Zsuzsa. 2007. *From the Cult of Waste to the Trash Heap of History: The Politics of Waste in Socialist and Postsocialist Hungary*. Bloomington: Indiana University Press.

———. 2009. The Tale of the Toxic Paprika: The Hungarian Taste of Euro-Globalization. In *Food and Everyday Life in the Postsocialist World*, ed. M. Caldwell, 57–77. Bloomington: Indiana University Press.

———. 2010. Is There a Global Postsocialist Condition? *Global Society* 24(1): 9–30.

Gomori, George. 1963. "Consumerism" in Hungary. *Problems of Communism* 12(1): 64–66.

Goven, Joanna. 1993. The Anti-Politics of Anti-Feminism. In *Gender Politics and Post-Communism: Reflections from Eastern Europe and the Former Soviet Union*, ed. N. Funk and M. Mueller. New York: Routledge.

Graan, Andrew. 2010. On the Politics of Imidž: European Integration and the Trials of Recognition in Post-Conflict Macedonia. *Slavic Review* 69(4): 835–58.

Greenberg, Jessica. 2011. On the Road to Normal: Negotiating Agency and State Sovereignty in Postsocialist Serbia. *American Anthropologist* 113(1): 88–100.

Gregory, Christopher A. 1982. *Gifts and Commodities: Studies in Political Economy*. London: Academic Press.

Groys, Boris. 1992. *The Total Art of Stalinism: Avant-Garde, Aesthetic Dictatorship, and Beyond*. Translated by C. Hanser. Princeton, N.J.: Princeton University Press.

Guano, Emanuela. 2002. Spectacles of Modernity: Transnational Imagination and Local Hegemonies in Neoliberal Buenos Aires. *Cultural Anthropology* 17(2): 181–209.
———. 2004. The Denial of Citizenship: 'Barbaric' Buenos Aires and the Middle-Class Imaginary. *City and Society* 16(1): 69–97.
Gullestad, Marianne. 1992. *The Art of Social Relations: Essays on Culture, Social Action and Everyday Life in Modern Norway*. Oslo: Scandinavian University Press.
Gyáni, Gábor. 1991. A polgári középosztály lakásviszonyai Budapesten a két háború között. In *Polgárosodás Közép-Európában. Tanulmányok Hanák Péter 70. születésnapjára*, ed. É. Somogyi, 109–21. Budapest: MTA-TTI Magyar Tudományos Akadémia Történettudományi Intézet.
Gyáni, Gábor, György Kövér, and Tibor Valuch, eds. 2004. *Social History of Hungary from the Reform Era to the End of the Twentieth Century*. Boulder, Colo.: Social Science Monographs.
György, Péter. 1992. The Mirror of Everyday Life, or the Will to a Period Style. In *Art and Society in the Age of Stalin*, ed. P. György and H. Turai. Budapest: Corvina.
Habermas, Jürgen. 1989. *The Structural Transformation of the Public Sphere: An Inquiry into a Category of Bourgeois Society*. Cambridge, Mass.: MIT Press.
Halász, Zoltan. 1965. The Town that Was Once a Wilderness. In *Projects Realized in Hungary: Some Achievements of the Last 20 Years*, 11–25. Budapest: Pannonia Press.
Hall, Edward T. 1969. *The Hidden Dimension*. Garden City, N.Y.: Anchor Books.
Hammer, Ferenc. 2002. A Gasoline Scented Sinbad: The Truck-driver as Popular Hero in Socialist Hungary. *Cultural Studies* 16(1): 80–126.
———. 2010. The Real One: Western Brands and Competing Notions of Authenticity in Socialist Hungary. In *Cultures of Commodity Branding*, ed. A. Bevan and D. Wengrow, 131–54. Walnut Creek, Calif.: Left Coast Press.
Hanák, Péter, ed. 1992. *Polgári lakáskultúra a századfordulón*. Budapest: MTA Történettudományi Intézete.
Haney, Lynne. 2002. *Inventing the Needy: Gender and the Politics of Welfare in Hungary*. Berkeley: University of California.
Hankiss, Elemer. 1989. *Kelet-európai alternatívák*. Budapest: Közgazdasági és Jogi Könyvkiadó.
Hanley, Eric. 2000. Cadre Capitalism in Hungary and Poland: Property Accumulation among Communist Era Elites. *East European Politics and Societies* 14(1): 143–78.
Hann, Chris M. 1990. Second Economy and Civil Society. In *Market Economy and Civil Society in Hungary*, ed. C. M. Hann. London: Frank Cass.
———. 1980. *Tázlár: A Village in Hungary*. Cambridge: Cambridge University Press.
Hanson, Phillip. 1974. *Advertising and Socialism: The Nature and Extent of Consumer Advertising in the Soviet Union, Poland, Hungary and Yugoslavia*. London: Macmillan.
Haraszti, Miklós. 1978. *A Worker in a Worker's State*. Translated by M. Wright. New York: Universe.
Hare, Paul G. 1988. Industrial Development of Hungary Since World War II. *East European Politics and Societies* 2(1): 115–51.
Harper, Krista. 2006. *Wild Capitalism: Environmental Activists and Post-Socialist Ecology in Hungary*. Boulder, Colo.: East European Monographs, Columbia University Press.

Heathcote, Edwin. 1997. *Imre Makovecz: The Wings of the Soul*. London: Wiley Europe.
———. 2006. Hungary: The Organic and the Rational Traditions. *Architectural Design* 76(3): 34–39.
Hegedűs, József. 1992. Self-Help Housing in Hungary: The Changing Role of Private Housing Provision in Eastern Europe. In *Beyond Self-Help Housing*, ed. K. Mathéy, 217–31. Munich: Profil Verlag.
Hegedűs, József, and Róbert Manchin. 1987. Az üdülőterületek expanziója (1965–1975) (Egyéni és kollektív stratégiák). *Szociológia* 2: 251–75.
Hegedűs, József, and Iván Tosics. 1983/1984. Lakásreform a nyolcvanas években. *Medvetánc* 1983(4)–1984(1): 177–200.
Herzfeld, Michael. 1997. *Cultural Intimacy: Social Poetics in the Nation-State*. New York: Routledge.
Hessler, Julie. 2000. Cultured Trade: The Stalinist Turn towards Consumerism. In *Stalinism: New Directions*, ed. S. Fitzpatrick, 182–209. London: Routledge.
Hixson, Walter L. 1997. *Parting the Curtain: Propaganda, Culture and the Cold War, 1945–1961*. New York: St. Martin's Press.
Hobsbawm, Eric J. 1978. Man and Woman in Socialist Iconography. *History Workshop* 6: 121–38.
Hódi Tóth, József. 1997. A Szögletesség Bűvöletében. *Családi ház: Építkezők, építtetők, építészek, vállalkozók és reménykedők lapja* 9(1): 61–62.
Hoensch, Jörg K. 1988. *A History of Modern Hungary, 1867–1986*. New York: Longman Inc.
Hofer, Tamás. 1984. Peasant Culture and Urban Culture in the Period of Modernization: Delineation of a Problem Area Based on Data from Hungary. In *The Peasant and the City in Eastern Europe: Interpenetrating Structures*, ed. I. P. Winner and T. G. Winner. Cambridge, Mass.: Schenkman Publishing Co., Inc.
———. 1991. Construction of the 'Folk Cultural Heritage' in Hungary and Rival Versions of National Identity *Ethnologia Europaea* 21: 145–70.
Hollos, Marida, and Béla C. Maday, eds. 1983. *New Hungarian Peasants*. Brooklyn, N.Y.: Social Science Monographs—Brooklyn College Press.
Holston, James. 1989. *The Modernist City: An Anthropological Critique of Brasília*. Chicago: University of Chicago Press.
Horváth, István. 2000. *Dunaferr 50. Dunai Vasmű Krónika*. Dunaújváros: Dunaferr Dunai Vasmű Részvénytársaság megbízásából a Dunatáj Kiadói Kft. gondozásában.
Hull, Matthew S. 2012. *Government of Paper: The Materiality of Bureaucracy in Urban Pakistan*. Berkeley: University of California Press.
Humphrey, Caroline. 1997. The Villas of the 'New Russians': A Sketch of Consumption and Cultural Identity in Post-Soviet Landscapes. *Focaal* 30/31: 85–106.
———. 2005. Ideology in Infrastructure: Architecture and Soviet Imagination. *Journal of the Royal Anthropological Institute* (N.S.) 39–58, Vol. 11.
Huseby-Darvas, Éva. 2001. Hungarian Village Women in the Marketplace During the Late Socialist Period. In *Women Traders in Cross Cultural Perspective: Mediating Identities, Marketing Wares*, ed. L. Seligmann, 185–209. Palo Alto, Calif.: Stanford University Press.
———. 2003. *Hungarians in Michigan*. East Lansing, Mich.: Michigan State University Press
Ingold, Tim. 2007. *Lines: A Brief History*. New York: Routledge.
Iordanova, D. 2003. *Cinema of the Other Europe: The Industry and Artistry of East Central European Film*. London: Wallflower Press.

Irvine, Judith, and Susan Gal. 2000. Language Ideology and Linguistic Differentiation. In *Regimes of Language: Ideologies, Polities, and Identities*, ed. P. V. Kroskrity, 35–84. Santa Fe, N.M.: School of American Research Press.
Irving, David. 1981. *Uprising! One Nation's Nightmare: Hungary 1956.* Lincoln, Neb.: Focal Point Publications.
Jameson, E. A. 1993 [1920]. *Milliók a semmiből.* Budapest: Új Vénusz Lap—és Könyvkiadó (orig. 1920s edition, Nova Irodalmi Intézet).
János, Andrew C. 1982. *The Politics of Backwardness in Hungary: 1825–1945.* Princeton, N.J.: Princeton University Press.
Jowitt, Ken. 1992. *New World Disorder: The Leninist Extinction.* Berkeley: University of California Press.
Jung, Yuson. 2009. From Canned Food to Canny Consumers: Cultural Competence in the Age of Mechanical Production. In *in Food and Everyday Life in Postsocialist Europe*, ed. M. Caldwell. Bloomington: Indiana University Press.
Kántor, Károlyné Éva. 1996. *Dunaújváros szociális helyzetének vizsgálata reprezentatív minta alapján, 1992.* Szocialis Problémak Vizsgálata. Dunaújváros, Hungary: Főiskola.
Keane, Webb. 1997. *Signs of Recognition: Powers and Hazards of Representation in an Indonesian Society.* Berkeley: University of California Press.
———. 2003. Semiotics and the Social Analysis of Material Things. *Language and Communication* 23(3–4): 409–25.
———. 2005. Signs Are Not the Garb of Meaning: On the Social Analysis of Material Things. In *Materiality*, ed. D. Miller, 182–205. Durham, N.C.: Duke University Press.
———. 2006. Subjects and Objects. In *Handbook of Material Culture*, ed. C. Tilley, W. Keane, S. Küchler, M. Rowlands, and P. Spyer, 197–202. London: Sage Publications.
Kelemen, Zsófi. 2010. Szürke, Szürkés, Szürkébb. *SzépLAK: Lakberendezés, ökológia, környezetkultúra* 15(11): 64–79
Kelly, Catriona, and Vadim Volkov. 1998. Directed Desires: Kul'turnost and Consumption. In *Constructing Russian Culture in the Age of Revolution: 1881–1940*, ed. C. Kelly and D. Shepherd. Oxford: Oxford University Press.
Kenedi, János. 1981. *"Tiéd az ország, magadnak építed." Szatírikus elbeszélés.* Párizs: Magyar Füzetek.
Kideckel, David A. 1993. *The Solitude of Collectivism: Romanian Villagers to the Revolution and Beyond.* Ithaca, N.Y.: Cornell University Press.
Kolankiewicz, George. 1994. Elites in Search of a Political Formula. *Daedalus* 123(3): 143–57.
Kolosi, Tamás. 1988. Stratification and Social Structure in Hungary. *Annual Review of Sociology* 14: 405–19.
Konrád, György. 1984. *Antipolitics.* Translated by R. E. Allen. San Diego: Harcourt Brace Jovanovich.
Konrád, György, and Iván Szelényi. 1969. *Az új lakótelepek szociológiai problémái.* Budapest: Akadémiai Kiadó.
———. 1979. *The Intellectuals on the Road to Class Power: A Sociological Study of the Role of the Intelligentsia in Socialism.* Translated by A. Arato and R. E. Allen. New York: Harcourt Brace Jovanovich.

Kopátsy, Sándor. 1993. Nemcsak Ház a Családi Ház. *Családi ház: Építkezők, építtetők, építészek, vállalkozók és reménykedők lapja.* 5(1): 52.
Kopytoff, Igor. 1986. The Cultural Biography of Things: Commoditization as Process. In *The Social Life of Things: Commodities in Cultural Perspective,* ed. A. Appadurai. Cambridge: Cambridge University Press.
Kornai, János. 1992. *The Socialist System: The Political Economy of Communism.* Princeton, N.J.: Princeton University Press.
Kőrősi, Katalin, and Mónika Tomán. 1996. A berendezés (néha) marad! *Cash Flow: Magyarországi gazdasági magazin,amiből ön profitál* 96(10): 106-10.
Kósa, László. 2000. The Age of Bourgeois Society, 1920-1948. Everyday Culture. In *A Cultural History of Hungary In the Nineteenth and Twentieth Centuries,* ed. L. Kósa, 177-210. Budapest: Corvina/Osiris.
Koselleck, Reinhart. 1985 [1979]. *Futures Past: On the Semantics of Historical Time.* Translated by K. Tribe. Cambridge: MIT Press.
Kostof, Spiro. 1985. *A History of Architecture: Settings and Rituals.* Oxford: Oxford University Press.
Kotkin, Stephen. 1995. *Magnetic Mountain: Stalinism as Civilization.* Berkeley: University of California Press.
Kovács, Katalin, and Mónika Váradi. 2000. Women's Life Trajectories and Class Formation in Hungary. In *Reproducing Gender: Politics, Publics, and Everyday Life after Socialism,* ed. S. Gal and G. Kligman, 176-99. Princeton, N.J.: Princeton University Press.
Kozma, Erzsébet. 1995. Az én házam, az én váram. *Dunaferr Hetilap,* June 29, 1995.
Kravets, Olga, and Örsan Örge. 2010. Iconic Brands: A Socio-Material Story. *Journal of Material Culture* 15(2): 205-32.
Kundera, Milan. 1981. *The Book of Laughter and Forgetting.* Translated by M. H. Heim. New York: Penguin.
Kunszabó, Ferenc. 1983. *Gyarapodásunk története.* Budapest: Magvető Kiadó.
Ladányi, János, and Iván Szelényi. 1997. Szuburbanizáció és gettósodás. *Kritika* 7 (July): 4-12.
Lampland, Martha. 1987. Working through History: Ideologies of Work and Agricultural Production in a Hungarian Village, 1918-1983, PhD diss., University of Chicago.
———. 1995. *The Object of Labor: Commodification in Socialist Hungary.* Chicago: University of Chicago Press.
Latour, Bruno. 1992. Where Are the Missing Masses? The Sociology of a Few Mundane Artifacts. In *Shaping Technology/Building Society: Studies in Sociotechnical Change,* ed. W. E. Bijker and J. Law, 225-58. Boston: MIT Press.
———. 1999. *Pandora's Hope: Essays on the Reality of Science Studies.* Cambridge, Mass.: Harvard University Press.
Lebow, Katherine. 1999. Revising the Politicized Landscape: Nowa Huta, 1949-1957. *City and Society* 11(1-2): 165-87.
———. 2001. Public Works, Private Lives: Youth Brigades in Nowa Huta in the 1950s. *Contemporary European History* 10(2): 199-219.
Le Corbusier. 1967. *The Radiant City: Elements of a Doctrine of Urbanism to Be Used as the Basis of Our Machine-Age Civilization.* New York: Orion Press.
Lefebvre, Henri. 1991 [1974]. *The Production of Space.* Cambridge: Blackwell.

Lemon, Alaina. 1991. Maiakovskii and the 'Language of Lenin.' *Chicago Anthropology Exchange* 19 (Winter): 1–26.
———. 1998. "Your Eyes are Green Like Dollars": Counterfeit Cash, National Substance, and Currency Apartheid in 1990s Russia. *Cultural Anthropology* 13(1): 22–55.
———. 2008. Writing Against the New Cold War. *Anthropology News* (November): 11–12.
———. 2011. Sensations to Superpowers. *Ab Imperio. Studies of New Imperial History and Nationalism in the Post-Soviet Space* (3): 313–29.
Liechty, Mark. 2003. *Suitably Modern: Making Middle-Class Culture in a New Consumer Society*. Princeton, N.J.: Princeton University Press.
Löfgren, Orvar. 1993. Materializing the Nation in Sweden and America. *Ethnos* 53 (3–4): 161–96.
———. 1994. Consuming Interests. In *Consumption and Identity*, ed. J. Friedman. Chur, Switzerland: Harwood Academic Press.
Losonczi, Ágnes. 1977. *Az életmód az időben, a tárgyakban és az értékekben*. Budapest: Gondolat.
Lovell, Stephen. 2002. Soviet Exurbia: Dachas in Postwar Russia. In *Socialist Spaces: Sites of Everyday Life in the Eastern Bloc*, ed. D. Crowley and S. E. Reid, 105–22. Oxford: Berg Press.
Lukovits, Judit. 1995. A Házigazda: Réz András. *Lakáskultúra* 30(7): 77–81.
———. 1996. Valóban lakótelepi? *Lakáskultúra* 31(7): 42–45.
Madigan, Ruth, and Moira Munro. 1999. 'The more we are together': Domestic Space, Gender and Privacy. In *Ideal Homes? Social Change and Domestic Life*, ed. T. Chapman and J. Hockney, 61–72. London: Routledge.
Major, Máté. 1981. "Sziget"-ház, "Sziget"-lakás vagy közösségi otthon? In *Új építészet, új társadalom 1945–1978: Válogatás az elmúlt évtizedek építészeti vitáiból, dokumentumaiból*, ed. M. Major and J. Osskó, 195–200. Budapest: Corvina Kiadó.
Major, Máté, and Judit Osskó, eds. 1981. *Új építészet, új társadalom 1945–1978: Válogatás az elmúlt évtizedek építészeti vitáiból, dokumentumaiból*. Budapest: Corvina Kiadó.
Manning, Paul. 2007a. Rose-Colored Glasses? Color Revolutions and Cartoon Chaos in Postsocialist Georgia. *Cultural Anthropology* 22(2): 171–213.
———. 2007b. 'Our Beer': Ethnographic Brands in Postsocialist Georgia. *American Anthropologist* 109(4): 626–41.
———. 2012. *Semiotics of Drink and Drinking*. New York: Continuum Books.
Manning, Paul, and Anne Meneley. 2008. Material Objects in Cosmological Worlds: An Introduction. *Ethnos* 73(3): 285–302.
Mark, James. 2005. Discrimination, Opportunity, and Middle-Class Success in Early Communist Hungary. *The Historical Journal* 48(2): 499–521.
Marody, Mira, and Anna Giza-Poleszczuk. 2000. Changing Images of Identity in Poland: From the Self-Sacrificing to the Self-Investing Woman? In *Reproducing Gender: Politics, Publics, and Everyday Life after Socialism*, ed. S. Gal and G. Kligman, 151–75. Princeton, N.J.: Princeton University Press.
Marosán, György. 1994. The Business of Business: The New Entrepreneurs in the Making. *The Hungarian Quarterly* 35(136): 72–78.
Marx, Karl. 1963 [1844]. Economic and Philosophical Manuscripts of 1844. In *Karl Marx: Early Writings*, ed. T. B. Bottomore. New York: McGraw-Hill Paperbacks.
Massumi, Brian. 2002. *Parables for the Virtual: Movement, Affect, Sensation*. Durham, N.C.: Duke University Press.

Mauss, Marcel. 1973 [1935]. Techniques of the Body. *Economy and Society* 2(1): 70–88.
———. 2000 [1923]. *The Gift: Form and Reason for Exchange in Archaic Societies*. Translated by W. D. Hall. New York: W. W. Norton & Company.
May, Elaine Tyler. 1988. *Homeward Bound: American Families in the Cold War Era*. New York: Basic Books.
Mazzarella, William. 2003. *Shoveling Smoke: Advertising and Globalization in Contemporary India*. Durham, N.C.: Duke University Press.
Meneley, Anne. 2008. Oleo-signs and Quali-signs: The Qualities of Olive Oil. *Ethnos* 73(3): 303–26.
Merkel, Ina 1998. Consumer Culture in the GDR, or How the Struggle for Antimodernity Was Lost on the Battleground of Consumer Culture. In *Getting and Spending: European and American Consumer Societies in the Twentieth Century*, ed. M. Judt, C. McGovern, and S. Strasser, 281–300. Cambridge: Cambrige University Press.
Miliutin, N. A. 1974 [1930]. *Sotsgorod: The Problem of Building Socialist Cities*. Translated by A. Sprague. Cambridge: MIT Press.
Miller, Daniel. 1984. Modernism and Suburbia as Material Ideology. In *Ideology, Power and Prehistory*, ed. D. Miller and C. Tilley, 46–47. Cambridge: Cambridge University Press.
———. 1987. *Material Culture and Mass Consumption*. Oxford: Basil Blackwell.
———. 1988. Appropriating the State on the Council Estate. MAN (N.S.) 23(2): 253–72.
———. 1994. *Modernity: An Ethnographic Approach. Dualism and Mass Consumption in Trinidad*. Oxford: Berg.
———. 1998. *A Theory of Shopping*. Ithaca, N.Y.: Cornell University Press.
———, ed. 2001. *Home Possessions: Material Culture Behind Closed Doors*. Oxford: Berg Publishers.
———. 2005. Introduction. In *Materiality*, ed. D. Miller. Durham, N.C.: Duke University Press.
Milosz, Czeslaw. 1990 [1953]. *The Captive Mind*. Translated by J. Zielonko. New York: Vintage International.
Miskolczi, Miklós. 1975. *Az első évtized. Dunapentelétől—Dunaújvárosig*. Dunaújváros: Dunaújvárosi Tanács.
———. 1980. *Város lesz, csak azért is . . .* Budapest: Szépirodalmi Könyvkiadó.
Molnár, Miklós. 1990 [1987]. *From Béla Kun to János Kádár: Seventy Years of Hungarian Communism*. Translated by A. J. Pomerans. New York: Berg.
Molnár, Virág. 2005. Cultural Politics and Modernist Architecture: The Tulip Debate in Postwar Hungary. *American Sociological Review* 70: 111–35.
———. 2010. In Search of the Ideal Socialist Home in Post-Stalinist Hungary: Prefabricated Mass Housing or Do-It-Yourself Family Home? *Journal of Design History* 23(1): 61–81.
Moore, R. 2003. From Genericide to Viral Marketing: on 'Brand'. *Language and Communication* 23: 331–57.
Mosse, George. 1985. *Nationalism and Sexuality: Middle-Class Morality and Sexual Norms in Modern Europe*. Madison: University of Wisconsin Press.
Mueggler, Erik. 2001. *The Age of Wild Ghosts: Memory, Violence, and Place in Southwest China*. Berkeley: University of California Press.
Munn, Nancy. 1971. The Transformation of Subjects into Objects in Walbiri and Pitjant-

jatjara Myth. In *Australian Aboriginal Anthropology*, ed. R. Berndt, 141–63. Nedlands: University of Western Australia Press.

———. 1986. *The Fame of Gawa. A Symbolic Study of Value Transformation in a Massim (Papua New Guinea) Society*. Durham, N.C.: Duke University Press.

———. 1994. Creating a Heterotopia: An Analysis of the Spacetime of Olmsted's and Vaux's Central Park. In *A Collection of Papers from a Conference on Place*, ed. Feld and Basso: Santa Fe, N.M.: School of American Research.

———. 2004. The "Becoming-Past" of Places: Spacetime and Memory in 19th Century, Pre-Civil War New York. *Finnish Journal of Anthropology* 29: 2–19.

Nadkarni, Maya. 2000. The 'Whisky Robber': Criminality as a Moral Discourse in Post-'89 Hungary. *Anthropology of East Europe Review* 18(2): 85–92.

———. 2002. "Csak a szépre emlékszem" [I only remember the beautiful]: Consuming Nostalgia in Post-Socialist Hungary. Paper presented at the Annual Symposium of Soyuz, Ann Arbor, Mich.

———. 2009. Remains of Socialism: Memory and Anxieties of the National in Postsocialist Hungary. PhD diss., Columbia University.

———. 2010. "But it's ours." Nostalgia and the Politics of Authenticity in Post-Socialist Hungary. In *Post-Communist Nostalgia*, ed. M. Todorova and Z. Gille, 190–214. Oxford: Berghahn Books.

Nadler, John. 1995. Troubled Youths Abandon 'Tomorrow.' *The Hungary Report*, June 12: 1, 11.

Norman, Donald. 2004. *Emotional Design: Why We Love (or Hate) Everyday Things*. New York: Basic Books.

O'Dougherty, Maureen. 2002. *Consumption Intensified: The Politics of Middle-Class Daily Life in Brazil*. Durham, N.C.: Duke University Press.

Offe, Claus. 1993. The Politics of Social Policy in East European Transitions: Antecedents, Agents, and Agenda of Reform. *Social Research* 60(4): 649–84.

Oláh, Sándor. 1970. *A családi ház kertje*. Budapest: Mezőgazdasági Könyvkiadó Vállalat.

Országh, László. 1987. *A Concise Hungarian–English Dictionary (Magyar–Angol Kéziszótár)*. Budapest: Akadémiai Kiadó.

Ortner, Sherry. 2002. Subjects and Capital: A Fragment of a Documentary Ethnography. *Ethnos* 67(1): 9–32.

Owensby, Brian P. 1999. *Intimate Ironies: Modernity and the Making of Middle-Class Lives in Brazil*. Stanford, Calif.: Stanford University Press.

Packard, Vance. 1960. *The Waste Makers*. New York: McKay Company.

Papp, Gábor Zsigmond (dir). 1998. *Budapest Retró: Életképek a 60-as, 70-es évekből*. Art Editor Stúdió. Hungary.

Patico, Jennifer. 2008. *Consumption and Social Change in a Post-Soviet Middle Class*. Washington, D.C., and Stanford, Calif.: Woodrow Wilson Center Press and Stanford University Press.

Patterson, Patrick H. 2011. *Bought and Sold: Living and Losing the Good Life in Socialist Yugoslavia*. Ithaca, N.Y.: Cornell University Press.

Pecz, Péter. 1996. Dunaújvárosi Lakóegyüttes: Szabálytalan építéstörténet. *Családi ház* 3: 36–38.

Peirce, Charles Sanders. 1955. *Philosophical Writings of Peirce*. New York: Dover Publications.

Pence, Katherine, and Paul Betts, eds. 2008. *Socialist Modern: East German Everyday Culture and Politics.* Ann Arbor: University of Michigan Press.
Pesmen, Dale. 1999. Normal and Not-Normal People in Perestroika Russia. Paper presented at the Annual Conference of the Central States Anthropological Society. Chicago, Ill.
———. 2000. *Russia and Soul.* Ithaca, N.Y.: Cornell University Press.
Pine, Frances. 1996. Naming the House and Naming the Land: Kinship and Social Groups in Highland Poland. *Journal of the Royal Anthropological Institute* 2(3): 443–59.
Pine, Jason. 2012. *The Art of Making Do in Naples.* Minneapolis: University of Minnesota Press.
Pinney, Christopher. 2005. Things Happen: Or, From Which Moment Does That Object Come? In *Materiality,* ed. D. Miller. Durham, N.C.: Duke University Press.
Pittaway, Mark. 2000. Stalinism, Working-Class Housing and Individual Autonomy: The Encouragement of Private House Building in Hungary's Mining Areas, 1950–54. In *Style and Socialism: Modernity and Material Culture in Post-War Eastern Europe,* ed. S. E. Reid and D. Crowley, 49–64. Oxford: Berg.
———. 2005. Creating and Domesticating Hungary's Socialist Industrial Landscape: From Dunapentele to Sztálinváros, 1950–1958. *Historical Archaeology* 39(3): 75–93.
Platz, Stephanie. 1996. Pasts and Futures: Space, History and Armenian Identity, 1988–1994. PhD diss., University of Chicago.
Polanyi, Karl. 1944. *The Great Transformation: The Political and Economic Origins of Our Time.* Boston: Beacon Hill.
Polster, Fred, ed. 1961 [1959]. *Nagy barkácskönyv. Politechnikai segédkönyv.* Budapest: Műszaki Könyvkiadó.
Rausing, Sigrid. 1998. Signs of the New Nation: Gift Exchange, Consumption and Aid on a Former Collective Farm in North-West Estonia. In *Material Cultures: Why Some Things Matter,* ed. D. Miller, 189–213. Chicago: The University of Chicago Press.
Ravetz, Alison, and Richard Turkington, eds. 1995. *The Place of Home: English Domestic Environments, 1914–2000.* London: Routledge.
Reid, Susan E. 1997. Destalinization and Taste, 1953–1963. *Journal of Design History* 10(2): 177–201.
———. 2006. Khrushchev Modern: Agency and Modernization in the Soviet Home. *Cahiers du Monde russe* 47(1–2): 227–68.
Reid, Susan E., and David Crowley, eds. 2000. *Style and Socialism: Modernity and Material Culture in Post-War Eastern Europe.* Oxford: Berg Press.
Rév, Istvan. 1987. The Advantages of Being Atomized. *Dissent* 34(3): 335–50.
———. 1991. In Mendacio Veritas. *Representations* 35(1): 1–20.
Révész, Gábor. 1990. *Perestroika in Eastern Europe: Hungary's Economic Transformation, 1945–1988.* Boulder, Colo.: Westview Press.
Ries, Nancy. 1997. *Russian Talk: Culture and Conversation during Perestroika.* Ithaca, N.Y.: Cornell University Press.
———. 2009. Potato Ontology: Surviving Postsocialism in Russia. *Cultural Anthropology* 24(2): 181–212.
Rist, Lilla, 1996. Ahol élni lehet. *Nők Lapja* Issue 26, 24–25.
Rivkin-Fish, Michele. 2009. Tracing Landscapes of the Past in Class Subjectivity: Prac-

tices of Memory and Distinction in Marketizing Russia. *American Ethnologist* 36(1): 79–85.
Robin, Régine. 1992 (1986). *Socialist Realism: An Impossible Aesthetic*. Translated by C. Porter. Stanford, Calif.: Stanford University Press.
Róna-Tas, Ákos. 1996. Post-communist Transition and the Absent Middle Class in East-Central Europe. In *Identities in Transition: Eastern Europe and Russia After the Collapse of Communism*, ed. V. Bonnell. Berkeley: University of California Press.
———. 1997. *The Great Surprise of the Small Transformation: The Demise of Communism and the Rise of the Private Sector in Hungary*. Ann Arbor: University of Michigan Press.
Ross, Kristin. 1996. *Fast Cars, Clean Bodies: Decolonization and the Reordering of French Culture*. Cambridge, Mass.: The MIT Press.
Rubóczki, Erzsébet. 1996. Szabálytalan tetőtér. *Lakáskultúra* 31(1): 26–29.
Rulwert, Joseph. 1991. House and Home. *Social Research* 58(1): 51–64.
Ryazanov, Eldar, dir. 1975. *Irony of Fate, or Enjoy Your Bath!* 184 min. Soviet Union.
S. Nagy, Katalin, 1987. *Lakberendezési szokások*. Budapest: Magvető Kiadó.
———. 1997. Fogyasztás és lakáskultúra Magyarországon a hetvenes években. *Replika* 26: 47–53.
Sahlins, Marshall. 1972. *Stone Age Economics*. New York: Adline Publishing Co.
Sampson, Steven. 1985/86. The Informal Sector in Eastern Europe. *Telos* 1985(66): 44–66.
———. 1987. The Second Economy of the Soviet Union and Eastern Europe. *Annals of the American Academy of Political and Social Science* 493 (The Informal Economy): 120–36.
———. 1994. Money Without Culture, Culture Without Money: Eastern Europe's Nouveaux Riches. *Anthropological Journal on European Cultures* 3(1): 7–30.
Sándor, András. 1951. *Sztálinváros*. Budapest: A Népművelési Minisztérium Kiadása.
Sasfi, Csaba. 1993. Polgárosodás. Körkérdés. *Replika. Társadalomtudományi folyóirat* 11/12: 72.
Schneider, Jane. 1994. In and Out of Polyester: Desire, Disdain and Global Fibre Competitions. *Anthropology Today* 10(4): 2–10.
Schudson, Michael. 1986. *Advertising, The Uneasy Persuasion: Its Dubious Impact on American Society*. New York: Basic Books.
Schwegler, Brian. 2002. 'Europe Place': Representational Space Among the Ruins of Slovak Socialist Modernity. Paper presented at the Soyuz Conference. Ann Arbor, Mich.
Scott, James. 1998. *Seeing Like a State: How Certain Schemes to Improve the Human Condition Have Failed*. New Haven, Conn.: Yale University Press.
Sennett, Richard. 1996. *Flesh and Stone: The Body and the City in Western Civilization*. New York: W. W. Norton & Company.
Shevchenko, Olga. 2009. *Crisis and the Everyday in Postsocialist Moscow*. Bloomington: Indiana University Press.
Shove, Elizabeth. 2003. *Comfort, Cleanliness and Convenience: The Social Organization of Normality*. Oxford: Berg Press.
Shryock, Andrew. 2004. The New Jordanian Hospitality: House, Host, and Guest in the Culture of Public Display. *Comparative Studies in Society and History* 46(1): 35–62.
Siegelbaum, Lewis H. 1988. *Stakhanovism and the Politics of Productivity in the USSR, 1935–1941*. Cambridge, Mass.: Cambridge University Press.

Sík, Endre. 1988. Reciprocal Exchange of Labour in Hungary. In *On Work: Historical, Comparative and Theoretical Approaches*, ed. R. E. Pahl, 527–47. New York: John Wiley & Sons.
Šiklová, Jiřina. 1993. Backlash. *Social Research* 60(4): 737–50.
Simmel, Georg. 1978. *The Philosophy of Money*. Edited by D. Frisby. London: Routledge and Kegan Paul Ltd.
Smith, Jeff. 2003. From Házi to Hyper Market: Discourses on Time, Money, and Food in Hungary. *The Anthropology of East Europe Review* 21(1): no pages.
Somogyi, Éva, ed. 1991. *Polgárosodás Közép-Európában. Tanulmányok Hanák Péter 70. születésnapjára*. Budapest: MTA-TTI Magyar Tudományos Akadémia Történettudományi Intézet.
Sparke, Penny. 1986. *Furniture: Twentieth-Century Design*. New York: E. P. Dutton.
Stade, Ronald. 1993. Designs of Identity: Politics of Aesthetics in the GDR. *Ethnos* 3–4: 241–58.
Stark, Tamás. 2006. *Magyar foglyok a Szovjetunióban*. Budapest: Lucidus Kiadó.
Stewart, Michael. 1993. Gypsies, the Work Ethic, and Hungarian Socialism. In *Socialism: Ideals, Ideologies and Local Practice*, ed. C. M. Hann, 189–203. London: ASA Monographs 31, Routledge.
Stokes, Raymond G. 2000. Plastics and the New Society: The German Democratic Republic in the 1950s and 1960s. In *Style and Socialism*, ed. S. E. Reid and D. Crowley, 65–80. Oxford: Berg.
Stretton, Hugh. 1978. *Urban Planning in Rich and Poor Countries*. Oxford: Oxford University Press.
Stukuls, Daina. 1997. Imagining the Nation: Campaign Posters of the First Postcommunist Elections in Latvia. *East European Politics and Societies* 11(1): 131–54.
———. 1999. Body of the Nation: Mothering, Prostitution and Women's Place in Postcommunist Latvia. *Slavic Review* 58(3): 537–58.
Swain, Nigel. 1992. *Hungary: The Rise and Fall of Feasible Socialism*. London: Verso.
Szabó, Miklós. 1988. Problems of Hungarian National Consciousness in the Second Half of the 20th Century. *Social Research* 55(4): 679–714.
Szalai, András. 1997. 1957. *Tér és Rend* 2: 34–35.
Szalai, Julia. 2000. From Informal Labor to Paid Occupations: Marketization from Below in Hungarian Women's Work. In *Reproducing Gender: Politics, Publics, and Everyday Life after Socialism*, ed. S. Gal and G. Kligman. Princeton, N.J.: Princeton University Press.
Szalkai, Sándor, dir. 1980. *Kojak Budapesten*. Budapest, Hungary: Budapest Film.
Szczepanski, Marek. 1993. Planning, Housing and the Community in a New Socialist Town: The Case of Tychy, Poland. *The Town Planning Review* 64(1): 1–21.
Szelényi, Iván, et al. 1988. *Socialist Entrepreneurs: Embourgeoisement in Rural Hungary*. Madison: University of Wisconsin Press.
Szelényi, Szonja, et al. 1998. *Equality by Design: The Grand Experiment in Destratification in Socialist Hungary*. Stanford, Calif.: Stanford University Press.
Szirmai, Viktória. 1988. *"Csinált" városok*. Budapest: Magvető.
———. 1998. 'Socialist' Cities (New Towns) in the Postsocialist Era. In *Social Change and Urban Restructuring in Central Europe*, ed. G. Enyedi, 169–88. Budapest: Akadémiai Kiadó.

Szirmai, Viktória, and Anna Zelenay. 1988. *A remények városa: Lakóhely és művelődés Dunaújvárosban.* Budapest: Marx Károly Közgazdaságtudományi Egyetem.
Szörényi, Levente, and János Bródy dirs. 1984. *István, a Király.* Budapest: MAFILM Budapest Filmstúdio.
Szűcs, Eszter. 1983a. Barkácsoló gyermekorvos: szenvedélyük a lakás (is). *Lakáskultúra* 18(1): 8–10.
———. 1983b. Hinnéd-e, hogy panellakás? *Lakáskultúra* 18(3): 16–18.
Tang, Xiaobing. 1998. Decorating Culture: Notes on Interior Design, Interiority, and Interiorization. *Public Culture* 10(3): 531–48.
Taylor, Mary. 2008. The Politics of Culture: Folk Critique and Transformation of the State in Hungary, PhD diss., City University of New York.
Thelen, Tatjana. 2003. The New Power of Old Men: Privatisation and Family Relations In Mesterszállás (Hungary). *Anthropology of East Europe Review* 21(2).
Tilley, Christopher. 2007. Materiality in Materials. *Archaeological Dialogues* 14(1): 16–20.
Tímár, Péter, dir. 1997. *Csinibaba (Dollybirds).* Budapest: MMA, Objektív Filmstúdió.
Torday, Aliz. 1979. *Lakni jó!* Budapest: Gondolat Könyvkiadó.
Vadas, József. 1992. *A magyar bútor száz éve: típus és modernizáció.* Budapest: Fortuna.
Valuch, Tibor. 1998/99. Toward the Middle Class—with Detours? (Social Changes in Hungary 1945–1995). *Hungarian Quarterly* 13(1): 139–49.
———. 2004. Changes in the Structure and Lifestyle of the Hungarian Society in the Second Half of the XXth Century. In *Social History of Hungary from the Reform Era to the End of the Twentieth Century,* ed. G. Gyányi, G. Kövér, and T. Valuch, 511–672. East European Monographs. Boulder, Colo.: Social Science Monographs.
———. 2006. *Hétköznapi élet Kádár János korában.* Budapest: Corvina Kiadó Kft.
Varga, Judit. 1983. Minilakások: szoba-konyha VOLT. *Lakáskultúra* 18(2): 22–23.
Várhelyi, Tamás, ed. 1963. *Családi ház—hétvégi ház.* Budapest: Tóth, László, Egyetemi Nyomda.
Veenis, Milena. 1999. Consumption in East Germany: The Seduction and Betrayal of Things. *Journal of Material Culture* 4(1): 79–112.
Verbeek, Peter-Paul. 2005. *What Things Do: Philosophical Reflections on Technology, Agency and Design.* University Park: The Pennsylvania State University Press.
Verdery, Katherine. 1991. Theorizing Socialism. *American Ethnologist* 18(3): 419–39.
———. 1996. *What Was Socialism, and What Comes Next?* Princeton, N.J.: Princeton University Press.
———. 2003. *The Vanishing Hectare: Property and Value in Postsocialist Transylvania.* Ithaca, N.Y.: Cornell University Press.
Vörös, Miklós. 1997. Életmód, ideológia, háztartás: A fogyasztáskutatás politikuma az állam-szocializmus korszakában. *Replika* 26: 17–30.
———. 1998. Navigating Malls and Markets: Mimesis and Alterity in Capitalist Hungary. Paper presented at the annual meetings of the American Association of Anthropologists. Philadelphia.
Warner, Michael. 1999. *The Trouble with Normal: Sex, Politics, and the Ethics of Queer Life.* Cambridge, Mass.: Harvard University Press.
Watson, Elisa. 1999. Reverse Ethnography: The Myth of America in Svanetia, Georgia. Paper presented at the Conference of the Central States Anthropological Society. Chicago.

Weber, Max. 1982. *A protestáns etika és a kapitalizmus szelleme: Vallásszociológiai írások.* Translated by A. Gelléri. Budapest: Gondolat.
Wedel, Janine. 1986. *The Private Poland.* New York: Facts on File Publications.
Weiner, Annette. 1985. Inalienable Possessions. *American Ethnologist* 12(2).
Weiner, Tibor. 1951. Sztálinváros, szocialista város. A városépítés módszere. (Stalin City, Socialist City: The City Planning Methods.) *Építész–Építészet: Special edition on Sztálinváros* 33(11–12): 589–98.
Weiss, Brad. 1992. Plastic Teeth Extraction: The Iconography of Haya Gastro-Sexual Affliction. *American Ethnologist* 19(3): 538–52.
———. 1996. *The Making and Unmaking of the Haya Lived World.* Durham, N.C.: Duke University Press.
———. 2012. Configuring the Authentic Value of Real Food: Farm-to-Fork, Snout-to-Tail, and Local Food Movements. *American Ethnologist* 39(3): 614–26.
Weiss, Srdjan Jovanovic. 2006. *Almost Architecture.* Stuttgart, Germany: Akademie Schloss Solitude.
———. 2009. Almost Architecture. Lecture presented at the Taubman School of Architecture, University of Michigan, Ann Arbor.
Wessely, Anna. 2002. Travelling People, Travelling Objects. *Cultural Studies* 16(1): 3–15.
Wilk, Richard. 1995. Learning to Be Local in Belize: Global Systems of Common Difference. In *World's Apart: Modernity Through the Prism of the Local,* ed. D. Miller. London: Routledge.
———. 1999. Consuming America. *Anthropology Today* 40(2): 1, 4–5.
Williams, Raymond. 1973. *The Country and the City.* New York: Oxford University Press.
Wright, Gwendolyn. 1981. *Building the Dream: A Social History of Housing in America.* New York: Pantheon Books.
———. 1985. *Moralism and the Model Home: Domestic Architecture and Cultural Conflict in Chicago, 1873–1913.* Chicago: University of Chicago Press.
Yurchak, Alexei. 2006. *Everything Was Forever until It Was No More: The Last Soviet Generation.* Princeton, N.J.: Princeton Univerity Press.
Zatlin, Jonathan. 2007. *The Currency of Socialism: Money and Political Culture in East Germany.* Cambridge: Cambridge University Press.
Zentai, Violetta. 1999. "The West" Envisions the West. *Ethnologia Europaea* 29(1): 69–84.
Živković, Marko. 2011. *Serbian Dreambook: National Imaginary in the Time of Milošević.* Bloomington: Indiana University Press.

Index

Page numbers in italics refer to illustrations.

advertising, 1, 7, 25, 95, 116–17, *136*, 171, 185; capitalist, 231, 249n3; houses in, 190, *214;* of "natural" materials, 160, 212–13; postsocialist, 30, 171, 225, 236, *237;* reactions to, 26; socialist, 12, 84, *85*, 88–89, *90*, 97–98, 111, 118, 120, *121*, 160

aesthetic regimes, 3, 5, 8, 112, 140. *See also* Organicist Modern; Socialist Generic; Socialist Modern; Socialist Realism; Super-Natural Organicism

agricultural labor, 11, 22; proletarianization of, 5, 54, 60, 76–77, 93, 250n18. *See also* agriculture; peasantry; second economy: and agricultural workers

agriculture, 53, 64, 70; in advertising, 191; collectivization of, 55, 70, 80; industrialization of, 61, 71. *See also* agricultural labor

antiques, 87, 97–99, 146, 163; and bourgeois intellectuals, 94, 151–52, 155; disdain for, 97, 185; and status, 183–84, 202, 205

apartments. *See* housing: apartments; panel concrete housing; privatization: of apartments

appliances, 30, 78–79, 241; kitchen, 87, 114. *See also individual names of appliances*

architects, 12, 16, 22, 82, 102, 146–47; magazines for, 160; Organicist, 155, 161; as social reformers, 13, 54, 62, 66, 81; and the "tulip debate," 149. *See also* architecture; Weiner, Tibor

architecture: modernist, 12, 54, 118–19, 255n8; politicization of, 25, 39, 147; postsocialist, 33, 152, 162; socialist, 16–17, 62, 83, 118–19. *See also* architects; Organicist school of architecture; panel concrete housing

Art Nouveau, Hungarian (*Szecesszió*), 146–47, 255n9

asthma, 144, 209

austerity measures, 157, 166

automobiles. *See* cars

bamboo, 145, 160

base/superstructure, 10–12, 59, 62, 130

bathrooms, 212, 235–38; in apartments, 31, 84, 132; as modern luxuries, 50, 89, 112, 216; reno-

vating, 202, 215; sharing of, 46, 200; size of, 132; and status, 49, 69, 101, 176, 218

Bauman, Zygmunt, 16, 54, 123, 243

bedrooms: and children, *104*, 105–106, 199; number of, 107, 204, 216; and privacy, 159; sharing of, 103, 131

birth rate, 146, 245n3

Bourdieu, Pierre, 5, 13, 24, 43, 251n8

bourgeoisie: embourgeoisement, 95, 152, 184, 222; and the family house, 190, 200, 209, 213; furnishings, 97–98, 129, 257n21; vs. new middle class, 188, 197; as "normal," 42, 233; and Socialist Realism, 3, 64–65, 82–83, 88; suppressed development of, 2, 44–45; veneration of, 92, 151–52, 182–83; vilification of, 4, 13, 56–58, 81, 86, 87, 91. *See also* cultural producers; middle class; *polgár*

brands: brand-name/Western goods, 35, 37, 48, 136–37; second economy, 241; socialist, 123–24, 125–30, 253n5, 253n10; state as Socialist Generic brand, 16, 11–12, 118, 138

breathing, 142, 201; of brick, concrete, and wood, 134, 255n6; and open spaces, 41, 88, 158–59, 211–12; and textiles, 96

built environments, 1, 12–13, 77, 112, 138, 161; agentive powers of, 52; distinguished from material worlds, 246n8; and social problems, 134; and system change, 29, 50. *See also* materialities

cameras, 111, 126

cars, 7, 38; luxury, 19, 50; Mercedes, 7, 175, 207; and status, 93, 173, 175, *194*, 215, 218; Trabant, 7, *194*, 226–27. *See also* transportation

Catholic, 48, 227–28; churches and cathedrals, 33, *35*, 81, 155, 189

cell phones, 37, 179; as status symbols, 48, 174. *See also* telephones

central planning, 12, 55, 56, 111, 132, 145; and goulash communism, 4, 44; and second economy, 15. *See also* socialist cities; unitary state

ceramic tiles: do-it-yourself remodeling, 202,

281

204, 220, 236; and Socialist Realism, 3, 69; and system change, 30, 156; and Organicist Modern, 160. *See also* roofing tiles
children: child care, 68, 69, 76, 99, 100, 114, 166; and class, 58, 62, 94, 101, 197; and deference, 184; and the family house, 192, 200, 211, 230; health, 144, 209–10; norms for, 45, 46; raising of, 130, 224–25, 228, 240, 242; room for, 75, 77, 103, *104*, 105–106, 131, 159, 199; sacrificing for, 233
Christian, 29, 57, 144, 168, 228
CIAM (International Congress of Modern Architecture), 54
citizen consumers/consumer citizens, 4–5, 10, 16, 79, 88, 91, 93, 116
citizenship, 2, 10, 22, 112, 158, 183, 221
civil society, 17, 57, 151
class: classless society, 81, 88–89, 93; consciousness, 95–96; hierarchies, 93, 252n12; and materiality, 7; mobility, 93–94; politicization and censuring of, 57–58, 59, 99, 151, 215; privilege, 225; revival of, *xi*, 150–52, 155, 172–73, 176, 182–83; underclass, 22, 167. *See also* bourgeoisie; middle class; peasantry; *polgár*; professionals; proletariat; upper classes; "X" class
cleaning, 46–48, 83, 87, 105, 141–42; the "clean room," 99, 101; and gender, 90, 142, 201, 229
clocks, 67, 120, *121*
coffee table, 91–92, 216, 221; books, 39
collectivization of agriculture, 55, 70, 80
colors: in advertising, 89, 107, 220; brown and masculinity, 142, 146; of capitalism vs. socialism, 1, 4, 8, 20; lack of, 135; in modernism and contemporary style, 78, 86, 95, 102; and Organicist Modern aesthetics, 142, 161–62; and panel housing, 147, 149; and qualisigns, 8–9, 87; red and socialism, 29; and shopping, 30, 35, *36*, 38, 111, 124, 152–53; and status, 73; and suburban housing, 162, 189, 216, 217; and synthetic materials, 96; and system change, 31, 33, 155–56, 239; television sets, 84, 87, 114; and Western goods, 137. *See also* gray
COMECON (Council for Mutual Economic Assistance), 126, 127, 149, 165, 253n11
commodity exchange, 19–20, 118, 130, 247n22. *See also* gift exchange
Communist Party, 53, 54–55, 79–80, 152, 154, 242; elites, 92, 171; ideology, 10, 11, 12, 52, 62–63, 245n4; and modernism, 82; and Steel XXI, 176. *See also* system change
companies. *See* firms/companies

compensation for property lost, 168–69, 171–72; coupons, 167
concrete, 83–84, 95; crumbling, 50, 141; drawbacks, 131, 134, 251n2; vs. Organicist Modern aesthetics, 139, 142; and plumbing, 72; qualities of, 3, 78, 145, 246n14. *See also* panel concrete housing
contemporary style, 86–87, 91, 95, 97, *106*, 128, 129, 141
cosmologies, 9, 13, 137
cosmopolitan, 83, 149, 161
Council for Mutual Economic Assistance. *See* COMECON
Csete, György, 147
cultural producers, 12, 59, 60, 62, 82–83, 93, 97; artists, 29, 98, 243; postsocialist, 151; promoting consumerism, 88, 107, 252n8; theater actors and directors, 48, 179; writers, 17, 18, 29, 151, 183, 210. *See also* professionals
currency, *x*, 150, 166; hard, 136, 149; Hungarian forints, 29, 242; materiality of, 127; Western, 138

debates: over aesthetics, 88, 149; over consumerism, 119; over socialism, 80–81; over Sztálinváros, 70
decorative objects: and individuation, 146; old vs. new, 78, 87, 96, 97–98; and wall units, 103; Western goods as, *136*, 137. *See also* folk; home decorating; peasantry: artifacts of
deference, 184
demands. *See igények/igényes*
dirt: healthy dirt, 142; modernism and, 87; peasant order and, 212. *See also* cleaning; pollution
do-it-yourself (DIY), 5, 20, 107–109, 140; and men, 142, 220–21; and norms, 241; and research, 25; self-provisioning, 68, 77, 110. *See also kaláka;* self-built housing
doors, 30, 159; to apartments, 18, 135; French, 69; to houses, 162, 177, *213*; removal of, 91, 105

economic crisis, 17, 151, 241, 242
economic reforms, 4; postsocialist, 20, 21, 39, 42, 99, 166; socialist, 15, 33, 101, 111, 130, 149–50
electricity. *See under* infrastructure
elevators, 84; broken, 160, 203; and social isolation, 134–35
entertainment, 7, 69, 71, 103, 111, 123, 174, 202; watching television, 39, 91, 105, 205
European Union, 28, 44, 166, 181, 211, 223, 239, 240–41, 242–43

factories: cities as, 67; furniture and porcelain, 97; nationalization of, 55–56, 59, 253n10; postsocialist, 31–32, 39, 175–77; presocialist, 53; privatization of, 33, 167, 240–41; quality of goods, 126–27; socialist, 11, 52, 56, 61, 72, 84, 124, 130. *See also* steel factory

family house with garden, 189–91, *191*, 220, 258n2; disdain for, 200–203; and emotional states, 230, 231–32; and entrepreneurs, 199–200; as heterotopia, 19, 234; idealization of, 210–11; ideological condemnation of, 81; as investment, 171; and marital relationships, 198–99, 205, 215–16; and middle-class status, 182, 188, 195–96, 208–209, 213–14, 217; as rejection of modernist and state socialist architecture, 160, 190, 218; renovation of peasant houses, 200, 207; and the second economy, 17, 80; size of, 30, 216, 252n16; troubles with, 192–95. *See also* housing; middle class: and the family house; self-built housing

fashion: consumption, 48, 89; do-it-yourself, 5, 20, 108, 138; folk, 143; jeans, 14, 47, 124, *136*; normative demands for, 47, 48–49; old-fashioned, 87, 97, 183, 185, 207; quality of, 126; in shops, 37, 111; Western, 43, 49, 92, 129; women's, 65, 69, 111

fences. *See* walls and fences

FIDESZ (Young Democrats), 157–58, 166, 240, 242–43, 257n20

Fifteen-Year Housing Plan, 80–81, 84

firms/companies: postsocialist, 21–22, 149–50, 153, 167–68, 169–70, 208, 227, 258n4; presocialist, 54–55, 253n10; socialist, 54, 84, 111, 113, 124–25, 126. *See also* multinational corporations; steel factory

five-year plan, 61–62, 70

folk, 43; artifacts, 142–43, 258n23; embroidery, 87, 142–43, 162, 202; motifs, 64, 140, *143*, 147, 225n9; music and dance, 6, 143–44

furnishings: aura of, 4, 184, 218; and color, 1, 129, 254n17; do-it-yourself, 108, 145, 220–21; exhibitions, 86, 102, 119; French bed, 105, 204, 220, 252n15; Organicist, 146, 160; Socialist Modern, 78, 82, 86, 88, 91; Socialist Realist, 64–65, 66, 88; traditional, 91, 185. *See also* coffee table; *Lakáskultúra*: on old and new furnishings; masculinity: and furnishings; *polgár*: furnishings; storage

gardens: decorative, 189, 195, 206, 207, 209, *210*; and leisure, 109, 201, 214–15; plots, 17, 38, 176, 205; productive, 80, 94, 108; zoning, 68. *See also* family house with garden

gender, 141–42, 211, 228–29. *See also* cleaning: and gender; labor: gendered division of; masculinity; *rend*: gendering of; women's employment

gift exchange, 14–15, 19–20, 56, 98, 115–16; commodities and, 110, 120, 127

Gorbachev, Mikhail, 168

goulash communism, 4, 44, 224

gray, 1–2, 142, 221, 257n16; buildings, 187, 189, 239; as qualisign, 8; qualities of, 3

gray economy. *See* second economy

habitus (Bourdieu), 24, 56

hallways: and social isolation, 16, 134–35; and waiting, 130

health: and Communist regimes, 60, 67, 76; and the normal, 40, 42; problems, 202, 240; retraction of services, 114, 166; and the rural, 142, 210, 215

heating, 18, 52; central, 86, 91, 134, 170; floors, 30, 216; fuel shortages, 113–14, 166; lack of, 73, 75

heterotopic spaces (Foucault), 16, 18–19, 141, 142, 163, 222, 238; and normalcy, 49–50, 233–35

home decorating, 30, 139, 142, 183–84, 235; advice, 25, 78, 105–106; books, 98; magazines, 1, 108, 162–63, 183, 233–34; painting, 30, 146, 162, 187, 258n1; and Western trends, 129. *See also* decorative objects; *Lakáskultúra*

homeless, 164, 180

hospitals, 31–32, 67, 69, 79; medical facilities, 167

housing, 80–82, 99–100; aesthetics, 118–19, 129, 139; apartments, 31, 72, 74–76, 134, 141; forms, 78, 192, 211, 252n12; shortages, 18, 33, 55, 70–71, 76, 80, 83–84, 101, 131, 250n18; size, 107; socialist, 3, 5, 17, 55, *68*, 74, 86, 130; state disinvestment in, 84–85; 150, 152. *See also* family house with garden; heterotopic spaces; panel concrete housing; privatization: of apartments; self-built housing

Hungarian Revolution: 1848, 32–33; 1956, 3–4, 44, 73–74, 79, 154

hygiene, 89, 235, 236, 238; products, 128

igények/igénye (demands or needs/demanding), 45, 165; and consumerism, 90, 112, 116, 252n9; cultivated by socialist state, 4–5, 69, 79, 84, 88–89, 91; and housing, 76, 77, 78, 159, 205, 213, 216, 220; *igénytelen* (undemanding) people, 47,

180–81; and middle stratum status, 93, 96–97, 110; postsocialist, 225. *See also* normal; *rend*
illegal economy, 38, 41, 135, 172, 174–75, 187, 229, 259n3; black market, 81, 119; corruption, 223, 241; labor, 195, 208; prostitution, 47, 178. *See also* second economy
industrial labor, 3; commuting to, 76–77; resentment to, 71; transformative powers of, 63, 250n10
industrial workers, 250n18; first generation, 73, 176; skilled vs. unskilled, 71–72, 73, 94, 251n8. *See also* proletariat; workers
informal economy. *See* second economy
infrastructure: dependency upon, 7, 18; electricity, 54, 84, 134, 194, 204, 252n16; and housing, 80, 133, 154; and ideology, 12–13; as "normal," 27; pipes, 72; rural vs. urban, 81, 190, 192, 251n2, 258n3. *See also* heating; roads; transportation; water
insulation: do-it-yourself, 109; and panel housing, 170, 239
International Monetary Fund (IMF), 22, 150, 155, 166
iron (and wrought iron), 54, 61, 144; bars on windows, 31; peasant artifacts, 142, 258n23; and postsocialist public space, 156, *157*, 224; and the second economy, 115

Jewish, 53, 57, 183, 197, 243

Kádár, János, 4, 79, 150–51, 154, 252n10; compromise, 79; regime, 111, 132, 156
kaláka (reciprocal labor), 81, 116, 195, 210–11; decline of, 211, 216, 220. *See also* do-it-yourself; self-built housing
Khrushchev, Nikita, 79, 82
kitchens, 235–38; American or "open," 50, 102–103, 159, *237*; appliances, 87, 114; and *igények* (demands), 89, *90;* size of, 107, 132, 211–12
kitsch, 87, 97

labor, 11, 52, 56, 247n12, 250n10, 253n7; cheap or illegal, 22, 195, 208, 216; diligence, 45, 48; gendered division of, 45, 46, 52, 159, 229; physical or menial, 60, 63, 69, 93, 94. *See also kaláka*; self-built housing
Lakáskultúra (home décor magazine), 25–26; and contemporary style, 87; and cultivating *igények* (demands), 89–91, 252n9; and do-it-yourself, 108; on kitchens, 89, 159, 236; on old and new furnishings, 98–99, 105–107, *106*, 151, 202, 257n21; on panel housing, 134, 145, 159; on

rearranging for children, *104*, 233; on socialist and postsocialist hardships, 110, 123
laundry, 35; as burden, 90–91, 105; and gender, 229; laundromats, 68, 81–82; rooms, 200, 216, 218, 235. *See also* washing machines
loans, 20, 76, 155, 169, 171, 187, 198, 243; for home improvement, 236, *237;* for housing, 85, 150, 181, 193, 205, 206, 214, 242

Makovecz, Imre, 147, *148*, 155, *156*, 162, 243
manners/etiquette, 43; bourgeois, 88, 185; hospitality, 182, 212
Marshall Plan, 54, 249n2
Marx, Karl, 10, 15, 56, 247n21; statues, 29
Marxism-Leninism (Marxist-Leninists), 11, 52, 60
masculinity, 224, 227, 256n20; and the family house/cottage, 141–42, 159, 211; and folk culture, 144; and furnishings, 220–21; labor of, 108, 142; and norms for order, 46, 48, 232; and postsocialist entrepreneurship, 174, 224–25, 228–29, 241, 259n6; and wood, 142. *See also* gender
materialities, 1, 6, 9, 20, 24–26, 28, 39, 163, 185; communist ideas about, 10–12; of currency, 127; definition of, 7, 245n5; disappointment with, 5, 110, 118–19, 134, 140; and houses, 191, 196, 208, 213–14, 217–18, 246n8; modernist, 83, 87–88, 91, 93, 95–96, 119; "natural" vs. synthetic, 142, 144–45, 160, 161; norms and standards, 45, 48, 164, 165, 178, 180, 225, 238; Organicist, 151, 154, 212, 243; public vs. private, 15, 16–17, 138, 210; rural vs. urban, 81–82; of the second economy, 15, 112, 115; Socialist Generic, 64, 78, 140, 147, 150, 158, 209; transformation through, 4, 13, 61, 221–22, 223; of Western goods, 136. *See also* qualisigns
materials. *See* bamboo; ceramic tiles; concrete; iron; plastic; roofing tiles; steel; stone; textiles; thatch; wood
Mauss, Marcel, 9, 15, 56, 247n22
MDF (Hungarian Democratic Forum), 154, 157, 166
medical facilities. *See* hospitals
middle class, 22, 185–86; as European or global, 49, 174, 205, 235, 243; and the family house, 190–92, 195–96, 209–10, 217–19, 234, 254n1, 258n2; new/postsocialist, 155, 160–61, 164, 178, 182–83, 188, 199, 212, 222–23; socialist middle stratum, 5, 41–42, 93–95, 98, 164, 176. *See also* family house with garden: and middle-class status; *polgár;* status: middle class
middle stratum. *See* middle class: socialist middle stratum

mobile phones. *See* cell phones
modern design, 82, 97; and alienation, 94, 118–19, 132; and atomized sociality, 102–103, 140; dictating behavior, 11–12, 54, 62, 66–67, 77; Pop design, 95. *See also* modernism; open plan
modernism, 4–5; avant-garde art/architecture, 11–13, 52; Hungarian, 83–84; ideology, 12, 65–67, 87, 130, 141; movement, 53, 129; rejection of, 149, 152, 155, 160, 163. *See also* Art Nouveau, Hungarian; modern design; modernist cities; Organicist Modern; socialist cities; Socialist Modern
modernist cities, 12, 52, 66, 76; renovated apartments as, 162–63; socialist vs. capitalist, 64, 67. *See also* socialist cities
money. *See* currency
mortgages, 170, 175, 193, 242
MSZP (Hungarian Socialist Party), 166
multinational corporations, 111, 172, 174, 239, 243; IKEA, 86
Munn, Nancy, 9
museums, 39, 58, 64–65, 69, 92; the home as, 185; and research, 22, 25

nationalization: by Communist Party, 54–55; by postwar government, 53. *See also under* factories
new towns. *See* socialist cities
normal: the abnormal, 19, 229–31; discourse of, 14, 27–29, 31, 39–43, 45, 140, 164, 238. *See also* fashion: normative demands for; heterotopic spaces: and normalcy; *igények/igényes*; materialities: norms and standards; *rend*; system change: and the normal

oil crisis of 1973, 21, 140, 149
open plan: original concept, 102–103, *106*; with private spaces, 159, 211–12; socialist, 78, 132. *See also* breathing: and open spaces
Orbán, Viktor, 154, 157, 242, 243
order. *See rend*
Organicist Modern, 5–6, 140, 142, 151, 154–56, 161, 163, 164, 246n7; and the family house, 191, 209, 211–12, 216, 222. *See also* Art Nouveau, Hungarian; Organicist school of architecture
Organicist school of architecture (Hungarian), 33, 35, *35*, 147, 155, 161–62

packaging, 12, 118, 120, 127, 128, 135, 241; of Western goods, *136*, 137
paintings, 151, 185
panel concrete housing, 32, 36, 83–86, *130*, *133*, 134–35, 152–53; antiques and, 97, 99, 185, 205; drawbacks of, 170, 251n2; and ideology, 130–32; rejection of, 92, 129, 140–41, 147, 158–60, 203–204, 209; renovation of, 145–46, 162–63, 220–21, 234, 239; size of apartments, 30, 84, 100, 107, 132, 201, 203, 233; and Socialist Modern aesthetics, 4, 5, 78, 112. *See also* colors: and panel housing; housing: apartments
peace and quiet, 204, 231–33, 247n23
peasantry, 6, 37, 53, 55, 58, 95, 198, 210, 252n12; artifacts of, 142, *143*, 145, 185, 255n8, 258n23; disdain for, 108, 179–80, 201, 212–13; houses of, 81, 99, 101, 189, *193*, 195, 205, 207, 214, 254n18; and norms for order, 45–46; peasant-workers, 58, 76, 94, 101, 152, 192, 214; proletarianization of, 56, 57, 60, 67, 71, 88–89, 93; romanticization of, 143. *See also* agricultural labor
Peirce, C. S., 7–8, 9, 245n5, 246n13
pensioners, 161, 164, 169, 172
Plan, the. *See* Fifteen-Year Housing Plan; five-year plan
planned cities. *See* socialist cities
plastic, 95–96, 102; aging of, 141; and cars, 227; décor, 146; vs. "natural" materials, 145, 213; packaging, 127, 194–95; vs. second-economy materialities, 115
Polanyi, Karl, 55
polgár (bourgeois-citizen, burgher), 151–52, 155, 182–85; and do-it-yourself/gardening, 108; and FIDESZ, 166; furnishings, 96–97, 98, 183, 202, 205, 216, 218; intellectuals, 94; and the new middle class, 199, 200, 203, 217; and status, 175, 180, 258n22. *See also* bourgeoisie; middle class
political prisoners, 92; labor of, 72, 215n19; 250n10; political repression, 58; release of, 79
pollution, 2, 6, 23, 30, 142; from steel factory, 144, 209
populists, 83, 149, 151, 157; and the second economy, 210, 211
porcelain: décor, 87, 97, 185; Hungarian, 97, 126–27; and Organicism, 151; vs. plastic, 96
posters: décor, *136*, 142, 160; and shopping, 37; socialist, 59, 60, 68
postmodern, 50, 238; architecture, 30, 152, 156; vs. Organicism, 212
poverty: postsocialist, 242; of proletariat, 95, 181; rural, 71; and socialism, 1, 5, 42; and state assistance, 150
privacy/intimacy, 16–17, 50–51, 135, 141–42, 159, 162, 191, 234; and bathrooms, 89, 235–36; lack of, 18, 37; marital, 103, 212. *See also* heterotopic spaces

Index

private property, 16–17, 155, 168–69, 257n5; elimination of, 54–55, 63, 81. *See also* real estate
privatization: of apartments, 33, 170, 257n6, 257n7; by FIDESZ government, 240; limited, 80; postsocialist, 22, 33, 155, 165, 169–72; of public spaces, 156, 166, 188
professionals, 24, 57, 59, 89, 93–94, 99, 150–51, 169, 192; civil servants, 57, 183, 192; doctors, 108, 197; engineers, 57, 73, 167, 169, 216, 231; lawyers/prosecutors, 167–68, 216, 258n4; and research, 22–23; white-collar workers, 22, 93, 99, 108, 110, 201, 231. *See also* cultural producers
proletariat: derogatory term (*proli*), 73, 180–81; idealization of, 60; and norms, 95; vs. *polgár*, 184; vs. skilled workers, 93–94; and Socialist Generic materialities, 6, 150, 178, 212; working classes, 62–63, 150, 181. *See also* agricultural labor: proletarianization of; industrial workers; workers
Protestant, 48, 186
publicity/propaganda campaigns, 12, 59–60, 78, 112; for bathrooms and kitchens, 237; for furnishings, 86, 97–98, 129; for socialist cities, 52, 61–62, 63–64, 69–70, 72, 248n3

qualisigns, 7–8, 10, 87, 145–46

radios, 57, 65, 91, 103; and *polgár*, 108, 183; and socialism, 56, 59, 61; and Western goods, 111
Rákosi, Mátyás, 59, 70
real estate, 17, 171, 220, 242; agents, 24, 117, 177–78; and anxiety, 18; developers, 240, 257n7
refrigerator socialism, 4, 119
regime change. *See* system change
religion, 57, 160, 186, 197; and Communism, 11, 54; and socialism, 71, 89–90. *See also* Catholic; Christian; Jewish; Protestant
rend (order), 28–29, 45–48, 249n13; and Communist regimes, 63; vs. disorderliness as marker of ethnic groups and proletariat, 46–47, 180; gendering of, 46, 141, 228; and peace and quiet, 232–33; vs. *polgár* status, 197; after system change, 48, 224–25. See also *igények/igényes*
roads, *191*; dependency upon, 7, 18; dirt, 204; and normalcy, 42, 50; paved, 81; and underdevelopment, 192, 194
robots for house cleaning, 90–91
Roma (gypsies), 48, 63, 172, 180, 197, 217, 243
roofing tiles: in advertising, 190, 191, 212–13; and private housing developments, 153; and status, 175; and Super-Natural Organicism, 6, 160, 212–13, *213*. *See also* ceramic tiles

roofs. *See* roofing tiles; thatch
rural underdevelopment, 81–82, 190, 192. *See also* suburbs/suburbanization; urbanization

science/scientific: and *igények* (demands), 89–90; and Marxism-Leninism, 10–11, 60. *See also* technology
second economy (informal economy, gray economy), 5, 6, 15, 19, 20, 113, 115–16, 123, 160; and agricultural workers, 49, 80, 99, 101, 192; and do-it-yourself, 109; and market reforms, 149–50, 152, 154–55; and the private sphere, 17, 151, 165, 222; tolerance for, 4, 21, 80, 111–12. *See also* illegal economy
second society (Hankiss), 151
second world, 22
self-built housing, 31, 82, 101–102, *153*, 175, *193*, *194*, 195, 210, 217. *See also* do-it-yourself; *kaláka*
shock therapy, 166
shop windows/displays, 30, *36*, *37*, 123; socialist, 97, 119–20, 124, 126
shortages, 113–15
"Show me your home, and I'll tell you who you are," 4, 79, 109, 197
show trials, 56
socialist cities (new towns/planned cities), 52, 61–62; after socialism, 2, 31, 239; aspirations of, 3, 12, 67–69; building of, 71–72; experiences of, 70–71, 73, 76–77, 133–34; vs. the family house, 101, 141, 188, 209, 255n11; and Socialist Realism, 64–65. *See also* modernist cities
Socialist Generic, 5, 16–17, 112–13, 118–19, 130, 138, 158, 181, 246n7; rejection of, 139–40, 144, 147, *157*, 209
Socialist Modern, 4–5, 78–79, 82–84, 102, 112, 120, 129, 246n7; dissolution of, 149, 152, 155, 162
Socialist Realism, 4, 12, *32*, 59, 60, 61, 64–65, *65*, 246n7; and the future, 41, 69; rejection of, 4, 82
Soviet constructivism, 54
sports, 166, 225; facilities, 60, 67; soccer, 23, 62
Sputnik, 79
stairwells, 16, 134–35, 203
Stalin, Joseph, 3, 12, 59; regime, 4, 39, 52, 55, 57, 61, 71, 88, 93. *See also* Socialist Realism
state socialist benefits, 5, 76, 116; loss of after 1989, 22, 42, 140, 164, 166, 222–23; of political elite, 93; retraction of during state socialism, 21, 150, 155; rights to as citizens, 57, 59, 69
status: anxiety, 167, 175, 182, 215; embodied, 23; vs. materialities, 6–7, 201; middle class, 5, 41, 69, 94, 186, 188, 195–96, 199; postsocialist, 176, 178–80, 184–85; and the second economy, 99;

symbols, 48, 105, 136–37, 201, 258n23; and urban vs. rural housing, 82, 101, 153; working class, 88
steel, 2, 54; vs. agriculture, 60, 64; and concrete panels, 35, 84. *See also* steel factory; Steel XXI
steel factory, 31, 38, 239, 240; building of, 61, 63; history of, 52, 70; and housing, 85, 152, 153; management of, 39, 177, 182, 198; monumental gates, 37, 72; pollution, 144, 209; privatization, 33, 227; and research, 22, 24; and system change, 32, 39. *See also* steel; Steel XXI
Steel XXI (*Acél XXI Kft.*), 176, 240
stereos, 91
sterile: bodies, 181; housing, 146, 180
stone: as "natural" material, 146, 160, 189; and postsocialist public space, 35, 155–56, *157;* and second-economy goods, 115
storage, 105, 216; bedding, 103; closets, 103; garages, 200; wall units, 92, 99, 103, *106,* 221, 252n14
stores, 27, 38; "Boutique Row," 35–37, 156, 170–71; clerks or retail salespeople, 1, 111, 115, 117, 122–23; convenience, 27, 30; department, 69, 88, 124; lack of, 81–82, 100; postsocialism, 37; shopping centers, 33, 35, 69, 74; specialty, 138; state socialist, 68, 108–109, 111, 120–24, 126; twenty-four-hour, 27, 38. *See also* shop windows/ displays
suburbs/suburbanization, 189–91, 209, 239; and research, 23; troubles with, 192–95, 201. *See also* family house with garden; rural underdevelopment; urbanization
Super-Natural Organicism, 6, 163, 187, 218–19; 246n7; and consumption, 185–86, 199, 222; materialities, 140, 160, 213
swimming centers, 17, 38–39, 69, 167
system change (regime change), 21–22, 31, 154–55, 157; and anxiety and insecurity, 165–68; compensation coupons, 171–72; disappointments of, 220–21; and marriages, 200; and the normal, 39–40, 48–49; and private property, 168, 170; and television programs, 187
SZDSZ (Free Democrats), 157, 166
Szecesszió. *See* Art Nouveau, Hungarian

technology: and base/superstructure, 10; and being modern, 82, 89, 120, 188, 235; ideological neutrality, 11, 79; and "normal" materialities, 27, 28, 37, 141, 235, 238; panel housing, 129, 131, 135, 152; promises of, 62, 77, 83, 95, 96; and the second economy, 15; state need for during socialism, 79, 111; and status, 179; and Super-Natural Organicism, 140, 160, 213, 216. *See also* science/scientific
telephones: availability, 22, 37, 81, 201; and norms, 27; and status, 179; tapped, 18, 241. *See also* cell phones
television programs: *Dallas,* 173, 187, 207, 257n12; do-it-yourself, 108; *Family, Inc.* and *Neighbors,* 186–88, 258n26
televisions, 4, 21, 78, 84, *85,* 95, 113, 124, 128, 204; channels, 87, 224, 258n24; and gender, 141; and images of the U.S., 181, 186; and research, 23, 25, 26; sales of, 75, 114. *See also* television programs
textiles, 142–43; and contemporary style, 87; crochet, 103, 108, 175; kitchen, 89, *90;* natural, 146, 151; rugs, 8, 98, 184; synthetic, 95
thatch, 189, *194, 214;* mimicked in shingles, 162, *213;* on peasant houses, *193*
tourism, 79; abroad, to west, 136; to east, 135; in Hungary, 29, 39, 80, 135, 187, 241
transformation. *See under* materialities
transportation, 64, 67, 182; bicycles, 38, 73; buses, 38, 42, 69, 123, 126, 155, 192, 201, 202; lack of, 81, 99, 100, 203, 230; and norms, 41, 164; public, 167, 182. *See also* cars; roads

unitary state, 16, 125, 137, 165; end of the, 164, 235. *See also* central planning
upper classes, 57, 58, 173; aristocracy, 53; gentry, 44, 48, 61, 94, 139, 151, 177, 180, 185; nobility, 177, 185, 207, 254n1
urbanization, 52, 81, 109, 258n3. *See also* rural underdevelopment; suburbs/suburbanization

vacuum cleaners, 216
ventilation, 255n16. *See also* breathing

walls and fences: and autonomy, 18; concrete walls, 83, 84, 131, 134; disguising, 142, 145; and norms for order, 45–46; and the open plan, 91, 102–103, 132, 140; tearing down, 30, 33, 158, 161, 221
washing machines (centrifuge), 78, 105. *See also* laundry
water: dependence upon, 18; financing, 154; metering, 170; running, 86, 194; wells, 81
wealth, 99; in American society, 186; and cars, *194;* and class enemies, 57–58, 60; collective redistribution of, 3, 56, 75, 80, 164, 227; legitimacy of, 172–74, 175, 177, 189; and normalcy, 42; and private property, 17, 171; and status, 179, 226; and suburban housing, 204–205

Weiner, Tibor, 62, 66–69, 77
Western goods, *x*, 111, 112–13, 120, 125, 135–37, *136*, 138, 176
white-collar workers. *See under* professionals
women's employment: the "double shift," 225; during socialism, 38, 58, 59, 63, 72, 93–94, 119; post-socialism, 225–26, 169, 202, 222, 228–29
wood, 75, 86, 96, 115, *143*, 151, 155; commodities, 6; and do-it-yourself, 108; and masculinity, 108, 142; and postsocialist houses, 153, 162, 189, 206, *213*; qualities of, 3, 8, 9, 145–46, 160, 255n6; and renovation, 30, 204, 215; and shops, 35, 156

work. *See* agricultural labor; industrial labor; labor
workers, 11, 52, 56, 60, 61, 154, 177, 247n21; and ATMs, 37–38; defend the city, 73–74; housing, 68, 69–71; illegal, 195; and research, 23; unskilled, 94–95, 172, 251n8. *See also* industrial workers; peasantry: peasant-workers; professionals; proletariat
working class. *See under* proletariat
World Bank, 155
World War I, 53
World War II, 5, 32, 53

"X" class (class enemies), 56–58, 63

NEW ANTHROPOLOGIES OF EUROPE

Algeria in France: Transpolitics, Race, and Nation
Paul A. Silverstein

Locating Bourdieu: An Ethnographic Perspective
Deborah Reed-Danahay

Women's Health in Post-Soviet Russia: The Politics of Intervention
Michele Rivkin-Fish

Divided Cyprus: Modernity, History, and an Island in Conflict
Edited by Yiannis Papadakis, Nicos Peristianis, and Gisela Welz

Colonial Memory and Postcolonial Europe: Maltese Settlers in Algeria and France
Andrea L. Smith

Empowering Women in Russia: Activism, Aid, and NGOs
Julie Hemment

Migrant Media: Turkish Broadcasting and Multicultural Politics in Berlin
Kira Kosnick

Getting By in Postsocialist Romania: Labor, the Body, and Working-Class Culture
David A. Kideckel

Women's Social Activism in the New Ukraine: Development and the Politics of Differentiation
Sarah D. Phillips

On the Social Life of Postsocialism: Memory, Consumption, Germany
Daphne Berdahl. Edited and with an introduction by Matti Bunzl

Corsican Fragments: Difference, Knowledge, and Fieldwork
Matei Candea

Masquerade and Postsocialism: Cultural Dispossession in Bulgaria
Gerald W. Creed

Serbian Dreambook: National Imaginary in the Time of Milošević
Marko Živković

Sharing Sacred Spaces in the Mediterranean: Christians, Muslims, and Jews at Shrines and Sanctuaries
Edited by Dionigi Albera and Maria Couroucli

The Euro and Its Rivals: Currency and the Construction of a Transnational City
  Gustav Peebles

Labor Disorders in Neoliberal Italy: Mobbing, Well-being, and the Workplace
  Noelle J. Molé

Jewish Life in Twenty-First-Century Turkey: The Other Side of Tolerance
  Marcy Brink-Danan

Political Crime and the Memory of Loss
  John Borneman

Secularism Soviet Style: Teaching Atheism and Religion in a Volga Republic
  Sonja Luehrmann

Hypersexuality and Headscarves: Race, Sex, and Citizenship in the New Germany
  Damani J. Partridge

Loyal Unto Death: Trust and Terror in Revolutionary Macedonia
  Keith Brown

Politics in Color and Concrete: Socialist Materialities and the Middle Class in Hungary
  Krisztina Fehérváry

Jewish Poland Revisited: Heritage Tourism in Unquiet Places
  Erica T. Lehrer

KRISZTINA FEHÉRVÁRY is Associate Professor of Anthropology at the University of Michigan.

www.ingramcontent.com/pod-product-compliance
Lightning Source LLC
Chambersburg PA
CBHW050431240426
43661CB00055B/2343